CHILDREN IN FOSTER CARE

Social Work and Social Issues

Columbia University School of Social Work

CHILDREN IN FOSTER CARE

A Longitudinal Investigation

David Fanshel and

Eugene B. Shinn

COLUMBIA UNIVERSITY PRESS
NEW YORK

David Fanshel is professor and director of the Child Welfare Research Program, Columbia University School of Social Work.

Eugene B. Shinn is professor at the School of Social Work, Hunter College of the City University of New York.

Library of Congress Cataloging in Publication Data

Fanshel, David.
  Children in foster care.

  Bibliography: p.
  Includes index.
  1. Foster home care—United States —Longitudinal studies. I. Shinn, Eugene B., joint author. II. Title.
HV881.F36   362.7'33'0973   77–2872
ISBN 0–231–03576–4

Columbia University Press
New York and Guildford, Surrey

**We dedicate this book to all foster children
and hope our work reflects our deeply felt concern for them.**

The Columbia University School of Social Work publication series, "Social Work and Social Issues," is concerned with the implications of social work practice and social welfare policy for solving problems. Each volume is an independent work. The series is intended to contribute to the knowledge base of social work education, to facilitate communication with related disciplines, and to serve as a background for public policy discussion. Other books in the series are

Shirley Jenkins, *editor*
Social Security in International Perspective 1969

George Brager and Harry Specht
Community Organizing 1973

Alfred J. Kahn, *editor*
Shaping the New Social Work 1973

Shirley Jenkins and Elaine Norman
Beyond Placement; Mothers View Foster Care 1975

Deborah Shapiro
Agencies and Foster Children

CONTENTS

FOREWORD

As a nation we are prone to describe our children as "our most precious asset." Yet, all too often we act in ways that run counter to what we say about children and their importance. Both lack of knowledge and lack of commitment to make use of what we do know contribute to our failures.

The special importance of this excellent book by David Fanshel and Eugene Shinn is that it makes a significant contribution in both these areas. It represents the only longitudinal study of foster children ever undertaken. It was made possible by a major investment by the federal government and was carried out by a university-based team of scholars functioning in the best traditions of scholarly research. The Columbia University School of Social Work is proud of having made available this longterm commitment of senior faculty and other resources to contribute to the empirical foundations of social work practice and to the development of more effective social policy for children.

Some of the earlier books and articles stemming from this study have already been positively received and used by U.S. Senate committees headed by Senators Russell Long and Walter Mondale. In addition, the findings have been recognized and used by state and city legislative bodies and program administrators. For example, the findings about the importance of parental visiting as a predicter of discharge of children from foster care and as an important factor related to the welfare of the children have begun to influence practice in New York City and other parts of the country.

The School of Social Work deeply appreciates the help of some 80 cooperating agencies without which this study could never have been carried out. From the beginning Professor Fanshel and his colleagues viewed the study as a way of illuminating practice problems and enhancing the capacity of agencies to meet complex service-delivery problems.

It is important to recognize that the work reflected in this book is continuing. The knowledge gained in the study is now being applied to the task of computerizing information about children in foster care. Through the efforts of Professor Fanshel, the school has developed a close working relationship with Child Welfare Information Services (CWIS) in New York City, a management information system that is already drawing national attention as an important innovation in service delivery. The Columbia University School of Social Work is committed to continuing and expanding its efforts in these and related areas.

In both research and training we recognize the importance of the relationship between social agencies and a university-based school of social work. Without access to practice the schools would soon find themselves irrelevant. Without access to scholars in universities the agencies would find their practice frozen and unchanging, with disastrous results to those they serve. Much remains to be done, but this study and its follow-up do represent a significant part of what must be a continuing effort.

Mitchell I. Ginsberg

ACKNOWLEDGMENTS

The completion of this longitudinal study has been an exercise in delayed gratification. It is with a genuine sense of pleasure—and relief—that we come to the end of our work. Our frustration of awaiting the final results has been shared by the many cooperating agencies who participated in this study. As we contemplate the many years of our labor, we realize how much of what we have produced has depended on the effort and cooperation of others. In the course of the investigation we have interacted with many persons, in Washington, D.C., New York City, and elsewhere, who have had a vital role and interest in our work, and we have also had a fairly large research and supportive staff over the years. All of these relationships have developed from formal work associations to more intimate levels and in many cases, to long-lasting friendships. We are grateful to a host of persons even though we cannot fully and explicitly recognize the contribution of each. However, certain persons and organizations stand out as having played special roles in the furtherance of this enterprise, and we wish to express our indebtedness to them.

The U.S. Department of Health, Education, and Welfare has participated by providing generous funding through the Child Welfare Research and Demonstration Grants Program. This study has entailed considerable expenditure and reflects the high priority assigned foster children in the Children's Bureau, where the grant was originally made, and in the Community Services Administration, Social and Rehabilitation Service, where support was continued over the years. We feel a special sense of gratitude for the encouragement received from Dr. Charles P. Gershenson of the Office of Child Development, who helped initiate the study. He has served as a wise mentor and friend over many years. We also appreciate the concerned interest shown by Dr. Abraham S. Levine of the Community Services Administration; he has been most helpful to us in a variety of ways.

As faculty members of the Columbia University School of Social Work, we received major support and encouragement for our research efforts from the school's administration and colleagues. The senior author has for many years had grant-supported exemption from some of his teaching duties and, at times, his heavy involvement in this research has diminished his availability in normal school affairs. Dean Mitchell I. Ginsberg hsd been a long-time friend and supporter of this research and early recognized the critical need for such empirical scholarship in professional social work. We have also appreciated the collegial interest of Associate Dean Sidney Berengarten and Professor Samuel Finestone, Director of the Research and Demonstration Center at the Columbia University School of Social Work.

We have been part of a larger scholarly effort than that reflected in this volume. Dr. Shirley Jenkins has directed parallel studies of the parents of the children included in our investigation and has facilitated our work in a variety of ways, not the least of which has been to secure preplacement developmental histories from the parents of our subjects as part of the field interviews that were conducted at the beginning of the study. We are grateful to both Dr. Jenkins and her colleague in the family study, Dr. Elaine Norman. Readers of this volume will want to review the reports of Jenkins and Norman also published by Columbia University Press: *Filial Deprivation and Foster Care* (1972) and *Beyond Placement: Mothers View Foster Care* (1975).

Dr. Deborah Shapiro carried out the Agency Study, as the third element of these programs of research. We have relied heavily on a number of measures developed from her studies, and our special debt to her should become clear as one reads this book. Her work, *Agencies and Foster Children*, (1976), complements our research.

Many voluntary and public child-welfare agencies participated in the study. Close to 80 agencies were involved. We often made outrageous demands on the time of their staff members, yet we received outstanding cooperation over the full five years of data gathering. We have a special sense of appreciation for their contribution. It is our strong hope that our work will be helpful to these agencies in carrying out their demanding service roles. We cannot single out individuals for special thanks but can report that almost all administrators of public and voluntary agencies were helpful to us at one time or another. As chairman of our Advisory Committee in the later years of our study, Father Joseph M. Sullivan, Executive Director of the Catholic Charities of Brooklyn, gave us warm understanding and support. We thank him and the members of the committee.

The collaboration of the Bureau of Child Welfare of the New York City Department of Social Services and the Family Court of the State of New York was indispensable to our effort.

We have enjoyed the help of a most industrious and committed staff. Their prodigious labors have helped to see this longitudinal effort to its conclusion. Dr. Brenda Steinberg organized the psychological testing program, trained the testing staff, and supervised the field operations for about three years. She played a major role in this program. We are, of course, accountable for our treatment of the data collected through her efforts.

John Grundy has been a bulwark of support in the computerization effort required to deal with the massive amount of data we collected. His consummate skills as a programmer and his ability to build and keep manageable a data file that had as many as 65 IBM cards for a single child was absolutely essential to the completion of the study. We are also indebted to Carlos Stecher for the special index-construction program developed during the course of the study.

We have had stalwart assistance from Joanne Hansen as a research assistant and Margarita Pizano, who served as administrative assistant in arranging for the psychological field studies on three separate occasions. Dorothy Schmidt performed specialized psychological testing and research tasks with admirable skill.

We employed a rather large staff during the course of the study, with a legion of interviewers and coders as well as testing psychologists and research assistants. Pauline Dougherty served in an executive capacity with the program for many years and handled well the administrative tasks required to keep us going. We appreciate her efforts on our behalf.

Frances Kroll was with the project for its first three years. A seasoned and wise practitioner, she was enormously helpful in orienting the research staff to the intricacies of the foster care system. Her support greatly facilitated the cooperation we received from agencies and significantly contributed to our work.

We depended heavily over the years on consultation on statistical methods from Dr. Jacob Cohen of New York University. He was more than a consultant—he was always the superb teacher—seeking to share his profound understanding of data-analysis problems and always attempting to broaden our understanding of statistical issues. We fear that we have not done justice to his years of consultation but very much appreciate his considered approach to the special problems of dealing with longitudinal data.

We are indebted to Dr. Edgar Borgatta, who played a crucial role in the development of the child behavior characteristics (CBC) form and has given us the benefit of his counsel over many years.

Ann Gerlock has been a very special person to us. She has done more than the usual secretarial chores, and has assisted our efforts in a variety of ways. We have particularly benefitted from her typing of the manuscript and the voluminous number of tables. Her patient help has been a blessing.

Last, but not least, we must thank the people who helped provide the data—the hundreds of social workers, parents, foster parents, and child care staff.

We have a special feeling for the foster children themselves. We hope that we have clarified somewhat the experiences they have gone through and assisted those who are trying to be helpful to them and the children who have come after them.

New York   David Fanshel
February 1977   Eugene B. Shinn

CHILDREN IN FOSTER CARE

ONE

THE FOSTER CARE PHENOMENON

Billy is a white Catholic child, born out of wedlock in New York City. Early in 1966, a judge of the Family Court ordered his placement in a temporary foster home, after a public assistance social worker had found him in the care of an unrelated male adult, filthy, and lying on a bed of rags. He had been found in similar conditions the previous month. His mother had moved eight times in eight months. The court was brought into the case, as the mother was considered seriously disturbed and incapable of caring for her child. Billy was a "hit" in the nursery where he was placed. Everyone who had contact with him seemed to like him. This was somewhat surprising since he showed initial crankiness and irritability which stemmed from a series of illnesses he experienced in the nursery—chicken pox, frequent upper respiratory infections, and tonsilitis. When he came into foster care he had many splinters in his feet which had to be taken out a few at a time. He also had an orthopedic problem of turned-in toes which was corrected at a hospital. In August 1966 Billy was placed with a foster family. He remained in foster care for five years, during which time his mother had borne two additional children, also out of wedlock and requiring foster care placement. Over time, her condition deteriorated. Although she had shown interest in Billy for a while and had taken him home for a month, she could not sustain the relationship. He was relieved to come back into foster care and he talked about his experiences at home. He had been left alone with responsibility for his two baby sisters. When he returned to care, he became frightened when being given even minor responsibility. His social worker thought that he had been mistreated and had perhaps witnessed his mother taking drugs.

Debbie is a black Protestant child who came into foster care at age two months. The main reason for placement was that her mother was still of school age and interested in finishing her schooling. She reported having been raped by a bus driver unknown to her. She impressed the social worker who interviewed her as a "disturbed, immature teenager." The infant went into foster care directly from the hospital where she had been born. She was described as alert, healthy, and easy to care for. She was developing well in all areas. She was friendly and cooperative and responded with great warmth to her very devoted foster parents. Two years later, Debbie was discharged to her mother, who had married and had a second baby. Debbie was subsequently returned to foster care, being described as a "battered child." The child had been seen at a local hospital with signs of severe beating; she needed stitches and had many bruises and signs of internal injury. The stepfather said the child was frightened by a dog and fell down the stairs. A psychiatric evaluation of the mother raised questions about her adequacy to care for the child. Debbie was frightened, timid, very dependent, and demanding in her new foster home. Gradually, however, she seemed to recuperate and while she showed many emotional scars, she was able to respond to the warm atmosphere of the foster home. Debbie's timidity gradually diminished and she became more outgoing and secure.

Tina entered foster care at eight years of age. A Puerto Rican child, she was born in wedlock in New York City. She was brought into care on an emergency basis at the request of her mother, who was unable to control her and feared that she might unintentionally kill Tina. There was also the problem of the 25-year-old maternal uncle living in the home who was indecently exposing himself to the child. Tina was also showing problems in school and had recently bitten a teacher. A school-ordered psychiatric examination of the child and the mother resulted in a request for consideration of placement. The psychiatrist felt that Tina was in actual danger. Subsequently the child was placed in a long-term children's institution. She seemed to do well for a while, was visited occasionally by her mother, and then suddenly developed severe symptoms. She was discharged to a state hospital because she attempted to stab and strangle her group mother and tried to commit suicide with a plastic bag. The staff psychiatrist, evaluating her difficulties in placement and her continued aggressiveness, diagnosed the child as suicidal and of danger to others in contact with her. For several years both the child and mother received intensive treatment from several agencies. They were united some five years after Tina had entered foster care.

Some children absorb early in their lives that strong sense of helplessness and futility that comes with being born into a sorely impoverished family. Other youngsters soon taste the bitter gall that has to be swallowed by those who have the misfortune to be born with the wrong skin color. Still others suffer the frailty associated with malnutrition, body deformation, or ill health. But the crowning insult—one that goes beyond all of these in its power to debase the human spirit—is for a child to be born without parents who are willing to take care of him. Being cared for in one's own family by one's own parents is a fundamental and almost universal fact of life in almost all societies. It is taken for granted by most Americans. For a child to find himself bereft of parental care is a condition so different from the nearly universal status of other children as to mark those so afflicted as abnormal in a most profound way.

We are concerned with the fate of 624 children who—like Billy, Debbie, and Tina—shared the common experience during 1966 of being separated from their parents and entering the foster care system in New York City. Some were newborn infants and others were as old as twelve years. Among them, black and Puerto Rican children were heavily represented, although 26 percent were white. They remained in care for at least 90 days. We studied their adjustment over a five-year time span, keeping in touch with those who returned home as well as those who remained in foster care.

Child development studies of a longitudinal nature have been quite few in number in the United States. This investigation is one of the first to employ longitudinal methods in studying the developmental progress of *foster children*. We share here the results of five years of data gathering to determine how children separated from their parents fare over time with extended tenure in foster care.

THE DESIGN LIMITATIONS OF PREVIOUS RESEARCH

The genesis of the research described here can be traced to a four-day working conference attended by a group of scholars and practitioners considered to be highly knowledgeable about child welfare research in the United States. The Institute on Child Welfare Research was held at Amherst, Massachusetts, September 8–11, 1963 and was sponsored by the Child Welfare League of America and the National Association of Social Workers.[1] The conference

[1] Miriam Norris and Barbara Wallace, eds., *The Known and Unknown in Child Welfare Research: An Appraisal* (New York: Child Welfare League of America and National Association of Social Workers, 1965).

was designed to provide current documentation and assessment of the status of child welfare research. Such consolidation of findings and analysis of research methodologies seemed especially timely in view of the availability, for the first time, of federal funds earmarked for research in the child welfare field under the Child Welfare Research and Demonstration Grants Program of the Children's Bureau, U.S. Department of Health, Education, and Welfare. At the conference, major attention was directed to children who had experienced—or faced the danger of experiencing—total separation from their natural parents, and to determine whether psychological damage to children caused by separation from parents could be reversed through either good placement experiences or the therapeutic services provided by agencies:

> Essentially the issue is to determine what research may offer on factors indicative of potential for corrective restoration of children and their families to normal psychological balance. An adequate level of parental care is theoretically so fundamental a requirement for the normal development of children that one wonders how the typical separated child can be expected adequately to overcome the profound role failure of his parents. Yet, some of the papers prepared for this Institute suggest that stressful experiences of childhood, even the overwhelming kind suffered by children in placement, are sometimes growth-producing. Whether this view is valid is, of course, open to debate. In any case, the child welfare field is concerned with the basic question: Do the skills and resources exist to save these children from the consequences of the severe trauma which they have suffered?[2]

Participants at the conference were particularly impressed with the findings reported by Maas and Engler in their study of foster children in nine communities in the late 1950s.[3] An analysis of their data appeared to lend support to the widely held view of clinicians that children who suffer extended placement in foster care—with associated frequent movement from one setting to another—show a behavioral pattern that is extremely disheartening and indicates possible maladjustment in adulthood. These clinical impressions, however, had not been firmly validated on the basis of the available

[2] David Fanshel, "Opportunity and Challenge in Child Welfare Research," in *Known and Unknown in Child Welfare Research*, Norris and Wallace, eds., 12–13.

[3] Henry S. Maas and Richard E. Engler, Jr., *Children in Need of Parents* (New York: Columbia University Press, 1959).

empirical research data. The participants also considered problems of research design to warrant serious attention as a key to future progress in building knowledge of child welfare activity. Development of research enterprises that adequately addressed the issue of what happens to the children in foster care was believed to be related to the way in which research was institutionalized as a part of child welfare service programs. Lack of adequate support often led to short-range research designs for studying foster children, which created uncertainty about the validity of reported findings. In order to properly assess the progress of children exposed to the risks of separation and placement, long-term follow-up was deemed necessary.

Prior to the Amherst conference no longitudinal investigation of foster children had been reported in the literature. The typical investigations had been designed on a one-shot basis with reference to the time factor. Such investigations were essentially static, concentrating on the exposure of children to the system over the course of their placement experience, through viewing the population in foster care cross-sectionally. The study by Maas and Engler exemplified the approach of dealing with the factor of *time* on the basis of a single data-gathering effort. Instead of taking measurements of children at the time they entered the foster care system and repeating such assessments over time, the investigators appeared on the scene for a single occasion and through case record analysis attempted to trace, in retrospective fashion, the nature of the child's condition from the time of his original entry to foster care. This approach—often dictated by the economics of social welfare research—is not an adequate substitute for the longitudinal endeavor. Its deficiencies include the following:

1. A static cross-sectional study can only include children currently in foster care. The view of the investigator is thus restricted to remnants of earlier cohorts of children who entered foster care over a number of years prior to the study. For example, if an investigator embarked on a study in 1970, he might have had available for scrutiny 80 percent of the children who entered foster care that year, with 20 percent having already returned home; he might also have been able to see 60 percent of the group entering in 1969, 50 percent of the 1968 group, and so forth. The discharged children would no longer have been available for the purpose of securing current adjustment data.

2. When the investigator seeks to determine whether the length of time a youngster spends in care is associated with the degree of disturbance manifested at the time a study is undertaken, he may find that children who have experienced extended care show more symptoms than those having less exposure to placement. However, this may not be *caused* by extended substitute care. The higher degree of disturbance may reflect the fact that the children who manifested a greater degree of pathology at the time of entry to foster care may have tended to remain in placement, while less afflicted youngsters may have been discharged more readily. The issue is an important one. The current weight of reported research tends to depict foster care as providing a kind of noxious environment for children. However, such a perspective may well stem from the inadequacy of the research designs employed in studies of separation and foster care.

3. Compared to the longitudinal study, the cross-sectional study provides a more tenuous basis for valid measurement of adjustment patterns. Typically, the earlier conditions of the children are recreated through case-reading schedules. The source of such data is case records, which have been maintained for purposes other than research. The available materials are often sporadic in the quality of their narrative description and prepared from perspectives unrelated to the concepts underlying the investigator's approach to child measurement.

Sample size

The above-stated criticisms do not exhaust the limitations of prior research in this area. Investigations concerned with the effects of maternal deprivation such as reported by Bowlby[4] as well as studies of foster care as a social service system have tended to include only small samples of children. As a result, it is rather hazardous to generalize from such efforts to the larger populations they presumably represent. Furthermore, data analysis is usually severely circumscribed. The use of multivariate analytic techniques is constrained in situations where the samples are small.

Focus of research

There are many influences helping to shape the adjustment of children in foster care, and few investigations have been able to

[4] John Bowlby, *Maternal Care and Mental Health* (Geneva: World Health Organization, 1951).

simultaneously account for the contribution of even several of these. How a child fares may reflect many factors operating in his situation, such as: (a) his condition on arrival, (b) the degree of family pathology, if any, before placement, and whether it continues to influence his experience in foster care, (c) the qualities of the responsible persons to whom he is exposed in the placement situation i.e., foster parents and institutional child-care workers, and (d) the quantity and quality of attention from caseworkers and other professional persons accorded him over time. To gather data in these important domains requires a number of parallel research undertakings in which the focus of attention may be the parent, the child, and agency staff persons. No investigation included in the research literature reviewed at the Amherst meeting appeared to have had sufficient funding to accomplish such expansive research objectives.

Research design as a reflection of the social arrangements for research. The constraints imposed by funding arrangements on the quality of child welfare research were recognized by Gershenson:

> The almost complete dependence upon project grants to support child welfare research perpetuates and fosters the further growth of the weak institutional structure. Paradoxically, financial support from project grants provides an immediate means for expanding research productivity; but if not balanced with other kinds of financing, it will eventually impede further research development. Project grants are meant for short-term, problem-focused studies that can be completed usually within three years. The funding agencies frequently use project grants because they are good insurance risks, particularly when a feed-back review system is used .... Project grants, because they are short-term, force professional workers to become research migrants .... The research facilities must reorganize themselves to carry on long-term as well as short-term research in child welfare. Such reorganization means that the university research center should become more than facilities for individuals to carry on research in any field of interest. There must be a full-time interested and competent staff to engage effectively in child welfare research .... What is lacking is money! This is where the funding sources should shift part of their programs from project grants to programmed research and research contracts. Programmed research implies long-term support from five to ten years, in a basic program area, with a specific research problem and research design left to the responsibility of the research facility ... In other words, there would be an attempt by

both the research facility and the funding source to maximize the combination of money, men, materials, and methods to produce research results.[5]

The research described in the present volume can trace its lineage to the Amherst conference. It arose out of the concept that programmatic research can contribute more significantly to the knowledge basic to child welfare services than can the more restrictive project enterprise. Indeed, our study of foster children in New York City is probably as clear-cut an example of programmatic research to be developed within the context of the Child Welfare Research and Demonstration Grants Program as any other enterprise. In a sense, the results of our endeavor constitute one test of the soundness of the concept.

LAUNCHING A RESEARCH PROGRAM

When the Children's Bureau encouraged the Columbia University School of Social Work to develop a programmatic research enterprise within the framework of the thinking cited above, the senior author proposed to focus on the phenomenon of foster care of children because of the awareness of the deficiencies of past research. This led to the following key decisions by the Columbia group:

1. Teams would be organized to perform three interdependent studies dealing with the same population base and focusing on the following: (a) a sample of foster children about whom data would be gathered on a repeated basis (this study is described in the present volume), (b) the parents of these children, about whom knowledge would be obtained through home interviews with the families at three points in time coinciding with the assessment of the children,[6] and (c) the role played by agencies providing services to the children. Team (c) would use the device of annual telephone research interviews as a

[5] Charles P. Gershenson, "Institutionalization of Child Welfare Research," in *Known and Unknown in Child Welfare Research*, Norris and Wallace, eds., pp. 200–201.

[6] This study eventually developed independent administrative status as the Family Welfare Research Program. See Shirley Jenkins and Elaine Norman, *Filial Deprivation and Foster Care* (New York: Columbia University Press, 1972) and, by same authors, *Beyond Placement: Mothers View Foster Care* (New York: Columbia University Press, 1975).

way of obtaining agency perspectives on the condition of the children and families as well as information about the nature of service delivered to them.[7] Thus the program grant would enable study in parallel fashion of three major aspects of the foster care phenomenon. Each study would be longitudinal in character.

2. A large sample of children and their families would be selected. Thus, 624 children were identified as study subjects in 1966, a sizable sample compared to most of the studies described in the literature on maternal deprivation.

3. The assessment of the children would be multidimensional. The goal was to view the child from more than one perspective. Our data-gathering procedure thus includes: (a) standard intelligence tests and two projective tests administered by the program's staff of three examining psychologists: (b) behavioral ratings and developmental profiles secured from agency caseworkers who filled out mailed schedules: (c) teacher assessments, also collected by use of mailed instruments: and, (d) reports by the children's parents during personal interviews regarding the condition of the children both at the time of entry into foster care and later after discharge to their homes. Older children in the sample were also interviewed about their foster care experience and given a sentence-completion test at the midpoint of the study. The availability of such diverse measures constituted a safeguard against the hazard of depending on findings stemming from only one source. In many of the previously reported studies of maternal deprivation and/or the foster care phenomenon, investigators relied on quite "soft" data as the sole basis for assessing the condition of children, that is, the judgment of an individual on a single rating scale.

4. The study would be longitudinal in design. Consequently, the data provided in the present volume reflect the repeated assessment of the children at three points in time over the five years of study. The program grant made it possible to engage in such an expensive undertaking. The expanded costs were not simply related to what was involved in gathering the data. Increased opportunities for data analysis in such a multifaceted undertaking required major investments of time and services. The cost of computer time and personnel involved in data analysis was of a magnitude not encountered in one-shot studies.

[7] See Deborah Shapiro, *Agencies and Foster Children* (New York: Columbia University Press, 1976).

FOSTER CARE: A SOURCE OF DAMAGE TO CHILDREN?

Underlying the research we report here is a conceptual framework that evolved from past studies and writing. A review in 1965 of the literature on children experiencing separation from their parents did not clearly indicate whether the sustained separation and transfer of a child from his own parents to foster care arrangements invariably results in ruinous impact on his evolving personality. The reports were uneven. A review of the research in this area was complicated by the fact that investigators had used highly varied approaches to conceptualizing the basis on which they measured the personal and social adjustment of foster children. Nevertheless, the aura pervading this literature quite strongly suggested that children exposed to sustained separation from their parents and long-term living experiences in foster care are most vulnerable to the development of serious cognitive and personality impairments. From a theoretical perspective regarding what is required for healthy personality development, separated children were widely seen as vulnerable from the moment of their entry into a foster care system. This concern was linked to the deprived conditions surrounding the youngsters before entry to a foster home or institution and also to the vicissitudes of substitute care arrangements. It was assumed that a family so unfortunate as to be unable to forestall the separation experience would likely have been able to provide only minimum security to its children in their preplacement upbringing. This observation is reflected in the Child Welfare League of America's *Standards for Foster Family Care Service*:

> Children who require placement away from their own families today tend to come largely from families where social disorganization or personality disorders of parents are so severe as to affect their ability to provide adequate parental care, thus bringing about the need for placement. These problems interfere with the child's normal development prior to removal from his home, and frequently result in injuries to his emotional well being which require corrective treatment.... It has become necessary to provide for treatment of the emotional problems of the child, which involves help to their parents with problems associated with impaired parental functioning, in order to assure the child the best opportunity for healthy personality development.[8]

In view of the commonly held assumption that families of children in foster care are the breeding ground for pathological development in children, it is not surprising that this is linked to observation that children entering foster care in the United States have tended, in recent years, to be more disturbed. Note Kadushin's statement:

> There is trend toward a changing composition of children coming into foster family care. The development of services to children in their own home implies that many situations that once led to foster care do not do so today. This suggests that the families of children needing foster family care are those that demonstrate the greatest disorganization, the greatest pathology. Children who have lived under such conditions for some time have suffered more deprivation and have more emotional difficulties than was true of children who came into foster family care earlier in our history.[9]

Some authorities have stressed the need for therapeutic treatment for the foster child and his family to help overcome the difficulties that surround an experience in foster care. Thus, Kline and Overstreet have observed:

> Any aspect of the human and non-human environment in which the child experienced continuity is lost when the child leaves it. The nuclear family as a unit, its ways, its customs, its dynamic system, of which he has been a part, have also been a part of him, his equilibrium, and his sense of identity... The familiarity of his home, the place he sleeps, his friends, his school, and the neighborhood to which he is accustomed have special meaning in the child's experiencing of his world and his place in it. The neighborhood may be deteriorated, the friends few and even undesirable, the educational opportunities inferior—but these are adult reactions. The child himself does not feel this way. To him they are known and familiar, and hold aspects of cherished intimacy which he has made privately his own. All of the small mysteries and rituals of a child and his absorbing feelings about these activities are a part of his life in a specific environment; they are his ways of gaining comfort and gratification, his ways of solving some of his problems of living....Ultimately, in his adult life, the placed child may always carry within him a specific

---

[8] *Standards for Foster Family Care Service* (New York: Child Welfare League of America, 1959), p. 2.

[9] Alfred Kadushin, *Child Welfare Services* (New York: Macmillan, 1967), p. 423.

vulnerability to separations and to strangeness. How he manages these stresses—by repetition-compulsion, by avoidance, or by active mastery—will depend to some extent on the help he receives in the placement experience and the capacity of his ego to master accompanying anxiety.[10]

In the research reported by Maas and Engler, findings are reported for some communities demonstrating that as many as 60 percent of the children studied showed evidence of confused self-identity. They further noted that children who returned home were less likely to display psychological symptoms and those who were adopted tended to be free of such symptoms:

> The child in foster care was much more likely to exhibit some psychological disturbance, although these symptoms did not appear more frequently at the time of our study than they had appeared at the intake of the children. It was found that children with psychological symptoms were often likely to have problems of self-identity and difficulties in interpersonal relationships, and the largest group of children with symptoms were those whose parents were markedly ambivalent about them. A circular process could be discerned in this situation. Ambivalent parents seldom relinquished their children for adoption. Thus the child remained in foster care, grew older, exhibited psychological symptoms, experienced many different placements because of these symptoms, his symptoms increased, and he became progressively less adoptable. It was found that symptomatic behavior in the children was positively associated, not with the length of time they spent in care but with the number of different moves they had made in foster care. . . . The child remaining in foster care was more likely to have a severe physical handicap which affected his social functioning, and he was more prone to be of a dull-normal intelligence or mentally retarded.[11]

A summary of the findings of the Maas and Engler study contained in a pamphlet produced by the Child Welfare League of America referred to children permanently locked into foster care as "difficult." Reference was made to the fact that half showed signs of emotional disturbance.[12]

[10] Draza Kline and Helen-Mary Forbush Overstreet, *Foster Care of Children: Nurture and Treatment* (New York: Columbia University Press, 1972), pp. 73, 76.

[11] Maas and Engler, *Children in Need of Parents*, pp. 353–54.

[12] *Children in Need of Parents* (pamphlet; New York: Child Welfare League of America, 1959).

Whether children tend to deteriorate in foster care has not been definitively resolved because of the rather primitive approach to assessing subjects used in most studies. As noted by Dinnage and Kellmer Pringle, "The measuring and assessment devices used to assess 'successful' fostering and adjustment among foster children have, generally speaking, been rather crude and unsophisticated." They further observe:

> While there appears to be a definite association between the break-down of fostering arrangements and emotional maladjustment, the causal relationship between these two sets of conditions is neither simple nor clear. The most important reason for breakdown may well lie in emotional disturbance due to the child's background and history, more particularly previous rejection by parental figures. It seems that the younger the child when first fostered, the greater the likelihood that the placement will be a "stable, successful" arrangement; however, findings differ regarding the interpretation of "young" and there is no accepted criterion of "successful."[13]

Dinnage and Kellmer Pringle also emphasize that inadequate research designs make it difficult to establish clear-cut findings about the effects of foster care placement:

> What are the short- and long-term effects of foster care in terms of later personality development, delinquency proneness, mental ill health, in short, general effectiveness as citizen, worker and parent? Do these effects differ—and if so, how—from those shown by adults who remained with their own families, but grew up emotionally neglected or rejected? Retrospective studies, available at present, have been carried out on too limited a scale and with too highly selected groups to permit valid generalizations. In any case, retrospective studies are suspect on a number of grounds: the fallibility of memory; the inadequacy of records; the self-selection of subjects, inherent in a high rate of refusals to cooperate; and the difficulty of tracing adults who have been in care. Only truly longitudinal studies carried out, if at all possible, on a national scale can be expected to overcome some of these limitations.[14]

---

[13] Rosemary Dinnage and M. L. Kellmer Pringle, *Foster Home Care: Facts and Fallacies* (New York: Humanities Press, 1967), pp. 30–31.

[14] Ibid., pp. 38–39.

CLINICAL PERSPECTIVES ON FOSTER CHILDREN

Examination of the professional literature before we began our study revealed that psychiatrists were concerned with the number of emotionally disturbed children brought to their attention by foster care agencies. They were in the forefront among those expressing alarm about the way in which separated children appeared to be damaged by the experiences they encountered. Eisenberg, for example, reported on more than 499 children for whom psychiatric consultation was requested in Baltimore; these children represented about 10 percent of the children in care for a year or more. He found such children to be largely unvisited and to have suffered multiple placements. They were relatively inarticulate and showed poor orientation to time, place, and person. Many were apathetic and mistrustful. He observed that:

> They have little reason to believe that any home will be permanent or that any parent will be constant.... The older children are troubled by a conviction that they are doomed to repeat the pattern of their own parents whose behavior they learned to see as violating the norms of school and foster home. Expecting rejection, they find it difficult to invest affection in others; foster parents often resent this apparent "lack of gratitude" and diminish or cease efforts to bridge the gap. These children approach peers with an anticipatory belligerence that induces the very antagonism they fear.[15]

An effort to provide specialized treatment services to children known to a public agency outside of New York City resulted in a report of a marked lack of success in helping these children. This was attributed to the inability of foster parents to cooperate with the therapeutic efforts of psychiatrists and most were found to be rejecting or ambivalent to the children. The authors noted that "although the actual number of disturbed children in foster care is not known, several studies indicate that emotional difficulties of varying degrees are present in a large number of foster children."[16]

---

[15] Leon Eisenberg, "The Sins of the Fathers: Urban Decay and Social Pathology," *American Journal of Orthopsychiatry* 32 (January 1962): 5–17.

[16] Zira DeFries, Shirley Jenkins, and Ethelyn C. Williams, "Treatment of Disturbed Children in Foster Care," *American Journal of Orthopsychiatry* 34 (July 1964): 615.

One psychiatrist observed that even the "nonproblem" foster child has feelings of despair:

> A child has many reactions to being placed. No amount of preparation can remove from deep down inside of him a feeling that he is being abandoned and that he feels himself responsible and seeks for some specific aspect of his own behavior upon which he can fix the blame. Maybe he wasn't as nice to his younger sibling as he should have been; or wasn't very neat. Or he wishes he hadn't been so angry at his father on several occasions.
>
> He often finds it difficult to extend himself to develop new social contacts, particularly in his transposed living situation. He may sit for hours staring into space or out the window, or digging his toe into the dirt aimlessly. Or he may be continuously restless and unable to sit still. Young children often regress in toilet habits and bed wetting and soiling are frequent occurrences. Sleeping may be disturbed by nightmares, bed rocking and head banging.[17]

Having observed many foster children in his work as staff psychiatrist with the Illinois Children's Home and Aid Society, Ner Littner made the following comment:

> A placed child, who becomes extremely afraid of yet another rejection by someone he loves, may either try to stop loving, by keeping everyone at an emotional distance, or may be involved constantly in rejecting people first.... Instead of attempting to provoke from others treatment reminiscent of his pleasant past, the child may attempt to provoke behavior that repeats his *painful* past.[18]

Hollander, who had seen many foster children in his work as staff psychiatrist at the Jewish Child Care Association in New York City, provided a similar observation:

> In evaluating a child in consultation with the worker and in psychotherapy, the psychiatrist frequently notes: separation anxiety; conflict of divided loyalties between parents and foster parents; identity problems; poor self-concept; depression; mistrust of close relationships; and disturbances of instinctual drives, ego, and superego functioning.... The shift in the nature of the population in foster care

---

[17] Quotation from Dr. Morris A. Wessel of Yale University School of Medicine, in *Orphans of the Living: The Foster Care Crisis*, Richard Haitch, ed., Public Affairs Pamphlet No. 418, 1968, pp. 16–17.

[18] Ner Littner, "The Child's Need to Repeat His Past: Some Implications for Placement," *Social Service Review* 34, (June 1960): 5, 7.

to more and more disturbed youngsters stimulates continued reexamination of the services and facilities which the agency offers. . . . Today's troubled child must have the benefits of closely coordinated efforts of worker, psychiatrist, and psychologist.[19]

PRELUDE TO EVALUATION

That many questions about foster care are absorbing the interests of policymakers and program planners is beyond doubt. A recent observer of one kind of substitute care, namely, foster family care, has commented:

> After more than a century of existence, the system of foster family care of children in the United States is undergoing a critical period of intense re-examination and reassessment. This has resulted from growing questions and doubts concerning its effectiveness and is reflected in numerous research undertakings, articles and books, and professional meetings at the national, regional, and state levels. . . . Foster family care has been viewed ambivalently. There has been a tendency to idealize the natural parent and to view the placement of a child in a substitute family as an inferior plan. Furthermore, practice has been characterized by considerable confusion between *value assumptions* regarding what might be "good" for people and *substantive knowledge* about what might be effective.[20]

The reader might well wonder whether it was our intention to conduct a formal evaluation of the foster care system with the goal of assessing its effectiveness in serving children in New York City. Such an expectation would not be farfetched, considering the amount of controversy generated about foster care. There is fairly widespread concern of observers of the system that it is not serving children well, that the longer they stay in care, the more disturbed they seem to become. Many fear that the services mobilized on behalf of foster children are inadequate and serve to compound the original misfortune experienced in the disintegration of their own family units.

[19] Leonard Hollander. "Foster Care Services in a Child Placement Agency," *Journal of the American Academy of Child Psychiatry* 4, (April 1965): 220–21.

[20] Anthony N. Maluccio, "Foster Family Care Revisited: Problems and Prospects," *Public Welfare* 31, (Spring 1973): 12.

The material presented in this volume does not constitute a formal evaluation of the system such as to enable social policy makers and program designers to refashion the structure of foster care with sure knowledge of cause-and-effect relationships. A much more rigorous design would be required and clearer conceptions about desired outcomes and measures of effectiveness would have to be spelled out to achieve such an end. Furthermore, an enterprise focused exclusively on evaluation would be more restricted in its focus, seeking to "zero in" on policy decisions as the major unit of attention. In contrast to such an orientation, our entry into this area of inquiry was as much theoretical and speculative as it was practical and applied. We ranged widely, seeking to illuminate theoretical issues that concerned child development researchers for several decades. Explorations of this kind do not always have an immediate payoff for the decisionmaker. As Suchman has noted:

> The problem-solving objective of evaluative research places a premium upon administrative decision making for some immediate need; hypothesis-testing in nonevaluative research seeks a generality which transcends the immediate phenomenon under investigation with as broad a generality in theory as is justified by the data. The more "controls" that an evaluative study can specify and the more specific it can make the various contingencies of success, the more useful it will be; the fewer "controls" or contingencies that have to be attached to a nonevaluative hypothesis, the greater will be its theoretical value.[21]

Our assertion that our investigation does not constitute a formal appraisal of the social service system of foster care does not gainsay the fact that a number of aspects of the study have *evaluative implications*. That is, our collection of data and our analysis were designed to provide information about the impact of the foster care experience on our subjects. The message that emerged from the Maas and Engler study of the late 1950s seemed to be, "Your system is hurting children." In the investigation we report here, we undertook to examine this issue in the context of a more powerful research design, the longitudinal study. We asked ourselves whether children really tend to deteriorate to an extent proportional to the

[21] Edward A. Suchman, *Evaluation Research: Principles and Practice in Public Service and Social Action Programs* (New York: Russell Sage Foundation, 1967), p. 78.

length of time they spend in foster care and were able to address the issue by gathering comparative data on the progress of children remaining in care and those returning home over the course of the five-year investigation. If we found children remaining in care to be in better condition than those returning home, this would obviously provide a less pessimistic view of the foster care system. However, we recognized that this might not serve as a reliable index in all cases, since most of the children returning home were apt to be rejoining families where conditions were extremely impoverished.

The contrasts between subgroups of the subjects included in our study, for example, those remaining in care versus those returning home, offers limited comparison and emphasizes the problem encountered in attempting a formal evaluation of foster care, namely, with whom the foster children should be compared. One could choose: samples of (a) children returning home, (b) children receiving alternative forms of care, and (c) children never requiring foster care. The choice of either group obviously sets the stage for flattering or unflattering evaluations.

In addition to the important goal of determining how children fare in foster care, some evaluative mileage can be gained from other components of our investigation. For example, our ability to examine the association between qualities of child care personnel, foster families, and institutional child care workers provided by the agencies and the progress shown by the children over the five years as assessed by various measures of their development constitutes a piece of program assessment. If the data demonstrate that certain qualities of child care personnel seem to be associated with beneficial changes over time, this obviously has important implications for agency staffing policies. Furthermore, we analyze in this volume the potential contribution of the social services provided by agencies in the form of social workers who vary in training from bachelor's degree with no experience or graduate training to highly experienced workers with master's degrees in social work. We are able to examine whether we find significant associations between the amount and quality of social services provided to the children and the various measures of their development incorporated in our study. This, too, has obvious evaluative implications.

It is our hope that the results of this longitudinal study will be useful to those seeking to better conceptualize evaluative efforts relative to foster care. By analyzing the effects of a number of influences that seem to be operating with respect to the foster child and presenting an analytic approach that seems best suited for dealing with the complexity of the phenomena to be studied, we may provide a useful backdrop for formal evaluations attempted in the future. It is our belief that any reader who goes through the entire report presented here will agree with us that there are many variables influencing how children develop in foster care, and that these should be considered in any thorough evaluation scheme.

It should be clear that there are two basic kinds of dependent variables in our study which could be regarded as evaluative in nature: (a) status changes and (b) changes in the characteristics of the children. In category (a) we include data about the movement of children back to their own homes and the movement of some children into adoptive homes as changes that are generally considered highly desirable. We also examine the amount of transfer from one foster home to another the children experienced while in care. Included in category (b) are measures related to the condition of the children, such as intelligence quotient (IQ) and projective test scores, observed behavioral characteristics, symptoms of disturbance, and school performance measures; in our study these data were gathered on a repeated basis. Our experience in analyzing such "outcomes" can be considered a kind of field trial for those who in the future would undertake more formal evaluation.

One further observation on the implication of our study for future evaluation efforts is as follows. As part of our analytic approach, we have made use of several indexes constructed from items secured from interviews with the mothers of the subjects in 1966, the first year of the study. The indexes are based on reports of the mothers about the existence of developmental problems that preceded the entry of the children into foster care. Looking at the condition of the children at a later point in time, we are able to account for the impairments the children brought with them into foster care as a prelude to analyzing the subsequent contributions of other influences. In evaluating any foster care system, it is one thing to hold an agency accountable for a child being three years retarded in school performance if he entered foster care at an appropriate grade level, and it is another thing if that child entered care severely retarded. It is a relatively simple but often overlooked notion, that evaluation schemes must account for the differential impairments among subjects at the time of their entrance into an agency's service system.

CONSEQUENCES OF SEPARATION: IMPACT OF THE FOSTER CARE EXPERIENCE ON SOCIAL AND PERSONAL ADJUSTMENT

To provide a context for our study, we attempt to compare the investigation of foster children reported here and the previous work on maternal deprivation described by Bowlby and others.[22] We observe that the literature on maternal deprivation has tended to highlight research projects that assess the consequences of separation for young infants cared for in large institutions, where a lack of sensory stimulation usually constituted an important feature of the environmental deprivation to which these children were exposed.

By contrast, the data presented here concern children ranging in age from infancy to twelve years at the time of entry to foster care. These children were exposed to a variety of forms of substitute care during the time we studied them, including early care in congregate shelters and subsequent long-term placement in institutions or foster family care. Furthermore, while the earlier literature largely focused on white children, this study has substantial representation of black and Puerto Rican children.

The reader may question whether our study will contribute to further understanding of the maternal deprivation phenomenon. We believe that our effort to understand what happened to more than

---

[22] For major reviews of research on maternal deprivation, See John Bowlby, *Maternal Care and Mental Health* (Geneva: World Health Organization, 1952); *Deprivation of Maternal Care: A Reassessment of its Effects* (Geneva: World Health Organization, 1962); Leon J. Yarrow, "Separation from Parents During Early Childhood," in *Review of Child Development Research*, Vol. I, Martin L. Hoffman and Lois Wladis Hoffman, eds. (New York: Russell Sage Foundation, 1964); Lawrence Casler, *Maternal Deprivation: A Critical Review of the Literature*, Monographs of the Society for Research in Child Development, vol. 26, no. 2 (1961); Michael Rutter, *Maternal Deprivation Reassessed* (Drayton, Middlesex, England: Penguin Books, 1972).

600 foster children in a five-year period takes its departure from prior work and extends the knowledge-building effort to a broader canvas. We emphasize that the children in our study did indeed suffer separation from their parents. Even if the substitute arrangement was more individualized and, for many, a close duplicate of the nuclear family—in contrast to the experiences of children in studies cited by Bowlby and others (see footnote 22)—there remains interest in determining the consequences of the switch from one parent figure to another. We have also attempted to pinpoint the nature of the substitute care arrangements, detailing such information as the number of times children were moved, the qualities of caretaker personnel with whom they lived, the degree of support provided subjects by contacts with social workers, and the nature of the role played by the child's own parents in the course of his placement experience. These factors focus on more refined issues than those pursued by previous investigators of the phenomenon of maternal deprivation.

A close linkage to Bowlby's major conceptual contribution is reflected in our effort to identify the degree to which our foster child subjects were able to adjust to the living arrangements provided for them by agencies. Bowlby placed great emphasis on the importance of the child being able to develop attachments to other people, sometimes referring to the phenomenon as "bonding." Empirical questions arise as to whether there is any negative consequence of the disruption of the primary family on the child's ability to develop other attachments and there is also need to establish whether the nature of the substitute living arrangement further affects the tendency of the child either to be withdrawn and incapable of developing close ties or to "bond" in a manner supportive of ego growth.

We report data on such aspects of the child's situation as the degree to which he: (a) was aware that he was not living with his own parents, (b) treated the foster care person as a natural parent, (c) manifested overt reactions to the substitute arrangement in the form of feeling rejected, unwanted, or unloved by his own parents, (d) appeared content to remain where he was placed, and (e) expected to remain there. We also examine the association between the relative adjustment of a child to his placement situation (i.e., the quality of his ongoing affectional relationship with his substitute caretakers and own parents as well) and his overall adjustment within a variety of domains that we measured.

We sought to answer the following questions about the personal and social adjustment of our subjects:

1. Do children who stay in foster care for longer periods show greater exacerbation of their problems when contrasted with those who return home after briefer placements?

2. Is the number of times children are moved in foster care a variable that is positively correlated with an increase in evidence of emotional disturbance?

3. Is the developmental condition of the children at the time of entry into foster care predictive of their condition when they are assessed at subsequent points in the study?

4. Are the qualities of the caretakers, foster parents, and institutional child care staff associated with the change of adjustment in the children over time?

5. Are the qualities of the child's natural parents and the frequency of their visits to the foster home predictive of later adjustment as measured on a longitudinal basis?

6. Does it seem to make a difference, as reflected in ongoing adjustment measures, whether a child receives the attention of caseworkers over time (i.e., do the frequency and quality of casework service contribute to our understanding of the child's adjustment)?

7. Can we expect a child who is able to settle into a stable living arrangement, in which some sense of permanency is developed in the placement, to be more likely to show an untroubled adjustment pattern?

IMPACT OF FOSTER CARE
ON COGNITIVE DEVELOPMENT

The research literature dealing with the effects of maternal deprivation emphasizes the issue of whether the intelligence of children is adversely affected by such experience. Bowlby's review cited a number of studies in which it was established that severely deprived children— particularly those separated from their mothers at an early age and raised for extensive periods in institutions— showed decline in IQ scores over time. His findings were later clarified by Ainsworth in her review of the research literature correlating maternal deprivation with intellectual development. She emphasized that in a number of studies there was confusion between the effects of separating a very young child who had developed an attachment to the mother, thus rupturing an important tie (with a consequent disorganizing effect), and of failing to provide adequate substitute mothering. Findings were also brought into question by the demonstrated low predictive validity of tests designed to measure the intelligence of infants. Despite the tenuous basis of the findings, however, Ainsworth observed that the research literature tended almost uniformly to reveal the vulnerability of children who have suffered depriving experiences. She observed:

> There is such a weight of evidence that children undergoing separation experiences under depriving conditions have lower IQs or DQs that this point need not be labored. Although less depriving environments seem to yield less deficient IQs, the extent to which intellectual development *can* be retarded by an extremely depriving environment boggles the imagination and can be fully believed only by those whose experience has brought them into contact with children so deprived.[23]

Ainsworth introduced a caveat to this doleful observation. She made the point that maternal care, when adequately rendered after the separation experience, can serve to reverse the tendency toward loss of intellectual capacity and that such care can be given by either the child's own mother or a substitute.

Since almost all of the studies reviewed by Bowlby and Ainsworth were focused on children who suffered maternal deprivation at very young ages and were subsequently cared for in institutional settings that were often limited in their capacity to individualize their wards, the knowledge gained from their reviews must be seen as being restricted in its applicability. There are almost no studies of the effects of deprivation on cognitive functioning of children, separated from their families, that include the full gamut of types of recipients of foster care in the United States today. The Maas and

[23] Mary D. Ainsworth, "Reversible and Irreversible Effects of Maternal Deprivation on Intellectual Development," in *Maternal Deprivation* (New York: Child Welfare League of America, 1962); Mary D. Ainsworth, "The Effects of Maternal Deprivation: A Review of Findings and Controversy in the Context of Research Strategy," in *Deprivation of Maternal Care*.

Engler study contained the observation that children remaining in foster care were more prone to be of dull–normal intelligence or mentally retarded, but there was no information as to whether this was a consequence of their foster care experience or whether the duller children tended to remain in care while those of higher intelligence were returned home.[24] In order to determine whether a prolonged separation from natural parents and placement in foster care are deleterious to children with respect to their intellectual functioning, it is necessary to assess these youngsters repeatedly over time, comparing them with others who have not been so exposed.[25]

Some investigators pinpointed retardation in language development as a particular handicap of deprived children. Pringle, for example, found that early first separations and subsequent complete deprivation of family contact appeared to have an adverse effect on language development and future capacity to read. This in turn was seen as being related to unsatisfactory school adjustment.[26]

In chapters 7–8 of the present volume we report findings based on an analysis of intelligence tests administered to our subjects at three points during the five-year developmental study. To our knowledge, this is the most ambitious effort yet undertaken to assess the intelligence of foster children. The questions we sought to answer were the following:

1. Is the length of time a child spends in foster care associated with changes in intelligence scores?
2. Do qualities of the child's own parents and their pattern of

[24] Maas and Engler, *Children in Need of Parents*, p. 354.

[25] The relative lack of attention to the cognitive development of foster children in the past several decades of research on foster care in the United States contrasts with the centrality of the issue for earlier scholars who saw the availability of adopted children and institutionalized children as providing an opportunity to examine basic questions regarding human intelligence. In the recent controversy generated by Jensen, a major source of his data is earlier studies of separated children reported by Burt, Skeels, and others. Even the more recent investigation of the role of intelligence as it relates to schooling and employment outcomes by Jencks and others relies on early studies of small samples of twins reared apart. See Christopher Jencks et al., *Inequality: A Reassessment of the Effect of Family and Schooling in America* (New York: Basic Books, 1972).

[26] M. L. Kellmer Pringle, *Deprivation and Education* (London: Longmans, 1965), pp. 35–60.

visitation while he is in foster care show significant correlation with
IQ change?

3. Do qualities of child caretakers provided by agencies (i.e.,
foster parents or child care personnel in institutions) significantly
account for changes in IQ?

4. Does the age when children enter foster care help us understand the course of their cognitive development?

5. Do we find that the variables associated with the foster care
experience operate differently with respect to changes in verbal as
opposed to nonverbal measures of IQ?

6. Do the frequency and quality of casework service offered
children over the five-year period show an association with IQ
change?

7. Is observed IQ change associated with changes in patterns of
school performance as revealed by reports of teachers who know the
children.

The issue of a child's cognitive development was one of our
major concerns because the course of a child's life experience is
obviously strongly influenced by the quality of his cognitive development. This facet had not been addressed with sufficient rigor in
previous foster care research. In undertaking such an investigation,
we hoped that our findings would provide useful data not only for
those interested in the foster care phenomenon but also for those
scholars interested in understanding how children respond in their
cognitive development to a variety of environmental influences.

STATUS CHANGES

An important criterion commonly used to judge the efficacy of
social services administered on behalf of foster children and their
families concerns the issue of whether and how soon the child is
able to return to his own home. If the child remains in foster care
indefinitely, this is construed by many observers of this field of
practice as a sign of failure in the performance of the service
mission. Such a point was made by Kadushin:

> One of the most serious problems faced by the foster home program
> is that it is failing, by a wide margin, to fulfill its purpose. The
> distinguishing aspect of foster care is that it is designed to be a
> temporary arrangement. The family is broken up only so that it can be

put together again in a way that will be less problematic for the child. Currently, however, many children moving into foster care never return to their own homes.[27]

Maas and Engler referred to children in foster care as "children in limbo." They observed:

> Their placement was not planned as a permanent solution. Yet in more than half the cases, cold fact shows that it has become so. A hundred thousand American children are growing up without the security of homes of their own, without the lasting guidance and companionship of mothers and fathers—or even the security of sympathetic long-term foster parents. Many of these children have not seen a home they could call their own for a decade or more, their initial bitterness increasing as year by year they see other youngsters return to their parents or find adoptive homes.[28]

A well-known figure cited from the Maas and Engler study is the conclusion that "under present conditions, if a youngster stays in foster care for more than a year and a half, there is great danger that he will stay indefinitely."[29]

It is almost uniformly assumed that arranging for a child to leave foster care and return to his own home—or to be placed in an adoptive home—is the most important test by which one can judge the outcome of a placement experience. Watson voiced such a point of view:

> Long-term foster care has represented something of an anathema to children's agencies, particularly to voluntary agencies. To a private agency children who remain in foster care often represent its failures! Many private agencies have assumed that their responsibility should be to use their increased resources to rehabilitate families and get children out of foster care and back with their parents.[30]

In New York City, the foster care system has frequently come under attack as one that fails to focus on the correct strategy, which is forestalling the need for placement. Thus, the Citizens Committee for Children of New York made the following charge:

[27] Kadushin, *Child Welfare Services*, p. 411.
[28] *Children in Need of Parents* (pamphlet of Child Welfare League of America), p. 5.
[29] Ibid., pp. 9–10.
[30] Kenneth W. Watson, "Long-Term Foster Care: Default or Design? The Voluntary Agency Responsibility," *Child Welfare* 47, (June 1968): 332.

Efforts in New York City in recent years to expand the goal of "child welfare" to include prevention of the need for placement have been half-hearted, small-scale and ineffective. The situation will not be remedied unless a fundamental defect is faced: an organization built around the process of child placement cannot create programs and policies that emphasize promoting the welfare of children while they live at home in their communities.... We seek a system of services incorporating many components that in the past have not been related to one another adequately, if at all.... The primary goal is to help families, not to find substitute care for children.[31]

As part of the overall effort to determine how the children in our study fared after being separated from their families, we attempted to account for the success of the agencies involved in returning children to their own homes or in placing them for adoption. The reader might well wonder whether a child is more apt to go home if he is white, has two living parents, was born in wedlock, is not markedly impaired in his personal and social functioning, belongs to a family that is not on public assistance, and so forth. Through use of multivariate statistical procedures, we have attempted to analyze the contribution of a number of background variables to explaining the variance in this important outcome domain.

FOSTER FAMILY CARE VERSUS INSTITUTIONAL CARE

Our study does not directly address the issue of whether foster family care has more beneficial consequences than institutional care for children deprived of their own parents. This is a matter that has been debated over many decades. The nature of the controversy has been thoroughly documented by Wolins and Piliavin.[32] While there seems widespread agreement that good community planning requires that a variety of living arrangements be available for children requiring care and their use dictated by individual need, there nevertheless remains concern as to whether one modality

[31] Citizens Committee for Children, "Toward a New Social Service System," *Child Welfare* 50, (October 1971): 448–49.

[32] Martin Wolins and Irving Piliavin, *Institution or Foster Family: A Century of Debate* (New York: Child Welfare League of America, 1964).

might not have more positive effects than another. For example, some investigators have expressed serious reservations about the ability of most foster parents to cope adequately with the emotional difficulties that afflict many foster children.[33] We also know that there is great variation among different nations in their predilection to use group care as opposed to the foster family arrangements that are so popular in the United States.

Our inability to shed light on this controversy in a direct way stems from the fact that our investigation was designed as a descriptive piece of scholarship. We studied the foster care phenomenon as it was operating in real life and studiously avoided intruding ourselves into the service-delivery situation in a way that would alter the kind of care a child would normally receive. Children were routed to foster family or institutional care on the basis of criteria employed by the agencies involved. If one sought to determine the relative benefits of each type of care, it would be necessary to carry out a field experiment involving the random assignment of children from a common pool of subjects to alternative modes of care. Out of concern for the welfare of children already faced with catastrophic life circumstances, neither the writers nor the agencies involved would have contemplated the manipulation of human subjects for such a scholarly purpose, laudable as the objectives might be.

In the context of a developmental study, which is exploratory–descriptive in its basic design, we deal with the issue of foster family versus institutional care in a somewhat tangential fashion. We present data in the body of this report concerning the degree to which some qualities or attributes of the caretakers (i.e., foster parents or institutional child care personnel) contributed to our understanding of changes with respect to intelligence and personal and social adjustment of the children as assessed over a five-year period. We also have occasion to divide our study population for analytic purposes, examining the experiences of the subjects in parallel fashion—in foster family care and in institutional care—scrutinizing the way in which a variety of child, family, and agency

[33] See Eisenberg, "The Sins of the Fathers," pp. 5–17; also DeFries, Jenkins, and Williams, "Treatment of Disturbed Children," pp. 615–24.

background variables contribute to explaining changes in the condition of the children. This is a quite limited mode of dealing with the issue of institutional versus foster family care.

LOCAL AND NATIONAL DIMENSIONS OF THE FOSTER CARE PHENOMENON

At the time the study subjects entered the New York City system of foster care, there were nearly 23,000 children in foster care, 95 percent of whom were being supported through public funds. Of these children, 53 percent were Catholic, 41 percent Protestant, and 6 percent Jewish, and 32 percent were white, 45 percent black, and 23 percent Puerto Rican. Over the last half decade, the number of children in foster care had increased almost 17 percent and had become increasingly black or Puerto Rican.[34] By June 30, 1971, some five years after the children had entered care, in New York City the population of children in foster care who were public charges had risen to about 26,500. In this five-year period, the proportion of minority children had increased about 36 percent.

Throughout the United States in 1966 there were 296,000 children in foster care; of these, 74 percent were living in foster family care and 26 percent, in institutional care. To gain some historical perspective, it should be pointed out that in 1933 there were 249,000 children living in foster care and of these, 42 percent were in foster family care and 58 percent in institutions. By 1969 there were 352,000 children living apart from relatives; almost 65 percent (226,000) were in foster family homes or group homes, about 18 percent (nearly 63,000) in institutions, and about 13 percent (45,000) in adoptive homes.[35] Thus, there has obviously been a marked rise in the absolute number of children living in foster family care since 1933, although the proportion of children placed

[34] Bureau of Child Welfare, New York City Department of Welfare, Summary Analysis of Monthly Population Reports Submitted by Foster Care Agencies, December 31, 1960 and December 31, 1965. (Dittoed.)

[35] National Center for Social Statistics, Social and Rehabilitation Service, U.S. Department of Health, Education, and Welfare, Child Welfare Statistics, 1969.

has declined from 5.9 to 4.1 per thousand children under 18 years of age.

For the fiscal year ending June 30, 1969, foster care payments of state and local public welfare agencies amounted to over $363 million; of this amount, 55.6 percent was payments for children living in foster family homes supervised by public welfare agencies, and 44.4 percent was payments for children and institutions supervised or administered by voluntary agencies.[36]

In New York City, appropriations from the New York City Charitable Institutions Budget for payments to private child-care agencies amounted to over $64 million in 1965/66 and almost $133 million for the fiscal year 1971/72. An analysis by the authors projected a cost of nearly $24 million covering payments for the care of children in the 467 families included in the study reported here.[37] Thus, foster care must be seen as an expensive social service. When parents break down and can no longer care for their own children, society picks up a substantial economic burden. For four families in the study, ranging in size from five to eight children, it was projected that the community would have to purchase 335 cumulative years of foster care services costing an estimated $2.5 million.[38]

The foster care system serving New York City consisted of a network of five public and 78 private agencies (or agency subdivisions) at the time our study was launched. The system was essentially the same at the termination of our study. Foster care is used here as a generic term and refers to full-time substitute living arrangements provided by licensed child welfare agencies. The term covers children being cared for in institutional facilities for the dependent and neglected child and those in foster family homes. Children cared for in foster homes housing groups of children and in facilities providing residential treatment for the emotionally disturbed child are also included within our frame of reference. Not included under the rubric of foster care are the adopted child, the child who has been adjudicated as delinquent and placed in a state

[36] Ibid., p. 37.

[37] David Fanshel and Eugene B. Shinn, *Dollars and Sense in the Foster Care of Children: A Look at Cost Factors* (New York: Child Welfare League of America, 1972), p. 19.

[38] Ibid., p. 25.

training school, and the retarded or mentally ill child placed in a institution.

Most communities in the United States provide foster care services primarily through agencies under public auspices. New York City is unusual in the degree to which foster care for children is purchased from private agencies; the City of New York purchases about 90 percent of required foster care placements from independent, private agencies. This division of responsibility makes the foster care system an extremely complex one to coordinate.[39]

LOOKING AHEAD

The present volume is divided essentially into seven parts. Chapters 1–3 present the background to the study, with discussion of the subjects, the methods used to assess them, and the placement processes to which they were exposed. Chapters 4–6 discuss the status changes affecting the children over the five years of the study, accounting for those who returned home, those who were placed for adoption, and those who remained in foster care. We also examine the extent to which the children experienced turnover in placements while in care. Chapters 7–8 discuss foster care and cognitive development, with analysis of the IQ data secured in three rounds of testing. Change in scores is related to child and parental characteristics and selected agency service variables. In chapters 9–10 we scrutinize the school performance of the older children in our sample, presenting a multidimensional approach for assessing their status, and also examine factors related to change in performance over time. Chapters 11–13 cover the personal and social adjustment of the children over the five-year study period and also projective tests, behavioral characteristics, and clinical assessment material. In chapters 14–15 we examine the condition of children who have returned home as well as those remaining in care. We also provide narratives that display the views of the children about foster care as

[39] See Eugene B. Shinn, "The New York City of Foster Care: A Descriptive Overview of Resources Serving the Child Through Age 12," Child Welfare Research Program, Columbia University School of Social Work, March 1970. (Mimeographed.)

well as the overall perspectives of their social workers. In chapter 16 we summarize the study by reviewing our major findings and set forth their implications for child welfare practice and future research on foster care.

TWO

CRITERIA
FOR SELECTION OF
STUDY SUBJECTS AND
THEIR CHARACTERISTICS

As indicated in chapter 1, the basic design of our study was longitudinal and called for the identification of children entering foster care in New York City in 1966 and their repeated assessment over a five-year period. This chapter describes the basis for sample selection and provides an analysis of the characteristics of the children.

The criteria for selection of the children resulted in the identification of subjects with the following characteristics. A group of 624 New York City children was selected. They were classified by age and sex, including dependent, neglected, delinquent, and "person in need of supervision" (PINS), and the age range was from birth to 12 years. These children entered foster care at partial or full expense to the New York City Charitable Institutions Budget during the 1966 calendar year and had never experienced previous placement nor had a sibling previously been in placement at a licensed voluntary or public child welfare agency, and remained in care a minimum of 90 continuous days. Subjects placed for adoption or in controlled residences or training schools were not included in the sample. No more than two children were selected randomly from among all siblings in a family.

Diverse considerations led to these sample specifications. Early in the planning stage we decided to focus on a single cohort—children entering foster care in 1966—rather than having a sequence of cohorts over the years of the study. Thus our investigation was fixed in time, constituting, so to speak, a study of "the class of 1966."

A decision reached early was to develop a rather homogeneous study population. While children who entered state hospitals, training schools, and institutions for the retarded were certainly being exposed to a separation experience, we decided to restrict our purview to children who were not physically or emotionally handicapped or socially deviant to the extent that these children were[1] Rather, we preferred to focus on children who would be considered much more within a normal range. Another important decision, encouraged by the federal agency, was to allow for a broad age representation among the subjects of our study. Children ranging in age from infancy to 12 years[2] were considered eligible for inclusion in the study. For analytic purposes, quota samples were established for age and sex variables to ensure adequate numbers of infants, toddlers, and school-age children, with both sexes given relative parity in their representation. Since there was planned follow-up for five years after the children had entered care, the oldest children would be reaching their 18th year at the termination of the study.

The specification that the subjects be exposed to at least 90 days in care was introduced out of consideration that shorter periods of separation would not justify the costly investment of five years of follow-up activity. It was considered desirable that the tenure in foster care be sufficiently long to constitute a relatively significant exposure to a substitute care arrangement. The specification that the child or his siblings had never experienced previous placement at a licensed child welfare agency was based on the desire to limit the study to a group of families and children who

[1] Over the course of five years of investigation, 20 of our subjects were transferred to state institutions for the mentally ill, retarded, or delinquent. Two of these subjects returned to foster care after treatment.

[2] The upper age limit of 12 years at the time of entry into foster care resulted in very few subjects entering foster care because of delinquent behavior or classification as PINS. These categories are seldom utilized by the Family Court for young children. Thus, only one subject entered care because his behavior was judged delinquent; six subjects came into care as PINS cases. We have reason to believe that some children came into court as PINS cases and that the court petitions were "reduced" to a charge of neglect or abuse to secure a more desirable child care placement.

were new to the foster care system. The perspectives of families regarding the impact of the system would thus be restricted to the period under investigation by the three research teams. Attitudes could be expected to derive from what was currently happening rather than previous placement experiences.

In the families with three or more children in foster care, subjects were selected through the use of a table of random numbers, and no family could be represented by more than two children. The intention was to maximize the number of families participating in the study. This procedure resulted in a final study sample of 624 children who represented 467 family groups. There were 157 families who contributed two children as study subjects to the sample.

A further limitation of our sampling procedure involved the exclusion of children who were not residents of New York City but who were using foster care facilities in New York City or whose care was not being charged to the public agency. In 1966 about 5 percent of the caseload of children in care was of this character. The exclusion of these children stemmed from our desire to have the study sample relatively homogeneous with respect to the responsibilities carried by the public agencies involved.

One final group of children should be cited as being excluded from our purview of direct interest. Children placed in adoptive homes were not included in the sample. Furthermore, if a child were placed for adoption after having been formally entered into the sample, it was agreed that no effort would be made to gather ongoing data about him. This specification was made necessary by the concern of agencies to protect the privacy of adoptive families. Since our study was not regarded as an investigation of adopted children, this exclusion was not seen as a serious restriction of our research.

We can now summarize the features of our exclusions that act as limitations on the degree to which our sample may be regarded as representative of children who entered foster care in New York City. Our sample was restricted to a single cohort, the "entering class" of 1966. It does not address the problems of children who: (a) were over age 12, (b) remained in foster care less than 90 days, (c) had been in care before, (d) had siblings who had experienced prior care, (e) were placed in training schools, state hospitals, or institutions for the retarded, (f) were in adoptive homes, or (g) had parents who purchased the total cost of care through their own means rather than having part of the cost underwritten by the New York City Charitable Institutions Budget.

With these exclusions made explicit, the selection of subjects was not biased in any other way, and our sample likely reflects a large core of the children in the foster care system for reasons of either parental inadequacy or the child's own behavioral difficulty.

SELECTION PROCEDURES

A sequential sampling procedure was utilized wherein every child entering the foster care system on or after January 1, 1966 was scrutinized to determine whether he (or she) met the eligibility criteria. As each child entered care, he was given a priority number based on the day of his entry. Monitoring activity took place at the intake sections of the Bureau of Child Welfare (now called Special Services for Children) of the New York City Department of Social Services and the Family Court, the two organizational entities through which children entered care.[3]

In order to complete the identification of all children entering care, it was also necessary to monitor the daily intake log of emergency cases entering the main congregate shelter[4] that received and collated the entries at the other two temporary shelters. In addition, since the Family Court placed all PINS and delinquency cases directly without referral through the Bureau of Child Welfare, a monthly letter of inquiry about admission of such cases was sent directly to all child care agencies known to accept this type of case. Monitoring the intake of all children into foster care required two staff persons from the research team to record entries for each

[3] Although intake was conducted in at least ten different locations in the city, all cases except PINS or delinquency cases entering through the Family Court were channeled for administrative purposes through the Allocation (referral) section of the Bureau of Child Welfare of the Department of Social Services. It took up to 30 days for records to arrive for processing at the Allocation Section, but this source was the most feasible for use in identifying most of the children entering foster care.

[4] The Children's Center of the New York City Department of Social Services.

calendar day; such identification normally occurred about two weeks after the child actually entered either a temporary shelter or one of the long-term care agencies.[5]

After 90 days, each potential study subject's case record was again reviewed at the Bureau of Child Welfare to verify that all other criteria had been met. The child was formally identified as a study subject if a positive determination had been made. If the child was excluded because of the criteria cited above, his age–sex quota position was filled by the next available subject according to the priority of the date of entry into foster care.

In establishing age and sex quotas, we had initially intended that 750 children be included in the study and that these be divided so as to include 10 percent infants (up to six months), 30 percent toddlers (six months to two years), 30 percent preschoolers (two to six years), and 30 percent children in midchildhood (six to twelve years). Because of the subsequent need to limit costs, the sample was eventually reduced to approximately 600.

The time required to fill age and sex quotas was quite varied. The infant quota was completed rapidly, taking only ten weeks for both male and female subjects. For toddlers, preschoolers, and children in midchildhood, it took about 32 weeks to fill all quotas for the female subjects and 24 to 26 weeks for the male subjects. The infant quotas were filled by March 16, 1966, whereas the last female child in midchildhood was registered in the project on August 1, 1966. If we had not developed age and sex quotas, we would have had a much larger infant group in the sample. The modified sampling plan called for inclusion of about 250 children in midchildhood, 175 preschoolers, 100 toddlers, and 75 infants. We subsequently increased the infant group to nearly 100 because we were already

---

[5] Once a child's entry was noted on the Allocation section's records, the daily log of the temporary shelters, or a returned letter from a child care agency, a research staff assistant was assigned to read available case material—usually a two-page form or face sheet of basic identifying information—to verify that the child met the sample selection criteria of: (a) entry into care on or after January 1, 1966, and (b) being under 12 years of age. If the child met these two criteria, the case name and number were recorded on a sample selection record card. If three or more children from a family were entering care, the research assistant utilized a randomizing procedure by which two children were identified as potential study subjects.

experiencing the loss of subjects who were being placed in adoptive homes.[6]

During the January–August period of sample selection, 2720 cases of children entering foster care in an age–sex bracket for which a sample quota opening still existed were reviewed to ascertain eligibility for the study. Of these, 2096 were determined ineligible; 26 percent of the potential subjects were excluded because their sex and age quotas had already been filled, and an additional 16 percent were being screened for eligibility when their quotas were filled. About 22 percent of the children were discharged before 90 days and 2 percent were placed in adoptive homes. One-third of the excluded cases reflected situations in which either the child or a sibling had been previously placed in foster care. Thus for every child we included in our sample there were three other children who entered care at the same time but were excluded for the reasons cited.

CHARACTERISTICS OF STUDY SUBJECTS

The reader may wish to refer to the work by Jenkins and Norman for a description of the family characteristics.[7] We review here the characteristics of the children included in our study, with the cautionary note that distributions may vary somewhat from the previously published volume because we are talking about children and not families.

In Table 2.1 we show the distribution of the children according to variables of ethnicity and religion. White Catholic or Protestant children constituted about 20 percent of the sample. We have included the 16 white Protestant children with the white Catholics in many of the analyses because they were too small a group to isolate and strongly resembled the white Catholic children with respect to

---

[6] Of the 624 designated as study subjects 90 days after their entry into care, 29 were subsequently adopted.

[7] Shirley Jenkins and Elaine Norman, *Filial Deprivation and Foster Care* (New York: Columbia University Press, 1972), pp. 19–51.

TABLE 2.1
ETHNICITY AND RELIGION OF CHILD SUBJECTS

	Number	Percentage
White Catholic or Protestant[a]	132	21.2
Jewish	31	5.0
Black Protestant	191	30.6
Black Catholic	68	10.9
Puerto Rican	202	32.3
Total	624	100.0

[a] Includes 116 Catholics and 16 Protestants.

key characteristics.[8] The 31 Jewish children constituted a small group (5 percent of the sample).

Black children constituted the largest group in the study (at least 40 percent). Something of a surprise to us was the finding that 68 children were black Catholic; they constituted almost 11 percent of the sample. In some of our subsequent analyses we treat the black Protestant and black Catholic children separately because they differed in a number of characteristics, especially the tendency for placement in different child care agency systems based on religious affiliation.

Puerto Rican children constituted 33 percent of the sample. Among them we have included 10 children for whom there was indication of other Latin American background. A child was designated as Puerto Rican either by birth or if at least one parent had been born there.

It is of interest to compare the characteristics of our sample with those identified for the foster care system as a whole on December 31, 1965, the day before the commencement of subject identification. White children made up 31.8 percent of the 23,258 children identified as public charges at this date, whereas they constituted 26.2 percent of our research sample. Black children constituted 45.5 percent of the larger system and 41.5 percent of the sample. Puerto Rican children were overrepresented in our sample;

[8] Also included along with the white Catholic children were two Moslem and four Oriental children who were arbitrarily placed within this group for analytic purposes.

they constituted 32.3 percent of our subjects compared to 22.7 percent of the system as a whole.[9] The differences between our study sample and the larger population can be partly explained by the following facts:

1. Eighteen percent of the larger system is composed of children 12 years and over, whereas we have excluded children 13 years or older.
2. We have excluded children in foster care under 90 days.
3. We have filled our age–sex quota cells at an uneven rate, depending on which was filled first.
4. The population in the foster care system includes "residual" children left over from all previously entering cohorts (years of admission). These were children who stayed on in care while others were discharged, whereas our sample represents an entering class of children rather than such a "residual" population.

We were pleased to find good representation from the three major ethnic groups to allow use of this information as a major independent variable in our analytic work.

Jenkins and Norman have pointed out that black and Puerto Rican families are nearly three times more prevalent in the study sample than in the general population of New York City.[10] It seems clear that children of minority groups are more apt to suffer separation and exposure to foster care than their white counterparts.

In Table 2.2 our sample is described by sex and age characteristics within the context of white, black, and Puerto Rican groups.[11] We observe the proportion of subjects under two years of age to be much lower among Puerto Rican than white or black groups. Whereas three to four out of every 10 white and black subjects were in the youngest age groupings, this was true of less than two out of 10 Puerto Rican subjects.[12] It also should be noted

[9] Source: Bureau of Child Welfare, New York City Department of Welfare, "Summary Analysis of Monthly Population Reports Submitted by Foster Care Agencies: December 31, 1960 and December 31, 1965." (Dittoed.)

[10] Jenkins and Norman, *Filial Deprivation and Foster Care*, p. 23.

[11] The mean age in years of the children at the time of placement, by ethnicity–religion, are as follows: white Catholic and Protestant (3.98), Jewish (8.23), black Protestant (3.81), black Catholic (3.34), and Puerto Rican (5.63).

[12] We have been informed by a number of observers of the foster care system that Puerto Rican infants enter care less frequently than those of other ethnic groups. This has been attributed to the availability of extended family members for the care of young children during times of parental crises. We have also been told that the "compadrazgo" and "hijos de

TABLE 2.2
AGE GROUPING OF CHILD SUBJECTS, BY SEX AND ETHNICITY

Sex and Age Group	Ethnicity			Number of Cases (N = 624)
	White	Black	Puerto Rican	
	(percentages)			
Male				
Under 2 years	31.8	41.9	18.7	99
2–5 years	24.7	24.2	36.4	90
6–12 years	43.5	33.9	44.9	127
No. of cases	85	124	107	316
Female				
Under 2 years	33.3	37.1	14.7	90
2–5 years	29.5	29.6	28.4	90
6–12 years	37.2	33.3	56.9	128
No. of cases	78	135	95	308

that older girls are more heavily represented in the Puerto Rican groups.

Table 2.2 shows males and females to be almost equally represented (boys 50.6 percent and girls 49.4 percent). Children under two years constituted 30.3 percent of the subjects, children two to five years, 28.8 percent, and those six years and over, 40.9 percent.

We saw the variable of birth status (i.e., subjects born in or out of wedlock) as providing an indication of the nature of the family-

crianza" institutions offer alternatives to foster care for Puerto Rican children. These have been described by Mizio:

> The *compadrazgo* is the institution of *compadres* (or "companion parents"), a network of ritual kinship whose members have a deep sense of obligation to each other for economic assistance, encouragement, support, and even personal corrections. *Hijos de crianza* ("children of upbringing") is the cultural practice of assuming responsibility for a child without the necessity of blood or even friendship ties, and raising the child as if he were one's own. There is no stigma attached to the parent for surrendering his child or to the child who is given up. This may be a permanent or temporary arrangement.

Emilicia Mizio, "Impact of External Systems on the Puerto Rican Family," *Social Casework* 55, (February 1974): 77.

TABLE 2.3
BIRTH STATUS OF CHILD SUBJECTS, BY AGE GROUP[a]

	Age Group			
	---	---	---	---
Birth Status	Under 2 years	2–5 Years	6–12 Years	Number of Cases
	(percentages)			
In wedlock	19.0	57.6	66.9	305
Out of wedlock	81.0	42.4	33.1	307
No. of cases	184	177	251	612

[a]Twelve cases omitted because child's birth status could not be definitely determined.

support systems available to the children. That is, unmarried mothers in crisis may have less surrounding family resources than other mothers.

Table 2.3 correlates birth status with age. In the sample as a whole there are almost equal proportions of both types of birth status, but examination of the table shows 81 percent of the very young children to be born out of wedlock. We subsequently identified many of these children as likely candidates for adoption.[13] Preschoolers and school-aged children included a higher proportion of those born in wedlock, particularly in the school-aged group, where almost 66 percent were born in wedlock.

Table 2.4 displays birth status information according to the ethnicity of the subjects. The black children stand out as having the largest proportion of children born out of wedlock; 62 percent were so characterized. The Puerto Rican group is almost evenly divided between both types of birth status. Of the white children, 67 percent were born in wedlock, with only one Jewish child born out of wedlock.

Jenkins and Norman developed an index to characterize the socioeconomic circumstances of the study families.[14] This index was constructed to be appropriate for a study population living under deprived economic circumstances. The majority of the families

[13] See chapter 5 of the present volume for information on this matter.
[14] Jenkins and Norman, *Filial Deprivation and Foster Care*, pp. 275–86.

TABLE 2.4
BIRTH STATUS OF CHILD SUBJECTS, BY ETHNICITY[a]

Birth Status	Ethnicity			Number of Cases
	White	Black	Puerto Rican	
	(percentages)			
In wedlock	67.1	37.7	51.3	305
Out of wedlock	32.9	62.3	48.7	307
No. of cases	161	252	199	612

[a] Twelve cases omitted because child's birth status could not be definitely determined.

included in our study could be so described. It must be understood that the families from which the children derived can hardly be considered as typical of American families. Over 33 percent of the mothers were single, with no previous marriage, and an additional 10 percent were divorced or widowed. The remaining women were married but most of them were not living with their spouses. Measures of socioeconomic status typically found in the literature presume an intact family unit in which the male's occupation and income is an important basis for classification. The index measuring socioeconomic circumstances included information about sources of support, the highest educational achievement of any adult in the household, the income rank of the neighborhood, the juvenile delinquency rank of the neighborhood, and the number of negative housing conditions. The families were divided into "higher," "middle," and "lower" families so that exactly one-third of the total sample was in each category.[15]

The families of Puerto Rican children in the study show the greatest impoverishment as reflected by the index of socioeconomic circumstances. Some 44 percent were in the lowest group, compared to 28 percent of the black children and only 4 percent of the white subjects (Table 2.5). The white children almost uniformly came from families of more favorable circumstances; 76 percent were from

[15] It is important for the reader to bear in mind that "high," "middle," and "low" refer to relative strata of a largely deprived study population.

TABLE 2.5
SOCIOECONOMIC LEVEL OF CHILD SUBJECT'S FAMILY, BY ETHNICITY

Socioeconomic Status	Ethnicity			Number of Cases
	White	Black	Puerto Rican	
		(percentages)		
Higher	76.1[a]	37.1	19.8	260
Middle	20.2	34.7	36.1	196
Lower	3.7	28.2	44.1	168
No. of cases	163	259	202	624

[a] Among the white families, all 31 Jewish families were in the higher socioeconomic level.

families in the higher socioeconomic bracket,[16] with Jewish children from the most advantaged circumstances. If we were to characterize the sample as a whole, we would have to identify the Puerto Rican families as those with the most impoverished circumstances, followed by the black families.[17] Table 2.6 cross-tabulates birth status with socioeconomic level. There was a higher proportion of children born out of wedlock in the lower socioeconomic group (some 59 percent), but the proportions were not dramatically different between the middle and the higher groups, where about 47 percent of the children were born out of wedlock.

Analysis of our data showed that 31 percent of the lower socioeconomic group entered foster care through the Family Court, compared to 18 percent of the middle and 17 percent of the high economic groups. Thus there appears to be an association between economic circumstances and mode of entry into foster care.

[16] We remind the reader that figures given here reflect child subjects, rather than the families, as the unit of count.

[17] Another indication of the association between socioeconomic circumstances and ethnicity is the percentage of each group where the child's mother or the household of the latter were receiving public assistance: white Catholic or Protestant (29.6 percent), Jewish (13.0 percent), black Protestant (59.7 percent), black Catholic (54.4 percent), and Puerto Rican (66.9 percent).

TABLE 2.6
BIRTH STATUS OF CHILD SUBJECTS, BY SOCIOECONOMIC LEVEL[a]

Birth Status	Socioeconomic Level			Number of Cases
	Higher	Middle	Lower	
		(percentages)		
In wedlock	53.3	52.6	41.1	305
Out of wedlock	46.7	47.4	58.9	307
No. of cases	255	194	163	612

[a]Twelve cases omitted because child's birth status could not definitely be determined.

REASONS FOR PLACEMENT

The reasons for placement of children in the sample provide a good indication of some of the main social problems existing in New York City. Essentially, the entry of children into foster care reflects major breakdowns in parental performance; in a minority of cases, it is the child himself who, by his behavior provides the major impetus for placement. Problems of inadequate health and social service delivery no doubt further contribute to the failure of parents and children to carry on within a community context.

Analysis of the situations leading to the need for the placement of the children led to a classification scheme consisting of nine reasons. The classification is based in part on established categories stated by intake workers and supplemented by case material and reasons given by respondents to interviews with social workers in the family study reported by Jenkins and Norman. It was recognized that any family could have multiple reasons related to a child's entering care, and considerable effort was invested in developing a reliable procedure for identifying the reason that seemed central. We made one modification in the Jenkins and Norman classification scheme by adding a category covering death of a parent as a main reason for placement; this applied to 14 children (see Table 2.7).

It is important for the reader to keep in mind that the codification of the main reason for placement used here is essentially based

TABLE 2.7
DISTRIBUTION OF CHILDREN ACCORDING TO
MAIN REASON FOR PLACEMENT IN FOSTER CARE

Reason	Number	Percentage
Mental illness of child-caring person	136	21.9
Neglect or abuse of child	91	14.6
Behavior of child	73	11.7
Physical illness of child-caring person	68	10.9
Abandonment or desertion by parent	67	10.7
Parent unwilling or unable to continue care	63	10.1
Family problem	57	9.1
Parent unwilling or unable to assume care	55	8.8
Death of a parent	14	2.2
Total	624	100.0

on parental perspectives, which were not always in accord with the views of agencies. It is also important to note that while coded categories were designed to be mutually exclusive, they were not so in an absolute sense. In other words, a family may have been coded as requiring foster care services mainly because of parental neglect and abuse, with mental illness of the parent or behavior difficulty of the child evidenced as a secondary reason.

In our study the largest group of children entered foster care because of mental illness of the child-caring person, typically the mother, who was usually institutionalized. This kind of situation was faced by 21.8 percent of the children in our sample. About 60 percent of these cases involved actual mental hospitalization, while the remaining cases clearly reflected severe emotional disturbance without consequent institutionalization. Such cases were more prevalent among the children who entered foster care through the public welfare agency, the Bureau of Child Welfare, where they constituted 25 percent of the cases, in contrast with the Family Court, where only 9 percent of the cases reflected the mother's mental illness as the main reason for placement (Table 2.8). The behavior of the child was identified as the main reason for placement for 12 percent of the sample, and there was little difference between the Family Court and the public welfare modes of entry. This was not the case with respect to physical illness, which

TABLE 2.8
REASON FOR PLACEMENT, BY JURISDICTION OF CASE AT ENTRY
(N = 624)

	Jurisdiction	
Reason	Bureau of Child Welfare, Department of Social Services	Family Court
	(percentages)	
Mental illness of child-caring person	25.1	9.2
Neglect or abuse of child	4.3	53.8
Behavior of child	11.9	10.8
Physical illness of child-caring person	12.8	3.8
Abandonment or desertion by parent	12.3	4.6
Parent unwilling to continue care	10.7	7.7
Family problem	9.5	7.7
Parent unwilling to assume care	10.9	.8
Death of a parent	2.4	1.5
No. of cases	494	130

constituted 11 percent of the total sample. Illness was the main reason for placement of 13 percent of the children who entered through the public welfare agency and only 4 percent through the Family Court.

Unmarried mothers unwilling to assume care of their babies accounted for 9 percent of the reasons for placement of the entire sample, and this reflected almost exclusively cases entering via the public welfare agency. Parents who were unable or unwilling to continue with the care of their children coped with a variety of problems. They constituted 10 percent of the sample and were reflected in both court cases (8 percent) and public welfare cases (11 percent).

By far the most common reason for placement among court cases was child neglect or abuse. While 15 percent of the total sample were in this category, 54 percent of the court cases were in it, in contrast with only 4 percent of the cases that involved entry through the public welfare agency. Abandonment or desertion, on the other hand, was more prevalent among the public welfare cases than among the court-admitted children; there were 12 percent in the former category and only 5 percent in the latter. Abandonment or desertion as the main reason for placement constituted 11 percent of the reasons for the total sample.

A residual category was developed in which were put, as a main reason for placement, a variety of personal or family situational problems that resulted in the child's entering care. These constituted 9 percent of the reasons for placement for the entire sample and were similarly distributed for the court and the public welfare admissions. Some 14 children entered care at the time of the death of a parent; this represented 2.2 percent of the entire sample and was fairly evenly distributed between the court and the public welfare admissions.

In Table 2.9 the main reasons for placement are cross-tabulated with age groupings. Behavior of the child as a major reason for placement was almost exclusively a problem of children aged six to 12 years. Similarly, the problem of a parent unwilling to assume care

TABLE 2.9

REASON FOR PLACEMENT, BY CHILD SUBJECT'S AGE GROUPING
($N = 624$)

	Age Grouping		
Reason	*Under 2 Years*	*2–5 Years*	*6–12 Years*
	(percentages)		
Mental illness of child-caring person	16.4	31.1	19.2
Neglect or abuse of child	12.2	17.8	14.1
Behavior of child	—	0.6	28.2
Physical illness of child-caring person	10.6	11.7	10.6
Abandonment or desertion by parent	12.2	15.6	6.3
Parent unwilling to continue care	7.9	10.6	11.4
Family problem	11.1	9.4	7.5
Parent unwilling to assume care	28.6	0.6	—
Death of a parent	1.1	2.8	2.7
No. of cases	189	180	255

of a child was almost exclusively a problem of the child under two years of age. Neglect or abuse of children tended to prevail across the three age groupings in equal proportions. However, abandonment or desertion was more apt to affect preschoolers. Mental illness of the child caring person was more prevalent for the parents of children aged two to five years. The physical health of the child caring person was not age-related.

Table 2.10 shows reason for placement according to enthnicity. A number of salient facts are readily identifiable. For white and Puerto Rican children, mental illness of the child caring person is the predominant category, while for black children, neglect and abuse is the most prevalent category. Behavior of the child was a prevalent category for white children (18 percent, with 58 percent of the Jewish children in the sample) compared to black and Puerto Rican children (each 9 percent). Abandonment was the reason for placement for 12 percent each of the black and Puerto Rican

TABLE 2.10
REASON FOR PLACEMENT, BY CHILD SUBJECT'S ETHNICITY

Reason	Ethnicity			
	White	Black	Puerto Rican	Number of Cases
		(percentages)		
Mental illness of child-caring person	27.6	17.4	22.8	136
Neglect or abuse of child	8.6	18.9	13.9	91
Behavior of child	18.4	9.2	9.4	73
Physical illness of child-caring person	7.4	9.2	15.8	68
Abandonment or desertion by parent	6.1	12.4	12.4	67
Parent unwilling to continue care	8.0	7.7	14.9	63
Family problem	5.5	12.4	7.9	57
Parent unwilling to assume care	14.7	9.7	3.0	55
Death of a parent	3.7	3.1	—	14
No. of cases	163	259	202	624

TABLE 2.11
REASON FOR PLACEMENT, BY SOCIOECONOMIC LEVEL
OF CHILD'S FAMILY[a]

Reason	Socioeconomic Level			Number of Cases
	Higher	Middle	Lower	
		(percentages)		
Mental illness of child-caring person	21.5	26.0	17.3	136
Neglect or abuse of child	11.5	12.8	21.4	91
Behavior of child	16.2	5.6	11.9	73
Physical illness of child-caring person	3.5	16.3	16.1	68
Abandonment or desertion by parent	12.3	7.1	12.5	67
Parent unwilling to continue care	10.0	12.2	7.7	63
Family problem	7.7	11.2	8.9	57
Parent unwilling to assume care	16.5	4.6	1.8	55
Death of parent	0.8	4.1	2.4	14
No. of cases	260	196	168	624

[a] The socioeconomic level for 156 children (25 percent) was estimated using a linear regression model, which accounted for 63 percent of the variance in the socioeconomic level of child subjects for whom SES scores were available.

children but only 6 percent of the white subjects. In Table 2.11, reason for placement is shown according to socioeconomic level.[18] It is significant that physical illness of the child caring person was rarely the major reason for placement of the higher status families (3.5 percent), while it constituted about 16 percent of the lower and middle status families' reasons for placement. On the other hand, among lower status families the unwillingness of the parent to assume care of a child born out of wedlock was rarely a reason (1.8 percent), in contrast with higher status families (almost 17 percent).

[18] The classification scheme was based on procedures developed by Jenkins and Sauber in their earlier study of the reasons for placement in New York City, as published in Shirley Jenkins and Mignon Sauber, *Paths to Child Placement* (New York: Community Council of Greater New York, 1966).

Neglect or abuse of a child was a more prevalent reason for placement among lower status families. Almost twice the proportion of such cases were found in the lower status families than in the other two groups. When we cross-tabulated reason for placement with ethnicity, controlling for wedlock status, a number of interesting findings emerged.[19] For white families, the mental illness of the child caring person of children born in wedlock constituted 33 percent of the cases, whereas this was true of only 13 percent of the families where the child was born out of wedlock. No such dramatic difference on the basis of birth status was found among the Puerto Rican or black children. For all three ethnic groups, behavior of the child as the major reason for placement was found to be more characteristic of children born in than out of wedlock.

Physical illness of the child caring person was rarely a reason for placement for a child born out of wedlock among the white children, but constituted 10 percent of those born in wedlock. Birth status was not a differentiating factor with respect to physical illness of Puerto Rican child caring persons, but was more apt to be a factor for children born in wedlock among the black children. Child neglect or abuse was more frequent with children born out of wedlock among all three ethnic groups.

One final note on the demographic characteristics of our study population is in order. Our data show the Puerto Rican children to enter care in the largest family units. In only 27 percent of the cases were Puerto Rican children placed as single children (i.e., with no siblings entering care with them), whereas 49 percent of the white Catholics or Protestants, 71 percent of the Jewish children, 42 percent of the black Protestants, and 46 percent of the black Catholics were placed as single children.

This chapter provides the reader with information about the sample selection criteria and the background characteristics of the subjects chosen for study. We now proceed to an examination of the methodology used in the study, with particular emphasis on the measures used to assess the condition of the children over the five years of investigation.

[19] To conserve space, these data are not tabulated here.

THREE

PROCEDURES
FOR STUDY
OF FOSTER CHILDREN

The purpose of this chapter is to orient the reader to the methods used to assess the foster children. We present our thinking about the measurement tasks we faced and provide description of the data-gathering procedures used. Some research instruments took the form of standardized tests, while others were constructed to suit our special purposes. We also describe measures we have employed in our analyses of the "outcomes" experienced by the foster children, involving description of other key actors in the foster care phenomenon, namely, parents, foster parents, and agencies. The chapter concludes with an orientation to the approaches we employed in organizing and analyzing our data.

CHOICE OF ASSESSMENT PROCEDURES

The task of assessing the adjustment of human beings for the purpose of gathering research data poses demands that differ significantly from those that arise when the examination procedure is intended to support a treatment effort. In the latter case, the results of assessment are seen as a guide for therapeutic intervention and what is learned constitutes information that can be tempered in the light of an ongoing appraisal of the patient. While the consequences of the examination might entail the designation of a label to be assigned to the individual's condition, this is hopefully secondary to the task of formulating a plan for remediation of the problem for which treatment was originally sought.

The act of assessing human beings for the purpose of meeting research goals serves the need to classify individuals. The information is important in its own right. The examination of the subject is not intended to have consequences in an immediate personal sense. If the rights of human subjects are well observed, the individual being studied does not suffer consequences from the inquiry into his personal life situation. A common task facing those involved in treatment and research is to obtain a *correct* assessment of the individual being appraised. This is often seen as fraught with possibility for error, since human beings can be most artful in giving false cues about the phenomenon under investigation. We approached the task of assessing our 624 foster child subjects with due appreciation of the hazards involved. The development of a valid portraiture of the children over time was our paramount goal. To carry out our assessment of the children over the course of their experience in foster care—and after discharge, for those who returned to their own homes—required resolution of a number of problems.

First, we attempted to define the major dependent variables in our study. We were clear that our interest was focused on two major kinds of "outcomes": (a) status changes experienced by the children and (b) changes in their personal and social adjustment. In the former category, we were concerned with such variables as the duration of a child's placement experience and whether he was returned home during the five years of longitudinal investigation. We were also interested in determining the nature of other status outcomes: (a) whether children who were "adoptable" were indeed adopted, (b) how often children "turned over" in care, that is, how many placements the children experienced, and (c) how many children deteriorated in care to the point of requiring institutionalization for mental illness.

In the category of outcomes dealing with the personal and social functioning of the children, we had to grapple with more subtle and less easily measured phenomena. Describing qualities in the children that could be assessed on a repeated basis over five years required explication of our views about child development and our notions of what constituted good or poor child adjustment. Past experience in research of this nature and our careful review of the literature had sensitized us to the fact that the territory we were becoming involved in was still in a highly undeveloped state, that it was more art than science.

One very critical choice confronting us was whether or not to rely on an overall clinical measure of the child's adjustment—by a social worker, psychologist, or psychiatrist—which would enable us to locate the condition of the child on a single scale. For example, in a well-known midtown Manhattan study, reported by Srole et al., field-survey questionnaire data concerning the mental health of subjects were converted into summaries of symptom formation and rated independently by two psychiatrists as: (a) well, (b) mild, (c) moderate, (d) marked, (e) severe, or (f) incapacitated.[1] The virtue of such a scale is its simplicity—it is easily understood by the layman and can be statistically analyzed with relative ease; but the procedure has limitations. A single global measure lacks subtlety. It does not differentiate areas of the child's life where the pressures of separation and foster care placement may give rise to evidence of stress and/or dysfunctional behavior. Furthermore, we cannot, so to speak, "get into the head " of the psychiatrist, to determine what mixtures of behavioral and symptomatic phenomena were put together to constitute an overall judgment. We also had misgivings about building an entire research structure upon a single measure and wondered whether it was not more sensible to spread the risk by securing measures in a number of domains and using multiple measures.

Second, we had to determine how to meet the longitudinal requirements of the study. It was important to develop measuring techniques that could be employed on a repeated basis, in keeping with our longitudinal design. Our measures had to be appropriate for subjects who ranged in age from infancy to 12 years at the time of entry into foster care. Thus, we sought assessment procedures that were clearly age-appropriate while at the same time allowing for repeated measurement of a child's progress on some common dimensions over a five-year period. Experience in developing multi-faceted measures for such a longitudinal enterprise that could

---

[1] Leo Srole et al., *Mental Health in the Metropolis* (New York: McGraw-Hill, 1962).

provide guidelines for our efforts was relatively rare in the child development literature at the time we launched our study.[2]

Third, we had to decide whether to rely on well-established standardized measuring instruments or to fashion approaches of our own creation that might be better suited to our goal, namely, assessing the consequences for children of suffering separation from their parents and experiencing varying kinds of living arrangements in foster care. In the area of cognitive functioning it seemed clear that persuasive arguments could be made for using standardized intelligence tests.[3] But what about measures of personal and social adjustment? As we had anticipated, this proved to be a much more complicated area of assessment activity than IQ testing, requiring custom-tailored construction of measures designed to meet the specialized purposes and circumstances of our investigation.

In selection of appropriate sources of data, there were a number of modes of data collection available to us, depending on our choice of informants about the children. We could test the subjects directly, using a standardized test, and supplement this by conducting structured research interviews with the older children in our sample, thus obtaining direct accounts of the foster care experience from those most directly involved. We also had the option of eliciting developmental data from each child's parent as part of the field interviewing of families, an enterprise that paralleled our own investigation. We additionally had the possibility of securing data from agency caseworkers who could provide information about the developmental progress of the children based on their own direct observations and reports of foster parents or institutional child care personnel to whom they had access.

A note of reality has to be introduced at this point. Our decisions relative to the problems we have set forth had to be made within the constraints of the budget allowed us by the funding agency. While our grant was generous, it was nevertheless not open-ended. For example, we could have advanced the idea that every child in our study ought be examined by a psychiatrist; whatever the merits of

---

[2] For an important recent exception, see Mary C. Jones, et al., eds., *The Course of Human Development* (Waltham, Mass.: Xerox College Publishing, 1971).

[3] See chapter 7 for a discussion of these reasons.

such a procedure, we simply would not have been able to use this form of data gathering because of the level of funding required. For similar reasons, we could not consider approaches involving systematic observation of the children.

It was also essential that our choice of procedures reflect the tolerances of subjects and agency personnel. We obviously could not make unreasonable demands on the busy practitioners, who often carried sizable caseloads. We also had to recognize the tolerances of the children, many of whom had experienced considerable trauma in their lives.

To summarize our overall approach to the measurement task with respect to the questions raised, we undertook to ensure the following:

1. We would not rely on a single assessment of a child's adjustment and instead would use multiple measures covering a variety of domains. In other words, we would not put all of our eggs into one basket.

2. Wherever possible, we would use age-appropriate measures that would permit coverage of behaviors coming into play as the child matured.

3. We would have recourse to a variety of informants: the child himself, his parents, social workers (and through them, foster parents and child-care personnel), and teachers.

4. We would use standardized tests as well as data stemming from familiar sociological and social–psychological approaches (i.e., survey data, ratings, and various kinds of information provided through mailed schedules). We would not use psychiatric examinations or systematic observation of the children.

5. Where possible, we would use repeated measures over time. We would not rule out, however, one-shot approaches that might seem appropriate as we proceeded into the study.

We next will describe our procedures and will clarify for the reader the basis of our choices in the light of the considerations we have outlined.

DEVELOPMENTAL HISTORIES OF CHILDREN

One way of obtaining an estimate of the condition of the children close to the time they arrived in foster care was to secure information from their mothers (or the person who had taken care of them prior to placement). We were able to include a series of questions about their developmental histories as part of the field interviews carried out in 1966 in the research reported by Jenkins and Norman.[4] We had prepared these questions to obtain an overall view of the degree to which the children had come into care with histories of physical and emotional difficulty. An analysis of parental responses resulted in the creation of three developmental indexes:

1. Health Index, which provides a basis for classifying data on the child's physical condition at time of admission to foster care, and focuses on: (a) illnesses and accidents since birth, (b) mother's condition during pregnancy, (c) history of any birth complications, and (d) child's general health status at birth. Of the subjects, 20 per cent were identified as showing health problems in any one of these areas.

2. Emotional Problem Index which focuses on: (a) difficulties of sleep, (b) toilet trainning, and (c) disciplinary problems. Problems in any one of these areas were reported for 33 percent of the subjects.

3. Developmental Problem Index, which focuses on: problems of the children with respect to eating, walking, talking, and body coordination.

The internal reliabilities of the indexes (using the Cronbach alpha as the reliability measure) showed them to be quite soft. The alpha for Index (1) was .37, for Index (2) .41, and for Index (3) .54. Although we were pleased to have some baseline measures of the children's condition at the time of arrival, we had to recognize that these indexes did not provide a particularly sturdy platform on which to predict the child's future development. Nevertheless, our experience in utilizing these admittedly crude measures in a variety of analyses has shown some capacity for the information covered to contribute to an understanding, albeit of a modest nature, of the children's adjustment over the course of the study.

PSYCHOLOGICAL TESTING OF THE CHILDREN

The children in our sample were tested at three times: (a) Time I, after being in foster care at least 90 days, (b) Time II, about two and

[4]Shirley Jenkins and Elaine Norman, *Filial Deprivation and Foster Care* (New York: Columbia University Press, 1972).

one-half years after entering care, and (c) Time III, about five years after entry. Two basic kinds of tests were administered, intelligence tests and projective tests.

Intelligence tests

Three intelligence tests were selected for administration on an age-appropriate basis.[5] The Psyche Cattell Infant Scale was chosen for subjects aged three months to two years and 11 months.[6] This is a standardized test to evaluate the mental growth of young children; it follows the groundwork used in constructing the Gesell and Merrill-Palmer tests.[7] The Minnesota Preschool Scale was administered to subjects aged three years to five years and 11 months.[8] This test is quite similar to the Stanford-Binet, with the added advantage that there are verbal and performance subscores. The children aged six years and over were given the Wechsler Intelligence Scale for Children (WISC).[9] This is a widely used test with a breakdown into verbal and performance subscores.

Because children advanced from one test to another as they matured over the five years of the study, it was necessary for analytic purposes to convert scores into "deviation IQs" relating the means and standard deviations to a common standard. This is discussed in chapter 7, where we also describe the conditions under which the subjects were tested, the losses incurred in the sample over the three testings, and the examiners who tested the children.

Projective Tests

The projective tests we used were limited to a drawing test and a picture test at Times I and II, administered to children of school age. The Draw-A-Person and Draw-A-Family tests were included (with

---

[5]The testing of intelligence and the rationale for our approach are discussed in chapter 7.

[6] Psyche Cattell, *The Measurement of Intelligence of Infants and Young Children*, rev. ed. (New York: Psychological Corporation, 1960).

[7] Arnold Gesell, *The Mental Growth of the Preschool Child* (New York: Macmillan, 1925); Rachel Stutzmann: *Mental Measurement of Preschool Children* (Yonkers, N.Y.: World Book, 1931).

[8] Florence Goodenough, et al., *Minnesota Preschool Scale (Manual)* (Circle Pines, Minn.: American Guidance Service, 1940).

[9] David Wechsler, *Wechsler Intelligence Scale for Children* (New York: Psychological Corporation, 1949).

children six years of age and older) to obtain information concerning the child's feelings about himself, his concept of a family, and his identification with his own (natural or foster) family. Rating scales were based on the responses of the children to these tests and were patterned after those of Machover and Harris.[10] The psychologists rated the child's drawings with reference to the following scales: (a) stability of sex role (unstable/marginal/stable) (b) internal conflict (much/some/little), (c) self-confidence (little/average/much), (d) avoidance of repression (much/some/little), (e) maturity (immature/average/unusually mature), (f) social relatedness (poorly related/somewhat related/well related), (g) sense of family cohesion (none/some/much), and (h) which family (fantasy/foster/own). The test was also used as the basis for calculating an intelligence score.

The Michigan Picture Test was the second projective test used with the children.[11] It is a test much like the Thematic Apperception Test (TAT) and the Child Apperception Test (CAT). It consists of a set of photographs about which the child is asked to tell a story. The advantage of this test over others of a similar nature is the scoring system, which is relatively objective and yields scores in such areas as interpersonal relationships and kinds and amount of tension. It was administered to children eight years of age or older.

The responses of the children were codified to produce objective scores based on four primary psychological needs: (a) love or the need for affection, (b) extrapunitive needs, including oral, physical, or psychological aggression, (c) submission needs as indicated by deference or passivity, and (d) personal adequacy, either physical or psychological. An index of the total number of needs expressed is considered a measure of tension related to unresolved psychological needs. The authors of the test report differences in verbalized expressions of unresolved conflict in groups of well- and poorly adjusted schoolchildren.

The responses of the children were also codified for mean

---

[10] Karen Machover, *Personality Projection in the Drawing of Human Figures* (Springfield, Ill., Thomas, 1949); Dale B. Harris, *Children's Drawings as Measures of Intellectual Maturity* (revision and extension of the Goodenough Draw-A-Man Test) (New York: Harcourt, Brace, World, 1963).

[11] G. Andrew, S. W. Hartwell, M. L. Hutt, and R. E. Walton, *Michigan Picture Test Manual* (Chicago: Science Research Associates, 1953).

percentages of past, present, and future verb tenses. The authors report that poorly adjusted children use significantly fewer present tense references than do well-adjusted children.[12]

Interview

During the second round of testing a structured interview was conducted with subjects seven years of age and older about their reactions to the foster care experience. There have been few systematic inquires into children's own perceptions of separation and how they have integrated the experience into their views of themselves and the world around them. One detailed investigation in this area was undertaken by Weinstein, who studied 61 children under the care of the Chicago Child Care Society.[13] The interview that we developed is influenced by Weinstein's research, although the emphasis is somewhat different. Both assume that a child's confusion over who he is, to whom he belongs, why he is not able to live with his parents, and what his future holds may be important in determining his ability to develop normally. The interview was designed to elicit information in the following areas: (a) the child's cathexis and integration of the separation experience, (b) the child's sense of identification with his family and/or substitute family persons, (c) his sense of identity and self-image, and (d) his concept of the causal basis for the events that transpired in his own life and led to the experience of separation and placement.

The interviewing schedule was prepared in three versions: (a) for children in foster family care (59 subjects), (b) for those in institutions (90 subjects), and (c) for those who had returned to their own homes (56 subjects). The interviews were tape recorded and their contents typed. While the interviews were rated by our psychologists and the ratings subjected to analysis, we do not present this material here owing to limited space. In chapter 15 we present the analysis of the child interview material, emphasizing the more qualitative and subjective aspects of the phenomena dealt with in the interview.

[12] Dr. Leonard Kogan of the City University of New York provided consultation in reviewing the test literature and advising on the selection of tests.

[13] Eugene A. Weinstein, *The Self-Image of the Foster Child* (New York: Russell Sage Foundation, 1960).

Sentence Completion
After each child over age seven had been interviewed at Time II, a sentence-completion test was administered. It was designed to elicit material similar to that covered by the interview. It provided the children with the opportunity to articulate their inner feelings in as spontaneous a manner as possible. When used to measure attitudes and orientations of subjects, the sentence-completion technique involves the construction of a list of beginning phrases or sentence stems such as:

> Children who are bad...
> When I grow up...
> My family is...
> A sad time for me was when...
> I felt happiest when...

It was necessary to deal with a wide range of answers to the sentence stems, and considerable effort went into developing a coding scheme for classifying them. After analyzing the responses of the children to this part of our investigation, we recognized that we had been permitted only limited access to inner emotional material and many of our subjects seemed quite restrained in their answers. Yet certain insights emerged, and we discuss these briefly in chapter 15.

Clinical Assessment
Because our examining psychologists had access to the children for up to two hours of testing, we thought it useful to have them appraise the subjects with respect to their emotional condition (abnormal/suspect/normal) and intellectual capability (defective/borderline/normal/advanced). We particularly desired the ratings on the emotional condition of the children for purposes of comparison with the estimates of other observers of the child (i.e., social workers and teachers). While we did not intend to use the psychologist's assessment as a validity check in a strict sense, it was nevertheless of interest to be able to determine the correlation between observers. Since the children who were discharged were often no longer seen by their caseworkers after a period of several months, we could not rely on such observers for progress reports on

how the children were faring after their return home. In contrast, the psychologists continued to examine children even after their discharge from foster care. We thus had the advantage of a measure that would be available throughout the study.

SCHOOL PERFORMANCE AND ACHIEVEMENT

We considered it important to determine how the children in our study fared with respect to school performance. Considering the depressed and disorganized family circumstances from which most of them came and the disruption they had experienced through separation and placement in foster care, it was clear that they would be vulnerable to some degree of scholastic failure. The attendant consequences of such failure need not be elaborated; it makes sense to assume that the spectrum of failures in adulthood characterizing the parents of children in foster care derive from earlier serious dysfunctions of childhood. It is reasonable to hold child care agencies and schools responsible for what happens in this vital area.

In order to study this phenomenon, a "school report form" was developed and sent to the schools the children attended. If the child was still in foster care, the agency was requested to forward the form to his school. A stamped envelope was provided for return of the form to the research project rather than to the agencies. If the child had returned home, the school was contacted directly by the research staff, after we had determined the school's identity from the child's parent. Early in the course of the study, cooperation had been secured for this part of our research effort from the New York City Board of Education and a copy of a letter of support from the administration of the board accompanied every form sent to a local school.

The data supplied by the teachers about the children were combined into indexes of achievement based on a number of subjects. Measures were also created in the areas of attendance, general behavior, and school performance. These are described in chapters 9 and 10.

The reader should be aware that this part of our research could only be relevant for those subjects old enough to attend school at the time they entered foster care. The three data-gathering occasions coincided with the psychological testing periods (Times I–III) and with the mailing of research forms to the agencies, designed to gather behavioral and developmental information. As children achieved school age, they were included in the school survey. In chapters 9 and 10 we present cross-sectional analyses of the school data for each of the three data-gathering occasions and analyze the changes in school performance of the children over time.

Teacher Ratings

At Time III we included a rating instrument published by Science Research Associates of Chicago with our request for information from the schools. This instrument, the Rating Scale for Pupil Adjustment, was to be filled out by teachers as a way of classifying the children with respect to personal and social adjustment as shown in the classroom.[14] There are 11 rating scales included in the form. Three indexes were created by grouping items according to the instructions of those who had constructed the instrument: (a) emotional adjustment score (4 items), (b) aggressive behavior score (4 items), and (c) inhibitory control score (3 items). We also found it useful to combine nine items into an overall adjustment score. We were pleased to find that this summary index showed high internal reliability (as measured by Cronbach's alpha) and gave evidence of fairly strong correlations between the teacher's perceptions and those of the caseworkers as measured by the Child Behavior Characteristics (CBC) scores.[15] These findings are discussed in chapter 12.

CHILD PROFILES

Coinciding with the three psychological testing occasions, a "child profile form" was sent to the child care agencies where the children

[14] The instrument was developed as part of the research undertaken in connection with the Michigan Picture Test. The *Rating Scale for Pupil Adjustment* is published with normative data by Science Research Associates, 259 East Erie Street, Chicago, Illinois 60611.

[15] The scale and an analysis of its properties can be obtained from the authors at the Columbia University School of Social Work, 622 W. 113th Street, New York, N.Y., 10025.

were placed. It was requested that the caseworker who best knew the child fill out the form. The research instrument on each occasion was fairly elaborate, ranging from 27 pages at Time I to 16 pages at Time III. The information could only be secured for children who had contact with caseworkers, that is, those remaining in care or receiving postdischarge service. Thus, the number of forms available for subjects declined over time; at Time III, 223 forms were received (representing 98 percent of the children still in care).

The child profile form covered a variety of topics, including physical and emotional health, growth and development, adjustment to being in foster care, modes of relating to substitute caretakers as well as own parents, and play behavior.[16]

Because of the volume and complexity of data gathered in this study, we have decided to limit our presentation of the profile material to quite specialized information gathered at Times II and III. The latter data-gathering occasion covered the children still in care at the end of five years.[17] In chapters 13 and 14 we analyze two types of data: (a) symptomatic behavior reported about the children and (b) the nature of the child's attachment behavior (to caretakers and/or own parents).[18]

Symptomatic Behavior

Included in the Time III child profile form was a list of 37 child behaviors chosen as a basis for characterizing the adjustment of the children. It had been developed by one of the authors for a longitudinal study of adopted children, with some interesting results.[19] The symptoms encompassed a variety of behaviors fairly common to children. They were the kind that most parents or other observers

[16] At Time I, specialized forms were developed for infants, toddlers, and school-aged children. At Times II and III, general forms were used without respect to age. The forms were developed by one of the present authors (Eugene B. Shinn).

[17] Summaries of these data have previously been made available in progress reports to the granting agency. For example, see Eugene B. Shinn, "Foster Care for Infants: A Three-Year Longitudinal Study of 84 Infants Entering Long-Term Care Before Age of Six Months," Child Welfare Research Program, Columbia University of Social Work, March 1, 1970. (Mimeographed.)

[18] In chapter 14 we also present analyses of symptomatic behavior reported by the mothers of those children who were returned home before the end of the study.

[19] David Fanshel, *Far From the Reservation:The Transracial Adoption of American Indian Children* (Metuchen, N.J.: Scarecrow Press, 1972).

of children could easily identify and were fairly straightforward and hardly subtle. The rater was requested to indicate on a three-part scale whether the symptomatic behavior was present "sometimes," "frequently," or "rarely or never." When summed into a single score in the earlier study, the symptom list had correlated fairly highly with an independent clinical judgment of the child's adjustment.[20] A factor analysis and item analysis procedure was used to create a number of multiple-item indexes, including emotional maturity, body and bowel control, fears, and aggressiveness (see chapter 14).

Attachments

An important aspect of the adjustment of the child who remains in foster care for several years concerns the attachments he is able to make with his own parents, foster parents, institutional personnel, and with other significant individuals. The literature on maternal deprivation is replete with reference to "bonding" and has emphasized the hazard that children deprived of maternal care may manifest "affectionless and psychopathic character."[21] Concern has been expressed that such children will not be able to develop meaningful relationships with others and that they will be confused about their own identities. We have relied on rating scales filled out by the caseworkers to develop several measures related to this area of our interest. In chapter 13 we describe and analyze such phenomena as: (a) the child's attachment to his own parents, (b) the degree to which he is entrenched in the foster care setting, (c) the degree to which he shows evidence of identity conflict, (d) how he is coping with the foster care environment.

Parent Reports on Child
Symptomatic Behavior

For children who had returned home it was not possible to secure reports from agency caseworkers—as it had been for children remaining in care—about symptomatic behavior. We decided to

---

[20] Ibid., pp. 306–37.

[21] John Bowlby, *Maternal Care and Mental Health* (Geneva: World Health Organization, 1952), p. 47.

secure this information from the mothers of the children (or other child-caring persons in a few instances). When our psychologists visited the homes of the children at Time III, they enlisted the cooperation of the mothers in an interview about the child that lasted approximately 15 minutes. The content of the interview was focused on symptomatic behavior and covered much the same ground as the child profile form. The responses were subjected to a factor analysis which served as a guide to the construction of several indexes reflecting such phenomena as: (a) evidence of behavioral problems, (b) quality of health, (c) quality of security and sociability, (d) evidence of toileting problems, and (e) evidence of sleep problems. The analysis of these measures is presented in chapter 14.

CHILD BEHAVIOR CHARACTERISTICS (CBC) FORM

The CBC is a rating instrument constructed in the form of an adjective check list. It was developed in a series of replication studies of the behavior of normal and disturbed children.[22] The form's development represents a convergence of two lines of investigation in child development research. One complements the work of a number of investigators (Becker, Lapouse, and Peterson) concerned with the basic task of describing the behavioral characteristics of representative groups of normal children (i.e., the nonpsychiatric samples).[23] The development of a parsimonious set of descriptive categories that can be replicated for children in many different social contexts is seen as particularly necessary to further research and professional communication among those concerned

[22] For full description of the form, see Edgar F. Borgatta and David Fanshel, "The Child Behavior Characteristics (CBC) Form: Revised Age-Specific Forms," *Multivariate Behavioral Research.* 5 (January 1970): 49–52.

[23] Wesley C. Becker and Ronald S. Krug, "A Circumplex Model for Social Behavior in Children," *Child Development* 35 (1964): 371–96; Rema Lapouse and Mary A. Monk, "Behavior Deviations in a Representative Sample of Children," *American Journal of Orthopsychiatry* 34 (1964): 436–46; Donald R. Peterson, "The Age Generality of Personality Factors Derived from Ratings," *Educational Psychology Measurement* 20 (1960): 461–74; Donald Peterson, "Behavioral Problems of Middle Childhood," *Journal of Consulting Psychology* 25 (1961): 205–29.

with child welfare programs and their assessment. The second line of investigation, pursued by Borgatta, Fanshel, and others, is concerned with the emotional problems of adopted and foster children.[24]

The preparation of the CBC form resulted from the need to modify previous approaches to child description undertaken by Borgatta and Fanshel to take into account the requirements of the longitudinal study reported here. Earlier studies had focused primarily on samples of school-aged children, generally from 7 to 17 years of age. Previous versions of the form now had to be modified to allow rating of infants and toddlers as well as school-aged children. The development of such rating forms for the description of human behavior requires "keying" to the appropriate age group.

Clearly, behaviors of children cannot be observed or described if they have not yet had the opportunity to develop. Complex emotions, obviously, cannot be judged in the infant and, similarly, certain intellectual skills cannot be tested where language capacity has not yet been achieved. Yet, if longitudinal investigation is to have any meaning, it is necessary that certain behaviors be charted over time for all age groups. That is, it was considered desirable for any factor that emerged in the factor analytic studies of item responses and was found to exist in the earliest age group to be carried through all of the other age groups.

The effort that went into the creation of the rating instrument was directed toward the goal of charting change in the child over time through use of a constant set of descriptive categories to which additional age-specific items might be added. In other words, it was considered desirable that items that appeared to belong together in the formation of a single factor maintain some unity, some belonging together as a group, when employed in a longitudinal analysis of the same children over time.

Candidate items for the development of the CBC were culled

[24] Edgar F. Borgatta and David Fanshel, *Behavioral Characteristics of Children Known to Psychiatric Outpatient Clinics: With Special Attention to Adoption Status, Sex and Age Groupings* (New York: Child Welfare League of America, 1965); David Fanshel, Lydia Hylton, and Edgar F. Borgatta, "A Study of Behavior Disorders of Children in Residential Treatment Centers," *Journal of Psychological Studies* 14 (1963): 1–24; Edgar F. Borgatta and Patricia Cautley, "Behavioral Characteristics of Children: Replication Studies with Foster Children," *Multivariate Behavioral Research* 1 (1966): 399–424.

from various studies, with emphasis in item selection placed on the previous work of the authors. Additional sources of items were interviews arranged with mothers, fathers, and pediatric nurses. Case records of foster care agencies were scrutinized for descriptive adjectives stemming from contacts with infants and toddlers.

On the basis of expert opinion, the candidate items initially compiled were reduced to a set of 95 items in a preliminary form. These items were subject to review by social workers, pediatric nurses, and mothers with direct experience with infants and younger children. Respondents were asked to consider each item with reference to the question, "What is the earliest age that you think you can tell that a child shows this behavior or quality?" A second question took the form, "How long do you think a person must watch a baby or child to be able to judge him on each behavior or quality?" Responses were utilized to develop preliminary age-specific forms for five age groups that were further tested by child welfare agencies on cases known to them.

The final organization of data from the five preliminary forms led to construction of three final age-specific versions utilized in the study of foster children reported here. No items were retained for younger children that were phrased in such a way as to render them inapplicable to the older age group(s). The form for the youngest age group (up to two years) consisted of 60 items. These items became the first part of the form for the middle age group (two to six years), and to these were added 55 items. The instruction for this age form states, "If the child is already four years old (or even if he is not four, but speaks fluently), please complete the following section" (the additional 55 items). The form for the oldest age group (7 years to 17 or over) includes all 115 items. The form also contains four items on the physical characteristics of the child and an open-ended question requesting information on the possible existence of physical or mental defects.

Based on factor-analytic treatment, 27 clusters of items were identified to constitute "component scores":

   1. Distractibility (B) items[25]—gets distracted easily, loses interest in things.

   [25] Letters A, B, or C in parenthesis indicate the age at which items can be used: (A) represents the infancy group, (B) the early childhood group (2 to 6 years), and (C) the general childhood group (7 to 17 and over).

2. Learning difficulty (B) items—is slow to understand people, has difficulty in learning things.

3. Alertness (A) items—is alert, is bright, is smart.

4. Intelligence (C) items—is rational and logical, is clearminded, is intelligent.

5. Attention–curiosity (A) items—is interested in what goes on, is curious about things around him, pays attention to things going on.

6. Responsibility (C) items—accepts responsibilities, is interested in getting things done, is conscientious, pays attention to the task at hand.

7. Unmotivated–laziness (C) items—is sluggish or listless, is lethargic or lazy, is slow in getting things done, is apparently unmotivated to do anything.

8. Cooperativeness (B) items—is cooperative, is easy to train, does what people want him to, is patient.

9. Compliance (A) items—is easily quieted or calmed down, is easy to take care of, is easily satisfied or pacified.

10. Defiance (B) items—is stubborn, is defiant, is resistant.

11. Hostility (C) items—is rough or unruly, is antagonistic toward others, is hostile to others, is rebellious.

12. Unsocialized (C) items—is dangerously daring, is reckless, risks self-harm without apparent concern.

13. Lies, steals, destroys (C) items—tells lies, destroys property, commits vandalism.

14. Likability (A) items—is friendly, is likable, is cheerful, is pleasant, laughs, shows warmth and affection, smiles.

15. Agreeableness (A) items—has a nice disposition, is agreeable.

16. Gloomy–sourness (A) items—is gloomy or sad looking, appears sulky or sour, is moody.

17. Irritability–tension (A) items—is fidgity, gets upset easily, is tense, is irritable, is restless, fusses and frets, is easily overexcited.

18. Tension–anxiety (B) items—is fearful, anxious, is overly emotional, is very tense, is overly nervous.

19. Withdrawal (B) items—rejects strangers, does not warm up to people, withdraws from people, is cautious with strangers.

20. Withdrawal (C) items—appears incapable of showing love, avoids contact with others of same age, is socially withdrawn, avoids ordinary friendly contact, shows lack of affection, resists attempts of others to be friendly.

21. Infantilism (C) items—requires constant reassurance, is overly dependent on others, clings to adults dependently, acts juvenile or babyish.

22. Appetite (A) items—has a good appetite, eats well.

23. Sex precocious (C) items—masturbates or plays with self, engages in sexual play with others, is sexually forward or precocious, tries to involve others in sexual play.

TABLE 3.1

ORGANIZATION OF COMPOSITE CBC SCORES DERIVED FROM CONSOLIDATION OF COMPONENT SCORES WITH INFORMATION ON AGE RELEVANCE

Composite Score	Component Score	Number of Items	Level	Age/Relevance[a] A/B	Age/Relevance[a] C
Ia = 3 + 5	Alertness–Attention–Curiosity	6	A	A/B	C
	3. Alertness	3	A		
	5. Attention–Curiosity	3	A		
Ib = 4	4. Intelligence	3	C		C
I = Ia + Ib	ALERTNESS–INTELLIGENCE	9	C		C
II = 1 + 2	LEARNING DIFFICULTY	4	B	B	C
	1. Distractability	2	B		
	2. Learning difficulty	2	B		
III = 6	6. Responsibility	4	C		C
IV = 7	7. Unmotivated-laziness	4	C		C
V = 8 + 9 + 15	AGREEABLENESS	9	B	A/B[b]	
	8. Cooperativeness	4	B	B	
	9. Compliance	3	B		
	15. Agreeableness	2	A		
VIa = 10	10. Defiance	3	B	B	
VIb = 11, 12, 13	11. Hostility	10	C		
	12. Unsocialized	4	C		
	13. Lies, steals, destroys	3	C		
VI = VIa + VIb	DEFIANCE–HOSTILITY	13	C		C

			A	A/B	C
VII = 14 − 16 + K^c	LIKABILITY	10	A	A/B	C
	14. Likability	7	A		
	16. Gloomy-sourness	3	A		
VIII = 17 + 18	EMOTIONALITY-TENSION	11	B	A/B	C
	17. Irritability-tension	7	B		
	18. Tension-anxiety	4	B		
IX = 21	21. Infantilism	4	C		
X_a = 19	19. Withdrawal B	4	B	B	
X_b = 20	20. Withdrawal C	7	C		
X = Xa + Xb	WITHDRAWAL	11	C		C
XI = 22	22. Appetite	2	B	A/B	C
XII = 23	23. Sex precociousness	4	C		C
XIII = 24	24. Overcleanliness	4	C		C
XIV = 25	25. Sexual inhibition	2	C		C
XV = 26	26. Activity	2	A	A/B	C
XVI = 27	27. Assertiveness	4	C		C

[a] A, B, and C refer to the age relevance as: (A) infancy, (B) early childhood, and (C) general childhood.
[b] A indicates the composite score would not have all component scores in the infancy group. There are 16 C scores and 9 B scores.
[c] K = constant added to make all scores positive.

24. Overcleanliness (C) items—is excessively neat, is rigid in habits, is overconcerned with cleanliness, is prim or prissy, overly proper.

25. Sex inhibition (C) items—shows fear in sexual matters, is inhibited in normal sexual exposure (e.g., bathroom, showers).

26. Activity (A) items—is physically active, vigorous, has lots of pep and energy.

27. Assertiveness (C) items—is assertive, does most of the talking in a group, has strong opinions, is authoritative.

On the basis of the simplex-type analysis of the component scores and, additionally, factor analysis of the scores themselves, the component scores were consolidated into a smaller number of composite scores. Table 3.1 shows the composite scores with information about their age relevance. There are 16 composite scores that can be used for children aged seven years and older and nine that can be used for younger children.

The reader should bear in mind that the behaviors included in the CBC form have no implications of pathogenicity and do not derive from psychiatric formulations. In other words, they do not reflect a "syndrome" with disease implications. Normal and disturbed children can be described using the form; the latter group would merely tend to fall within the extreme while so-called normal children would tend to fall well within the middle of the normal distribution.

Scores were available for children about 30 days after they entered care, again at 90 days, two and one-half years after their entry, and at the end of five years.[26] The fact that children increased in age by five years in the course of the longitudinal investigation did not pose problems because of the feature of the CBC that permits replication on some component scores from infancy into general childhood.

The CBC was filled out by social workers who best knew the children in the agencies that cared for them. (For tests of reliability in the instrument-construction stage, the form was also filled in independently by foster parents and institutional personnel).

---

[26] Scores developed on the basis of 90-day ratings constituted Time I CBC scores. Where the 90-day ratings were missing, 30-day ratings were used as Time I measures.

Measures of internal reliability using Cronbach alpha coefficients and inter-rater reliabilities have already been reported.[27]

Because CBC scores were based on caseworkers' reports, scores were only available for children remaining in care or for those having follow-up contact with a caseworker. Thus, the number of children for whom CBC scores were available diminished over time. Analysis of change in behavior at the end of the study was limited to the proportion of the original sample who were still in care.

In chapter 12 the reader has opportunity to examine the correlations between the CBC scores and the previously cited measures of the children related to their adjustment.

MEASURES OF PARENT AND AGENCY INFLUENCES

In line with our purpose of seeking to analyze the sources of change in the adjustment of the children over the five years of longitudinal investigation, we utilized a number of measures reflecting influences that seemed to us to be worthy of study. In this regard we first considered the contribution of the child's parents. We were aware that there was considerable variability in the quality of parents in the study, which could have grave importance for their children. Some of the parents of our subjects had never provided direct care to their children or exposed them to intermittent or multiple mothering. It was also determined that some were highly disturbed individuals requiring hospitalization in mental hospitals or having histories of drug abuse and in need of detoxification. Some parents, on the other hand, appeared relatively intact in their ability to function as individuals and to carry out some of their parent roles. We were also interested in determining whether the parents visited their children while they were in foster care, and saw this as having a potentially strong influence on the adjustment of the youngsters.

To secure relevant measures in this area we relied on the research effort taking place parallel to our own, the agency study, under the direction of Deborah Shapiro.[28] As explained in our

[27] Borgatta and Fanshel, *Behavioral Characteristics of Children*, pp. 70–79.

[28] The agency study and the child assessment study reported here constituted the Child Welfare Research Program at the Columbia University School of Social Work and were carried out under the direction of David Fanshel.

prefatory acknowledgments, both of these studies were concerned with the same cases. In the agency study, four rounds of interviews were conducted with agency caseworkers: Time I (1966/67), Time II (1967/68), Time III (1969/70), and Time IV (1971).

Parent Measures

The following measures related to parents were used in analyzing changes in the condition of the children over time:

1. Principal preplacement child caring person—a single item of information dichotomized to indicate whether the child had received care mainly from his own mother or some other person.

2. Stability of care before placement—a single variable in which the responses of the caseworker were codified to indicate whether the child had received continuous care from a single mother figure before entering foster care or had received multiple or intermittent mothering.

3. Evaluation of the mother—a multiple-item index based on information provided by caseworkers on the four data-gathering occasions.[29] The index reflected the worker's assessment of the mother and included such items as a judgment of the mother's capacity to function in her maternal role, the degree of emotional disturbance, the outlook for working with her, prediction as to the likelihood that the mother would lose contact with the agency, the extent to which the mother was disturbed by separation from her child, the mother's attitude toward her worker and the agency, and the interviewer's assessment of the worker's interest in the mother.[30]

4. Parental visiting—in chapter 4 we analyze in considerable detail the matter of frequency of parental visiting over the course of the five years of longitudinal investigation. On each of the four data-gathering occasions of the agency study, the visiting scale developed by Shapiro was used to classify the parent's visiting behavior as reflecting no visiting, minimum visiting, frequent irregular visiting, or maximum permitted visiting. For Times II, III, and IV, we also had information as to whether a child predominantly visited his own home. We have given close attention to the phenomenon of parental visiting because it emerges as one of the best predictors of the

[29] For description of the index, see Deborah Shapiro, *Agencies and Foster Children* (New York: Columbia University Press, 1976), pp. 93–98.

[30] As described by Shapiro, the list of items included at each of the four data-gathering occasions was not uniform since some items that correlated highly with others at one cycle did not on other occasions. The four versions of the index were seen as essentially comparable, however.

discharge of the subjects. It also proves to be a relevant variable in the analyses of changes shown by the children in IQ scores and in their personal and social adjustment as measured on a repeated basis over time.

In addition to the frequency of parental visiting, we have included in a number of our analyses a variable measuring the stability of visiting (i.e., visiting decreased or increased over time).[31]

Agency Measures

We considered it important to take into account the amount and kind of casework contact to which the child and his family had been exposed. We reasoned that the investment of professional time was potentially an important source of explained variance in the two kinds of "outcome" that interested us, status changes and changes in the cognitive and personal functioning of the child. Shapiro made the service variables the heart of her study, and we relied on two of her indexes as the basis for our work in this area. One variable is an index of the total average monthly contact invested by the caseworker (transformed into logarithmic form to deal with the fact that the distribution of the index scores was quite skewed). The variable is a summation of the average monthly contacts with the child, child caring person, his parents, and other agencies; it also includes contacts within the agency, collateral contacts, and average monthly written communications. A second variable we have used is an index of the caseworker's skill. It is based on two items: (a) education of the worker with respect to social work training and (b) years of experience (in logarithmic form).[32]

Another important source of influence on the children, reflecting the resources provided by the agencies, was the child caring persons who assumed responsibility for direct care. These included the foster parents for children living with foster families and child care personnel for children placed in institutions. The material that follows describes our approach to assessing these agency-connected influences.

---

[31] The reader should be aware that we have deviated somewhat from the procedure developed by Shapiro, in that her volume reports the mother's visiting behavior, whereas the data we present reflect the optimal visiting of either parent.

[32] See Deborah Shapiro, *Agencies and Foster Children*, p. 6.

Appraising Foster Parents
We considered the role of foster parents as sources of influence on
the children living in foster family care to be highly important. As
substitute parents, they had daily contact with the children, com-
forted them when they were upset, disciplined them when they
misbehaved, and in many ways assumed the responsibilities and
behaviors we associate with biological parenthood. They obviously
were in a position to help shape the adjustment of the children in a
very direct way.

To secure data about the qualities of the foster parents, we
utilized a rating instrument, the Foster Parent Appraisal Form
(FPAF), designed to be filled out by caseworkers who knew them
best. The instrument was adapted from one previously used in a
study of foster parents in Pittsburgh; its use had also been replicated in Montreal.[33] Although a factor analysis had been completed on the Pittsburgh data, for the study we report here we had
to undertake new factor analyses using the revised rating instrument
as the source of items. A full description of the approach to index
construction has been made available.[34]

The foster parents were rated on two occasions. The first
assessment took place when the children had been in care for an
average of 10.5 months. A repeat assessment took place about 30
months later. At both times, 152 foster families were rated, although
there was not a complete overlap of families rated twice. About 52
percent of the foster families were black, while 32 percent were
white. The Puerto Rican foster families represented about 15 percent
of the sample. The white foster families were equally divided
between Catholic and Protestant families, with a small addition of
Jewish families. The foster fathers tended to be blue-collar workers
earning relatively modest incomes. Eighty percent of the families
lived in homes they owned; 10 percent lived in apartments in public

[33] David Fanshel, *Foster Parenthood: A Role Analysis* (Minneapolis: University of
Minnesota Press, 1966); Louise Boivin, et al., "A Study of the Role Performance of
French-Canadian Foster Mothers" (Montreal: Société de Service Sociale Aux Familles, June
1966). (Mimeographed.)

[34] David Fanshel and John Grundy, "Foster Parenthood: A Replication and Extension of
Prior Studies, "Report of Child Welfare Research Program, Columbia University School of
Social Work, April 15, 1971. (Mimeographed.)

housing projects; and the remainder lived in other types of rented facilities.

The foster parents were rated by agency caseworkers; 31 percent of the raters at Time I and 20 percent at Time II were graduates of schools of social work holding Master's of Social Work degrees.

The factor analyses were carried out for Time I and Time II ratings in parallel. The results were used as a guide to the selection of items for inclusion in eight indexes. These were subsequently consolidated for our analyses into the following four compact measures:

1. Intellectual climate (FPAF 1)—a measure of the climate of the foster family with respect to its potential for stimulating the child's intellectual development. A positively rated family also tends to be intellectually oriented in its disciplinary techniques and to have both a diversity of interests and a larger number of community contacts.

2. Democratic permissiveness (FPAF 2)—a high score indicates family is observed to avoid harsh, rigid discipline or physical punishment. Little stress is placed on social conformity. There is a kind of free spirit to the family.

3. Perseverance–altruism (FPAF 3)—describes families who take on some of the harder placements in foster care, for example, physically handicapped or mentally retarded children. The family tends not to cling to the foster child, permitting easy access of natural parents to their home and tends to facilitate the departure of children going into adoptive homes.

4. Age suitability (FPAF 4)—assesses the degree to which age preferences of foster parents are being met by the attributes of the foster child actually placed in their home.

For some analyses a fifth index was included, which provided an overall assessment of the role competence shown by the foster families.

Institutional Care

The agency study gathered several kinds of information about the situations faced by children in institutional care. While in the form of individual items of information, these measures are not as elaborately developed as those used to describe foster parents. We nevertheless found them potentially useful as sources of explanation of changes in the adjustment of the children:

1. Routine of institutional care—measures the quality of attention received by the child from child care staff (ranging from routine care, in which there is no indication of special attention from staff, to care involving considerable attention and a strong relationship with a staff person).

2. Experience of institutional staff—provides a measure of the experience of the child care counselor most actively involved with the child (ranging from no experience to three or more years).

3. Evaluation of institutional counselor—reflects the caseworker's assessment of the counselor (coded acceptable, valued, or highly valued).

4. School setting—dichotomous variable indicating that the child attends school on the institution's grounds or attends school in the community.

These variables were available on a repeated basis for the four data-gathering occasions of the agency study.

PREPARATION OF DATA AND ANALYSIS

As can be surmised from our previous discussion, we gathered a considerable amount of information over the course of five years. The accumulation of data is of course the hallmark of a longitudinal investigation. In our case, it was not only the use of repeated measures over time that led to the proliferation of variables; our decision to utilize a variety of approaches to assessing the children rather than resorting to a simplified single measure of adjustment considerably expanded the amount of data collected. Thus we had CBC scores, IQ scores, projective test scores, measures of school performance, measures of symptomatic behavior, and assessment of the "attachments" of the child to foster parents and own parents. In addition, we monitored a variety of measures of status changes (adoption and discharge, interagency transfers, etc.). We also had measures of parents and agencies that were repeated over time (e.g., total casework contact with family, parental visiting, and evaluation of the mother). This may seem to be an excess of riches for the reader. However, we do not feel that the inclusion of so many variables reflecting diverse domains reflects a lack of cohesiveness of the investigation; rather, this represents a conscious choice of what is important to monitor. The complexity of the data reflects the complexity of the phenomenon we wish to study.

We invested much effort in the preparation of codebooks, recruitment and training of coders, and supervision of the coding operation. Samples of the data were continuously subjected to code checks and the results scrutinized to ensure that errors were random and within prescribed tolerance limits. Similarly, the punching of IBM cards was routinely subjected to verification and results were inspected to detect out-of-range punches. The data included in this study are as free of "static and noise" as meticulous attention to detail could provide.

We created a data file for each child in the study, encompassing as many as 65 IBM cards.[35] Most often, only summary measures were included in the file and much of the preliminary analytic work (for example, the creation of indexes through factor analyses and item-analysis procedures) was carried through as separate analytic operations.

Our approach to the task of analyzing the voluminous data we had organized in the data file was, by necessity, varied. Many of our measures were in the form of categorical scales, and it was possible to pursue some lines of analysis through cross-tabulation procedures. However, when we desired to go beyond three-variable contingency tables, we often found that our sample size was a barrier to such elaboration.

Multiple regression and correlation analysis (MRC) procedures appeared best suited for the purpose of analyzing the potential contribution of a fairly large number of independent variables in "explaining" some of the phenomena we were interested in. For example, in seeking to analyze the status outcomes experienced by our subjects, that is, whether they were discharged or still in care at the end of five years, we identified such sources of explanation as the child's birth status, age, reason for placement, frequency of parental visits, evaluation of the mother by the caseworker, and amount of casework service given to the family. Such a list of variables—each plausible as a source of explanation of discharge—

---

[35] The file was created to conform with the data-format specifications of the Harvard Data-Text System, the computer software program predominately used by the present authors.

required statistical analytic procedures that could assign to each variable an explanation of its contribution to explained variance in outcome without attributing to it the effect of something correlated with it, in other words, holding the effect of other variables constant. Our resort to correlation procedures required that we transform categorical variables into sets of dichotomies in the form of "dummy variable" codes (with binary values of 0 or 1). For example, the ethnic identification of subjects could be converted into three variables (e.g., Variable $1 = 1$ if white, 0 if other; Variable $2 = 1$ if black, 0 if other; and Variable $3 = 1$ if Puerto Rican, 0 if other).

We must emphasize that our analyses were not predicated on a theoretical model of the influences at play during a child's experience in foster care. No such model exists and one is not likely to emerge for some time. The basic underpinning of research in this area to provide a clear notion of the dependencies involved has not been done as yet. The effort reported here will, we hope, serve this purpose for future investigators. Much of our analytic effort entailed the identification of a sequence of independent variables that seemed promising to us as potential sources of explanation without a theoretical statement of our sense of the causal relationships involved. We ran many multiple regression analyses, attempting to determine which variables would recurrently produce significant pieces of explained variance. We thus attempted to build a credible portrait of the forces at play in producing various outcomes and particularly sought to determine whether certain dependencies were obtained across different measures and subpopulations. While our findings may perhaps have capitalized on chance, we rely on repetition of some of them in different analytic contexts as one way of coping with this problem.

A point should be made about one aspect of the analyses that follow. We often present to the reader findings in which we indicate that an independent variable has contributed a significant amount of explained variance in an outcome measure, and this turns out to be a relatively modest figure, say 2–3 percent of explained variance. Some readers may react with the feeling that much is being made of a trivial finding. In this regard, we should point out that experienced social scientists have come to appreciate that many of the complex social phenomena they are attempting to bring under predictive control do not typically account for large proportions of explained variance.[36] This certainly holds true for child development studies.

To illustrate the matter of "variance accounting," one can consider the task of accounting for changes in IQ scores of the children upon repeated testing, say changes from Time I to Time II. First we must appreciate the fact that a major portion of variance in the Time II scores is accounted for by the child himself (i.e., the score he achieved at Time I). That is to say, there is stability of IQ scores over time; thus, if the correlation of WISC scores from Time I to Time II is .80, this means that some 64 percent of the variance in the child's Time II score is accounted for by the earlier testing. This has already markedly constricted the amount of variance that remains to be explained. When we subsequently view the contribution of such variables as the length of time the child has spent in foster care, the number of moves he has experienced while in care, the qualities of his foster parents, and the nature of parental visiting he has experienced, we are apt to find that collectively these seemingly important variables have only added 7 or 8 percentage points of explained variance in the Time II scores. If a single variable makes a significant contribution of 2–3 percent in the context of such limited possibilities, this becomes significant. Human beings are subject to an extraordinary variety of influences, some redundant and others making unique contributions— but they are almost always modest in their effects.

Further comment is in order about our analytic procedures. A key task we faced was measuring changes in our subjects when they were tested on the same measures over time. While we occasionally looked at "raw change" or "raw gain" scores obtained by subtracting pretest from posttest scores—and examined the correlations of independent variables with these measures—we knew that we could not comfortably rely on such analyses. It is well known that "raw gain" scores are unreliable in that they may be systematically related to random errors of measurement.[37] We have relied mainly

[36] Derek Phillips, "Sociologists and Their Knowledge," *American Behavioral Scientist* 14 (1971): 563–822.

[37] Chester W. Harris, ed., *Problems in Measuring Change* (Madison, Wis.: University of Wisconsin Press, 1967); Lee J. Cronbach and Lita Furley, "How Should We Measure 'Change'—or Should We?" *Psychological Bulletin* 74 (1970):63–80.

on the use of multiple regression and correlational analysis (MRC), in which we have taken the approach of first entering into the regression equation the earlier score, say the Time I IQ, in which the Time II score was the criterion measure whose variance we were seeking to account for as a function of other variables. By doing this, we are essentially studying "regressed change" in which the earlier score has been partialed out. The first covariate, the Time I score, makes the variables that come later in the analysis predictors of IQ change rather than that of IQ status.

Time Perspectives

A longitudinal study such as we have conducted provides different time perspectives than a single-time investigation such as Maas and Engler's study.[38] In their ground-breaking research, much of the information about the conditions of the children over time was gathered in retrospective fashion. We refer to the limitations of this in chapter 1. In the study reported here, we collected our data close to the time at which the events we were interested in were occurring. We did this in an ongoing fashion over a five-year period. We are thus in a position to undertake analyses that are only possible within the context of a longitudinal investigation. For example, we can look at a child's IQ score or CBC score at Time II and analyze the factors that have contributed to change from the Time I score. We can also analyze Times II–III and Times I–III changes. Since we have invested heavily in the task of repeated measurement over time, we of course wish to exploit the data fully so that forces acting on the foster child can be seen as time unfolds.

It has occurred to us that it may not seem much of a blessing to the reader to have data presented in this manner rather than in a seemingly more straightforward single time perspective. To refer to changes at Times I–II, Times II–III, and Times I–III introduces a complexity of phenomena that does not lend itself to simple understanding. It also requires many more statistical tables to examine. The mind can become fatigued trying to maintain differentiation of the time perspectives. We trust the reader will see the analyses

[38] Henry S. Maas and Richard E. Engler, Jr., *Children in Need of Parents* (New York: Columbia University Press, 1959).

through, however, because the assessment of change is at the heart of this study and we believe the varying time perspectives provide insights not heretofore available. For example, we later present data in which some children do not show significant change from Time I to Time II but then show spurts from Time II to Time III.

Let us move on to a second aspect of the matter of time as reflected in our data analysis. In looking at the phenomenon of the discharge of the children from foster care, we provide the reader with information about the saliency of various child, family, and agency characteristics from the perspective of an increasingly diminished sample, namely, predicting departure from care in the second year after entry, with the first year's discharged children excluded. That is, putting ourselves in the position of the social planner seeking to better understand the foster care phenomenon, we can raise the question, "Given the fact that a part of the sample left care this past year, which variables best predict the future departure of the residual group that is *now* in care?"

Contributing to the complexity associated with time is the fact that the data-gathering occasions do not coincide for all of the data presented in the study. The reader will need to keep in mind that child-assessment data (psychological tests, child profiles, CBC assessments, and school reports) are reported for three data-gathering occasions:

1. Time I—collection of data took place in 1966, after the child had been in foster care 90 days, and collection of such data continued well into the first year after the subjects had entered care.
2. Time II—collection of data took place in the period 1968/69 at a point about two and a half years after the child had entered care.
3. Time III—collection of data took place in 1971, five years from the time of the child's entry into care.

There is a fairly close correlation between the above data-gathering occasions and the field interviewing of the families as reported by Jenkins and Norman.[39] However, the agency study—from which a number of key variables we utilized have derived—

---

[39] Shirley Jenkins and Elaine Norman, *Beyond Placement: Mothers View Foster Care* (New York: Columbia University Press, 1975).

has a somewhat different time perspective because data were gathered on four separate occasions:

1. Time I—data collection took place in 1966/67, when most of the 616 children covered had been in placement between six and nine months.

2. Time II—data collection took place in 1967/68 and covered 496 children at a time when most had been in placement between 18 and 23 months.

3. Time III—data collection took place in 1969/70 and covered 389 children, most of whom had been in care between 35 and 48 months.

4. Time IV—data collection took place in 1971 and covered 275 children, most of whom had spent the entire five-year span in care.

Adding complexity to the situation, we remind the reader that foster parents providing care for the children in the study who were placed in foster family homes were rated on two occasions: (a) Time I, when the children had been in care for an average of 10.5 months and (b) Time II, about 30 months later.

We are now prepared to examine, in the chapters that follow, what transpired over the course of the five-year period following the entrance of the children into care.

FOUR

PARENTAL
VISITING
OF CHILDREN
IN FOSTER CARE

In this chapter we provide data about parental visitation of the children in foster care and explore the ramifications of visiting patterns for the discharge of the subjects over the five years of longitudinal investigation. By way of prelude to this subject, we should mention that throughout the study we viewed parental visiting as highly important for the welfare of the children. We were sensitized to this by our previous clinical experience in working with foster children. Both of the present authors had occasion to witness the dismay and acute pain caused children by the failure of their parents to visit. Anyone who has observed this phenomenon soon becomes appreciative of the emotional turmoil often experienced by the unvisited youngster.[1]

The matter of parental visitation has tended to receive limited attention as a research topic, but we did find some references that impressed us. In the study reported by Maas and Engler, for example, there is a commentary by Joseph H. Reid, executive director of the Child Welfare League of America, indicating that

---

[1] We assume that for most children in foster care, contact with their own parents is to be desired. There are, of course, cases where parents are so disturbed or destructive in relationship to their children that contact may not be in the latter's interest. In this study, restriction of parental visiting by agencies ranged from 2 to 4 percent over the course of the four research interviews encompassing five years of investigation.

The contents of this chapter have appeared previously in the *Social Service Review*, 49 (1975): 493–514.

there was massive failure of parents to visit their children in the nine communities studied:

> We can only conclude that there are roughly 168,000 children today who are in danger of staying in foster care throughout their childhood years. And although in a third of the cases at least one parent did visit the child, in approximately half the parents visited infrequently or not at all.[2]

More recently we have learned of similar findings about the low level of parental visiting in a statewide study of children in foster care in Massachusetts:

> Related to the issue of parental interest, the social workers were asked about the frequency of parent contact with the child. The statistics remained consistent on this point. It was found that less than thirty percent of the children had seen one of their parents in a given three month period. Approximately 38 percent had seen their parent(s) sometime within the last six months. The remaining children have no substantial parental contact.[3]

In a study of foster children in Arizona, less than 30 percent of the children interviewed reported receiving visits from their parents, and only 14 percent reported visiting their parents in their own homes.[4]

In addition to the fact that a low level of parental visiting is likely to lead to a child's remaining in care for an extended time, we were also interested in the visiting phenomenon in terms of its impact on the children.[5] We were encouraged to consider this by the report of a study of foster children in Chicago; the evidence presented indicated that children who are visited by their parents

---

[2] Henry S. Maas and Richard E. Engler, Jr., *Children in Need of Parents* (New York: Columbia University Press, 1959), p. 380.

[3] Alan R. Gruber, *Foster Home Care in Massachusetts*, Governor's Commission on Adoption and Foster Care, Commonwealth of Massachusetts, Boston, Mass., 1973, p. 18.

[4] Edmund V. Mech, *Public Welfare Services for Children and Youth in Arizona*, Joint Interim Committee on Health and Welfare, 29th Legislature, State of Arizona (April, 1970), p. 72.

[5] In this chapter we consider only the relationship between parental visiting and the discharge of children from foster care. We subsequently consider its potential impact upon the adjustment of the children.

while in care show a better sense of wellbeing than those who are unvisited.[6]

THE VISITING SCALE

Our data on visiting are derived from the series of four sequential interviews carried out by the agency study staff over the course of five years of longitudinal investigation. The social workers who had primary responsibility for work with the children and their families were queried about the nature of the contact between the parents and their children. The questions covered such details as the frequency with which fathers and mothers visited, restrictions imposed by the agency on visiting, conditions preventing the parents from availing themselves of opportunity to visit, and whether the child visited his parent(s) at home.

In our presentation here we focus on frequency of parental visiting, and for this purpose a visiting scale was created reflecting the following categories of visitation:

    1. No visiting—neither parent had visited during the time span covered by the interview with the social worker.[7]
    2. Minimum visiting—a parent had visited rarely or occasionally in the period covered; many had visited only once or twice.
    3. Frequent irregular visiting—a parent had visited fairly often but visiting was irregular and not up to the maximum permitted.
    4. Maximum permitted visiting—a parent had visited very regularly, at each opportunity.
    5. Child visits home—the predominant form of contact was the child visiting in his own home.[8]

    [6] Eugene A. Weinstein, *The Self-Image of the Foster Child* (New York: Russell Sage Foundation, 1960), pp. 68–69.
    [7] The first round of agency study interviews (Time I, 1966/67) took place when most of the 616 children covered had been in placement between six and nine months. The second round (Time II, 1967/68) covered 496 children at a time when most had been in placement between 18 and 23 months. The third round (Time III, 1969/70) covered 389 children, most of whom had been in care between 35 and 48 months. The fourth round (Time IV, 1971) covered 275 children, most of whom had spent the entire five-year span of the study in care. The declining number of subjects in each round of interviewing reflects the discharge of children from care; social workers were no longer available for reports when the cases were closed. Parental visiting was, of course, not a relevant matter for discharged children.
    [8] This category was not coded separately in the Time I interview, and such children were included under "maximum permitted visiting."

It should be noted that the visiting scale was created on the basis of each child being classified according to an optimal criterion. The parent whose visiting was most frequent became the source of codification. Thus, if a mother of a child was reported as having engaged in "minimum visiting" and the father as having visited on the basis of "maximum permitted visiting," the visiting pattern was categorized according to the father's behavior.[9]

PARENTAL VISITING OVER FIVE YEARS OF STUDY

Table 4.1 displays the pattern of parental visiting over the five years of longitudinal investigation. The data show a dramatic decline in visitation from Time I to Time IV; as children were discharged from care over time, the residual populations of children showed an increasing proportion of those who were unvisited. Whereas 18 percent of the children in foster care at Time I were not visited at all, this is true of 31 percent at Time II, 36 percent at Time III, and 57 percent at Time IV. Consolidating the cases where there was *no visiting* with those where there was *minimal visiting*, we can report that about two-thirds of the children remaining in care five years after their entry had essentially lost contact with their parents. This is a striking and dismaying finding but not very different from those of the studies previously cited.

The data we provide here tend to be in agreement with a 1970 survey of the New York City foster care system undertaken to determine the number of children who should be considered for adoptive planning. The investigators found that nearly 33 percent of all children in foster homes and institutions had had no communication with either parent for six months or longer.[10] Since this reflected a cross-sectional analysis of all children in care, including

[9] The reader may observe that the presentation of data here differs somewhat from the agency study report. This is due to the fact that the latter presents the mother's visiting behavior whereas the data discussed here represent the optimal visiting of either parent. See Deborah Shapiro, *Agencies and Foster Children* (New York: Columbia University Press, 1976).

[10] Gwen Bellisfield, Miriam Allen, and Virginia Hyde, "Census of Children Who May Need Adoptive Planning," New York City Department of Social Services, July 1971, p. 2. (Mimeographed.)

TABLE 4.1
FREQUENCY OF PARENTAL VISITATION OVER FIVE YEARS
OF LONGITUDINAL INVESTIGATION[a]

Visitation Pattern	Time I		Time II		Time III		Time IV	
	No.	%	No.	%	No.	%	No.	%
No visiting	112	18.2	146	31.3	136	36.0	153	56.9
Minimum visiting	125	20.3	49	10.5	58	15.3	20	7.4
Frequent irregular visiting	75	12.2	90	19.4	45	11.9	16	5.9
Maximum permitted visiting	304	49.3	150	32.3	96	25.4	58	21.6
Child visits home[b]	—	—	30	6.5	43	11.4	22	8.2
Total	616	100.0	465	100.0	378	100.0	269	100.0

[a] Each data-gathering occasion represents a round of telephone interviewing of agency caseworkers over the course of the five-year study.

[b] At Time I this category was included within "maximum permitted visiting."

recent arrivals who were more apt to be visited (in contrast to the data reported here for children in care for five years) the findings can be seen as quite compatible.

We will not dwell here on the significance of the social data we have provided. We explore this issue analytically in the material that follows. We are aware, however, that the fact that large masses of foster children are unvisited must awaken considerable consternation among those charged with program planning and legislative responsibility in this area of service.

Ethnicity as a Factor in Visiting

We undertook an analysis of parental visiting according to the ethnic backgrounds of our children. We wished to determine whether the children were differentially handicapped with respect to having ongoing contact with their parents. For this purpose, we

TABLE 4.2.

FREQUENCY OF PARENTAL VISITATION FOR FOUR TIME OCCASIONS, BY ETHNICITY–RELIGION

	Ethnicity–Religion				
Visitation Pattern	White Catholic and Protestant	Jewish	Black Catholic	Black Protestant	Puerto Rican
Time I (N = 616)					
High visiting (%)[a]	66.7	93.5	47.1	48.9	70.2
Low visiting (%)	33.3	6.5	52.9	51.1	29.8
(No. of cases)	(126)	(31)	(68)	(90)	(201)
		$\chi^2 = 64.117$, 16 df, $p < .001$[b]			
Time II (N = 465)					
High visiting (%)	59.8	92.6	48.1	38.6	72.7
Low visiting (%)	40.2	7.4	51.9	61.4	27.3
(No. of cases)	(87)	(27)	(52)	(145)	(154)
		$\chi^2 = 82.758$, 16 df, $p < .001$			

Time III ($N = 378$)					
High visiting (%)	48.6	100.0	40.9	35.9	54.9
Low visiting (%)	51.4	—	59.1	64.1	45.1
(No. of cases)	(72)	(21)	(44)	(117)	(124)
		$\chi^2 = 51.176$,	16 df,	$p < .001$	
Time IV ($N = 269$)					
High visiting (%)	34.8	70.0	50.0	22.2	39.6
Low visiting (%)	65.2	30.0	50.0	77.8	60.4
(No. of cases)	(46)	(10)	(36)	(86)	(91)
		$\chi^2 = 49.045$,	16 df,	$p < .001$	

[a] In this and subsequent tables, "high" visiting includes children who received frequent irregular visiting, maximum permitted visiting, or who visited their own homes. "Low" visiting includes children whose parents engaged in minimum visiting or did not visit at all.

[b] Chi-squares were calculated on basis of 5×5 contingency tables reflecting full visiting scale (instead of collapsed version presented here

grouped the children within the following five categories: (a) white Catholic and white Protestant, (b) Jewish, (c) black Catholic, (d) black Protestant, and (e) Puerto Rican. We grouped white Catholic and white Protestant children together because there were relatively few of the latter in our sample and because the two groups appeared relatively undifferentiated for almost all of our measures of child adjustment. We separated the black children into two groups on the basis of religion because we had a fairly substantial number of black Catholic children, who tended to be cared for by a different network of agencies than those in charge of the Protestant children.

Table 4.2 displays the visiting patterns of the parents according to the ethnicity–religious breakdowns cited. Parental visiting was characterized as "high" if the parent(s) engaged in frequent irregular visiting, the maximum visiting permitted by the agency, or the child visited his own home. It was characterized as "low" if the parent(s) engaged in minimum visiting or did not visit at all. At Time I, reflecting the situation in the early phase of our study, we find that all groups show a significant proportion of children whose parents engaged in a high degree of visiting. However, distinct intergroup differences are readily apparent. The Jewish children, coming most often from intact family units, tended to receive the most frequent visitation; more than nine out of ten were visited to a high degree. The white Protestant and Catholic children fared almost as well, with about 67 percent frequently visited. The Puerto Rican children also fared well, with 70 percent visited for the maximum amount permitted or on a frequent but irregular basis. The black children, both Catholic and Protestant, experienced the least amount of parental visiting. Fully half of both groups were either unvisited or visited minimally, compared to 33 percent of the white Catholic and Protestant children and 30 percent of the Puerto Rican children. Less than seven percent of the Jewish children were visited minimally.

For the children remaining in care at Time II, we observed the visiting of the Jewish and Puerto Rican children to be high and comparable to that reported at Time I. The white Catholic and Protestant children showed a small decline in the group of highly visited children, while the black Protestant children showed a decline of about 10 percent. Only 39 percent of the latter received a high degree of visiting. The black Catholic children were visited to about the same degree as at Time I.

Finally, at Time IV, we observe an erosion in the proportion of visited subjects for those still left in care. Only 22 percent of the black Protestant children were receiving frequent visits, as were 35 percent of the white Catholic and Protestant and 40 percent of the Puerto Rican children. Frequent visits were received by 50 percent of the black Catholic children and 70 percent of the few (10) Jewish children remaining in care. The special disadvantage of the black Protestant children is noteworthy.

Reason for Placement

The major reasons for the placement of the children as displayed in Table 4.3 provide some clues about the different patterns of parental visitation. We observe that children entering foster care because of their own behavioral and/or emotional disorders received a quite high degree of visiting at all four times. They tended to come from intact families whose economic circumstances were relatively superior. Surprisingly, children who entered care because of the mental illness of a parent were relatively advantaged with respect to parental visiting. By the end of the study only one out of three children in the neglect or abuse category was visited, and only one in five of those who had been abandoned by a parent.

As might be expected, unmarried mothers unwilling to assume care of their newly born babies were among those who visited less frequently. By the end of the study when their children were about five years old, only one in ten of such mothers frequently visited their children.

Parental Visiting and Discharge from Care

In approaching the task of analyzing the relationship between parental visiting and the discharge of children from foster care, we were prepared to find a significant association between the phenomena. It seemed reasonable to expect that parents who maintained steady contact with their children would be more likely to arrange to take them home than those who hardly visited or who completely dropped out of the picture. The latter were apt to include the most disabled among the parents as well as the most socially

TABLE 4.3

**FREQUENCY OF PARENTAL VISITATION FOR FOUR TIME OCCASIONS,
BY REASON FOR PLACEMENT**

	Reason			
Visitation Pattern	Mental Illness of Child-caring Person	Neglect or Abuse of Child	Behavior of Child	Physical Illness of Child-caring Person
Time I (*N* = 616)				
High visiting (%)	77.2	55.0	84.9	57.4
Low visiting (%)	22.8	45.0	15.1	42.6
(No. of cases)	(136)	(91)	(73)	(68)
				$\chi^2 = 102.792,$
Time II (*N* = 465)				
High visiting (%)	70.0	46.5	86.5	54.3
Low visiting (%)	30.0	53.5	13.5	45.7
(No. of cases)	(100)	(71)	(67)	(35)
				$\chi^2 = 100.288,$
Time III (*N* = 378)				
High visiting (%)	56.0	41.8	81.2	42.0
Low visiting (%)	44.0	58.2	18.8	58.0
(No. of cases)	(84)	(55)	(48)	(31)
				$\chi^2 = 79.285,$
Time IV (*N* = 269)				
High visiting (%)	48.3	33.4	68.0	37.9
Low visiting (%)	51.7	66.6	32.0	62.1
(No. of cases)	(56)	(42)	(25)	(29)
				$\chi^2 = 88.360,$

deprived. One would also anticipate that those not motivated to visit—or prevented from doing so by circumstances beyond their control— would feel under less pressure from their children to take them home than parents who had regular face-to-face contact with their offspring. We should point out, however, that although we anticipated a fairly strong association between parental visiting and child discharge, we were not sure how visiting behavior interacted with

TABLE 4.3 (*cont.*)

		Reason		
Abandonment or Desertion by Parent	Parent Unwilling to Continue Care	Family Problems	Parent Unwilling to Assume Care	Death of Parent
43.3	68.2	40.4	49.0	35.7
56.7	31.8	59.6	51.0	64.3
(67)	(63)	(57)	(47)	(14)
24 df, $p < .001$[a]				
50.9	42.0	45.5	40.0	72.7
49.1	58.0	54.5	60.0	27.3
(57)	(50)	(44)	(30)	(11)
32 df, $p < .001$				
47.0	37.1	38.4	29.2	27.3
53.0	62.9	61.6	70.8	72.7
(51)	(35)	(39)	(24)	(11)
32 df, $p < .001$				
18.9	33.3	32.1	10.0	12.5
81.1	66.7	67.9	90.0	87.5
(37)	(24)	(28)	(20)	(8)
32 df, $p < .001$				

[a]Chi-squares were calculated on basis of five categories of visiting instead of collapsed high–low version presented here.

other variables, nor were we well informed about the influence of visiting in the later years of the child's placement experience as opposed to the first year after entry into care. That is, we desired to know more, from a longitudinal perspective, about the relationship between visiting and discharge.

In Table 4.4 we provide cross-tabulations between the reported visiting of parents and the discharge of children. For simplicity of presentation, we have dichotomized the status of the children as discharged or still in care after five years rather than indicating the year in which the child exited from foster care (e.g., first year or second year). We also should note that we have excluded from this analysis 29 cases of adopted children since their exit from the foster care system is a phenomenon not related to parental visiting. We have also excluded 16 cases where the children left foster care through transfer to state mental institutions and two cases involving transfer to state training schools for delinquent children. While the discharge of children is generally construed as a positive outcome, such orientation is not appropriate for these latter cases.

Table 4.4 shows a strong association between the frequency of parental visiting and the discharge of children from foster care. Examining visiting data for the first year we see that subjects whose parents visited the maximum permitted by the agency or who visited frequently but irregularly were almost twice as likely to be discharged eventually as those not visited at all or only minimally. Sixty-six percent of the children whose parents engaged in no visiting at Time I were still in foster care five years after their entry. This was true of 54 percent of those whose parents visited on a minimum basis. By contrast, 31 percent of the children whose parents visited on a frequent but irregular basis and 27 percent of those whose parents visited on all occasions permitted by the agency were still in care at the end of five years. The strength of the relationship between visiting and discharge is impressive and demonstrates the centrality of visiting as a key element in the return of foster children to their own homes.

Inspection of the data in Table 4.4 shows the visiting behavior of parents to be significantly associated with discharge status on the three subsequent data-gathering occasions. Even at Time IV, when the children had been in care over five years, highly visited children left the system in significantly greater proportions than those whose parents visited either not at all or minimally. Put another way, for all four data-gathering occasions high parental visiting appears to be a good omen with respect to discharge. It is also important to observe that the association between visiting and discharge becomes

TABLE 4.4
**DISCHARGE OF CHILDREN FROM FOSTER CARE ACCORDING TO
FREQUENCY OF PARENTAL VISITING FOR FOUR TIME OCCASIONS**[a]

	Visitation Pattern				
Discharge Status	No Visiting	Minimum Visiting	Frequent Irregular Visiting	Maximum Permitted Visiting	Child Visits Home
Time I (N = 577)					
Discharged (%)	34.0	46.2	68.9	73.4	—[b]
Still in care (%) after 5 years	66.0	53.8	31.1	26.6	—
(No. of cases)	(97)	(117)	(74)	(289)	(—)
			$\chi^2 = 60.799$,	3 df,	$p < .001$
Time II (N = 422)					
Discharged (%)	31.7	24.4	44.7	64.0	76.7
Still in care (%) after 5 years	68.3	75.6	55.3	36.0	23.3
(No. of cases)	(123)	(45)	(85)	(139)	(30)
			$\chi^2 = 47.630$,	4 df,	$p < .001$
Time III (N = 349)					
Discharged (%)	17.3	27.3	35.7	48.3	78.0
Still in care (%) after 5 years	82.7	72.7	64.3	51.7	22.0
(No. of cases)	(122)	(55)	(42)	(89)	(41)
			$\chi^2 = 57.756$,	4 df,	$p < .001$
Time IV (N = 245)					
Discharged (%)	7.9	—	7.1	29.6	28.6
Still in care (%) after 5 years	92.1	100.0	92.9	70.4	71.4
(No. of cases)	(139)	(17)	(14)	(54)	(21)
			$\chi^2 = 22.411$,	4 df,	$p < .001$

[a] Table excludes 29 children who left care because they were adopted, 16 who were transferred to state mental institutions, and 2 who were transferred to state training schools for delinquent children.

[b] At Time I, this category was included within "maximum permitted visiting."

attenuated over time so that high visiting at Time I is more closely linked to discharge than is high visiting at Time IV.

We believe that we have amply demonstrated the saliency of visiting as a predictive variable in the discharge of children from foster care. The association is indeed striking. The reader should also bear in mind that while patterns of no or minimal parental visitation bodes ill for the discharge of children, the absolute number of nonvisiting parents continually increased in our sample even as the study population in care diminished over the five years of the study. Thus, it is of concern that nonvisiting parents at Time I not only do poorly in retrieving their children from foster care but also that their ranks are added to over time by parents who have slipped into a nonvisiting pattern, that is, a number of parents who visited frequently in an earlier period have shown diminished frequency of visiting.

Five-Year Visitation Patterns and Discharge

Since during the five-year longitudinal study there were four data-gathering occasions when information on parental visiting could be obtained, a variety of visiting patterns could logically emerge. Some parents could maintain a uniformly high level of visitation over time, while others could uniformly engage in no visiting. For many parents, it was expected that changes in visiting patterns would reflect the ebb and flow of events in their lives—departure from mental hospitals, movement to new housing, or new responsibilities with the birth of a baby.

In Table 4.5 we display the various patterns of parental visiting. Our first procedure was to dichotomize the visiting scale information as previously cited into a "low" degree of visitation category (including children whose parents did not visit at all or visited only on a minimum basis), and a "high" category (including children whose parents visited frequently but irregularly, engaged in maximum permitted visitation, or situations where the child visited the parent at home). Inspection of Table 4.5 shows that 246 children (43 percent) were the recipients of uniformly high degrees of visitation. They were never exposed to foster care without the active presence of their parents. The table demonstrates a very high proportion of discharges for these children. An exception is the pattern identified as Hi_1, Hi_2, Hi_3, Hi_4. These are children who remained in foster care despite consistently frequent visiting by a parent. These were mainly situations involving totally disabled mothers; the fathers could not take care of their children but nevertheless sustained contact with them. These also involved a few situations where the child came into care because of behavioral disturbance and was still in care five years later.

About 22 percent of the children were exposed to uniformly low degrees of visitation. Almost all of the 71 children whose parents showed this pattern at all four times assessed (Lo_1, Lo_2, Lo_3, Lo_4) remained in care; only 3 percent were discharged. On the other hand, it should be observed that 37 of the children who returned home during the first year after their entry had parents who were reported to engage in infrequent visiting during that period. These tended to reflect cases in which the mother was not able to visit because she was hospitalized or otherwise disabled. As soon as she recovered, she resumed care of her children.

About 35 percent of the children were exposed to parental visiting that included a high degree of visiting during one period and low visiting during another. The table presents data bifurcated into two mixed patterns: (a) those cases in which the last visiting pattern was high (14 percent of the study population) and (b) those cases in which the last reported visiting pattern was low (21 percent). Where parental visiting moved into a high direction, the discharge rate was fairly good; about 53 percent of the children affected by this pattern were discharged within five years after entering care. This was true of only 36 percent of the children whose parental visiting pattern alternated between high and low visiting and where the last reported level of visiting was low.

Visiting Patterns and Discharge, by Race/Ethnicity

Having established that visiting patterns of parents are strongly associated with discharge rates and that such visiting is highly differentiated by race, we proceed to a somewhat more elaborate three-variable analysis. We inquired whether the strength of association between visiting and discharge held within racial and ethnic groups. For simplicity of presentation we have consolidated the ethnicity variable into three categories (white, black, and Puerto

TABLE 4.5
PATTERN OF PARENTAL VISITING OVER FIVE-YEAR
PERIOD RELATED TO DISCHARGE OF CHILDREN[a]
($N = 577$)

Selected Patterns of Visiting	Number of Children	Number Discharged
Uniformly high visiting patterns		
$Hi_1 {-}_2 {-}_3 {-}_4$	107	107
$Hi_1 {-}_2\ Hi_3 {-}_4$	2	2
$Hi_1\ Hi_2 {-}_3 {-}_4$	45	45
$Hi_1\ Hi_2\ Hi_3 {-}_4$	49	47
$Hi_1\ Hi_2\ Hi_3\ Hi_4$	43	11
Total	246	212
Uniformly low visiting patterns		
$Lo_1 {-}_2 {-}_3 {-}_4$	37	37
$Lo_1 {-}_2 {-}_3\ Lo_4$	3	0
$Lo_1\ Lo_2 {-}_3 {-}_4$	8	8
$Lo_1\ Lo_2\ Lo_3 {-}_4$	9	5
$Lo_1\ Lo_2\ Lo_3\ Lo_4$	71	2
Total	128	52
Mixed pattern—low to high		
$Lo_1\ Lo_2\ Lo_3\ Hi_4$	5	1
$Lo_1\ Lo_2\ Hi_3 {-}_4$	6	5
$Lo_1\ Lo_2\ Hi_3\ Hi_4$	7	0
$Lo_1\ Hi_2 {-}_3 {-}_4$	12	12
$Lo_1\ Hi_2\ Lo_3\ Hi_4$	2	0
$Lo_1\ Hi_2\ Hi_3 {-}_4$	10	9
$Lo_1\ Hi_2\ Hi_3\ Hi_4$	6	4
$Hi_1 {-}_2\ Lo_3\ Hi_4$	1	0
$Hi_1\ Lo_2\ Lo_3\ Hi_4$	8	3
$Hi_1\ Lo_2\ Hi_3 {-}_4$	6	4
$Hi_1\ Lo_2\ Hi_3\ Hi_4$	4	3
$Hi_1\ Hi_2\ Lo_3\ Hi_4$	13	1
Total	80	42

Rican) and the visiting variables into the dichotomy employed
earlier (low and high visiting). The results of our analysis are set
forth in Table 4.6. A close examination of the data shows that, with
few exceptions, parental visiting is linked to discharge from foster
care and that this holds across ethnic groups and persists over time.
Put another way, it would appear that there is a beneficial payoff in

TABLE 4.5 (*cont.*)

Selected Patterns of Visiting	Number Discharged	Number of Children
Mixed pattern—high to low		
Lo_1 Lo_2 Hi_3 Lo_4	9	0
Lo_1 Hi_2 Lo_{3-4}	5	2
Lo_1 Hi_2 Lo_3 Lo_4	15	2
Lo_1 Hi_2 Hi_3 Lo_4	9	0
Hi_{1-2} Lo_{3-4}	2	2
Hi_{1-2} Lo_3 Lo_4	1	0
Hi_{1-2} Hi_3 Lo_4	2	2
Hi_1 Lo_{2-3-4}	15	14
Hi_1 Lo_2 Lo_{3-4}	5	5
Hi_1 Lo_2 Lo_3 Lo_4	12	0
Hi_1 Lo_2 Hi_3 Lo_4	3	0
Hi_1 Hi_{2-3} Lo_4	1	1
Hi_1 Hi_2 Lo_{3-4}	14	12
Hi_1 Hi_2 Lo_3 Lo_4	14	1
Hi_1 Hi_2 Hi_3 Lo_4	16	3
Total	123	44

Summarized Data

Summary:	No.	Percent	Percent Discharged
Uniformly high	246	42.6	86.2
Mixed: low to high	80	13.9	52.5
Mixed: high to low	123	21.3	35.8
Uniformly low	128	22.2	40.6
Total	577	100.0	

ªThe symbol "Lo" signifies low parental visiting (either no visiting or minimum visiting); "Hi" signifies high visiting (either frequent irregular visiting, maximum permitted visiting, or child visits home). Subscript indicates numbered interview as source of data in series of four agency interviews. Symbol — signifies that interview was not held, usually because child was discharged and visiting phenomenon was no longer relevant. Cases involving adoption or transfer to a hospital or training school are excluded from this table.

superior discharge rates for the black and Puerto Rican subjects, as well as the white.

We further interpret our findings to indicate that while there is an apparent advantage within each ethnic group for highly visited children, white children experience a higher degree of discharge

TABLE 4.6

DISCHARGE OF CHILDREN FROM FOSTER CARE BY FREQUENCY OF PARENTAL VISITING FOR FOUR TIME OCCASIONS, CONTROLLING FOR ETHNICITY

Discharge Status	White		Black		Puerto Rican	
	Low Visiting	High Visiting	Low Visiting	High Visiting	Low Visiting	High Visiting
Time I (N = 577)						
Discharged (%)	44.5	85.0	37.0	69.2	45.8	65.4
Still in care (%) after 5 years	55.5	15.0	63.0	30.8	54.2	34.6
(No. of cases)	(36)	(107)	(119)	(120)	(59)	(136)
	$\chi^2 = 23.574$, 1 df, $p < .001$		$\chi^2 = 24.865$, 1 df, $p < .001$		$\chi^2 = 6.612$, 1 df, $p < .01$	
Time II (N = 422)						
Discharged (%)	48.5	72.6	21.5	58.1	35.9	50.4
Still in care (%) after 5 years	51.5	27.4	78.5	41.9	64.1	49.6
(No. of cases)	(31)	(73)	(98)	(74)	(39)	(107)
	$\chi^2 = 5.638$, 1 df, $p < .05$		$\chi^2 = 24.279$, 1 df, $p < .001$		$\chi^2 = 2.438$, 1 df, NS	

Time III ($N = 349$)						
Discharged (%)	34.5	72.0	14.3	44.7	22.2	44.0
Still in care (%) after 5 years	65.5	28.0	85.7	55.3	77.8	56.0
(No. of cases)	(32)	(50)	(91)	(56)	(54)	(66)
	$\chi^2 = 11.291$, 1 df, $p < .001$		$\chi^2 = 16.667$, 1 df, $p < .001$		$\chi^2 = 6.227$, 1 df, $p < .05$	
Time IV ($N = 245$)						
Discharged (%)	18.5	42.1	5.1	20.0	3.9	22.9
Still in care (%) after 5 years	81.5	57.9	94.9	80.0	96.1	77.1
(No. of cases)	(27)	(19)	(78)	(35)	(51)	(35)
	$\chi^2 = 3.060$, 1 df, NS		$\chi^2 = 6.081$, 1 df, $p < .05$		$\chi^2 = 7.242$, 1 df, $p < .01$	

than the minority subjects when compared within the high and the low visiting categories. Factors other than visiting are obviously operating to depress the discharge rates of the black and Puerto Rican children. We particularly note the rapid decline in discharge of the black children who receive low visiting; only 14 percent are discharged at Time III and five percent at Time IV. For the low-visited Puerto Rican children, 22 percent are discharged at Time III and four percent at Time IV. In contrast, 35 percent of the low-visited white children are discharged at Time III and 19 percent at Time IV.

Further Understanding of Visitation Pattern

Thus far we have examined the role of two independent variables in seeking to determine the sources of variation in parental visiting behavior, namely, ethnicity and reason for placement. In an effort to develop further understanding of the visiting phenomenon through use of a larger group of explanatory variables, we now switch from contingency tables to multiple regression procedures; this permits us to assess the predictive utility of a fairly large number of variables. We chose this approach because the limited sample size prohibited extending the contingency analysis much further than already carried out.

In the search for predictive correlates of parental visiting, a number of variables were examined in terms of their correlations with the dependent and other independent variables. Some were discarded because they showed little potential for enhanced understanding of the visiting phenomen. Among others, these included the sex of the child, birth status, and source of placement (court vs. public welfare). We selected the following independent variables for our multiple regression analysis:

1. Child's age at placement—we theorized that older children, having experienced longer living contact with their parent(s), would have more solid ties with them than would infants.
2. Number of children in family—we theorized that having multiple children would provide greater pull of the parent to offspring than in the case of the single child.

3. Ethnicity—this was a dummy variable coded in binary form (coded 1 if the observation falls into the category, 0 if not).[11]

4. Reason for placement—as demonstrated earlier, categories such as unwillingness to assume care of an infant, neglect and abuse, and abandonment are associated with low degrees of parental visiting, while child behavior as a reason for placement showed a positive correlation. Through dummy-variable coding, we created seven reasons-for-placement variables.

5. Evaluation of mother—this is a five-item index covering the agency caseworker's assessment of the mother: (a) adequacy of maternal functioning, (b) degree of disturbance, (c) outlook for working with her, (d) prediction of whether she would drop out, and (e) the quality of the caseworker's attitude toward the mother as rated by the agency study staff. This information was collected on the same four data-gathering occasions during which visitation patterns were recorded.

6. Log total contact rate of caseworker with parent—this variable is a seven-item index measuring the average monthly case contacts by the agency's caseworker. Data on contacts with the child, child-caring persons, parents, collaterals, and other agencies are included. The contacts include personal interviews, home visits, and extended telephone calls. A logarithmic form of the index was developed to pick up some of the nonlinearity of the scores. Contact scores were created to reflect each of the four time phases.

In Table 4.7 we provide the zero-order correlations between the variables just cited and the visitation patterns of the parents at Times I–IV. There are fairly numerous instances where the correlations are statistically significant, but none is higher than .36. The correlations must thus be seen as relatively modest.

We observe that, for all four time phases, older children tend to be visited more frequently. The correlations are statistically significant for each time phase. This finding tends to support our view that older children, having had more extended contact with their parents, enjoy a greater claim on their loyalty and attentiveness than

[11] As pointed out by Jacob Cohen, in creating dummy variables from nominal scales, it requires no more than $g - 1$ independent variables to represent g of a G nominal scale. Thus it is not necessary to create a dummy variable for the white group after black and Puerto Rican children have been accounted for. See Jacob Cohen, "Multiple Regression as a General Data-Analytic System," *Psychological Bulletin* 70 (1968); 428.

TABLE 4.7
CORRELATIONS OF SELECTED BACKGROUND AND OTHER VARIABLES
WITH VISITING BEHAVIOR OF PARENTS (TIMES I–IV)[a]
(decimals omitted)

	Time I (N = 577)	Time II (N = 422)	Time III (N = 349)	Time IV (N = 245)
Child's age at placement	16***	32***	27***	21***
Number of children in family	00	10*	04	07
Ethnicity: black vs. others[b]	−22***	−29***	−19***	−10
Ethnicity: Puerto Rican vs. others	10*	20***	08	07
Reason for placement[b]				
Child behavior vs. others	15***	25***	25***	21**
Unwilling to assume care vs. others	−02	−09	−10	−12
Abandonment vs. others	−12**	−04	01	−15*
Neglect or abuse vs. others	−05	−11*	−07	−03
Mental illness of parent vs. others	17***	14**	05	14*
Physical illness of parent vs. others	−04	−03	−04	02
Unwilling continue care vs. others	04	−10*	−06	−06
Evaluation of mother (Times I–IV)[c]	21***	35***	30***	36***
Log total casework contact rate[c]	22**	26***	35***	08

*p < .05   **p < .01   ***p < .001

[a]The visiting behavior variable is a dichotomy: *low* (coded as 0) and *high* (coded as 1).

[b] Ethnicity and reason for placement variables are dummy variable coded (each category is coded as 1 and "others" as 0).

[c]Variables come from the same time phase as the visiting behavior variable with which it is correlated.

do younger children, such as newborns, whose mothers decided not to assume their care early after birth.

The variable specifying the number of children in the family tended to show trivial and insignificant correlations with parental visitation except for Time II, when there was greater visiting by parents of larger family units ($r = .10$). On the whole, this variable is not impressive in its ability to contribute to the prediction of visiting behavior.

As previously displayed in our contingency tables, ethnicity is one of the stronger predictors of parental visiting, at least through Time III. Black children tended to be significantly undervisited for Times I, II, and III, while Puerto Rican children received somewhat higher degrees of visiting. As previously shown in the contingency tables, white, particularly Jewish, children, fared better than minority children as recipients of frequent visiting by their parents.

The reason-for-placement variables, coded in dummy-variable form, show a number of selected reasons that are significantly correlated with parental visiting. This information reflects the findings previously reported for Table 4.3. Children entering care because of their own behavior difficulties tended to be visited at a higher level when contrasted with others for all four time phases. Also, children entering care because of mental illness of parents were visited on a significantly greater basis for Times I, II, and IV. Abandoned children tended to be visited significantly less than the other children at Times I and IV, and children who were admitted into care because of neglect or abuse were significantly less visited at Time II.

Children of mothers who received more positive evaluations by the caseworkers, as reflected in the five-item index, showed significantly higher visitation over each of the four time phases. The correlations for each data-gathering occasion are significant beyond the .001 level. The fairly strong correlations are not surprising; one would expect that parents perceived as functioning on higher levels would visit their children more steadily. It would also seem logical that caseworkers' assessments would be influenced by the knowledge of the parent's visitation pattern.

The index measuring the amount of investment of caseworker effort in a case showed significant association with parental visiting for Times I, II, and III, but little association for Time IV. The fact that frequency of casework contact is associated with frequency of parental visitations does not necessarily suggest a causal relationship between the two phenomena. It is quite possible that an underlying dimension of accessibility of the parent accounts for the correlations we have found; this point is examined in the material that follows.

Multiple Regression Analysis of Visitation Pattern

Table 4.8 shows the standardized regression coefficients (beta weights) that relate parental visiting, the dependent variable, to the independent variables just cited. The multiple regressions were carried out for each of the four time phases in which visitation data were secured through agency study research interviews.

We observe that among the statistically significant variables in the Time I analysis were mental illness of the mother and child behavior as reasons for placement. Both were linked to enhanced visiting of the parent. Interestingly, the influence of these variables was greatly diminished in accounting for visiting behavior at Times II, III, and IV. Ethnicity was also a significant factor in Time I parent visitation, with black children generally less visited than either whites or Puerto Ricans. A similar inverse relationship is noted in the Time II analysis, but ethnicity is less salient as a predictor at times III and IV. This may be due to the discharge of visited children over time, leaving those behind in a greater state of parity with respect to conditions militating against discharge and hence rendering ethnicity less salient as a predictor.

We find that evaluation of the mother and the logarithm of total contacts made by the caseworker (with child, parents, collaterals, etc.) show fairly substantial beta weights, and these are sustained through Times II and III. At Time IV, the evaluation of the mother still looms large but casework activity is diminished in importance in accounting for variability in visiting.

When the effects of other relevant variables are removed, the age of the child at placement is not very salient at Time I, although some predictive variance is contributed. However, the variable does show greater usefulness as a predictor for the Time II, III, and IV analyses.

TABLE 4.8

STANDARDIZED REGRESSION COEFFICIENTS (BETA WEIGHTS) AND UNIQUE VARIANCE CONTRIBUTIONS OF SELECTED VARIABLES IN ANALYSIS OF PARENTAL VISITING (TIMES I–IV)

Independent Variables[a]	Time I Beta Weight[b]	Time I Unique Variance	Time II Beta Weight	Time II Unique Variance	Time III Beta Weight	Time III Unique Variance	Time IV Beta Weight	Time IV Unique Variance
1. AGE	.04	0.10	.17	1.70**	*.13*	1.10*	*.09*	0.50
2. NO. CHN	.01	0.00	.05	0.20	.00	0.00	.05	0.20
3. ETHN-BL	−.16	1.40**	−.14	1.10	−.10	0.60	−.08	0.30
4. ETHN-PR	−.02	0.00	.09	0.40	−.03	0.10	−.01	0.00
5. REASON-1	.21	2.20***	.10	0.40	.13	0.70	.12	0.80
6. REASON-2	.08	0.40	.01	0.00	.01	0.00	−.06	0.20
7. REASON-3	.06	0.20	−.02	0.00	.07	0.30	−.05	0.20
8. REASON-4	.13	0.90	−.03	0.10	.02	0.00	−.01	0.00
9. REASON-5	.27	3.00***	.07	0.20	.03	0.00	.08	0.30
10. REASON-6	.05	0.20	−.04	0.10	−.03	0.10	−.03	0.00
11. REASON-7	.13	1.00*	−.11	0.70	−.01	0.00	−.04	0.10
12. EVAL-MO.	*.15*	2.00***	*.24*	5.10***	.28	7.40***	*.31*	8.50***
13. CASEWORK	.15	2.10***	*.11*	0.90*	.23	4.40***	−.04	0.10
Multiple R	.41		.53		.50		.44	
Multiple R²	.17		.28		.25		.19	
No. of cases	577		422		349		245	

*p < .05   **p < .01   ***p < .001

[a]Variable labels represent the following: 1—age of child; 2—number of children in family; 3—ethnicity: black; 4—ethnicity: Puerto Rican. Variables 5–11, reasons for placement: 5—child behavior; 6—unwilling to assume care; 7—abandonment; 8—neglect or abuse; 9—mental illness of parent; 10—physical illness of parent; 11—unwilling to continue care; 12—evaluation of mother (Times I to IV); 13—log total caseworker contact rate (Time I–IV).

[b]Italicized standardized regression coefficients are at least twice as large as their standard errors.

For Times II, III, and IV, we note the lack of cogency of reason for placement as a set of explanatory variables. On the other hand, evaluation of the mother, extent of casework investment, and age of the child at placement appear fairly potent. We also observe that the number of children in a family makes a small predictive contribution at Times II and IV, with children in larger family units receiving greater visitation. We point out to the reader that the coefficient of determination (R^2) ranges between .17 and .28 for the four analyses. This reflects a relatively modest amount of variance accounted for and indicates that other sources of explanation of visitation patterns should be examined in future research.

Implications of Findings

One must be impressed with the fact that the proportion of parents who visit their children declines rapidly as one proceeds from the Time I to the Time IV data. At the end of five years, 57 percent of the children still in care were not being visited. Behind this figure may well exist acute feelings of pain for the children involved. The finding that discharge rates are quite closely linked to the frequency of parental visitation underscores the need to assign high priority to monitoring this phenomenon.

The present writers believe it should be mandatory for all agencies to keep a log on the visitation of parents to their children in foster care. This information should be available on a ready-state basis as part of the computerized management-information systems currently being developed in this area of service. The requirement that this information be available should be formalized into state law, and agency practices in this regard should be carefully monitored by the state departments of social service as part of their licensing function. Like the frequent monitoring of body-temperature information for assessing the health of patients in hospitals, parental visitation patterns should be carefully scrutinized as the best available index of the long-term fate of children in care. Consider the fact that 66 percent of the children who received no visiting during the first year of their entry were still in care five years later.

The reader should be aware that only a modest amount of the variance in parental visiting was accounted for by the variables utilized in our analyses. Further work remains to be accomplished in illuminating the factors that deter parents from maintaining contact with their children. The extent to which agencies encourage visiting demands attention, as well as other "systems" variables.[12]

Parental failure to visit their children cannot long be tolerated unless the parent is physically or mentally incapacitated. The question of termination of parental rights naturally arises when a parent drops out of a child's life. Agencies should be held accountable for efforts made to involve the parent in more responsible visitation. The finding that frequency of casework contact, independent of the evaluation of the mother, is associated with greater frequency of visiting is a good omen.

Further research to replicate and extend the findings reported here should be encouraged.

[12] In interviews with the parents of the children during the last year of the study, complaints of lack of encouragement of visitation were numerous. See Shirley Jenkins and Elaine Norman, *Beyond Placement: Mothers View Foster Care* (New York: Columbia University Press, 1975), pp. 67–69.

FIVE

DISCHARGE
AND OTHER
STATUS OUTCOMES

Billy P. is a lively and healthy Puerto Rican boy who entered foster care at the age of eight years, when his mother was hospitalized for serious surgery. He had never seen his father. The mother's prospects for recovery were good but the healing process was slow and she was physically unable to resume her home responsibilities for an extended period. During this time Billy was cared for by a foster family. The mother visited him as frequently as her circumstances permitted and always planned to take him home. With the help of two voluntary social agencies and the public welfare department, her home was restored and resumption of maternal responsibilities were finally effected some eighteen months after Billy had entered care. He did not appear to have suffered emotionally from the experience and had been quite secure with the foster family.

Carol T. came into care as an infant born out of wedlock to a mother who was heavily involved in the use of hard drugs. The mother was a young white woman who had performed well in high school but revealed serious emotional problems. She was ambivalent about releasing Carol for adoption and visited only sporadically. Agencies found it extraordinarily difficult to work with her concerning treatment plans for herself and planning for her child. After the mother had disappeared and could not be contacted for about a year, legal action was taken to terminate parental rights and an adoptive home was found for Carol. Although the child was three years old at the time of adoptive placement, she settled in rather quickly and seemed well integrated within her new family in about a year.

Tommy is a black 12-year-old, one of four children in the G. family, who entered foster care when his mother attempted suicide and was

The contents of this chapter appeared previously in *Child Welfare*, 55 (1976): 143–71.

admitted to a city hospital. She was diagnosed as suffering from schizophrenia and transferred to a state mental institution. She had a long history of emotional disturbance going back to a severely traumatized childhood in which she had witnessed her own mother's death in a household fire. She made little progress in the institution and the outlook for her release appeared increasingly dim over the years. After several placements in foster family homes where Tommy was restless and unhappy, he was finally placed in an institution in Westchester County where he seemed more at ease with himself and his surroundings. His siblings remained in foster family care. Prospects are strong that Tommy will be in care until adulthood.

David C. is an 11-year-old Jewish boy who was admitted to residential care because of his own serious emotional problems. He came from a family of fairly comfortable economic means; both of his parents were successful professional persons. From early childhood he had appeared "different" and had been exposed to a variety of treatment efforts including child psychoanalytic therapy. These were unsuccessful and he deteriorated to the point where residential care was recommended. For a time, David seemed to respond positively to his new institutional environment and seemed less disassociated with what was going on around him. He could not sustain this, however, and six months after placement reached the point of such severe withdrawal that institutionalization in a mental hospital became necessary.

These case vignettes typify different outcomes of the foster care experience and are provided as a way of orienting the reader to the content that follows. We examine here what is perhaps the most crucial point about a child's fate in foster care; namely, whether he will return home. We have briefly looked at this issue in the preceding chapter and have seen that parental visiting is a significant predictor of the discharge of children from care. We now examine this matter further, seeking to illuminate the factors that appear to favor a child's return home as well as those that stand in the way of such an outcome.

As a prelude to our discussion of findings we observe that the discharge phenomenon provides an important dimension for evaluating the foster care system. The failure to restore children to their own homes contradicts the concept of foster care as a temporary living arrangement for children. The failure to remedy conditions which have prompted the need for such care is regarded as a serious shortcoming by many child welfare experts. Indeed, the system of foster care has been severely criticized in New York City as one that tends to lock children into care.[1]

A note on our approach to studying status changes is in order. While the discharge of children over the five years of longitudinal investigation would seem simple enough to study, it turns out there are complexities to the phenomenon that need clarification: (a) whether we should treat children placed in adoptive homes as "discharged" in the same sense as those who have returned home, (b) how we should treat children who have been transferred out of the foster care system to other systems (e.g., children moved to mental hospitals or training schools), (c) how we should treat children who are discharged and then returned to foster care, and (d) how we should treat children who are transferred from one agency to another but remain within the system.

There were 29 children from our sample of 624 who were adopted. This resolution of the indeterminate status of the children can be construed as a positive outcome since it affords the children permanent homes. We have chosen to exclude these children from our analysis of factors leading to "discharge," but do include later in this chapter some contrast of the adopted children with others in our sample who were considered adoptable at the time they entered foster care but who were still in care five years after their entry.

We consider the transfer of children to other state institutions as apparent failures of the foster care system.[2] Some of the children in our sample were transferred to state mental institutions for the mentally retarded or for the mentally ill. A few children were referred to state training schools for delinquent children. These cases were removed from our analysis of discharge since their exit from care did not represent a positive outcome. While the number of cases involved is too small for any meaningful analysis, some

---

[1] For example, see Citizen's Committee for Children of New York, "Toward a New Social Service System," *Child Welfare*, 50 (1971): 6–7.

[2] We recognize that agencies often agree to accept children who are severely disturbed and whose care poses major problems; the foster care agency is often the last alternative for a child who seems destined to enter a mental institution. Evaluation of such "failures" needs to take this factor into account.

descriptive information is provided at the end of this chapter as a way of developing insight about the phenomenon.

Since we are concerned here with status changes—the movement of the child from one living situation to another—we also seek to clarify the amount of inter- and intra-agency transfers experienced by our subjects. To have a child remain in foster care for most of his childhood years is a legitimate cause of community concern; to have him experience repeated changes in the living arrangements afforded him would compound the matter. We undertake to provide answers to such questions as how many placements children experience while in foster care and what types of children are more prone to experience multiple placements. In subsequent chapters we examine the association between number of placements as a variable and the adjustment of the children.

In Table 5.1 we enumerate status outcomes experienced by the subjects five years after entry into foster care.[3] We observe that 56 percent had been discharged; we subsequently provide data showing that most of these children returned to their own homes. Another 5 percent of the children were placed in adoptive homes. About 3

TABLE 5.1
STATUS OF SUBJECTS FIVE YEARS AFTER ENTRY INTO FOSTER CARE

	Number	Percentage
In care	227	36.4
Discharged	350	56.1
Placed in adoptive home	29	4.6
Transferred to mental institution or training school	18	2.9
Total	624	100.0

[3] The child's status was determined by his whereabouts on the anniversary date of his entrance into foster care. Information about changes in the living arrangements of the children were monitored systematically over a six-year period. Approximately every three months a computerized report was mailed to each child care agency where study subjects were located to ascertain whether subjects under care in the agency had been discharged or transferred on an inter- or intra-agency basis. In addition, files of the Bureau of Child Welfare, New York City Department of Social Services were monitored periodically to determine whether discharged subjects had reentered foster care.

percent of the subjects could not "make it" in the foster care system and had to be transferred to state institutions; fourteen went to mental hospitals, two to institutions for the retarded, and two were placed in state training schools for delinquent children. Some 36 percent of the original study population remained in care at the end of the longitudinal investigation. These four status categories can be viewed as important outcomes of the foster care experience, and the major thrust of this chapter is to analyze some of the factors which help account for children experiencing such different end results.

It should be further noted that 61 of the children—almost 10 percent of the sample—were discharged more than once. There were 21 children still in care at the end of five years who had experienced discharge; 16 had been discharged once and reentered, and five had been discharged and reentered twice. There were 40 children who were discharged at the end of five years and had experienced more than one discharge. Of these, 32 had experienced two discharges and one reentry, six had experienced three discharges and two reentries, and two had experienced four discharges and three reentries.

DISCHARGE FROM FOSTER CARE

We begin our analysis of status outcomes by examining the phenomenon of central importance to any study of foster children, namely, their discharge from foster care. For this analysis of the status of the children at the end of five years, we have excluded the 29 cases where the children were adopted and the 18 involving transfers to state institutions. This reduces our study population to 577 children; of these, 350 were discharged (60.7 percent) and 227 remained in care (39.3 percent).

In Table 5.2 we present two-variable cross-tabulations of the number discharged versus those still in care. When we examine the role of age as an explanatory variable, we find a significant association; the youngest group of children showed a greater proportion who remained in care. Of this group, 50 percent were still in placement at the end of five years compared to the oldest group of children, 75 percent of whom had left care by the end of the fifth

TABLE 5.2
DISCHARGE STATUS, BY SELECTED INDEPENDENT VARIABLES
(N = 577)

	Discharged		Still in Care	
	%	No.	%	No.
Age at Entry				
Under 2 years	49.7	80	50.3	81
2–5 years	62.1	108	37.9	66
6–8 years	59.0	69	41.0	48
9–12 years	74.4	93	25.6	32
$\chi^2 = 18.292$, df = 3, $p < .001$				
Sex				
Male	59.4	174	40.6	119
Female	62.0	119	38.0	108
$\chi^2 = 0.404$, df = 1, NS				
Birth Status				
In wedlock	68.3	198	31.7	92
Out of wedlock	52.5	145	47.5	131
Not determined	63.6	7	36.4	4
$\chi^2 = 14.722$, df = 2, $p < .001$				
Mode of Entry into Care				
Court	63.5	80	36.5	46
Bureau of Child Welfare	59.9	270	40.1	181
$\chi^2 = 0.542$, df = 1, NS				
Ethnicity–Religion				
White Catholic or Protestant	71.7	81	28.3	32
Jewish	86.7	26	13.3	4
Black Catholic	55.6	35	44.4	28
Black Protestant	52.3	92	47.7	84
Puerto Rican	59.5	116	40.5	79
$\chi^2 = 20.242$, df = 4, $p < .001$				

year. The two middle groups fall in between with respect to discharge. One explanation of the differential outcome based on age is that the children entered care for age-related reasons. Infants often were placed because of the unwillingness of their mothers to assume care, while older children included a sizable group whose behavior difficulty was the reason for their entry. One might also conjecture that older children, having experienced longer years of relationship with a parent than an infant, had the advantage of stronger claims for ongoing parental involvement and responsibility.

We observe only trivial difference in proportions of children discharged when we compare boys with girls, and a similar finding obtains for court-committed cases as opposed to those entering voluntarily through the public welfare agency. The fact that court cases were no more obdurate with respect to discharge than other cases may cause some surprise. The aura surrounding court cases is that of quite dramatic parental failure which has required societal intervention.[4]

Ethnicity–religion is defined by five groups: white Catholic or Protestant,[5] Jewish, black Catholic, black Protestant, and Puerto Rican. The data in Table 5.2 show that minority children tended to experience a lower proportion of discharges than white children; the differences are statistically significant. Almost nine out of ten Jewish children and seven out of ten white Catholic or Protestant children returned home. By contrast, less than six out of ten black or Puerto Rican children were discharged. These differences in outcome constitute important social data. As in many other areas of social life, race and ethnicity are powerful predictors of life outcomes. We will seek to gain more insight about the meaning of our finding as we proceed further into our analysis.

We now proceed to an examination of Table 5.3, which displays discharge information according to the reasons for the child's placement. Here the discharge data are shown in more elaborated form, that is, broken down for the percentage who left each year over the five years of longitudinal investigation. This gives a sense of the flow of the children out of care over the five years being monitored. We observe that almost 25 percent left care the first year, and 7 percent during the last year. Our data tend to contradict the notion originating from earlier research which main-

---

[4] Throughout the study we have failed to find significant differences between court cases and those involving voluntary admission to foster care.

[5] We combined white Catholic and white Protestant children because we had so few of the latter, and on many measures of child description the two groups of children were quite similar.

tains that unless children leave foster care within the first or second year after entry, they are doomed to spend the remainder of their childhood years in care.[6] We note that almost 25 percent of the children from our sample left care after a sojourn of two years. The practice implications of these data would seem obvious; even three, four, and five years after a child's entry into care, one need not relinquish hope of his eventual return to his own home or to the home of relatives or friends.

Turning to the differentiation in discharge related to reason for placement, we can report findings pertinent to understanding the discharge phenomenon:

1. Children who enter care because of their own behavior difficulties show the smallest proportion returning home during the first year—less than 8 percent—but by the end of the study they also show the smallest proportion remaining in care, 24 percent. Given the fact that treatment of emotional disturbance is a time-consuming process, the minimal early movement is understandable. The fact that *they* rather than *their parents* are the source of the need for placement would also indicate that an intact home is more likely available to them than is true of other categories of children and would thus likely explain their higher discharge rate over time.

2. Children whose entry into care was due to physical illness of a parent or child caring person left care in proportionately larger number during the first year—some 43 percent.

3. Children who were abandoned or deserted showed the largest proportion still in care at the end of five years—57 percent. The next highest group consisted of children who entered care because of neglect or abuse; 48 percent were still in care at the end of five years.

In Table 5.4 we hold reason for placement constant while we examine variation in discharge by ethnicity. For purpose of our analysis, we have consolidated the latter variable into three categories: white, black, and Puerto Rican. Mental illness of the child caring person accounted for more children coming into foster care than any other category. We observe in Table 5.4 that white children of such parents fared much better than black and Puerto Rican

[6] See statement by Joseph H. Reid in Chapter 8, Henry S. Maas and Richard E. Engler, Jr., *Children in Need of Parents* (New York: Columbia University Press, 1959). He observes, "In community after community, it is clear from the data in the study that unless children move out of care within the first year to year and a half of their stay in care, the likelihood of their ever moving out sharply decreases" (p. 390).

TABLE 5.3
DISCHARGE STATUS, BY REASON FOR PLACEMENT[a]
(N = 577)

Discharge Status	Reason			
	Hospitalization (mental) of Child-caring Person	Child's Own Behavior	Hospitalization (physical) of Child-caring Person	Unwilling Assume Care
	(percentages)			
Discharged first year	25.6	7.6	43.3	30.6
Discharged second year	13.5	19.7	9.0	19.4
Discharged third year	8.3	16.7	1.5	5.6
Discharged fourth year	6.8	22.7	3.0	—
Discharged fifth year	8.3	9.1	10.4	2.8
Still in care after five years	37.5	24.2	32.8	41.6
No. of cases	133	66	67	36

[a] Table excludes 29 children who were adopted, 16 transferred to state mental institutions, and 2 transferred to state training schools for delinquent children.

children. We are unable to account for this variation in discharge, within the limitations of our data. We wonder whether differences in the severity of disturbance of the mothers in the three ethnic groupings accounts for the variations in outcome. We also would be interested in knowing whether discrepancies in quality of mental health care made available to them plays a role here.

When we look at the group of children who entered care because of parental neglect or abuse, we observe that noticeably

TABLE 5.3 (*cont.*)

Reason

Unwilling Continue Care	Neglect or Abuse of Child	Abandonment or Desertion	Family Dysfunction	Death of Parent	Total
		(percentages)			
26.7	22.1	14.5	27.3	25.0	24.4
16.7	16.3	4.8	5.5	—	12.8
6.7	9.3	4.8	7.3	—	7.6
11.7	2.3	12.9	10.9	16.7	8.8
5.0	2.3	6.5	5.5	25.0	6.9
33.2	47.7	56.5	43.5	33.3	39.3
60	86	62	55	12	577

$\chi^2 = 19.367$,   df $= 8$, $p < .05$ (discharge treated as dichotomy; discharged/in care)

more black children entered care for this reason than did white or Puerto Rican subjects. Furthermore, the proportion of black children leaving care within five years is much less than that of other children. The disproportionate failure to restore black neglected or abused children to their homes must be studied in greater depth. Again we ask whether their parents were more disabled than other parents in the sample who were also charged with neglect and

TABLE 5.4
RELATIONSHIP BETWEEN DISCHARGE STATUS AND ETHNICITY OF
SUBJECTS, CONTROLLING FOR REASON FOR PLACEMENT[a]
(N = 577)

Reason for Placement[a]	White	Black	Puerto Rican
	(percentages)		
Mental illness of child-caring person			
Discharged	76.7	42.4	46.7
Still in care	23.3	57.8	53.3
(No. of cases)	(43)	(45)	(45)
	$\chi^2 = 5.758$, df = 2, p = .057		
Neglect or abuse of child			
Discharged	76.9	37.8	64.3
Still in care	23.1	62.2	35.7
(No. of cases)	(13)	(45)	(28)
	$\chi^2 = 8.576$, df = 2, p < .05		
Behavior of child			
Discharged	85.7	71.4	64.7
Still in care	14.3	28.6	35.3
(No. of cases)	(28)	(21)	(17)
	$\chi^2 = 2.856$, df = 2, NS		
Physical illness of child-caring person			
Discharged	75.0	47.8	78.1
Still in care	25.0	52.2	21.9
(No. of cases)	(12)	(23)	(32)
	$\chi^2 = 5.977$, df = 2, p < .05		

abuse, and whether quality of service delivery is part of the problem.

There is only one other category of reason for placement where we find statistically significant ethnic variation in the proportion of children discharged—children who entered foster care because of physical illness of their parents. Black children were discharged significantly less often than white or Puerto Rican children. The questions raised above are obviously pertinent here as well.

Although the remaining analyses in Table 5.4 do not reveal statistically significant ethnic differences in discharge rates, we note

TABLE 5.4 (*contd.*)

Reason for Placement[a]	White	Black	Puerto Rican
	(percentages)		
Abandonment or desertion by parent			
Discharged	33.3	41.4	50.0
Still in care	66.7	58.6	50.0
(No. of cases)	(9)	(29)	(24)
	$\chi^2 = 0.844$, df = 2, NS		
Parent unwilling to continue care			
Discharged	84.6	66.7	58.6
Still in care	15.4	33.3	41.4
(No. of cases)	(13)	(18)	(29)
	$\chi^2 = 2.729$, df = 2, NS		
Family problems			
Discharged	55.6	63.3	43.8
Still in care	44.4	36.7	56.3
(No. of cases)	(9)	(30)	(16)
	$\chi^2 = 1.630$, df = 2, NS		
Parent unwilling to assume care			
Discharged	66.7	55.0	50.0
Still in care	33.3	45.0	50.0
(No. of cases)	(12)	(20)	(4)
	$\chi^2 = 0.549$, df = 2, NS		

[a] Twelve cases involving death of a parent as reason for placement are not shown here.

the relative disadvantage of Puerto Rican children among those who entered care because of generalized family dysfunctional problems and among those whose parents were unwilling to continue care.

Correlates of Discharge
Because of the limits of sample size it was not possible to perform more elaborate cross-tabulations in our analysis of discharge. We

instead chose to move to multiple correlational procedures as a way of dealing with a larger number of independent variables. In Table 5.5 we provide the zero-order correlations between selected background and other variables and a criterion variable signifying the child's discharge status five years after his entry into care (coded as a dichotomy: in care/discharged). The data are presented for four prediction occasions: (a) at Time I, when the five-year status of all the children in the sample is analyzed except for those adopted or transferred to mental institutions or training schools, (b) at Time II, when children discharged during the first year have been excluded from the analysis, (c) at Time III, with children discharged during the second year excluded, and (d) at Time IV, covering only children still in care at the beginning of the fifth year. Essentially, the analytic task is to make repeated predictions with the sample increasingly diminished by the discharge of children over the years.

The reader should be aware that some of the independent variables are time-specific for each prediction occasion, reflecting information secured in the sequence of four agency study interviews. These include: (a) parental visiting information, (b) the amount of casework contact during the recent period, and (c) the composite index reflecting an overall evaluation of the child's mother. Examining the situation at Time I, we find to make the strongest correlation of discharge status is the variable we have previously highlighted, namely, parental visiting. The correlation is .32 and, while statistically significant, must be seen as a relative modest predictor of the criterion variable. We also find that variables reflecting evaluation of the mother and the measure of casework activity are among the more important predictors. These three variables persevere in strength over the sequence of prediction occasions. Parental visiting is a fairly strong predictor at Time III ($r = .39$) as is the measure of overall casework activity ($r = .32$). Concerning the latter variable, the reader should be aware that from the correlation coefficient alone, it is not possible to determine whether a high level of casework investment "causes" discharge or whether a child's readiness to be returned home results in a flurry of activity which is reactive, that is, readiness for discharge "causes" casework activity. Nevertheless, levels of casework activity do help forecast the departure of children from care.

TABLE 5.5
CORRELATIONS OF SELECTED BACKGROUND AND OTHER VARIABLES WITH DISCHARGE STATUS[a] OF CHILD SUBJECTS FIVE YEARS AFTER ENTRY INTO FOSTER CARE (TIMES I–IV)
(decimals omitted)

Variable[b]	Predicting at Time I (N = 577)	Predicting at Time II (N = 422)	Predicting at Time III (N = 349)	Predicting at Time IV (N = 245)
1. Child's age at placement	16***	26***	34***	15*
2. Birth status (in/out of wedlock)	16***	17***	22***	24***
3. Ethnicity—black vs. others	-13**	-17***	-18***	-11
4. Ethnicity—Puerto Rican vs. others	-02	-01	-03	-05
5. Mental illness of parent vs. others	02	01	00	02
6. Child behavior vs. others	11**	22***	25***	10
7. Physical illness of parent vs. others	05	-06	-04	08
8. Unable to continue care vs. others	04	05	02	00
9. Unwilling to assume care vs. others	-01	-05	-09	-10
10. Abandonment vs. others	-12**	-10*	-08	-03
11. Neglect or abuse vs. others	-07	-07	-11*	-11
12. Parental visiting pattern	32***	31***	39***	27***
13. Log total casework contact rate	19***	21***	32***	18**
14. Evaluation of mother	24***	25***	26***	21**

*$p < .05$ **$p < .01$ ***$p < .001$

[a]Discharge status is a dichotomy (in care/discharged). Independent variables 12–14 are specific to the time predicting occasions.

[b]Ethnicity and reason for placement variables (5–11) are dummy-variable coded (each category is binary coded as *1* and "others" as *0*).

Examination of Table 5.5 shows age to be significantly correlated on all four prediction occasions with discharge status. As
previously indicated, older children tend to return home more often
than their younger counterparts. Similarly, birth status is significantly correlated on each prediction occasion with discharge,
with the children born in wedlock tending to be discharged with
greater frequency over the course of the five years of longitudinal
investigation. The correlations range from $r = .16$ at Time I to
$r = .24$ at Time IV.

Ethnicity has been previously established as predictive of
discharge status. We observe that the dummy variable contrasting
black children with all other children is a significant correlate of
outcome for Times I, II, and III, but not at Time IV. The children
who entered foster care because of their own behavioral difficulty
tended to return home in greater proportions than those coming for
other reasons—the zero-order correlations are significant for the
first three prediction occasions. By contrast, abandoned children
show significantly fewer proportions being discharged as predicted
at Times I and II, and this is also true of neglect or abuse cases as
predicted at Time III. These correlations are, of course, consonant
with the findings reported for the cross-tabulations presented earlier.

We now present the results of multiple regression analyses of
the discharge phenomenon for four prediction occasions using the
regressor variables previously cited. Table 5.6 summarizes the
empirical results in terms of standardized regression coefficients and
the unique variance accounted for by each variable. For the Time I
prediction occasion, parental visitation has the highest coefficient
and it has noticeably greater predictive power than any other
variable, contributing almost 5 percent of explained variance in the
discharge phenomenon beyond that explained by all other independent
variables in the analysis. The amount of variance accounted for is
particularly impressive since this prediction spans the five years of the
study. The index constituting an evaluation of the child's mother is also
a predictor of some potency. It would appear that mothers who
revealed better parental capacity, as judged by their caseworkers,
were more successful in arranging for their children to be returned
home.

It is of interest that the measure of casework activity as

reported during the first year contributes quite trivially to our ability to predict discharge—less than 1 percent of variance accounted for—but assumes greater importance when we look at the later prediction occasions. We further note that at Time I the variables of the age and ethnicity of the child contribute significantly but modestly as predictors of discharge. With respect to variation in discharge rate at five years being explained by the independent variables we have employed at Time I, we can report that the multiple correlation is .42 and that 18 percent of the variance is thus accounted for. Although statistically significant, this is a relatively slight result. Such low predictive yields are not uncommon in the social sciences,[7] however, and simply indicate that much exploratory work involving new types of variables remains to be done if the discharge phenomenon is to be brought under firmer predictive control.

The analytic effort taken from the vantage point of Time II as a predictive occasion—with the exclusion of children discharged during the first year after entry—essentially tells the same story as that reported for Time I. The variance accounted for by the regression analysis is 19 percent and hardly improves our predictive capacity in comparison with Time I.

At Time III there is a noticeable enhancement in the amount of variance accounted for; at this time children discharged within two years after entry have been excluded from the analysis. The multiple correlation for this analysis is .55, and 31 percent of the variance is thus accounted for. While still not large, this is nevertheless an improvement over the previous analyses. This gain in predictive capacity is largely accounted for by two variables, namely, the logarithm of total casework contact rate and evaluation of the mother. It is interesting that at a point two years after entry—and with a truncated sample of children remaining in care— casework activity appears to have more saliency as a predictor of discharge. We also find it of interest that the age of the child makes a significant contribution to prediction at this time.

When we examine the Time IV predictive effort, with the

[7] Derek Phillips, "Sociologists and Their Knowledge," *American Behavioral Scientist* 14 (1971): 563–82.

TABLE 5.6
STANDARDIZED REGRESSION COEFFICIENTS AND UNIQUE VARIANCE CONTRIBUTIONS RELATING DISCHARGE STATUS OF CHILD SUBJECTS FIVE YEARS AFTER ENTRY INTO FOSTER CARE TO SELECTED INDEPENDENT VARIABLES[a]

Independent Variables[b]	Predicting at Time I		Predicting at Time II		Predicting at Time III		Predicting at Time IV	
	Standardized Regression Coefficient	% Unique Variance Explained	Standardized Regression Coefficient	% Unique Variance Explained	Standardized Regression Coefficient	% Unique Variance Explained	Standardized Regression Coefficient	% Unique Variance Explained
1. Child's age at placement	.10*	0.60	.13*	1.00	.21***	2.70	-.01	0.00
2. Birth status	.02	0.00	.00	0.00	.01	0.00	.13	1.10
3. Ethnicity—black vs. others	-.09	0.50	-.16*	1.30	-.17**	1.60	-.21*	2.20
4. Ethnicity—Puerto Rican vs. others	-.13**	1.00	-.17**	1.50	-.21***	2.50	-.22**	2.50
5. Mental illness of parent vs. others	-.13*	0.60	-.07	0.20	-.14*	0.90	-.14	0.90
6. Child behavior vs. others	-.07	0.20	.00	0.00	-.07	0.20	-.12	0.80
7. Physical illness of parent vs. others	-.04	0.10	-.06	0.20	-.10	0.70	-.04	0.10

8. Unwillingness to continue care vs. others	-.04	0.10	.05	0.10	-.01	0.00	-.05	0.20
9. Unwillingness to assume care vs. others	-.05	0.10	.00	0.00	-.03	0.10	-.08	0.50
10. Abandonment vs. others	-.10	0.50	-.07	0.30	-.10	0.50	-.06	0.20
11. Neglect or abuse vs. others	-.09	0.40	-.02	0.00	-.12	0.80	-.17*	1.50
12. Parental visiting pattern	.25***	4.90	.17**	2.10	.20***	2.90	.18*	2.20
13. Log total casework contact rate	.08*	0.60	.09	0.60	.18***	2.40	.16*	2.00
14. Evaluation of mother	.17***	2.30	.16**	2.00	.19***	3.30	.13	1.30
Multiple R	.42		.43		.55		.42	
Multiple R²	.18		.19		.31		.18	
No. of Cases	577		422		349		245	

$*p < .05$ $**p < .01$ $***p < .001$

[a] The dependent variable is defined as the child's discharge status five years after entry into care (in care/discharged). Variables 5–11 represent reason for placement, and variables 12–14 are specific to the time predicting occasions.

[b] Italic coefficients are greater than twice their standard deviation.

exclusion of all children discharged within four years, we find the amount of variance accounted for to be diminished to 18 percent.

Our overall impression regarding the saliency of variables predicting discharge is that parental visiting, evaluation of the mother, activity of the caseworker, ethnicity, and age of child at placement are the most promising variables. Birth status contributes little to our understanding of discharge, as does the set of dummy variables representing reason for placement. These were previously seen to have some predictive value in cross-tabulations, but their effect is trivial when all variables are considered in the multiple regression analysis. A parallel multiple regression analysis was undertaken of length of time in care as a continuous dependent variable—rather than discharge status at five years treated as a dichotomy—and the results were quite similar to those we have reported. To save space, we do not present these data here.

ADOPTION AS AN OUTCOME

Most informed opinion about the foster care system would assume that if a child cannot be returned to his own family, placement in an adoptive home should be considered as the next best alternative. As stated in the Child Welfare League of America's *Standards for Adoption Service*, three principles have long guided child welfare practice with respect to adoption:

1. The primary purpose of an adoption service is to help children who would not otherwise have a home of their own, and who can benefit by family life, to become members of a family.
2. Adoption is an appropriate service for any child who is deprived of care by his natural parents, who either is or can be made legally free for adoption, and who has the capacity to form a relationship with new parents and to develop in a family.
3. No child should be deprived of the opportunity to have a permanent family of his own by reason of his age, religion, race, nationality, residence, or handicaps that do not preclude his living in a family or community.[8]

---

[8] Child Welfare League of America, *Standards for Adoption Service: Revised* (1968), p. 2.

Of the 624 children who made up our sample, 29 (4.6 percent) were placed for adoption. This will, no doubt, strike the reader as a small group. Why so few adopted children? The question merits investigation. It must be kept in mind, however, that our subject selection criteria called for the exclusion of adoption cases. It took seven months to complete the process of building our sample. Any child placed for adoption during this period was dropped from the study and replaced by another child in the same age and sex quota. Thus, our sample is biased in the direction of children who may be considered to have been either more difficult to place for adoption or for whom *early* adoption was not feasible.

Despite the above consideration we must nevertheless deal with the issue of why only some children were eventually placed for adoption. We must keep in mind the fact that 227 children (36 percent) were still in care at the end of five years, and 57 percent of these were unvisited by their parents. For the community at large, it is reasonable to raise questions about a situation where many unvisited children remain in care. This questioning is justified because of humanistic concern about the fate of these children as well as the consideration that foster care imposes a heavy financial burden on the community.[9]

Since our study focused on child assessment rather than agency perspectives, we can only address the issue of adoptive outcomes in terms of characteristics of the children.[10] We approached this task by first identifying among the 624 children those for whom adoption had been suggested, even in cases where this did not seem feasible. We defined a group six years or younger at the time of entry, which included: (a) the 55 cases where reason for placement was unwillingness of an unmarried mother to assume care of her infant, (b) 78 additional children where Time I agency study interviews specifically mentioned the possibility of adoption as an outcome,

[9] We estimated after the study had been underway for four years that the children in our sample and their siblings remaining in foster care until 18 years of age would cost the community close to $24 million. See David Fanshel and Eugene B. Shinn, *Dollars and Sense in the Foster Care of Children* (New York: Child Welfare League of America, 1972), p. 17.

[10] The reader is referred to the agency study report, Deborah Shapiro, *Agencies and Foster Children* (New York: Columbia University Press, 1976).

and (c) 25 cases identified through review of the subsequent agency study interviews where adoption was reported as a possibility (but had not been reported at Time I). We thus defined a group of potential "adoptables" totaling 187 subjects. At the end of five years after their entry into care, 29 (15.6 percent) of these children had been adopted, 79 (42.2 percent) had been discharged, and another 79 (42.2 percent) were still in care. It is worth noting that half of the children not adopted did indeed manage to return home.

We now proceed to an examination of factors associated with the three kinds of outcome: adoption, discharge, and remaining in care. We first determined that ethnicity was linked to status outcomes. Of the 29 adopted children, 17 (59 percent) were white, nine (31 percent) were black, and three were Puerto Rican. In Table 5.7 we show that 32 percent of the white adoptables were adopted, compared to nine percent of the black and a similar percentage of the Puerto Rican children. We thus note a familiar national pattern—white children available for adoption stand a stronger chance of being adopted than do minority youngsters.[11] Table 5.7 shows that

TABLE 5.7
STATUS OUTCOMES, BY ETHNICITY, AT FIVE YEARS AFTER ENTRY FOR SUBJECTS IDENTIFIED AS "ADOPTABLES"
($N = 187$)

Status Five Years After Entry	Ethnicity		
	White	Black	Puerto Rican
	(percentages)		
Adopted	31.5	9.1	8.8
Discharged	40.7	41.4	47.1
In care	27.8	49.5	44.1
No. of cases	54	99	34
	$\chi^2 = 16.660$, df = 4, $p = .003$		

[11] One observer has reported, "Blacks adopt almost in proportion to their percentage in the population, but more black children than white children ultimately fail to achieve adoption." Alfred Kadushin, "Child Welfare," in Henry S. Maas, ed., *Research in the Social Services: A Five Year Review* (New York: National Association of Social Workers, 1971), p. 31.

among the adoptables, the proportion of white children still in care at the end of five years was about half that of black and Puerto Rican subjects.

With respect to age, we found that 46 percent of the adoptables were young babies (infancy to two years of age) and 54 percent were preschoolers (aged three to five years). Almost 75 percent of the 29 children who were actually adopted were in the youngest grouping; these 21 adopted younger children represented 25 percent of the baby grouping among those who were classified as adoptables. Only 6 percent of the preschoolers were adopted. We have thus established that age is a fairly strong correlate of adoptive outcome. However, 49 percent of the older group were discharged, compared to only 35 percent of the younger subjects. The resulting disparity between the two age groupings with respect to the percentage remaining in care is thus small (40 percent of the babies and 45 percent of the preschoolers).

Girls had a somewhat more favorable outcome with respect to adoptions; 19 percent were adopted, compared to 12 percent of the boys. The difference was not statistically significant.[12]

As shown in Table 5.8, 78 percent (146) of the adoptables were born out of wedlock. The remaining children reflected situations where the unavailability or breakdown of the parents had necessitated consideration of adoption. Birth status turns out to be a fairly strong correlate of adoptive outcome; 86 percent of the 29 adopted children were born out of wedlock. Put another way, 17 percent of the out-of-wedlock children were adopted, compared to eight percent of the in-wedlock children. We note, however, that 64 percent of the in-wedlock children were discharged by the end of five years, compared to only 37 percent of the out-of-wedlock subjects. Hence, birth status is obviously an important variable in predicting outcomes among the adoptables.

When we analyzed the status outcomes for the adoptables by main reason for placement, we found that 62 percent of the 29 children adopted were in the category of infants born out of wedlock whose mothers were unwilling to assume responsibility for

[12] To save space, data relating age and sex to adoptive outcome have not been shown in the table form.

TABLE 5.8
STATUS OUTCOMES, BY BIRTH STATUS, AT FIVE YEARS AFTER ENTRY
FOR SUBJECTS IDENTIFIED "ADOPTABLES"
(N = 187)

Status Five Years After Entry	Birth Status		
	In Wedlock	Out of Wedlock	Not Ascertainable
		(percentages)	
Adopted	8.3	17.1	20.0
Discharged	63.9	37.0	40.0
In care	27.8	45.9	40.0
No. of cases	36	146	5

$$\chi^2 = 8.708, \quad df = 4, \quad p = .07$$

their care; the adopted children constituted a third of all children in this category. Five abandoned children were also placed for adoption; they represented 23 percent of the 22 abandoned children among the adoptables. Of concern is the fact that 14 children (55 percent of the abandoned children) were still in care at the end of five years. Another group arousing concern were the 22 neglect and abuse cases among the adoptables; none were adopted and 64 percent were still in care at the end of five years.

In order to determine what happened to the adoptables, we need to understand the fate of 79 children who were discharged (42 percent of the adoptables). Do they reflect a change in orientation to the placement phenomenon on the part of the parents or a change in circumstances faced by the child, parents, or agency? This matter will be dealt with in chapter 6, where we examine the circumstances surrounding the discharge of children from foster care.

HOSPITALIZATION AS A STATUS OUTCOME

One of the "outcomes" of the foster care experience that is saddening and evokes concern is the transfer of a child from the foster care agency to a state mental hospital. The necessity for such a move usually is seen as a failure, an admission that the system has been unable to cope with the child's condition. Sometimes the breakdown in arrangements comes as no surprise, since there was recognition at the time of admission that the child was emotionally disturbed and the agency was willing to take a risk in seeking to avoid hospitalization. In other situations, the child shows a marked deterioration while in care; such breakdowns are more clearly recognized as failures of the foster care system.

Sixteen of the children in our sample required transfer to state mental institutions; 14 were hospitalized because of mental illness and two because of mental retardation; two additional children were transferred to mental hospitals but were able to return to the foster care agency after a period of treatment. Two subjects were sent to state training schools for the care of delinquent children. These 18 children represent 2.9 percent of the study population. This proportion of breakdown would seem modest given the fact that the children have been exposed to loss of parental figures and tend to come from impoverished families where evidence of personal and social disorganization has been starkly present. Nevertheless, the transfer of these children must evoke considerable concern about the efficacy of services made available to them.

The small size of the group tends to prevent any meaningful statistical analysis. However, some descriptive characteristics of the cases may be helpful to the reader in obtaining a better sense of who these children are:

1. The children tend to be older; the mean age at the time of entry into care was 8.31 years (standard deviation = 3.63). One subject was an infant who proved to be severely retarded. At the time of entry, the two delinquent children were aged 11 and 13 years.

2. The transfer of the children was spread over the five years of investigation; 75 percent of the children were transferred after at least two years in care and 44 percent were transferred during the fourth and fifth years. The two delinquent children were transferred during the second year after entry.

3. Only seven of the children entered care because of their own behavior difficulty; these included the two delinquent children. Five children had entered care because of parental neglect or abuse.

4. In terms of social characteristics, nine of the children (50 percent) were black Protestant, two were black Catholic, two were

white Catholic or Protestant, four were Puerto Rican, and one was Jewish. The socioeconomic status index showed 50 percent of the children to come from higher status families, 75 percent were born in wedlock.

5. Almost 70 percent of the children were frequently visited by their parents, and 85 percent had been reared by their own parents prior to entering care.

The following case vignettes typify the problems presented by these 18 children:

Jackie is a five-year-old white Catholic child. His mother had deserted his family four years prior to his entering care with his sister. At that time he was six months old. He and his sister lived with his father, but he was often cared for by neighbors on a short-term basis—"he was pushed from one person to another." The father had himself been in placement and was very sensitive to the children's needs. He was a lonely man who tried to hold the family together. The mother had been a prostitute and an alcoholic. Jackie was hyperactive, nervous, always in trouble, and had difficulties in group situations. With his peers, he was always nervous, unsure, and had little confidence. He was placed in a children's institution where he was seen regularly by a psychiatrist. He was placed on medication as a way of reducing his hyperactivity. He deteriorated in the care of the agency, becoming very violent with other children and increasingly withdrawn. He was unable to sit for the duration of the school day. He could not concentrate. He suffered from hyperactivity, low frustration tolerance, intense rivalry, and inability to control impulses. Jackie did not respond to a sustained effort to help him through intensive psychotherapy, and the agency felt it necessary to arrange for his transfer to a state hospital some two years after his entry into care.

John is a black child who was six years old when he entered care. His mother had been attempting for some time to have him placed but had been unsuccessful. Just prior to his emergency placement she had been asked to take him home from a hospital where he had been admitted because of a broken leg. The request for his discharge had been made because he was found to be a difficult patient. The mother was reported to have become hysterical and threatened to kill John. She was hospitalized overnight and emergency placement for John was arranged. Her longstanding desire for placement of her son, her fear that she would hurt him, and her hospitalization precipitated the placement on an emergency basis. John experienced great difficulty in adjusting to congregate shelter care. He was transferred from one group to another because of a behavior problem—he often hit younger children, and required attention from five counselors. After a transfer to a long-term agency, John seemed to settle down and accept placement. However, this only lasted about three months and his behavior again deteriorated. He reacted strongly against the mother's inconsistent visiting patterns and the various manifestations of her rejection of him. It was evident that he needed a more controlled environment; his deep rage, his violent acting-out, and signs of bizarre and disassociated behavior became an increasingly permanent pattern. The agency arranged for transfer to a state hospital after an incident in which John seriously injured another child in an uncontrolled outburst.

Marie is a Puerto Rican child who entered care at ten years of age because of a long history of maladjustment. Her problems were especially pronounced in school, where she was reportedly continuously aggressive with classmates, needed constant watching, was wild and unruly at recess, and would work only spasmodically. Her school behavior became continuously worse and she was placed on home instruction at age nine. Efforts to help her through psychotherapy were unsuccessful, and placement in a children's institution was arranged on the recommendation of a psychiatrist. The placement experience over an 18-month period showed "ups and downs" in Marie's behavior. She was transferred to a state hospital because of suicide attempts and attacks on other children and counselors. The child could not control her violence.

NUMBER OF PLACEMENTS

The extent to which children experience turnover while in care (transfer from one setting to another) is an important index of the stability of the care provided them. Most child welfare experts would agree that children who have already suffered separation from their own parents should be spared unnecessary transfer while living under substitute living arrangements, as such children have a strong need for continuity of environment and continuity of relationships with significant others, particularly parents.[13]

In our five-year study we carefully traced all of the moves of

[13] For an excellent discussion of the child's need for continuity of relationship, see Joseph Goldstein, Anna Freud, and Albert J. Solnit, *Beyond the Best Interests of the Child* (New York: Free Press, 1973).

our 624 study subjects while in foster care. For each agency, computerized lists of children in foster care were sent for scrutiny approximately every three months. The agencies were asked to report discharges, intra-agency transfers (e.g., from one foster home to another), and interagency transfers. In addition, the return to care of subjects previously discharged was monitored at the central administrative entry point, the Bureau of Child Welfare, New York City Department of Social Services.

In Table 5.9 we present frequency distributions for the number of moves experienced by our subjects with respect to: (a) interagency transfers, (b) intra-agency transfers, (c) reentries into foster care of discharged children, and (d) the total number of placements experienced by the children. Category (d) reflects the simple addition of the three prior categories. Sixty percent of the children remained exclusively within the care of the agency of their entry; they experienced no transfer to another agency. Almost 31 percent experienced one agency transfer; this almost always involved the transfer of children from temporary care to a long-term care placement. It appears that transfer between agencies after the child leaves temporary care is a relatively infrequent event but

TABLE 5.9

INTER- AND INTRA-AGENCY TRANSFERS, REENTRIES INTO CARE OF DISCHARGED CHILDREN, AND TOTAL NUMBER OF PLACEMENTS OVER FIVE-YEAR PERIOD

Number of Placement Transfers	Interagency Transfers		Intra-agency Transfers		Reentries of Discharged Children		Total Placements[a]	
	No.	%	No.	%	No.	%	No.	%
0	377	60.4	467	74.7	562	90.1		
1	191	30.6	101	16.2	49	7.9	261	41.8
2	50	8.0	44	7.1	11	1.8	186	29.8
3	5	0.8	11	1.8	2	0.3	115	18.4
4+	1	0.2	1	0.2	—	—	62	10.0
Total	624	100.0	624	100.0	624	100.0	624	100.0

[a] Reflects the sum of inter- and intra-agency transfers and reentries into care after discharge.

nevertheless a source of concern for the children involved; 50 children (8 percent) experienced two interagency transfers, five children were reported to have experienced three transfers, one child was transferred four times.

Intra-agency transfers were reported to have been experienced by one-quarter of the subjects. Sometimes agencies provided both temporary and long-term care arrangements, and intra-agency transfers were carried out because of this.

Of the 229 subjects still in care at the end of five years, 16 had experienced one discharge and reentry and five had gone through this experience on two occasions. Of the 367 who had left care, with 29 adopted children excluded, 33 had experienced two discharges and one reentry, six had experienced three discharges and two reentries, and two had experienced four discharges and three reentries.

As indicated earlier, the total number of placements presented in Table 5.9 reflects the sum of the moves experienced by a child through inter- and intra-agency transfers and reentries. Three or more placements would reflect what many experts consider excessive moves, going beyond the transfer from temporary to long-term care. Almost 42 percent of the children experienced only one placement, and another 30 percent, two placements. Thus, 72 percent experienced "normal" moves or none, while 18 percent experienced three placements, and 10 percent, four or more transfers.[14]

The number of placements reported for the children is our best summary measure of the amount of movement experienced by our subjects. As the reader may have anticipated, the length of time a child spends in care is probably the best predictor of the number of placements. That is, the longer a child is in care, the more exposed he is to the possibility of being transferred. This is well reflected in Table 5.10, where we present the number of placements experienced by the children according to the year of last discharge from care. The relationship between the two variables is quite linear. Only 2 percent of the children discharged during the first year

---

[14] Thirteen children experienced five placements, two experienced six placements, and one child experienced seven placements.

TABLE 5.10

NUMBER OF PLACEMENTS BY YEAR OF LAST DISCHARGE
FROM FOSTER CARE[a] ($N = 577$)

	Year of Last Discharge					
Number of Placements	Dis- charged First Year	Dis- charged Second Year	Dis- charged Third Year	Dis- charged Fourth Year	Dis- charged Fifth Year	Still in Care Five Years After Entry
	(percentages)					
1	79.5	56.7	38.6	45.1	25.0	15.9
2	18.4	24.3	36.4	19.6	32.5	38.3
3	2.1	17.6	22.7	15.7	22.5	28.6
4+	—	1.4	2.3	19.6	20.0	17.2
No. of cases	141	74	44	51	40	227
Mean no. of placements	1.23	1.64	1.89	2.10	2.38	2.47
Standard deviation	0.47	0.82	0.84	1.19	1.08	0.96

$\chi^2 = 182.059$,   df $= 15$, $p < .001$;

F-test (differences of column means) $= 39.818$, $p < .001$.

[a] Twenty-nine adopted children and 18 children transferred to state institutions not included in this analysis.

had three or more placements. By contrast, 19 percent of the children discharged in the second year, 25 percent in the third year, 35 percent in the fourth year, and 43 percent in the fifth year experienced three or more placements; 46 percent of children still in care had likewise experienced three or more placements. About a fifth of the children discharged during the fourth year and after experienced four or more placements.

In Table 5.11 we examine the number of placements experienced by the subjects according to ethnicity–religion. Jewish children experienced the lowest number of placements—80 percent had only one placement experience. Most of these went directly into residential treatment on a long-term basis. Only 16 percent of the Jewish children had three or more placements, compared to 22

TABLE 5.11
NUMBER OF PLACEMENTS, BY ETHNICITY–RELIGION
(N = 624)

Number of Placements	White Catholic or Protestant	Jewish	Black Catholic	Black Protestant	Puerto Rican
			Ethnicity–Religion		
			(percentages)		
1	48.5	80.6	36.7	39.8	35.1
2	29.5	3.2	29.4	27.7	36.2
3	11.4	6.5	20.6	23.6	19.3
4+	10.3	9.7	13.3	8.9	9.4
No. of cases	132	31	68	191	202

$\chi^2 = 45.662$, df = 24, p = .006 (χ^2 calculated for up to 7 placements)

percent of the white Catholic or Protestant children. About 33 percent of the black children had three or more placements, and this was true of 29 percent of the Puerto Rican youngsters. Thus minority children have been exposed to somewhat more turnover in care. This finding has to be understood in the context of minority children tending to remain in care longer than white children.

When we analyzed the number of placements experienced by the children according to the main reason for placement, we found that factors of child behavior and the parent being unwilling to assume or continue care were linked to fewer placements. On the other hand, children who entered care because of family problems, neglect or abuse, or abandonment showed a relatively high number of placements.[15]

To help assess the relative importance of a number of background variables in "understanding" variation in the number of placements experienced by the subjects, a multiple regression analysis was carried out using as regressors the variables shown in Table 5.12. The reader might first wish to examine the zero-order correlations shown. We observe that the most important correlate of

[15]These findings have not been displayed in table form here.

TABLE 5.12
ANALYSIS OF NUMBER OF PLACEMENTS
(N = 577)

Independent Variables	Zero-Order Correlation	Standardized Regression Coefficient[a]	Percentage Unique Variance Explained
Child's age at placement	.03	−.08	0.20
Sex of Child	.05	.01	0.00
Age-sex interaction	.07	.07	0.10
Number of children in family	.04	.01	0.00
Ethnicity—black vs. others	.04	.03	0.10
Ethnicity—Puerto Rican vs. others	.04	.01	0.00
Reason for Placement:			
Child behavior vs. others	−.10*	−.15**	1.40
Unwilling assume care vs. others	−.10*	.05	0.20
First setting (institution/ foster home)	−.17***	−.16***	2.00
Index of emotional problems at entry	−.01	.01	0.00
Index of developmental problems at entry	−.03	−.01	0.00
Child Behavior Characteristics Score:			
Unmotivated-laziness	−.01	−.07	0.20
Defiance-hostility-unsocialized	.07	.13*	0.50
Emotionality-tension	.04	−.02	0.00
Log days in care over 5 years	.44***	.44***	16.30
Parental visiting pattern— Time I	−.13**	−.02	0.00
Log total casework contact rate—Time I	−.06	.05	0.20
Evaluation of the mother— Time I	−.16***	−.03	0.10
Multiple R		.51	
Multiple R²		.26[b]	

*p < .05   **p < .01   ***p < .001

[a] Italic coefficients are greater than twice their standard error.

[b] R² corrected for degrees of freedom = .24.

number of placements is the logarithm of the length of time in care (in days) experienced by the children ($r = .44$). This merely confirms what we have displayed in the cross-tabulation previously shown. The correlation of the dependent variable with the type of setting in which the child was placed ($r = .17$) shows that children in congregate-shelter care experienced more placements; this is likely accounted for by the need for interagency transfers. Evidently, children placed in foster family homes have been exposed to fewer placements.

Children whose parents visited less frequently suffered less replacement ($r = -.13$), as was true of children whose mothers were evaluated negatively ($r = -.16$). The implications of these small (but statistically significant) correlations are not absolutely clear; they seem to suggest that less active involvement of able parents is associated with higher stability of placement. Put another way, the more the parents are out of the picture, the fewer the replacements experienced by the children. As previously indicated, children who entered care because of their own behavior difficulties or because a parent was unwilling to assume care tended to experience fewer placements.

The results of the regression analysis confirm that the logarithm of length of time experienced in care by a child over the five years of the study is a strong predictor. The standardized regression coefficient is sizable and the variable accounts for 16 percent of unique variance. Other variables that play a significant role are the child's first placement setting (institution/foster home) and child behavior as a reason for placement. These coefficients, however, are not much greater than the standard errors of the variables. Of interest is the fact that children whose behavior was characterized as defiant and hostile (CBC score) tended to experience more replacement than other children.

The amount of adjusted variance accounted for in the analysis performed here is relatively modest (24 percent), and is heavily influenced by time in care as the influential regressor variable.

The analysis of number of placements experienced by foster children as developed here represents, as far as we know, the first analytic treatment of this phenomenon to appear in the professional literature. We hope that other investigators will be attracted to a study of the issue and will build upon the findings we have produced here.

We thus conclude our analysis of changes in the status of the children over the five years of longitudinal investigation. We should make one final observation, namely, that three children in our sample died during the five-year period after entry. Two died after discharge and one while in care. The latter case involved a child with severe congenital handicaps. One of the discharged children died of injuries sustained falling down a flight of stairs; there was some indication of failure to secure prompt medical attention for him. The second discharged child died as a result of falling into a hot bath; some suspicion of neglect surrounded the death. A fourth discharged child died after the five-year period; the circumstances of death were not available to the research staff.

In chapter 6 we examine the circumstances surrounding the departure of the children from care and the factors that enable some children to leave care. We also provide the perspectives of the agencies about the desirability of the discharges and future outlook for the children.

SIX

CIRCUMSTANCES
AT TIME
OF DISCHARGE

While there is widespread acceptance of the notion that the discharge of children from foster care is a highly desired goal, many questions accompany the termination of placement. Was the child's departure a well-prepared event or did it take place precipitously, with the likelihood that the child would eventually return to care? We might further ask what events prompted the discharge—did it stem from the action of the parent, the child, or the agency? Did the agency support the discharge as being in the best interest of the child?

A child may return home only to live in serious jeopardy because of his parent's tendency to engage in physical violence against him. It is not possible to regard such a discharge as a positive outcome. Indeed, return to such a home might well reflect the most serious violation of the child's welfare and rights. In this chapter we examine questions such as these as we focus on the circumstances surrounding the child's discharge from foster care.

In order to gather discharge information of this type, a research schedule was created that could be utilized in several ways:

1. It could be filled out by the caseworker who best knew the child and the family at the time of discharge.

2. It could be used as a case-reading schedule to be filled out by a research staff person in instances where the worker was no longer available; this would involve visits to agencies for the purpose of reading and abstracting records.

3. The schedules could be filled out by agency study interviewers on the basis of the telephone research interviews, which were com-

pleted on the four regular data-gathering occasions conducted by the study or when it was learned that a child had been discharged through routine computerized inquiries of the agencies.[1]

Before presenting some of the findings from this special inquiry into the discharge phenomenon, we should comment on the quality of the data that we present here. In many ways, we regard the information as "soft" and impressionistic, representing the views of informants who best knew the family and child. The information most often came from the caseworker assigned to the case by the under-care agency; sometimes it came from the caseworker assigned by the Bureau of Child Welfare as part of the public agency's ultimate responsibility for case planning and disposition. We are somewhat guarded about the information because of the variability in training and experience of the social workers interviewed. Furthermore, some had longstanding knowledge of the cases while others had been recently assigned responsibility. Such variability in backgrounds could serve to bias the information we received. We also recognize that agency perspectives can well differ from those of their clients with respect to many of the issues that we raised.[2]

The caveat introduced here has not deterred us from presenting the data because, with their limitations recognized, the caseworkers nevertheless represented the best sources available; in any future research of this kind they would again have to be used as informants. Also, as far as we have been able to determine, the information has not been previously reported in the professional literature. We thus present a first engagement with the phenomenon, which can provide some groundwork for future investigators.

We now proceed to examine the data we have collected on the

[1] The Report on Discharge Planning and After-Care (CWRP Form D-1) was not developed until the study was well into its first year. The alternative procedures for filling out the schedule reflected the exigencies of the data-gathering circumstances. For instance, we were confronted with the fact that some caseworkers, in situations were the child had been discharged for an extended time, had resigned their jobs and cases were not taken care of. Fifty-one percent of the schedules were filled out by agency study telephone interviewers, 36 percent were filled out by research staff on the basis of reading agency records, and 13 percent were filled out directly by agency caseworkers.

[2] See the report of interviews with parents of the children for contrasting perspectives. Shirley Jenkins and Elaine Norman, *Beyond Placement: Mothers View Foster Care* (New York: Columbia University Press, 1975).

basis of the procedures just outlined. We will be looking at 381 children who experienced at least one discharge from foster care. Sixty of these experienced multiple discharges and reentries. For the purpose of our analysis, we have restricted our examination to the *first* discharge only. We have excluded adopted children, those transferred to state hospitals and institutions, and those still in care at the end of five years who had never experienced discharge.[3]

CIRCUMSTANCES AT DISCHARGE

An analysis of the conditions that prevailed at the time of discharge reveals that 12 percent of the departures of the children were sudden and unplanned, and an additional 12 percent were somewhat sudden but not totally unplanned. About 75 percent of the children returned home on a planned basis; their departures were expected and not subject to surprise actions.

The nature of unplanned departures is reflected in the following anecdotal reports:

Mary T., a seven-year-old black child who had been in a foster home for eleven months, visited her father's home on the weekend. On Monday, the agency was called by the father and informed that he and his new wife were prepared to take care of Mary; the child wanted very much to stay with them. The decision to change living arrangements was presented as a *fait accompli*, and while there had been no prior inkling of the father's plans, the agency supported the move because of Mary's apparent unhappiness about being in foster care. Mary's mother had disappeared some time ago and had not been heard from. While follow-up service was offered the father, he made it clear that he could carry on without assistance.

Francisco R., a 12-year-old Puerto Rican child, had entered foster care because his mother was hospitalized with a serious health problem. He was unhappy in the institution in which he was placed and ran away several times. Placement was terminated abruptly when the mother returned home from the hospital and, against medical

---

[3] Eleven cases are included among the 381 discharges analyzed here where forms were returned although the discharge had taken place after the fifth anniversary of their entrance into care. Their inclusion had not been recognized until much of the analysis had been completed.

advice, resumed her household responsibilities. Francisco refused to return to the institution after a weekend visit.

Sarah P., a six-month-old white Catholic infant, was in care because her young unmarried mother had indicated she wanted to release her for adoption. Before legal surrender was carried through, the mother appeared at the agency stating that she had a job, had set up an apartment, and desired her baby. She was willing to wait several weeks so that the baby could receive treatment for a lung infection.

An important aspect of the discharge phenomenon is the nature of the living arrangements to which the child is being returned. Does he return to a home in which a mother and father are living together, to a mother living alone, or to a relative? Table 6.1 provides such information for the total group of 381 first discharges; there is also provided the familiar five-way breakdown by ethnicity–religion.

Most of the children returned to mothers who lived alone (58 percent of the discharges). Twenty-two percent returned to a home in which the mothers and fathers were living together. These percentages closely reflect the parameters that existed at the time the children entered care.[4] Fathers separated from the mothers took their children home in only 4 percent of the cases. Maternal and paternal grandparents provided homes for 7.5 percent of the children, while other relatives, such as aunts or uncles became the resource for an additional 7 percent of the subjects. Nonrelatives provided homes for only about 1 percent of the sample.

Table 6.1 shows fairly distinct ethnic differences with respect to the kind of homes available to children upon discharge from foster care. The Jewish children were obviously the most advantaged, 62 percent returned to a home where the parents were living together; this was true of 30 percent of the white Catholic or Protestant dischargees and 20 percent of the Puerto Rican youngsters. Black children were least likely to return to an intact family situation where their parents were living together. Relatives were an important resource for the black Protestant children; 14 percent of these subjects returned to their grandparents and another 9 percent returned to the homes of other relatives.

---

[4] Eighteen percent of the families at the time children entered placement represented intact family units with parents living together. See Shirley Jenkins and Elaine Norman, *Filial Deprivation and Foster Care* (New York: Columbia University Press, 1972), p. 39.

TABLE 6.1

**IDENTIFICATION OF HOME RECEIVING CHILD AT DISCHARGE,
BY ETHNICITY–RELIGION**

	Ethnicity–Religion					
Home Receiving Child	White Catholic or Protestant	Jewish	Black Catholic	Black Protestant	Puerto Rican	Total Number and Percent
	(percentages)					
Mother and father living together[a]	30.3	61.6	5.4	13.9	19.5	22.0% (84)
Mother	47.2	26.9	78.4	60.3	63.5	57.8% (220)
Father	5.6	3.8	8.1	2.0	3.1	3.9% (15)
Maternal grandparent	1.1	7.7	—	5.0	3.1	3.1% (12)
Paternal grandparent	—	—	2.7	8.9	2.3	3.4% (13)
Other relative	12.4	—	2.7	8.9	3.9	6.9% (26)
Nonrelative	—	—	2.7	1.0	2.3	1.3% (5)
Other[b]	3.4	—	—	—	2.3	1.6% (6)
No. of cases	89	26	37	101	128	381

[a] Includes mother and stepfather living together.
[b] Arrangements not clarified at time of data collection, or child ran away.

The events leading to the child's discharge were extremely varied. The task of codifying them provided considerable challenge, and despite our strong efforts we wound up with a miscellaneous category that contained 16 percent of the cases. The results of our codification are contained in the frequency distribution shown in Table 6.2 .[5] The elaborated code did not allow for easy breakdown

TABLE 6.2
EVENT LEADING TO CHILD'S DISCHARGE FROM FOSTER CARE

Event	Number	Percentage
Mother recovered from mental illness	60	17.4
Parent had desired time-limited placement in order to work out personal plans (e.g., job training, treatment)	47	12.2
Relatives offered acceptable plan for care of child	36	9.3
Mother recovered from physical illness	34	8.8
Parent changed mind about placement; not happy with placement	22	5.7
Child admitted for treatment—gains enabled him to return home	17	4.4
Court approved return in neglect or abuse case	17	4.4
Agency felt placement was not serving child's needs	15	3.8
Mother obtained public assistance—set up stable home	15	3.8
Mother failed return child from home visit	13	3.3
Child achieved sufficient maturity to function within context of family home	10	2.5
Child refused to return after home visit	8	2.0
Child precipitated discharge by running away	7	1.7
Relative changed mind about placement	6	1.5
Mother released from prison	5	1.2
Agency terminated; parent being habituated to placement	4	1.0
Mother of out-of-wedlock child changed mind about adoption	4	1.0
Miscellaneous categories	61	16.0
Total	381	100.0

[5] The code may be construed as signifying the main reason for discharge.

by ethnicity, and we simply present the findings for the 381 dischargees as a whole. The largest group of children, 60 subjects (17 percent), returned home because their mothers had sufficiently recovered from mental illnesses to resume their responsibilities. Most had been hospitalized and had been recently released. Another nine percent of the cases involved the mother's return to her responsibilities after a physical illness.

The next largest group, 47 subjects (12 percent), returned home because a parent had succeeded in using the respite from parental responsibility to work out personal plans. The placement of the child had originally been seen as a time-limited phenomenon affording the parent the opportunity to carry out such goals as completing vocational training, obtaining treatment, or resolving acute personal problems.

Relatives who offered an acceptable plan for the child's care provided the basis for the return home for nine percent of the children. Other leading events in the return of children include: (a) parents changing their minds about placement, (b) children improving so that disordered behavior became less of a problem, (c) the court returning children claimed to be neglected or abused, (d) agencies feeling that placement served no further useful purpose, and (e) mothers being accepted to receive public assistance.

CHANGES IN CHILDREN AND FAMILIES RELATED TO DISCHARGE

The research schedule also called for the informant to provide a summary judgment by designating one of the following as the main reason for discharge:

1. Change in family's capacity to care for child (e.g., health, housing, or return of child caring person).
2. Change in child (e.g., movement in child's capacity to adjust).
3. Change in agency's capacity to serve child (e.g., lack of appropriate facility or unusual circumstances affecting services).
4. Change in family's and/or child's capacity to accept placement.
5. Change in agency's views about the need and appropriateness of placement.

Table 6.3 contains information about these types of change for

TABLE 6.3

MAIN REASONS FOR DISCHARGE (SOURCES OF CHANGE), BY ETHNICITY-RELIGION

	Ethnicity–Religion					
Sources of Change	White Catholic or Protestant	Jewish	Black Catholic	Black Protestant	Puerto Rican	Total
			(percentages)			
Family's capacity to care for child	71.9	26.9	67.6	67.4	62.5	64.1% (244)
Child adjustment	7.9	34.7	—	5.9	9.4	8.9% (34)
Family's and/or child's capacity to accept placement	7.9	19.2	16.2	9.9	12.5	11.6% (44)
Agency's capacity to serve child	1.1	15.4	—	7.9	2.3	4.2% (16)
Agency's views about the need for placement	4.5	3.8	2.7	7.9	7.0	6.0% (23)
Other source of change	6.7	—	13.5	1.0	6.3	5.2% (20)
No. of cases	89	26	37	101	128	381

the 381 discharged children as a group and displays the ethnicity–religion breaks. Changes in the family's capacity to care for
the child were by far the leading reason for the departure of children
from care; 64 percent of the discharged children went home for this
reason. Changes in the family's and/or the child's capacity to accept
placement was the source of change in another 12 percent of the
cases. We observe that the Jewish children were more apt to return
home because of change in their own behavior; about 35 percent of
their discharges involved child change, and another 19 percent
involved change in the capacity of family or child to accept
placement. Changes in agency capacity to serve the child was also
important for Jewish children. For all other children, family change
was overwhelmingly the most important reason for their return home.

In only 4 percent of the cases was discharge carried out
because of a change in the agency's capacity to serve the child. In
another 6 percent, the changed agency view of the desirability of
placement resulted in the child's return home, 8 percent of the black
Protestant and 7 percent of the Puerto Rican children went home
for this reason, compared to about 4 percent of the remaining
children.

The informants were requested to provide information about
changes in the social circumstances faced by the child's family at
the time of discharge from care, as contrasted with conditions when
he entered. The areas specified included housing, family finances,
parental health, or the presence of a parent. In Table 6.4 we present
information in each of these areas for the 381 children as a group
and for ethnic subgroupings. We provide information on the
percentage of situations where the changes were characterized as
positive or presented in neutral terms.[6] For the discharged children
as a group, a fairly substantial amount of change in housing circumstances was reported between the time of the child's entry and his
discharge. Eighteen percent were said to have moved to better
housing; another 25 percent moved to other quarters with no estimate available as to whether or not this represented an improvement in living conditions. There was no noteworthy differentiation

---

[6] For each category, 2–3 percent of the subjects' families were reported to have experienced negative changes. These data are not included in the table.

TABLE 6.4

CHANGES IN SELECTED AREAS OF FAMILY LIFE PRECEDING CHILD'S DISCHARGE, BY ETHNICITY–RELIGION

	Ethnicity–Religion					
Selected areas	*White Catholic or Protestant*	*Jewish*	*Black Catholic*	*Black Protestant*	*Puerto Rican*	*Total*
			(percentages)			
Change in family housing						
Moved to better housing	12.4	19.2	16.2	20.8	18.0	17.3
Moved—condition undetermined	31.5	19.2	27.0	24.8	20.3	24.7
Change in family finances						
Accepted for public assistance	6.7	3.8	27.0	12.9	14.8	12.9
Becoming self-maintaining or improving income	19.1	26.9	18.9	13.9	9.4	15.0
Change in parent health						
Improved in health status	39.3	34.6	27.0	20.8	35.2	31.5
Change in presence of a parent						
Return of a parent to the home	21.3	11.5	32.4	14.9	11.7	16.8
No. of cases	89	26	37	101	128	381

among the five ethnic groups with respect to changes experienced in housing.

Considering changes in family finances, the table shows that 13 percent of the families who had applied for public assistance had been accepted. The black Catholic group was outstanding in this regard; 27 percent of the families became new recipients of assistance.[7] In contrast, this was true of only 4 percent of the families of the Jewish children. The white Catholic or Protestant, black Protestant and Puerto Rican families fell in between these extremes.

Fifteen percent of all of the subjects' families were reported to have become self-maintaining or have improved their income since the child's admission; this excluded those who had become new recipients of public assistance. The Jewish, white Catholic or Protestant, and black Catholic groups had the highest proportions where this was reported, (19–27 percent). In contrast, only 9 percent of the Puerto Ricans were reported to have achieved improved income.

Almost a third of the cases were reported to have involved improved health status of a parent. The highest group was the white Catholic or Protestant, where this was reported for 39 percent of the cases. The families of the black Catholic children constituted the lowest group; 27 percent were said to show such improvement.

About 17 percent of the cases involved the return of a parent to the home. The black Catholic cases showed the highest proportion in this category (32 percent) and the Jewish and Puerto Rican cases the lowest (12 percent).

When we examined reason for placement and family change, we found that for 66 percent of the children who entered care because of mental illness or physical illness of the parent, a change in parental health was reported.

---

[7] By "new" recipients, we mean receipt of public assistance on a newly opened case basis; this does not mean that the family had not ever received public assistance previously.

AGENCY PERSPECTIVES ON DISCHARGE

We sought to determine how the agency had viewed the child's departure by asking the question, "With respect to *your agency's* opinion about the child's discharge, please check the response that is most appropriate: *strongly approved, moderately approved, mixed or neutral reaction, moderately opposed,* or *strongly opposed.*"

In Table 6.5 we present the frequency distributions of responses for the total group of discharges with accompanying breakdowns by ethnicity. We observe that agencies strongly approved of the child's discharge in 47 percent of the cases. Moderate approval was indicated in another 20 percent of the cases. Thus, for 67 percent of the discharges, there was a general tendency to support the move as being in the child's interest. In an additional 17 percent of the cases, the response of the agency to the discharge was either mixed or neutral. The proportion of cases where agencies had misgivings about the discharge was relatively small. In 14 percent of the cases there was moderate or strong agency opposition.

Although space limitations do not permit us to elaborate further, in 66 percent of cases which involved agency doubt about the discharge of children, this doubt was based upon a negative assessment of the parent's (or relative's) capacity to provide adequate care. In the remaining cases the negative orientation was based on the timing of the discharge with respect to the readiness of child or family to resume the former living arrangement.

There is no strong ethnic differentiation apparent in Table 6.5 except that the discharge of the Jewish children was less likely to occasion support. Some opposition was expressed in 23 percent of the cases. The lowest opposition was reflected among the black Protestant cases; in only 9 percent was any doubt or opposition indicated.

One of the questions that evoked our interest was whether the discharged children were vulnerable to being returned to foster care. We sought estimates about this in our inquiry about the discharge cases and present our findings in Table 6.6. We asked the informant, "What is your estimate of the likelihood of the child's return to care? Would you say: *no possibility, slight possibility, 50–50 percent possibility,* or *substantial possibility?*" In only 16 percent of the

TABLE 6.5
AGENCY ATTITUDE REGARDING SUITABILITY OF DISCHARGE OF CHILD, BY ETHNICITY–RELIGION

Agency Attitude	Ethnicity–Religion					
	White Catholic or Protestant	Jewish	Black Catholic	Black Protestant	Puerto Rican	Total
	(percentages)					
Strongly approved	51.8	38.4	37.9	40.5	53.2	47.0% (179)
Moderately approved	19.1	15.4	35.1	29.7	10.9	20.4% (78)
Mixed or neutral reaction	14.6	23.1	10.8	17.8	17.2	16.5% (63)
Moderately opposed	4.5	15.4	10.8	4.0	7.0	6.6% (25)
Strongly opposed	6.7	7.7	5.4	5.0	9.4	7.1% (27)
Other or unknown	3.3	—	—	3.0	2.3	2.4% (9)
No. of cases	89	26	37	101	128	381

TABLE 6.6
ESTIMATE OF LIKELIHOOD OF RETURN TO FOSTER CARE OF DISCHARGED SUBJECTS, BY ETHNICITY-RELIGION

Likelihood of Return	White Catholic or Protestant	Jewish	Black Catholic	Black Protestant	Puerto Rican	Total
			Ethnicity–Religion			
			(percentages)			
No possibility	20.2	19.2	24.3	8.9	14.7	15.7% (60)
Slight possibility	51.7	30.9	37.9	46.6	41.1	44.0% (168)
Moderate (50–50 percent) possibility	9.0	19.2	32.4	12.9	14.7	14.9% (57)
Substantial possibility	4.5	11.5	2.7	5.9	17.1	9.4% (36)
Unable to estimate	14.6	19.2	2.7	25.7	12.4	16.0% (61)
No. of cases	89	26	37	101	129	382

cases was there a firm indication that there was no possibility that the child would return to care. For another 44 percent of the cases, the child's return was seen as only a slight possibility. Thus, for 60 percent the caseworker's outlook for the stability of the home arrangement could be construed as optimistic. In 15 percent it was estimated that there was a 50 percent chance that the child would be returned to care; in another 9 percent of the cases there was indication of a substantial possibility of the child's return. Thus we find that in 25 percent discharged cases, there is concern expressed about the stability of the arrangements available to the child after placement.

We have previously pointed out that by the end of the five years of longitudinal follow-up, 62 of the 381 discharged subjects (some 16 percent) had experienced at least one return to foster care. When we cross-tabulated the estimate of the caseworkers of the likelihood of return of the children with what actually transpired by the end of the five-year period, we came up with the following statistically significant findings:

1. Of 60 children rated as having "no possibility" of return, three (5 percent) reentered care at least once.
2. Of 168 children rated as having "slight possibility" of return, 25 (14.9 percent) reentered care at least once.
3. Of 57 children rated as having a "50–50 chance" of returning, 13 (22.3 percent) reentered care at least once.
4. Of 36 children rated as having "a substantial possibility" of return, 11 (30.5 percent) reentered care at least once.

We thus see that the perceptions of the caseworkers have already shown some substantial basis by the end of the five years of study.[8]

Table 6.7 fails to show differentiation among the five ethnic groups with respect to the estimate of the child's likely return. The situations of the black Protestant children and the white Catholic or Protestant children were seen in a somewhat more sanguine fashion than those faced by the Jewish and Puerto Rican children.

The research schedule used to study discharges contained the following open-ended question, "In your opinion, what are the problems present in this family that will affect the capacity to offer

[8] Chi square = 41.021, df = 18, p = .002.

TABLE 6.7

CASEWORKER'S REPORTS OF SELECTED FAMILY-BACKGROUND PROBLEMS THAT MIGHT ADVERSELY INFLUENCE CARE AVAILABLE TO CHILD AT DISCHARGE, BY ETHNICITY–RELIGION

| | | | | Ethnicity–Religion | | | |
Family Problem Areas Cited[a]	White Catholic or Protestant	Jewish	Black Catholic	Black Protestant	Puerto Rican	Total
			(percentage manifesting problem)			
Background of mental illness	25.8	26.9	21.6	18.8	25.0	23.4
Personality problem of parent(s)	40.4	73.1	37.8	44.6	35.2	41.7
Marginal finances	7.9	—	13.5	22.8	6.3	11.3
Poor child-rearing capacity of parents	13.5	26.9	18.9	16.8	23.3	19.1
Child's personality problem	20.2	53.8	8.1	19.8	29.5	24.3
No. of cases	89	26	37	101	128	381

[a] Information codified from open-ended inquiry directed to caseworker, "In your opinion, what are the problems present in this family that will affect their capacity to offer adequate care to the child?"

adequate care to the child?" The responses were examined as the forms were returned and a coding scheme was developed to reflect the topics most often mentioned. These included: (a) background of mental illness in the family, (b) personality problems of the parent(s), (c) marginal finances of the family, and (d) poor child-rearing capacity of the parents. In Table 6.7 we show the percentages of discharges where such problems were identified.[9]

In almost 25 percent of cases concern was expressed about the background of mental illness in the family. This was manifested with fairly equal frequency across the five ethnic groups. The most frequent commentary about the families referred to personality problems of the parents. For 42 percent of the families, the child care arrangements were judged to be vulnerable on this account. The Jewish group stands out because in 73 percent of the cases, concern was expressed about this matter. This is understandable since many of the Jewish children entered care because of a behavioral difficulty that might well have reflected pathology in their overall family situations. The remaining ethnic groups were not strongly differentiated in this regard.

Marginal family finances were raised as a possible threat to the child's ability to stay in the community in 11 percent of the cases. This may be seen as a relatively low percentage, given the fact that most of the families in the study were of poor or modest circumstances. The families of black Protestant children were most often cited as having this problem; 23 percent were so described. Financial problems as a threat to the stability of the living arrangement was not mentioned for any of the Jewish subjects.

The perceived poor child-rearing capacity of the child's parent(s) was cited in almost 20 percent of the cases. There was no evidence of strong differentiation among the ethnic groups in this area, although the Jewish subjects were most often described as being affected by this problem.

The child's personal adjustment difficulty was mentioned in 24

[9] From a methodological standpoint, the reader should bear in mind that use of an open-ended question to obtain this information has likely had the consequence of lowering the percentage of problems identified. In other words, asking the respondent about each coded area would have likely produced a larger number of positive identifications of problems. We thus provide a conservative estimate of the problems present in the families.

percent of the cases. Among Jewish subjects 54 percent of the cases were cited in this manner, as were 30 percent of the Puerto Rican children. There was much less of a tendency to identify the other ethnic groups as having this kind of problem.

One final interesting category of data related to discharge concerns the overall personal and social adjustment of the subjects at the time of discharge. Table 6.8 shows the frequency distributions for the rating scale used to secure an estimate for each child. Twenty percent of the children were rated as showing an excellent overall adjustment and another 38 percent as showing a good adjustment, accounting for almost 60 percent of discharged children. Thirteen percent of the subjects were said to show somewhat poor or poor adjustments. Jewish subjects were more often characterized as showing poor adjustment than the remaining ethnic groups.

This assessment of the child by the caseworkers was significantly correlated with independent assessments of the children made by our research psychologists at Times I and II, but not at Time III.[10]

DISCHARGE OF THE "ADOPTABLES"

We now turn briefly to the cases of the 79 children described in chapter 5 who were included in the "adoptable" group but who were discharged from care.[11] We wish to examine the conditions under which this group left care. We have previously established that they tended to be older than the children who remained in care or who were adopted, more likely to have been born in wedlock, and more likely to include black children. The following information summarizes their characteristics:

1. The discharged adoptables were returned to family situations in a pattern that closely resembled what was found for all discharged children, 19 percent returned to homes where a mother and father lived together, 65 percent returned to a mother living alone, and only one percent returned to a father living alone. About four percent went

[10] At Time I, the correlation was .135 ($p = .05$); at Time II, it was .231 ($p = .001$).

[11] The breakdown for the 79 discharged adoptables by ethnicity is 28 percent white, 51 percent black, and 21 percent Puerto Rican.

TABLE 6.8
ESTIMATE OF THE CHILD'S OVERALL PERSONAL AND SOCIAL ADJUSTMENT AT TIME OF DISCHARGE

Overall Adjustment	White Catholic or Protestant	Jewish	Black Catholic	Black Protestant	Puerto Rican	Total
			Ethnicity–Religion			
Excellent, almost no signs of maladjustment	22.5	7.7	27.0	17.8	21.1	20.2
Good, very few signs of maladjustment	37.1	34.6	46.0	32.7	41.4	38.1
Fair, some signs of maladjustment	23.6	26.9	24.3	26.7	21.1	23.9
Somewhat poor, quite a few signs of maladjustment	6.7	15.4	—	5.0	7.0	6.3
Poor, many signs of maladjustment	4.5	7.7	2.7	7.9	8.6	6.8
Other (or unknown)	5.6	7.7	—	9.9	0.8	4.7
No. of cases	89	26	37	101	128	381

to live with grandparents and nine percent were discharged to other relatives.

2. Five black children (12.5 percent of black children) were returned home because of an agency's unwillingness or lack of capability in keeping them. Almost all other discharges were related to change in the parent's attitudes or circumstances.

3. Agency opinions regarding discharge closely resembled what was found for all discharges. Strong approval was expressed for 50 percent of the discharges, and in 22 percent of the cases, moderate approval was expressed. In only 9 percent was opposition to the discharge manifested.

4. There was a somewhat higher percentage of planned discharges among the adoptables than for the discharged cases taken as a whole. Only 4 percent were sudden and unplanned, compared to 12 percent in the larger group of discharges.

5. About 45 percent of the families had changed housing since the child's entry into care (compared to 42 percent of the larger group). Thirty-four percent of the families were newly admitted to public assistance benefits (compared to 28 percent of the larger group). Twenty-six percent of the families had experienced improvement in the health status of a parent (compared to 32 percent of the larger group).

6. Only 15 percent of the families were affected by problems of mental illness in the family (compared to 23 percent of the larger group). Parental personality problems were identified for 40 percent of the families (compared to 42 percent of the larger group). The proportion of families beset by problems related to finances was higher (21 percent compared to 11 percent). Fewer cases were reported to have problems related to poor parental child-rearing capacity (12 percent, compared to 19 percent).

7. The estimate of the likelihood of the child's returning to foster care showed a more positive perspective with respect to the adoptables. Twenty-seven percent were rated as showing no possibility of return (compared to 16 percent of the larger group) and 47 percent were rated as having only a slight possibility of return compared to 44 percent of the larger group).

8. Twenty of the cases involved the recovery of parents who had been severely ill (mentally or physically); 16 cases involved unmarried mothers managing to establish households for themselves.

We consider it important for agencies to identify adoptable children in their caseload and to seek early clarification about the feasibility of adoption. Where this is ruled out by circumstances, it appears that there is still an even chance of returning the child to his own home. From our data it would seem that such discharges are in the interest of the children and as viable as for those children leaving care who are not among the adoptables.

This brings to a close our discussion of status changes as a way of assessing the outcome of the foster care experience of children. We now move to another approach: assessing changes in the cognitive and personality functioning of the children as related to their experience in foster care.

SEVEN

MENTAL ABILITIES
OF FOSTER CHILDREN

Psychiatrists and psychologists interested in understanding factors influencing the development of children have naturally gravitated to the study of separation to test their notions about the effects of catastrophic events—such as the loss of parent figures—on the mental abilities of those exposed to such phenomena. The fact of being deprived of parental care is recognized as being such an unusual occurrence in the lives of children, such a departure from widely held notions about what they require in the way of support and emotional sustenance, that there is sound basis for grave concern about the consequences of such experiences. We state this even though we recognize that some children may emerge from a deprivation experience relatively intact while others succumb pitifully to the mean and pathogenic circumstances to which they have been exposed. Loss of intellectual functioning with concomitant impairment in school performance—and the subsequent danger of being relegated to the bottom of the ladder in the world of work—would indeed be a bitter price for a child to pay for earlier depriving experiences. Those who have responsibility for picking up the pieces by offering care to children after their families have disintegrated must be concerned with what happens to the minds of these youngsters—their power to think, to reason, to make sense of the world around them.

We view the testing of intelligence as providing an important barometer of how a child is reacting to the separation experience. In this sense, we find ourselves in accord with the statement of Gavrin and Sacks that tests tend to provide us with an indication of how the child is doing developmentally in a quite useful way:

While an IQ test by no means represents the entire spectrum of relevant variables, such sources, especially when repeated at standard intervals, provide a relatively objective measure of general developmental functioning. Particularly at the preschool ages, it would seem that decrease or increase in the child's IQ score would depend on his general emotional stability and comfortableness within the setting.[1]

The decision to administer standardized intelligence tests to children experiencing sustained separation from their parents was made with a full sense of the hazards involved. There was question about the validity of tests administered to a population of children whose composition included major proportions of blacks and Puerto Ricans. There have been cogent questions raised in many quarters about whether such tests are "culture fair." We were aware that these questions had not been decisively dealt with. In addition, the fact that many of the children had been recently exposed to acute family crises and separation experiences that were potentially traumatic in their consequences raised the point of whether the results would be affected by the impaired capacity of children to produce responses that truly reflected their cognitive capacities during such periods. Furthermore, the children were located in a variety of settings: congregate shelters, large and middle-sized long-term institutions, foster family homes—and some had already returned to their own homes after having received a minimum of ninety days of care. Conditions for testing were subject to uncontrolled factors including lack of privacy, noise, and distractions for the children.

Despite these risks, we chose to make a major investment of our research resources in intelligence testing using standardized tests. We did this for several reasons:

1. The importance of the issue for the well-being of foster children has been well demonstrated.
2. The relative richness of past research in this area with important leads to be followed relates us to the scholarship of others in a significant way.
3. Imperfect as they are, intelligence tests have received the longest and most concentrated attention of scholars around the world in comparison with any other way of assessing the personal and social functioning of children.

[1] Joseph B. Gavrin and Lenore S. Sacks, "Growth Potential of Preschool-Aged Children in Institutional Care: A Positive Approach to a Negative Condition," *American Journal of Orthopsychiatry* 33 (1963): 402.

We desired very much to relate ourselves to the work of others rather than to go our own way by creating novel and unstandardized procedures for intellectual assessment. We wanted to further understand our own findings in the light of what others had found—and we wanted to add to the understanding of future scholars in this field. To rely exclusively on tests we might create in ad hoc fashion would have reflected a kind of privateness and self-indulgence that was unconscionable considering the public expense involved in gathering these data. We also believed our analyses would shed further light on the testing phenomenon and problems in validity that arise from circumstances we would be able to monitor through our extensive data gathering.

Since most of the agencies caring for our study subjects had the resources to test children, why did we undertake an expensive and demanding field enterprise to test them through our own staff? A major consideration was our desire to standardize the tests to be administered. Our cooperating agencies, some 80 in number, varied considerably in both testing procedures and tests administered routinely. Some tested all children coming under their aegis while others tested only when special problems arose requiring evaluation, for example, a child showing behavioral difficulties in a foster home. Adding to the laissez-faire aspect of the situation is the fact that even when intelligence tests were given, there was no agreement among the agencies providing care for our study population as to what tests to administer. The agencies had their own preferred test batteries and this made it impossible to summarize tendencies across agency populations. Furthermore, the agencies were not uniform in their patterns of repeating tests of children over time, so it became impossible to secure trend data that could be used in a longitudinal analysis.

METHODS AND MATERIALS

Tests Administered

Since our sample specifications called for us to include children whose ages ranged from infancy to 12 years—with repeated testing over a five-year period after their entry into care—it was necessary to choose age-appropriate tests. There is no single intelligence test that can be administered to infants, toddlers, latency-aged children, and adolescents. We therefore had to select three age-related tests, knowing that as the children grew older, quite a number would be shifted from one test to another in our repeated testings.

The three tests that we selected were: (a) the Cattell Infant Scale for children two years and under, (b) the Minnesota Preschool Scale for children two to five years of age, and (c) the Wechsler Intelligence Scale for Children (WISC) for youngsters six years or older.

The Cattell was chosen because it is considered especially good in detecting retardation, is useful in determining approximate developmental levels, and has been found valuable in longitudinal studies of mental development since it runs easily into older-age mental tests. It provides a single IQ score.

The strong points of the Minnesota scale are its careful standardization, its two parallel forms, and a reported high interform reliability. Of particular importance in our selection of this test was the fact that part scores could be developed for nonverbal as well as verbal content.

The WISC was chosen as a relatively well-established test, standardized on a sample of 2200 cases (only white children were included) showing quite high reliability and validity coefficients. There is a fairly extensive research literature available on the use of the WISC for widely diversified populations of children. The test provides performance and verbal IQ scores.[2]

The first round of tests was administered by three trained psychologists whose testing experience ranged from six to 11 years. Two psychologists were white females, and the third was a male of Puerto Rican background. The latter tended to have more Puerto Rican older children assigned to him, while the former tended to do more infant testing. Otherwise, the children were randomly assigned to the three psychologists. Over the five years of the study and three

[2] See Psyche Cattell, *The Measurement of Intelligence of Infants and Young Children*, rev. ed. (New York: Phychological Corporation, 1960); Florence Goodenough, et al., *Minnesota Preschool Scale (Manual)*, (Circle Pines, Minnesota: American Guidance Service, 1940); David Wechsler, *Wechsler Intelligence Scale for Children* (New York: Psychological Corporation, 1949).

rounds of testing, 11 psychologists were employed by the program.[3]

While it had originally been planned that most of the testing would be performed at the Research and Demonstration Center of the Columbia University School of Social Work, and an attractive testing room had been prepared for this purpose, it soon became clear that we could not ask the child care agencies to have foster mothers or institutional staff persons transport children to our offices for this purpose. The travel was too burdensome, considering the other responsibilities these individuals carried. They were, however, quite willing to have our staff test the children in the foster homes, institutions, or agency offices. In the long run, we came to feel that field testing was actually a wiser choice than having children brought to strange offices. Despite the considerable travel, inconvenience, and cost involved, our psychologists soon came to the firm conclusion that more representative scores would be achieved if the children were tested in surroundings familiar to them.

Number of Children Tested

Over the three rounds of testing in the five years of longitudinal investigation, 1302 tests were administered. Sometimes our psychologists were required to make five or six field visits before the right circumstances presented themselves for locating and testing a child. For Time I, 577 children, or 92.5 percent of our 624 study subjects, were tested. At Time II, we were able to test 84.1 percent of the children already tested plus five children not previously seen, for a total of 490 children. At Time III, we tested 403 children, or 82.2 percent of those seen at the time of the second round. In all, 392 children out of 624 were tested on all three occasions (62.8 percent); 103 on two occasions (16.5 percent); 89 had been tested once (12.8 percent), and 40 had never been tested (6.5 percent). Adopted children were concentrated in the latter category.

Tables 7.1 and 7.2 contain information about the number of children tested and the reasons for not testing the remaining sub-

---

[3] In subsequent rounds we had to replace testers, so it was rare for a child to have been tested by the same person on two occasions. The new testers were all white, with males and females represented in a ratio of two to one.

TABLE 7.1
FREQUENCY DISTRIBUTION OF PSYCHOLOGICAL
TESTING OF CWRP SUBJECTS

	No.	Percentage
Tested Times I, II, and III	392	62.8
Tested Times I and II	93	14.9
Tested Time I	83	13.3
Tested Times I and III	9	1.5
Tested Times II and III	1	—
Tested Time II	4	.7
Tested Time III	2	.3
Not tested	40	6.5
Total	624	100.0

TABLE 7.2
FREQUENCY DISTRIBUTION OF REASONS FOR FAILURE
TO ADMINISTER PSYCHOLOGICAL TESTS TO CWRP SUBJECTS
ON THREE TESTING OCCASIONS

	Time I	Time II	Time III
		(percentages)	
Unable to locate family	12.8	16.4	23.2
Family refusal	36.2	29.1	26.8
Child refusal	4.3	3.0	2.3
Child found not testable	10.6	6.0	0.9
Adopted child—not available for testing	25.5	13.4	12.3
Child in hospital or training school	2.1	6.7	5.0
Family moved out of area	8.5	15.7	23.6
Agency request not to test	—	5.2	2.3
Other	—	4.5	3.6
Total number of children not tested	47	134	220

jects. The major reasons for all nonexamined children at Time III were: (a) inability to locate family (23.2 percent), (b) family refusal (26.8 percent), (c) family moving out of area (23.6 percent), and (d) adopted child not available for testing (12.3 percent). Considering the impoverished circumstances of many of the families, their high geographic mobility, and the ambivalent or hostile feeling some of them harbored against social agencies, we tend to view the number of successfully completed examinations reported here as a positive accomplishment.

Data on children not examined on each of the three testing occasions is contained in the Appendix. At Time I, the infants placed for adoption represented the group least available for testing. At Times II and III, children who came into foster care because of their own behavioral difficulties showed the highest proportion not tested. In terms of ethnicity and religion, white Catholic and Protestant children showed the highest rate of nonavailability for testing; some of this was due to adoptees being no longer available to the project because of previous agreement with the agencies not to test such children.

The location of the children when tested at each testing occasion is presented in Table 7.3, which shows that a heavy amount of the testing at Time I took place in institutions, usually congregate shelters. By Time III, the testing sites had shifted so that a preponderance of the examinations took place in foster family homes or, for discharged children, in the subjects' own homes.

FINDINGS AT TIME I: CONDITION ON ARRIVAL

Infants

The Cattell Infant Scale was administered to 164 children whose average age was 17.5 months. The mean IQ score of the group was 91.71 (Table 7.4). There was no significant variation in performance between males and females. When the children were contrasted according to racial or ethnic identifications (white, black, and Puerto Rican), the white children showed mean IQ scores about four points higher than the others. The one-way analysis of variance did not show the differences to be statistically significant.

The test was designed so that items would be age-appropriate. Therefore we did not expect that we would find a significant correlation between the age of the subjects and the IQ scores. There was, however, a correlation of $-.29$ ($p < .05$) between the variables,

TABLE 7.3

**LOCATION OF CHILDREN WHEN TESTED BY PSYCHOLOGISTS
IN RELATION TO ETHNICITY**

Ethnicity	Time I			Time II			Time III		
	Institution	Foster Home	Own Home	Institution	Foster Home	Own Home	Institution	Foster Home	Own Home
				(percentaged across)					
Puerto Rican (195/167/146)[a]	67.2	16.9	15.9	38.3	25.7	35.9	23.3	30.1	46.6
Black Protestant (174/152/124)	44.3	47.7	8.0	13.2	55.3	31.6	11.3	54.8	33.9
Black Catholic (64/54/47)	62.5	29.7	7.8	29.6	46.3	24.1	14.9	44.7	40.4
White Catholic or Protestant (115/90/62)	50.4	38.3	11.3	23.3	47.8	28.9	11.3	40.3	48.4
Jewish (29/25/20)	69.0	24.1	6.9	40.0	24.0	36.0	15.0	5.0	80.0
Total (577/488/399)[b]	56.5	32.2	11.3	26.8	41.2	32.0	16.3	39.8	43.9
	$\chi^2 = 46.100$, df = 8, $p \leq .001$			$\chi^2 = 43.317$, df = 8, $p \leq .001$			$\chi^2 = 33.578$, df = 8, $p \leq .001$		

[a] Data in parentheses give the total number of children tested at Times I, II, and III.
[b] Three children tested at Time III were excluded from the table because the results were not valid.

TABLE 7.4
MEAN IQ SCORES ON TIME I CATTELL INFANT SCALE
FOR WHITE, BLACK, AND PUERTO RICAN CWRP STUDY SUBJECTS
(UP TO TWO YEARS OF AGE)

Group[a]	N	Mean	SD[b]
White	41	94.68	14.04
Black	96	90.68	16.71
Puerto Rican	24	90.75	17.74
Total	161	91.71	16.23
F-test		0.924	
Significance		p*.399	

[a]Three cases omitted for children of group classification other than those listed above.
[b]SD = standard deviation.

indicating that the younger infants within the two-year age span of these subjects achieved significantly higher scores than the older infants. This suggests a line of investigation for further study, namely, whether the older infants have been more traumatized by the separation from their mothers than the younger ones. It might reasonably be conjectured that the older subjects, having enjoyed longer contact with their mothers and being more cognitively aware of their environments, would experience their loss with greater impact. It is also possible, of course, that the allocation of test items to age categories in the original test construction was faulty and would account for the age-related outcomes. Since infant tests are commonly recognized as resting on debatable foundations, this is not an unlikely source of explanation.[4]

Toddlers

The Minnesota Preschool Scale was administered to 149 children who were slightly over four years of age on the average (Table 7.5). They achieved a mean verbal IQ of 87.71 and a nonverbal IQ of 90.86. Their average produced a mean total IQ of 88.61. These

[4] See Murray Levine, "Psychological Testing of Children" in Lois Wladis Hoffman and Martin L. Hoffman, eds, *Review of Child Development Research*, vol. 2 (New York: Russell Sage Foundation, 1966), p. 277.

TABLE 7.5
MEAN VERBAL, NONVERBAL, AND TOTAL IQ SCORES
ON TIME I MINNESOTA PRESCHOOL SCALE FOR WHITE,
BLACK, AND PUERTO RICAN FOSTER CHILDREN
(AGED 3 TO 6 YEARS)

Group	N	Verbal IQ		Nonverbal IQ		Total IQ	
		Mean	*SD*	*Mean*	*SD*	*Mean*	*SD*
White	43	90.88	15.04	91.28	22.13	90.98	16.42
Black	61	86.02	13.97	86.59	17.97	86.00	14.54
Puerto Rican	45	86.98	13.88	96.24	16.13	89.89	12.45
Total	149	87.71	14.31	90.86	19.07	88.61	14.60
F-test		1.56		3.44		1.73	
Significance		$p = .215$		$p = .035$		$p = .181$	

means are fairly well below the standardization population for which normative behavior is available. We observe that while the scores appear on the low-average side, the children evidently did somewhat better, in the aggregate, on the nonverbal elements of the test. Of particular interest is the performance of the Puerto Rican children, who achieved a mean nonverbal IQ almost 10 points higher than their mean verbal IQ. Since the Puerto Rican children in this age group had not been exposed to school as yet, their lack of knowledge of English may have been a factor in accounting for the lower verbal IQ scores. The black youngsters showed the lowest mean scores on both the verbal and nonverbal parts of the test, scoring 10 points lower than the Puerto Rican children in the nonverbal.

The differences in performance between boys and girls on the Minnesota test were trivial for the verbal IQ and modest and nonsignificant for the nonverbal IQ. The correlation of the IQ scores with the ages of the children was not significant.

School-aged Children

The performance of 258 children on the WISC revealed patterns similar to those reported for the Minnesota test. The mean verbal IQ was 89.17, while the mean performance IQ was somewhat higher, at 96.45. The mean full-scale IQ was 92.04. As a group, the youngsters performed on a somewhat lower level than the group of children who served as subjects when the test was standardized. Generally, we note that on all three versions of the test the means fall within the low-normal range. The mean age of the subjects was about nine and one-half years. On the WISC, the variable of age shows a different pattern of association than reported on the previously discussed tests. The older children performed significantly better on the verbal part of the test and moderately so on the performance part.

Boys performed significantly higher on the verbal IQ, showing a mean of 91.26, compared to 87.00 for the girls. There was less difference between the sexes with respect to performance IQ. The weighting of the verbal part of the examination was sufficient to differentiate the means of the full-scale scores significantly according to the sex of the subjects. Among the white boys were a number of subjects who came into care for residential treatment and who achieved superior scores.

The more substantial size of the group of children who were administered the WISC made it possible to analyze their scores using religion as an analytic variable, as well as ethnicity. Six groups of children were identified for analytic purposes: (a) white Catholic, (b) black Catholic, (c) Puerto Rican, (d) white Protestant, (e) black Protestant, and (f) white Jewish children. The size of the groups ranged from 99 Puerto Rican children to a small group of eight white Protestant children. The comparisons reveal a number of significant differences among the groups of children (Table 7.6).

With respect to the verbal IQ's, the Jewish children achieved a considerably higher mean than all other groups of children, ranging from 30 points higher than the Puerto Rican children to 15 points higher than the white Catholic children. A one-way analysis of variance to examine the effect of ethnic group membership in accounting for differences in verbal IQ proved to be statistically significant ($F = 22.44$, df = 5/251, $p < .001$). Pairwise comparisons were made to further clarify the nature of the differences between groups. Since the sizes of the groups were quite variable, Kramer's

TABLE 7.6
SCORES OR CWRP CHILDREN ON WISC SCALE AT TIME I
ACCORDING TO RELIGIOUS, RACIAL, AND ETHNIC BACKGROUNDS
(N = 257)

		Verbal IQ	Performance IQ	Full-scale IQ
White Catholic Children (40)	Mean SD	97.43 15.72	104.75 14.82	100.93 13.95
Black Catholic Children (25)	Mean SD	94.32 15.69	98.16 14.12	95.88 13.91
Puerto Rican Children (99)	Mean SD	81.47 11.78	94.31 17.71	86.71 13.22
White Protestant Children (8)	Mean SD	97.13 23.16	103.38 23.99	100.25 25.18
Black Protestant Children (63)	Mean SD	84.83 12.94	89.40 12.33	85.76 11.92
White Jewish Children (22)	Mean SD	112.36 19.17	103.64 19.55	108.91 19.35
F-test Significance		22.44 $p = .001$	6.06 $p = .001$	15.54 $p = .001$

extension of multiple range tests was utilized for this purpose.[5] This analysis revealed the Jewish children to be significantly higher in verbal IQ scores than the children of the five other groups ($p < .01$ for all comparisons). The white Catholic children were significantly

[5] Clyde Young Kramer, "Extension of Multiple Range Tests to Group Means with Unequal Numbers of Replications," *Biometrics* 12 (1956): 307–10.

higher in their scores than the Puerto Rican children ($p < .01$) and the black Protestant children ($p < .05$), but this was not the case with respect to the black Catholic or white Protestant children. The white Protestant children were significantly higher in verbal IQ than the Puerto Rican children ($p < .01$) and the black Protestant children ($p < .05$). The white Protestant children were not significantly superior in verbal IQ to the black Catholic children. The scores of the black Catholic children were, however, significantly superior to those of the Puerto Rican ($p < .01$) and the black Protestant children ($p < .05$). The black Protestant children were not significantly higher in verbal IQ scores than the Puerto Rican children.

An analysis of group differences with reference to WISC performance IQ scores reveals a quite different pattern of findings. All of the groups except the Jewish children showed mean performance IQ scores higher than the verbal IQ. Levinson has previously reported the tendency of Jewish subjects ranging from preschool to college levels to show a significantly higher verbal than performance IQ score.[6] It should also be noted that the Jewish children tended more than the other subjects to come into foster care because of their own emotional and behavioral difficulties. Thus, it is possible that the discrepancy between the two types of intelligence scores may be a reflection of the emotional disturbance of many of the Jewish children.[7]

The three groups of white children performed in relatively undifferentiated fashion, with the white Catholic children scoring the highest mean performance IQ of the six ethnic groups. The Puerto Rican group is notable because the children showed a marked difference between mean verbal and performance IQs, their mean performance IQ being some 13 points higher than the mean verbal IQ. This appears to reflect the language handicap affecting the test performance of the Puerto Rican children. Although most of them were tested by a

[6] B.M. Levinson, "Traditional Jewish Cultural Values and Performance on the Wechsler Tests," *Journal of Educational Psychology* 50 (1959): 177–81.

[7] See David Rapaport, Merton M. Gill, and Roy Schafer, *Diagnostic Psychological Testing* (New York: International Universities Press, 1968), p. 79. The authors note that most characteristic of neurotic groups is the mild tendency to have an impaired performance efficiency and increased verbal scatter. Extreme impairment on performance tests is also characteristic of certain psychotic groups.

psychologist who himself was a Puerto Rican, the use of the Spanish language was reserved for only a few instances in which the child obviously did not understand English. As noted in a review of psychological measures used in the national Health Examination Survey, "where bilingualism is known to exist, verbal tests may be expected to be invalid measures and greater reliance on performance-type tests such as Block Design and Draw-A-Man is indicated."[8]

The previously observed difference between black Catholic and black Protestant children has its parallel for the performance IQ, where the Catholic children scored an average of nine points higher than the Protestant children. A one-way analysis of variance test on the performance IQs for the six groups revealed that it was significant at the .001 level. Further analysis by the multiple range test showed fewer significant differences in paired comparisons than in the case of the verbal IQ. The only significant differences were the higher mean scores achieved by the white Catholic, Jewish, and white Protestant children over the black Protestant children ($p <$ .05). No group among the three white groups was significantly superior to the other two.

For those who are tempted to generalize from these findings to children in the community, we should stress that this would not be warranted. The children from each ethnic group tended to enter foster care for different concentrations of reasons. Jewish children, for example, tended to enter foster care because of their own adjustment difficulties to a much greater extent than did the other children. Black children were much more heavily represented in the neglect or abuse cases. There were almost no cases among Puerto Ricans where the mother was unwilling to assume care of an infant.

It is noteworthy that the examining psychologists rated 7 percent of the 577 children examined at Time I as "defective" and 13 percent as "borderline." The great majority of the children (73 percent) were rated as "normal" and 6 percent were rated as "advanced." Older children tended to predominate among those seen as "advanced." There was no significant sex difference in the distribution of ratings.

[8] National Center for Health Statistics, series 2, 15, *Evaluation of Psychological Measures Used in the Health Examination Survey of Children Ages* 6–11 (Washington, D.C.: Public Health Service, HEW, March, 1966), p.15.

By way of summarizing what we have learned about the condition of the children on arrival, we emphasize that at the time the children entered care, their test scores were on the average about 10 points below the normative population on which the respective tests had been standardized. Differences among the infants and toddlers were insignificant when their IQ scores were analyzed for Puerto Rican, black, and white children. Significant ethnic differences characterized the older children. We noted differences in verbal and performance scores that were particularly pronounced for Puerto Rican children, suggesting a language handicap. From this point on we are less interested in absolute differences among groups and more on the shifts in IQ taking place over time.

IQ SCORES ACHIEVED ON THREE TESTING OCCASIONS

We now proceed to examine how the children performed on later testing occasions. The Time II examinations were administered about two and one-half years after the children entered care, and Time III, about five years after entry. We examined the children who had returned home (almost 66 percent of the study population at Time III), as well as those who had remained in care.

We will first take what might be considered a static or snapshot view of how the children performed at each testing occasion and then proceed to our major concern with assessing factors related to changes in their measured intelligence over time. The measurement of change must be identified as the most important feature of our study.

We report first on the stability of the IQ assessments over time. We can do this for those children who had the WISC at Times I–III or Times II–III; other children had a mixture of tests (i.e., Cattell, Minnesota, and WISC) that were selected to be age-appropriate. The correlation between Time I and Time II verbal WISC scores is .796; for Time II and Time III, it is .796; and for Time I and Time III, it is .733. For the performance IQ the correlations are .700, .711, and .638, respectively (Table 7.7).

In Table 7.8 we display the zero-order correlations between Times I and II, Times II and III, and Times I and III for the WISC

TABLE 7.7
ZERO-ORDER CORRELATIONS
OF WISC IQ SCORES FOR THREE TESTING OCCASIONS
(N = 167)

	Verbal IQ	
	Time II	Time III
Time I	.796	.733
Time II	—	.796

	Performance IQ	
	Time II	Time III
Time I	.700	.638
Time II	—	.711

	Full-Scale IQ	
	Time II	Time III
Time I	.789	.733
Time II	—	.799

verbal, performance, and full-scale IQs, carrying out the analyses separately for Puerto Rican, black, and white subjects. Most of the correlations are between .700 and .750, indicating that the WISC is quite stable. Our findings are similar to those reported by Gehman and Matyas in their four-year follow-up study.[9] Our data show that the verbal IQ tends to be more stable than the performance IQ. This is a matter that bears consideration since we later demonstrate more impact of variables relating to the foster care experience on performance measures than on the verbal IQ. One can view the greater stability of the verbal scores as more solidly established in the construction of the test or consider the hypothesis that the scores assess domains that are less influenced by changes in environmental circumstances.

We observe greatest stability in the scores of the white children

[9] Ila H. Gehman and R. P. Matyas, "Stability of the WISC and Binet Tests," *Journal of Consulting Psychology* 20 (1956):150–52.

TABLE 7.8
ZERO-ORDER CORRELATIONS
OF WISC IQ SCORES COMPARING TIMES I, II, AND III[a] SCORES
FOR PUERTO RICAN, BLACK, AND WHITE SUBJECTS

| | Puerto Rican | | |
Comparisons	Verbal IQ	Performance IQ	Total IQ
Times I–II	.651 (91)[b]	.564 (91)	.703 (91)
Times II–III	.716 (103)	.659 (103)	.739 (103)
Times I–III	.673 (79)	.655 (79)	.682 (79)

| | Black | | |
	Verbal IQ	Performance IQ	Total IQ
Times I–II	.731 (69)	.648 (69)	.750 (69)
Times II–III	.770 (82)	.728 (82)	.799 (82)
Times I–III	.716 (57)	.518 (57)	.720 (57)

| | White | | |
	Verbal IQ	Performance IQ	Total IQ
Times I–II	.793 (51)	.750 (51)	.809 (51)
Times II–III	.732 (46)	.772 (46)	.766 (46)
Times I–III	.707 (36)	.684 (36)	.760 (36)

[a] The number of cases increase from Time I to Time III because younger children given the Minnesota preschool at Time I were tested on the WISC at Time II and Time III, when the latter became age-appropriate. All correlations shown in this table are significant ($p < .001$).

[b] Number of cases involved in the correlation shown in parentheses.

and least in those of the Puerto Rican subjects. However, the differences are not major and one can point to a fairly substantial firmness of association of scores on repeated testing for all three ethnic groups.

In Table 7.9 we present the zero-order correlations between WISC scores on the three testing occasions and a number of key background variables as well as measures associated with the child's experience in care. The table shows that older children achieved significantly higher scores than the younger subjects. The correlation of the scores with age was statistically significant for Times I and III verbal IQs and on all three testing occasions for the full-scale IQs. In accounting for these correlations, we again note the presence of older children from families of relatively higher socioeconomic status who came into foster care because of the emotional difficulties they were experiencing at home. Boys were predominant in this group and their higher WISC scores contributed to the significant sex differentiation.

When children born in wedlock were compared with those born out of wedlock, the correlations with WISC scores favored the former, although the magnitude of the associations was not impressive. On the other hand, the correlations between the measure of socioeconomic circumstances and the IQ scores was more substantial, ranging as high as $r = .44$. On all three occasions, the correlations were highest between this measure and the verbal IQ.[10]

Some significant associations are revealed in Table 7.10 between caseworkers' evaluations of the subjects' mothers, patterns of parental visiting, and IQ scores (see chapter 8 for further discussion of this).

Deviation IQ Scores

As already indicated, our study included a broad age range. Since the design called for repeated testing of the children over a five-year period, it was necessary to deal with the fact that the subjects would not be given the same intelligence tests each time because of the age factor. As the reader is aware, some subjects started with one test and subsequently moved on to a different test that took into account their increased age. In other words, they moved from the Cattell Infant Intelligence Scale or from the Minnesota to the WISC. The statistical approach used here to deal with the problem of divergent tests has been described by Anastasi; test scores are standardized to achieve a desired mean and standard deviation.[11] The new scores are called "deviation IQs." We applied this transformation to the Cattell IQ, the Minnesota total IQ, and the WISC full-scale IQ for each testing occasion taken separately. The raw scores were standardized

[10] For information on the construction of the index of socioeconomic circumstances, see Shirley Jenkins and Elaine Norman, *Filial Deprivation and Foster Care* (New York: Columbia University Press, 1972), pp. 275–86.

[11] Anne Anastasi, *Psychological Testing*, 2nd ed. (New York: Macmillan, 1961), p. 95.

TABLE 7.9
ZERO-ORDER CORRELATIONS BETWEEN SELECTED BACKGROUND
VARIABLES AND WISC IQ SCORES ACHIEVED BY FOSTER CHILDREN ON
THREE TESTING OCCASIONS OVER A FIVE-YEAR PERIOD (N = 167)

	Time I		
Variable	Verbal	Performance	Total
Age at entry	.248**	.282***	.297***
Sex (Female; MALE)	.110	.116	.127
Birth status (out of wedlock; IN WEDLOCK)	.180*	.107	.162*
Socioeconomic status (low; HIGH)	.447***	.246**	.401***
Log days in care^a (low; HIGH)	.221**	.107	.188*
Setting—institution^b (not in institution; IN INSTITUTION)	.061	.163*	.120
Setting—foster family home^b (not in foster family home; IN FOSTER FAMILY HOME)	.114	−.053	.036
Reason for placement: child's behavior (other reasons; CHILD BEHAVIOR)	.124	.196*	.176*
Evaluation of mother—Time I (negative; POSITIVE)	−.021	.101	.038
Evaluation of mother—Time II (negative; POSITIVE)	−.052	.082	.010
Parental visiting behavior—Time II (no visiting permitted; MAXIMUM VISITING PERMITTED)	.095	.048	.085
Parental visiting stability—Time II (decreased visits over time; INCREASED VISITS)	−.072	−.050	−.067
Ethnicity: black (other; BLACK)	−.032	−.253***	−.149
Ethnicity: Puerto Rican (other; PUERTO RICAN)	−.349***	−.026	−.233**
Religion: Catholic (other; CATHOLIC)	−.147	.142	−.018
Religion: Jewish-white (other; JEWISH-WHITE)	.437***	.165*	.357***
Ethnicity: black Catholic (other; BLACK CATHOLIC)	.093	.066	.093
Age and sex interaction^c	.135	.177*	.174*

TABLE 7.9 (*cont.*)

	Time II			Time III	
Verbal	*Performance*	*Total*	*Verbal*	*Performance*	*Total*
.110	.243**	.194*	.155*	.204**	.197*
.110	.253***	.200**	.165*	.283***	.251**
.147	.091	.134	.138	.131	.157*
.334***	.196*	.294***	.344***	.214**	.318***
.274**	.169*	.249**	.254***	.152*	.232**
.021	.232**	.138	−.017	.098	.045
.215**	−.039	.101	.141	−.039	.061
.025	.141	.094	.110	.257***	.204**
.000	.123	.069	.011	.138	.045
−.030	−.048	−.043	−.005	.058	.061
.130	.099	.128	.177*	.215*	.031
−.172*	−.123	−.162*	−.220**	−.034	−.219**
−.001	−.187*	−.099	−.048	−.220**	−.150
−.277***	−.026	−.172*	−.228**	.097	−.081
−.115	.158*	.020	−.086	.138	.027
.353***	.128	.269***	.303***	.125	.251**
.088	.068	.088	.049	.033	.050
.102	.276***	.208**	.181*	.293***	.263***

*p < .05   **p < .01   ***p < .001

[a]For Times I and II correlations, variable represents the days a child was in foster care up to Time II testing; for Time III correlation, variable represents days in care up to Time III testing.

[b]Location of child at Time II testing.   [c]Product of age and sex.

to be in accord with the norms of the WISC (i.e., having a mean of 100 and a standard deviation of 15).[12]

The reader should be aware that our transformation of the three sets of IQ scores—Cattell, Minnesota, and WISC—into a single standard score was carried out as a matter of necessity. For one thing, we desired to work with our full sample for a number of our analyses. Also, in analyzing change, we had to cope with the fact that younger subjects were given different tests as they got older. We could not treat the IQs of each of the three tests as if they were interchangeable and could not assume equality of the original standardization populations from one test to another.

The creation of deviation IQs, by which we fixed the mean of our subjects' test scores at 100 with a standard deviation of 15 for each test, creates limitations on what we can say about the overall results of our analysis. We can make no statement about our sample's absolute change in IQ. This has been fixed through our transformation procedure. Nevertheless, we can observe for any subgroup within our study population whether the children show an increase or decrease relative to the rest of the sample or to another subgroup. Within a test where there is no rescaling—such as the group of children entering care at age six and over and who were administered the WISC on each of the three testing occasions—we will be able to look at the absolute number of mean points of change. But when the tests are pooled, we must forego any such statement and restrict our comments to relative change. We can say that one group is showing a relatively more positive or more negative shift than another but not whether this represents an absolute change.

The transformation of test scores into deviation IQs also tends to have the effect of reducing age differences in scores quite considerably. This is so because age tends to be very closely related to the tests that were used, and each test was standardized to the same mean. The consequences of standardization has been to make the children more or less equal by age despite known probable

---

[12] These new "deviation IQs" were created in the following manner: the IQs achieved on each test—Cattell IQ, total IQ of the Minnesota, and full-scale IQ of the WISC—were converted into Z-scores using the means and standard deviations of each test population. The Z-scores were multiplied by 15 and 100 was added.

differences in age groups with regard to other concomitant factors such as socioeconomic circumstances and religion.

In Tables 7.10–12 we present the means and standard deviations of the deviation IQs grouped by three age levels: (a) under two years, (b) two to five, and (c) six or over. We further differentiated with regard to sex and the following ethnic groupings: (a) Puerto Rican, (b) black Protestant, (c) black Catholic, and (d) white. Analysis of variance was employed to determine the extent to which variation in performance on the tests at each testing occasion is accounted for by these variables. The means used in the analyses were unweighted averages of cell means, that is, they were the means of the cell means, disregarding the number of cases in the cells.

Table 7.10 reveals that there were no significant relative differences in deviation IQs between the three age levels, and none between boys and girls. There were, however, significant differences between ethnic groups and a significant second-order interaction between age levels and ethnicity and a third-order interaction involving all three independent variables. The second-order interaction clarifies that the relative ethnic differences are age-related, and the third-order clarifies even further that ethnic differences are linked to specific age–sex groupings. Inspection of Table 7.10 shows a small group of black Catholic girls aged six or over with a mean IQ of 117.00, in contrast with a group of black Protestant girls, also aged six or over, with a mean IQ of 91.88. This disparity no doubt accounts for the significant higher-order interactions. Similarly, the mean IQ of the older white boys (114.22) is strikingly higher than the older Puerto Rican (97.85) and black Protestant (95.90) boys.

Table 7.11 presents the results of the three-way analysis of variance for the deviation IQs calculated for the Time II testing. Again, age and sex do not produce significant main effects, but ethnicity does. The only interaction effect is the third-order interaction of age, sex, and ethnicity. White older males score about 16 points higher than Puerto Rican and black Protestant older males. Similar relative disparities are noted between white and black Catholic older females and Puerto Rican and black Protestant older females.

For Time III, there is again evidence that age and sex do not

TABLE 7.10

MEANS AND STANDARD DEVIATIONS OF DEVIATIONS IQ'S OF CWRP SUBJECTS BY SEX AND AGE AT ENTRY INTO FOSTER CARE, BY ETHNICITY, TIME I (N = 577)

Age at Entry		Puerto Rican		Black Protestant		Black Catholic		White	
		Male	Female	Male	Female	Male	Female	Male	Female
Under 2 years	Mean	98.60	99.71	98.06	100.44	99.81	94.42	103.46	104.62
	SD	15.34	15.20	14.55	14.32	10.43	24.00	11.50	13.35
	N	(15)	(14)	(32)	(36)	(16)	(12)	(22)	(21)
2–5 years	Mean	98.24	100.00	96.95	98.76	98.60	98.00	103.42	100.86
	SD	14.29	15.89	16.85	13.28	17.14	11.19	14.92	17.54
	N	(37)	(27)	(21)	(21)	(5)	(15)	(19)	(21)
6+ years	Mean	97.85	94.61	95.90	91.88	100.33	117.00	114.22	109.63
	SD	12.67	12.27	11.94	11.70	6.23	12.25	18.03	12.57
	N	(48)	(54)	(31)	(33)	(9)	(7)	(37)	(24)

Summary of Analysis of Variance for Time I Deviation IQ Scores

Source	df	Percent of Total SS	F
Age at entry	2	0.71	2.191
Sex	1	0.01	0.072
Ethnicity	3	4.07	8.419***
Age at entry by sex	2	0.03	0.092
Age at entry by ethnicity	6	3.61	3.734**
Sex by ethnicity	3	0.33	0.693
Age at entry by sex by ethnicity	6	2.23	2.308*
Error	553	89.02	

*p < .05   **p < .01   ***p < .001

TABLE 7.11

MEANS AND STANDARD DEVIATIONS OF DEVIATION IQ'S OF CWRP SUBJECTS BY SEX AND AGE AT ENTRY INTO FOSTER CARE, BY ETHNICITY, TIME II (N = 488)

Age at Entry		Puerto Rican		Black Protestant		Black Catholic		White	
		Male	Female	Male	Female	Male	Female	Male	Female
Under 2 years	Mean	98.00	95.69	92.43	101.09	96.13	106.11	106.00	98.29
	SD	16.44	16.13	14.35	14.67	14.58	11.57	13.40	17.80
	N	(14)	(13)	(28)	(32)	(15)	(9)	(19)	(14)
2–5 years	Mean	97.69	99.00	101.95	93.65	111.00	95.21	105.53	101.20
	SD	12.30	13.69	9.64	13.87	19.78	11.78	17.20	14.77
	N	(32)	(23)	(19)	(20)	(4)	(14)	(15)	(20)
6+ years	Mean	99.00	96.95	100.12	92.82	104.00	112.25	116.10	104.00
	SD	12.63	12.99	12.37	12.83	7.48	13.67	18.14	16.43
	N	(42)	(43)	(25)	(28)	(8)	(4)	(31)	(16)

Summary of Analysis of Variance for Time II Deviation IQ Scores

Source	df	Percent of Total SS	F
Age at entry	2	0.85	2.221
Sex	1	0.56	2.924
Ethnicity	3	4.31	7.542***
Age at entry by sex	2	1.08	2.835
Age at entry by ethnicity	6	0.87	0.762
Sex by ethnicity	3	0.88	0.536
Age at entry by sex by ethnicity	6	3.14	2.753*
Error	464	88.32	

*p < .05   ***p < .001

TABLE 7.12

MEANS AND STANDARD DEVIATIONS OF DEVIATION IQ'S OF CWRP SUBJECTS BY SEX AND AGE AT ENTRY INTO FOSTER CARE, BY ETHNICITY, TIME III (N = 402)

Age at Entry		Puerto Rican		Black Protestant		Black Catholic		White	
		Male	Female	Male	Female	Male	Female	Male	Female
Under 2 years	Mean	98.71	96.86	94.65	96.58	97.36	107.71	101.78	102.54
	SD	13.18	20.63	18.60	12.36	19.78	11.03	10.61	10.94
	N	(14)	(11)	(23)	(24)	(14)	(7)	(14)	(13)
2–5 years	Mean	104.57	104.23	104.00	91.94	110.50	98.08	100.78	101.50
	SD	18.11	9.92	13.91	14.10	15.78	12.36	20.97	16.62
	N	(28)	(22)	(17)	(16)	(4)	(12)	(9)	(10)
6+ years	Mean	100.10	96.46	100.07	91.31	103.50	107.25	112.43	101.33
	SD	12.42	14.08	13.22	14.00	2.51	17.78	14.96	11.51
	N	(39)	(35)	(18)	(26)	(6)	(4)	(21)	(15)

Summary of Analysis of Variance for Time III Deviation IQ Scores

Source	df	Percent of Total SS	F
Age at entry	2	0.39	0.799
Sex	1	0.62	2.563
Ethnicity	3	2.99	4.138**
Age at entry by sex	2	1.21	2.514
Age at entry by ethnicity	6	1.09	0.756
Sex by ethnicity	3	0.49	0.676
Age at entry by sex by ethnicity	6	2.03	1.403
Error	378	91.17	

**$p < .01$

produce significant main effects but ethnicity does. However, there is no significant higher interaction effect evidenced, and the tendency is for somewhat greater equalization of scores across groups (Table 7.12).

In Tables 7.13–15 we display mean changes in deviation IQs for the three testing occasions: (a) Times I–II, (b) Times II–III, and (c) Times I–III. The means are again presented for groups organized by age, sex, and ethnicity. For Times I–II, infants and older white females have lost relative ground (4–6 points), as have older black Catholic females (7.5 points). On the other hand, relative gains have been made by infant black Catholic females (6.1 points), black Protestant male toddlers (6.3 points), and black Catholic male toddlers (6.2 points). For Times II–III we see gains by Puerto Rican male toddlers, white female infants, and black Catholic male infants. Losses were sustained by white male infants, black older Catholic females, and black Protestant females.

For the five-year span, the biggest relative gains were made by black Catholic infant females, black Protestant male toddlers, and black Catholic male toddlers. Notable relative losses were made by white older females, black Catholic older females, and black Protestant infant females.

The reader should be aware that shifts in IQ over time are presented in Tables 7.13–15 as aggregates in a way that does not take into account loss of subjects in repeated testing. Also, while the mean change of a group might be small, individual children could be showing extreme changes, say 20 points or more.

One final note: we found considerable variation in the mean IQs of our subjects according to reasons for entering foster care. For example, children who came into care because of neglect or abuse scored the lowest of all children, whereas higher mean scores were achieved by children who came into care because of their own behavior problems or because their unmarried mothers refused to assume care of them (Table 7.16). We also observed that the mean IQ scores varied significantly with respect to the socioeconomic status of subjects.[13]

[13] The means of the index measuring socioeconomic circumstances of the groups were: (a) Puerto Rican 12.34, (b) black Protestant 14.94, (c) black Catholic 16.83, (d) white Catholic or Protestant 18.84, and (e) Jewish 24.83.

TABLE 7.13

MEAN CHANGE IN DEVIATION IQ'S OF CWRP SUBJECTS FROM TIME I TO TIME II BY SEX AND AGE AT ENTRY INTO FOSTER CARE, BY ETHNICITY   (N = 484)

Age at Entry		Puerto Rican		Black Protestant		Black Catholic		White	
		Male	Female	Male	Female	Male	Female	Male	Female
Under 2 years	Mean $T_2 - T_1$ change	-0.64	-2.92	-4.22	0.25	-3.20	6.10	2.26	-6.21
	SD	13.00	9.94	13.05	16.54	12.85	10.61	12.32	18.65
	N	(14)	(13)	(27)	(32)	(15)	(9)	(19)	(14)
2–5 years	Mean $T_2 - T_1$ change	-0.88	-1.78	6.33	-2.56	6.25	-2.21	3.33	-0.55
	SD	12.62	13.83	14.51	12.99	16.46	10.45	10.29	13.01
	N	(32)	(23)	(18)	(18)	(4)	(14)	(15)	(20)
6+ years	Mean $T_2 - T_1$ change	1.26	1.93	4.20	1.39	3.00	-7.50	1.42	-4.69
	SD	9.24	10.00	9.59	7.20	6.37	15.72	11.36	6.70
	N	(42)	(43)	(25)	(28)	(8)	(4)	(31)	(16)

TABLE 7.14

MEAN CHANGE IN DEVIATION IQ'S OF CWRP SUBJECTS FROM TIME II TO TIME III BY SEX AND AGE AT ENTRY INTO FOSTER CARE, BY ETHNICITY (N = 367)

Age at Entry		Puerto Rican		Black Protestant		Black Catholic		White	
		Male	Female	Male	Female	Male	Female	Male	Female
Under 2 years	Mean $T_3 - T_2$ change	3.54	1.73	-0.05	-4.46	4.31	0.71	-4.57	4.33
	SD	18.16	16.76	18.52	9.93	18.51	15.00	13.13	14.09
	N	(13)	(11)	(22)	(24)	(13)	(7)	(14)	(12)
2–5 years	Mean $T_3 - T_2$ change	5.32	3.48	2.81	-0.38	-0.50	5.25	0.78	-2.00
	SD	12.13	8.91	13.77	7.35	19.98	6.70	12.57	11.57
	N	(28)	(21)	(16)	(16)	(4)	(12)	(9)	(10)
6+ years	Mean $T_3 - T_2$ change	1.85	-0.49	-0.33	-1.58	-3.83	-5.67	-2.30	-2.40
	SD	9.61	7.92	8.30	8.44	5.04	9.45	10.70	11.22
	N	(39)	(33)	(18)	(24)	(6)	(3)	(20)	(15)

TABLE 7.15

MEAN CHANGE IN DEVIATION IQ'S OF CWRP SUBJECTS FROM TIME I TO TIME III BY SEX AND AGE AT ENTRY INTO FOSTER CARE, BY ETHNICITY

$(N = 399)$

Age at Entry	Puerto Rican		Black Protestant		Black Catholic		White	
	Male	Female	Male	Female	Male	Female	Male	Female
Under 2 years								
Mean $T_3 - T_1$ change	2.00	−0.82	−4.22	−6.00	−3.00	8.86	−0.50	−1.92
SD	16.18	16.78	23.68	17.68	18.71	19.05	12.09	12.02
N	(13)	(11)	(23)	(24)	(14)	(7)	(14)	(13)
2–5 years								
Mean $T_3 - T_1$ change	4.96	1.23	10.12	−1.88	5.75	1.25	−0.33	1.10
SD	17.13	12.34	16.33	13.02	10.05	10.40	12.58	13.98
N	(28)	(22)	(17)	(15)	(4)	(12)	(9)	(10)
6+ years								
Mean $T_3 - T_1$ change	3.87	1.54	4.11	0.76	1.00	−10.00	−1.48	−7.40
SD	17.13	9.57	10.19	9.02	5.22	10.74	9.23	9.37
N	(39)	(35)	(18)	(25)	(6)	(4)	(21)	(15)

TABLE 7.16
MEAN DEVIATION IQ SCORES FOR CWRP SUBJECTS AT TIMES I, II, AND III TESTINGS, BY REASON FOR ENTRY INTO FOSTER CARE

Reason	Time I (N = 577)				Time II (N = 488)				Time III (N = 402)			
	Mean	SD	N	F-test	Mean	SD	N	F-test	Mean	SD	N	F-test
Mental hospitalization of parent	102.09	14.69	131		101.83	14.14	109		101.43	15.28	96	
Behavior of child	104.77	17.44	70		105.59	17.89	51		104.15	14.90	41	
Physical hospitalization of parent	97.97	12.84	62		96.59	14.74	56		96.62	18.74	53	
Parent unwilling to assume care	103.54	15.88	41		102.85	14.33	33		105.31	8.93	22	
Parent unwilling to continue care	99.78	12.95	60		98.83	13.70	46		103.49	12.64	37	
Neglect or abuse of child	95.94	15.81	88		95.98	14.05	79		95.81	14.53	64	
Abandonment or desertion	99.00	13.70	60		99.82	14.42	56		99.88	14.76	45	
Family dysfunction	95.84	13.07	51		98.00	14.91	45		97.49	11.76	37	
Other family crises (death, eviction, etc.)	102.00	16.52	14		106.23	14.98	13		98.86	16.09	7	
	Mean Square	df		F-test	Mean Square	df		F-test	Mean Square	df		F-test
Among Groups	672.784	8		3.082**	612.937	8		2.827**	492.761	8		2.248*
Within Groups	218.265	568			216.844	479			219.195	393		

*p < .05   **p < .01

SUMMARY

In this chapter we have provided data on the results of three rounds of testing of the intelligence of foster children. We have described the nature of sample loss over time and the reasons for it. We emerge, nevertheless, with information about a substantial number of our subjects. We have observed that the children tend to score in the low-normal IQ range, with the toddlers and school-aged children showing means about 10 points below those of the normative populations on which the tests were standardized. We also have shown that ethnic differences at the time of arrival in foster care are trivial for the infants, moderate for the toddlers, and quite pronounced for the school-aged children. Puerto Rican subjects are noteworthy for the discrepancy between verbal and nonverbal scores, indicating a language handicap for these bilingual children. We also found notable differences in the performance of black Protestant and black Catholic children, with the latter performing in relatively superior fashion.[14] Jewish children were noteworthy because of their superior verbal IQs and their comparatively less outstanding performance in nonverbal tasks.

We find IQ scores are generally quite stable on repeated testing. Ethnic differences persevere. Age and sex do not show significant main effects, but some interaction effects have been noted. We provide data on change on mean IQ changes for various subgroups in the sample.

---

[14] The superior performance of black Catholic children has its counterpart with respect to the performance of Puerto Rican children in our sample. We found that 14 Protestant Puerto Rican children performed significantly higher in their IQ scores than did 152 Puerto Rican Catholic children.

EIGHT

ANALYSES
OF IQ CHANGE
OVER FIVE YEARS

In this chapter we examine the IQ changes in the child subjects as revealed by testing on three occasions over the five years of investigation. We are particularly interested in determining whether the extended tenure in foster care is linked to decline in cognitive functioning, as might be predicted from a reading of the literature on the consequences of maternal deprivation. We are able to examine this issue because of the special features of our research design, which called for continued assessment of the children in our study even after they had returned home. This permits us to look at changes in intelligence scores associated with the length of time children have remained in care (the variable is used in its logarithmic form).[1]

As we discussed previously, we have transformed all of the raw score IQs into "deviation IQ" form, using the norms of the WISC as the standard (mean = 100, standard deviation = 15).[2] This was necessary because children who were administered the Cattell or the Minnesota preschool scales were later examined with tests ap-

---

[1] We use the logarithmic transformation of the number of days in care rather than the raw number as the measure of length of time in care. This tends to produce a regression curve that is closer to linear than the original curve. Such transformations generally increase the correlations that can be obtained.

[2] These new "deviation total IQs" were created by converting the IQs achieved on each test (e.g., Cattell, Minnesota total, and full scale IQ of the WISC) into Z-scores using the means and standard deviation of each test sample. The Z-scores were multiplied by 15 and 100 was added. Similar transformations were used to create "deviation verbal IQ" and "deviation nonverbal IQ" scores.

propriate for older children (i.e., the Minnesota or the WISC) over the course of five years.

In our analytic effort, using multiple regression, we have focused not only on the total IQ scores as a criterion variable (the variable to be "explained") but also on the component verbal and nonverbal scores. We were led to this approach by the concept that the influences at play in the foster care experience were apt to have different consequences for each of these domains. We reasoned that children benefiting from the surcease of tension associated with living with very disturbed or disorganized parents might display an "opening up" of cognitive abilities in the performance (nonverbal) areas, even when placed in working-class foster homes with adults who had modest educational backgrounds and were unlikely to influence verbal cognitive functioning.

In the multiple regression analyses we present here, we have used 12 variables as predictors; each seemed promising as a potential contributor to explaining change in IQ. We have included the following regressor variables in our analyses: age, sex, age–sex interaction,[3] socioeconomic status of the child's family, birth status, ethnicity, reason for placement, logarithm of days in foster care, evaluation of the mother, parental visiting behavior, and total casework contact rate (in logarithmic form). The last three variables are time-specific, that is they coincide with the four data-gathering occasions of the agency study (explained in chapter 3). Ethnicity and reason for placement are dummy-variable coded.[4] We have only included three reasons for placement categories as dummy variables in the set, for parsimony: child behavior, abandonment, and neglect and abuse. These are referenced to all the remaining children in the regression analysis.

[3] As Cohen has pointed out, the joint effect of two variables can be carried by a third variable that is the product of the two. This variable contains the joint effect, which is identical with the first-order interaction effect of analysis of variance. See Jacob Cohen, "Multiple Regression as a General Data Analytic System," *Psychological Bulletin* 70 (1968): 436.

[4] Dummy-variable coding involves the successive dichotomizing of subgroups in a nominal (categorical) scale. For example, for children to be classified by race–ethnicity, one dummy variable can be created where 1 = black children and 0 = other children. A second variable can be created where 1 = Puerto Rican children and 0 = other children. In multiple regression analysis, a third variable covering the white children is not required; it becomes the reference group for the other two variables.

EXAMINING IQ CHANGE

Before proceeding to our discussion of the analyses of IQ change, we refer the reader to Table 8.1, which presents the correlations between the length of time the children spent in foster care (log transformed) and their deviation IQs (verbal, nonverbal, and total) at Times II and III, with the earlier scores partialed out.[5] We observe that children who remained in foster care longer tended to show significant gains in verbal, nonverbal, and total IQs during the first two and one-half years of testing (Times I–Time II), but not during the final two and one-half years (Times II–III). Regarding the role of the length of time in care over the course of the full five years of the study, we see that children who remained in care achieved higher IQ scores relative to those who returned home, for all three categories (verbal, nonverbal, and total). This seems to reflect the persistence of gains associated with the earlier period under review.

TABLE 8.1
CORRELATIONS BETWEEN LENGTH OF TIME SPENT IN FOSTER CARE (LOG TRANSFORMED) AND TIMES II AND III DEVIATION IQ'S WITH EARLIER SCORES PARTIALED OUT

Time	Score Being Predicted	Partial Correlation
II	Verbal IQ (partialing out Time I score)	.23*** (375)[a]
II	Nonverbal IQ (partialing out Time I score)	.20*** (375)
II	Total IQ (partialing out Time I score)	.18*** (490)
III	Verbal IQ (partialing out Time II score)	−.01 (404)
III	Nonverbal IQ (partialing out Time II score)	.01 (404)
III	Total IQ (partialing out Time II score)	.08 (404)
III	Verbal IQ (partialing out Time I score)	.13** (404)
III	Nonverbal IQ (partialing out Time I score)	.13** (404)
III	Total IQ (partialing out Time I score)	.16*** (404)

**p < .01   ***p < .001

[a] Number of cases on which correlation is based is shown in parentheses.

[5] Space does not permit us to present the partial correlations of the independent variables we employed in addition to length of time in care. These variables uniformly showed quite trivial partial correlations with the later IQ measures.

How do we interpret these findings to the reader? First, we emphasize that, contrary to the expectations one would have from reviewing the professional literature, we do not find significant loss of intelligence associated with tenure of children in foster care. On the contrary, we find evidence of gain in IQ. We would introduce a caveat, however, and point to the quite modest sizes of the correlations displayed, albeit they are statistically significant. These would hardly call for rapturous statements about the benefits of foster care. The more prudent stance would be to raise strong questions about the presumption that the experience of placement is injurious to many children. We will have more to say about this matter in our examination of the multiple regression analyses of IQ change.

Times I-II IQ Change
In Table 8.2 we present the results of regression analyses of changes in deviation IQ scores (verbal, nonverbal, and total) for all subjects tested from Times I–II, covering approximately the first two and one-half years after the children had entered care. The number of subjects is reduced in the analysis of verbal and nonverbal IQ change because younger subjects received only total IQ scores in their earlier testing on the Cattel scale. They are included, however, in the analysis of total IQ change.

The standardized regression coefficients, commonly referred to as "beta weights," are shown in Table 8.2.[6] As might be expected, the major contribution to "explaining" the Time II IQ scores is made by the Time I testing. Thus, the beta weight for the Time I verbal IQ score is quite massive (.67), reflecting the fact that it accounts for 35 percent of unique variance in the criterion.[7] There is only one other variable among the predictors that shows a significant beta weight, namely, log days in care. This variable also shows significant beta weights in the analysis of the nonverbal and total IQ change.

---

[6] Standardized regression coefficients are often called "beta weights"; these are measures of the relative importance of predictor variables in this sample. Each variable is expressed in units of its own standard deviation; comparison can thus be made without regard to the original coding or scoring systems employed in the definition of each variable.

[7] The correlation between Times I and II Verbal IQ scores is .70.

TABLE 8.2
RELATION OF SALIENT BACKGROUND AND OTHER
INDEPENDENT VARIABLES TO VERBAL, NONVERBAL, AND TOTAL
DEVIATION IQ CHANGE, TIMES I–II

Independent Variables	Time II Deviation Verbal IQ	Time II Deviation Nonverbal IQ	Time II Deviation Total IQ
	(standardized regression coefficients)		
Deviation IQ Time I			
(verbal/nonverbal/total)	.67***	.61***	.64***
Child's age at placement	.09	.14*	.13*
Sex of child	−.01	.02	.02
Age–sex interaction	−.05	−.17	−.13
Socioeconomic status			
of family	−.01	−.06	.02
Birth status (OW/IW)	.00	.06	.02
Ethnicity:[a]			
Black	−.06	−.10	−.06
Puerto Rican	−.11	−.12	−.09
Reason for placement:[b]			
Child behavior	−.05	−.04	−.07
Abandonment	.03	.07	−.02
Neglect or abuse	−.03	.00	−.05
Evaluation of the mother	−.02	−.07	−.03
Log days in care	.15**	.13**	.13***
Parental visiting pattern	.04	.11*	.05
Log total casework			
contact rate	−.02	−.02	−.03
Multiple R	.73	.69	.69
Multiple R^2	.53	.47	.48
No. of cases	341	341	485

Significance, based upon t-tests for regression coefficients: *$p < .05$ **$p < .01$
***$p < .001$
    [a]Referenced to white children.   [b]Referenced to all other children.

These findings confirm the partial correlations presented in Table 8.1. They signify that during the first two-and-one-half-year period, the longer a child remained in care, the more apt he was to show improvement in his IQ score. This finding runs counter to the notion that children will deteriorate as a result of extended time spent in foster care. These findings lead us to conjecture that many of the children who returned to their families in the early phase of the study were encountering home situations in which there persisted much of the same personal and social disorganization that had contributed to their entry into foster care. Viewed positively, it seems that foster care offered benefits to the children remaining in care in the form of stable living arrangements with exposure to parental figures who were less sorely troubled than their own.

We observe that in addition to the contribution of log time in care two other variables made significant contributions to explained variance in the Time II nonverbal IQ scores: (a) the age of the child and (b) parental visiting. The older the child, the more apt he was to show improvement in his score on repeated testing. This carried over to the total IQ scores, where age also contributed a significant proportion of explained variance in the criterion. While we cannot be certain about the meaning of this finding, one potential explanation lies in the fact that older children might have been more sensitive to the chaos that prevailed in their families at the time of placement and therefore the foster care experience may have come as something of a relief to them.

The fact that more frequent parental visiting is associated with improvement in the nonverbal IQ scores is of considerable interest. It suggests to us that such visiting has some general salutary effect and that there is an improved sense of well-being associated with the child's having an ongoing contact with his parents. Such a notion has its echo in Weinstein's research over a decade ago at the Chicago Child Care Society.[8]

The Time II deviation total IQ scores show three significant predictor variables: (a) the Time I score (36 percent of unique variance explained), (b) the child's age, and (c) log time in care. Parental visiting does not contribute significantly to explaining the criterion.

The multiple correlations for the analyses of the three measures of IQ range from .69 to .73, and the explained variance ranges from 47 percent to 53 percent. There are obviously many influences at

---

[8] Eugene Weinstein, *The Self-Image of the Foster Child* (New York: Russell Sage Foundation, 1960).

play that are important but not identified by us. We further note the relative unimportance of a number of the independent variables we utilized in explaining change in IQ: sex, age–sex interaction, socio-economic status, ethnicity, reason for placement, evaluation of the mother, and the quantity of casework attention.[9]

Times II–III IQ Change

When we examine the IQ changes associated with the last two and one-half years of the study, we find that log time in care ceases to make a significant contribution to the explanation of IQ change. This was anticipated on the basis of the partial correlations presented in Table 8.1. Stated another way, in the latter phase of the study the children who have returned home are doing as well, on the average, as those who have remained in care. This holds true whether we consider the verbal, nonverbal, or total IQs.

There is only one variable other than the earlier IQ scores (Time II) that shows a significant standardized regression coefficient in predicting the Time III deviation verbal IQ scores, namely, the caseworker's evaluation of this mother. The contribution of this variable is very small but suggests that children of mothers who are evaluated more positively by the caseworkers tend to show better outcomes as reflected in gains in IQ (Table 8.3).

With respect to the analysis of nonverbal IQs, the only significant regressor variable is one related to ethnicity. Puerto Rican children appear to show enhanced scores more frequently than do white or black children. With reference to total IQ change, we find no variables other than the earlier IQ scores (Time II) contributing significant explained variance.

Times I-III IQ Change

In Table 8.4 we present the analysis of IQ change from Time I to Time III, spanning the full five years of longitudinal investigation. We find that the changes associated with length of time in care

---

[9] We should explain that we had no reason for including quantity of casework attention other than our desire to determine whether such service contacts had *unanticipated* beneficial effects. The fact that they did not contribute significantly to the analysis of IQ change should not reflect adversely on the reputation of casework; it would be ludicrous to assume that such service is designed to improve IQ scores.

TABLE 8.3
RELATION OF SALIENT BACKGROUND AND OTHER
INDEPENDENT VARIABLES TO VERBAL, NONVERBAL, AND TOTAL
DEVIATION IQ CHANGE, TIMES II–III

Independent Variables	Time III Deviation Verbal IQ	Time III Deviation Nonverbal IQ	Time III Deviation Total IQ
	(standardized regression coefficients)		
Deviation IQ Time II			
(verbal/nonverbal/total)	.73***	.66***	.63**
Child's age at placement	−.01	−.11	−.02
Sex of child	.07	−.05	−.03
Age–sex interaction	−.10	.05	−.03
Socioeconomic status			
of family	.03	.06	.03
Birth status (OW/IW)	−.05	.02	.00
Ethnicity:[a]			
Black	−.03	.08	.03
Puerto Rican	.01	.22***	.07
Reason for placement:[b]			
Child behavior	.01	.11	.04
Abandonment	−.01	−.07	−.01
Neglect or abuse	−.05	−.03	−.04
Evaluation of the mother	.08*	.01	.06
Log days in care	.00	.02	.06
Parental visiting pattern	−.02	−.06	−.04
Log total casework			
contact rate	.00	.01	.00
Multiple R	.75	.70	.67
Multiple R^2	.56	.49	.45
No. of cases	298	298	393

Significance, based upon t-tests for regression coefficients: *$p < .05$ **$p < .01$ ***$p < .001$
   [a]Referenced to white children.   [b]Referenced to all other children.

identified for the first two and one-half years of the study are sufficiently strong to account for significant amounts of explained variance in the Time III deviation verbal, nonverbal, and total IQs, after Time I scores have been partialed out as covariates. Thus, we again provide evidence that exposure to foster care has had some beneficial effect, as opposed to expected deleterious consequences, with respect to intelligence measures. It would appear that children who have returned home—especially those who were discharged from care relatively early—have not shown as much gain as those who have remained in care.

Also of interest is the fact that parental visiting again emerges as being associated with IQ gain, only this time it is related to

TABLE 8.4
RELATION OF SALIENT BACKGROUND AND OTHER
INDEPENDENT VARIABLES TO VERBAL, NONVERBAL, AND TOTAL
DEVIATION IQ CHANGE, TIMES I–III

Independent Variables	Time III Deviation Verbal IQ	Time III Deviation Nonverbal IQ	Time III Deviation Total IQ
	(standardized regression coefficients)		
Deviation IQ Time I (verbal/nonverbal/total)	.65***	.58***	.51***
Child's age at placement	−.01	−.04	.05
Sex of child	.01	−.09	−.04
Age–sex interaction	−.09	−.02	−.09
Socioeconomic status of family	.02	.05	.06
Birth status (OW/IW)	−.07	.04	.01
Ethnicity:[a]			
Black	.00	.07	−.02
Puerto Rican	.01	.18**	.07
Reason for placement:[b]			
Child behavior	−.07	.05	−.02
Abandonment	.03	−.02	−.01
Neglect or abuse	.05	−.01	−.05
Evaluation of the mother	.03	−.03	.01
Log days in care	.12**	.10*	.14**
Parental visiting pattern	.12**	−.00	.03
Log total casework contact rate	.01	−.01	.01
Multiple R	.67	.64	.58
Multiple R^2	.45	.41	.33
No. of cases	404	404	404

Significance, based upon t-tests for regression coefficients: $*p < .05$ $**p < .01$ $***p < .001$
[a]Referenced to white children. [b]Referenced to all other children.

enhancement of verbal scores rather than nonverbal, as was the case for the Times I–II analysis. There is no noteworthy association between parental visiting and IQ scores with respect to nonverbal and total measures.

We also observe that the only other regressor variable that shows a significant beta weight is ethnicity, Puerto Rican children show significant gains in nonverbal IQ scores for the five-year span relative to the other children.

The reader will note that the amount of variance accounted for when predicting IQ over the five-year span of the study is smaller than when this is undertaken for each of the two-and-one-half-year segments (Times I–II and II–III).

PREDICTING IQ WITHIN ETHNIC GROUPS

We were interested in determining whether an analysis of IQ change undertaken separately for white, black, and Puerto Rican children would reveal different findings with respect to the saliency of our predictor variables than was found for the study group as a whole. We were led to this query by our awareness that the minority children in our sample, black and Puerto Rican, had been exposed to greater deprivation in family and environmental conditions than many of the white children. Length of time in care might thus operate differently as an influence on children according to their ethnicity. For some children, time in foster care might constitute a reprieve from unsettled home conditions, with resultant improvement in personal adjustment and cognitive performance.

Table 8.5 presents the zero-order correlations between the length of time the children spent in foster care and their IQ scores at Times II and III with the earlier scores partialed out. The correlations have been calculated separately for white, black, and Puerto Rican children. The findings are of interest and tend to show different associations between time in care and IQ change according to race–ethnicity. There is also variability with reference to the time spans being considered.

When we examine the association between length of time in care and IQ at Time II (partialing out the Time I IQ score), we find

TABLE 8.5
CORRELATIONS BETWEEN LENGTH OF TENURE IN FOSTER CARE (LOG TRANSFORMED) AND TIMES II AND III DEVIATION IQ WITH EARLIER SCORES PARTIALED OUT, ANALYZED SEPARATELY FOR WHITE, BLACK, AND PUERTO RICAN SUBJECTS

| | | Partial Correlations for: | | |
| | | | | |
Time	Score Being Predicted	White	Black	Puerto Rican
II	Verbal IQ (partialing out Time I score)	.06 (88)[a]	.21** (144)	.32*** (143)
II	Nonverbal IQ (partialing out Time I score)	.13 (88)	.15* (144)	.26** (143)
II	Total IQ (partialing out Time I score)	.06 (116)	.14* (207)	.33*** (167)
III	Verbal IQ (partialing out Time II score)	−.25* (83)	.06 (171)	.03 (150)
III	Nonverbal IQ (partialing out Time II score)	−.16 (83)	.22** (171)	−.07 (150)
III	Total IQ (partialing out Time II score)	−.04 (83)	.19* (171)	.03 (150)
III	Verbal IQ (partialing out Time I score)	−.18 (83)	.12 (171)	.27** (150)
III	Nonverbal IQ (partialing out Time I score)	−.09 (83)	.30*** (171)	.07 (150)
III	Total IQ (partialing out Time I score)	−.12 (83)	.22** (171)	.24** (150)

*p < .05   **p < .01   ***p < .001
[a] Number of cases upon which correlation is based is shown in parentheses.

the association to be positive for all three groups of children. That is, the longer children have been in care, the more they tend to show gains over their earlier performance for verbal, nonverbal, and total IQs. However, the correlations fail to achieve statistical significance for the white children (correlations for the three measures of IQ are .06, .13, and .06), while for the black children, they do achieve significance (correlations are .21, .15, and .14). The association is even stronger for the Puerto Rican children (correlations are .32, .26, and .33).

When we look at the second time span (Times II–III), covering the last half of the five-year investigation, we find an altered association between length of time in care and IQ gain. The white children show a loss in IQ associated with remaining in care; the negative correlation is significant with respect to verbal IQ but not for nonverbal or total IQ (correlations are − .25, − .16, and − .04).

The black children, on the other hand, continue to show improvement in IQ related to tenure in foster care, and the correlations are significant for nonverbal and total IQ measures (correlations are .06, .22, and .19). For the Puerto Rican children, the Times II–III span fails to show a significant association between time in care and IQ gain (correlations are .03, − .07, and .03).

Looking at the full five-year span (Times I–III), we find that white children tend to show negative associations with respect to time in care ($r = − .18$, − .09, and − .12), while black and Puerto Rican children show associations reflecting gains (for black children, $r = .12, .30$, and .22; for Puerto Rican children, $r = .27, .07$, and .24). It is of interest that black children show a significant association only for nonverbal scores and the Puerto Rican children for verbal scores. In the latter case, we might speculate that these bilingual children have improved in the verbal aspects of the test procedures by virtue of extended exposure to English-speaking environments.

The findings we have reported become important when we consider their meaning. White children who have extended tenure in foster care—going beyond the first two and one-half years—show declines in IQ, while black children show sustained gain, in the aggregate, over the full five-year period after entering care. Puerto Rican children show rather impressive IQ gain during the first two and one-half years, but continuance in care after this period is not associated with noticeable gain or loss in scores.

In Tables 8.6–8 we present the multiple regression analyses of IQ change shown separately for the three ethnic groups. We are compelled to somewhat alter our perspective regarding the association between length of time in care and IQ change for Times I–II when all of the independent variables are considered. It is only with respect to the Puerto Rican children that we find length of time in care showing significant standardized regression coefficients indicating significant gains in verbal, nonverbal, and total IQ for children who have remained in care as opposed to those who have returned to their homes. The black children show positive effects but these are not statistically significant. The beta weights for the white children are also positive for Times I-II but negative for Times II–III and Times I–III.

Times I–II Change

When we examine the role played by other variables in accounting for Times I–II IQ change (Table 8.6) we find the following.

White children. There is a significantly higher IQ gain achieved by white girls than white boys with respect to nonverbal IQ scores, but this does not apply to verbal or total scores. There is also a significant age–sex interaction effect for nonverbal scores. Younger boys have made significant gains while older girls have lost ground. We also find that abandoned children and children who have been the object of intensive casework attention are those who have lost most ground with respect to total IQ change. Another significant variable is the fact that children of poorly evaluated mothers have not performed as well as previously in their nonverbal IQ scores.

Black children. Only two variables in the Times I–II analysis are predictive of IQ change for black children, and these apply only to the total IQ change: age and age–sex interaction. Older children have shown significant gains and older females have fared less well than younger males.

Puerto Rican children. Aside from the contribution of time in care, only one variable is significantly associated with IQ change for Puerto Rican children. Abandoned children have shown more improvement in nonverbal IQ in contrast with the other children.

Times II–III IQ change

We now proceed to examine Times II–III change (Table 8.7), again in the context of the three ethnic groups.

White children. Other than the premeasure (Time II IQ), none of the independent variables is a significant predictor of the Time III verbal IQ. The major influence of the independent variables is manifested in the realm of nonverbal IQ. Age, sex, and age–sex interaction show significant standardized regression coefficients. These are interpretable as indicating that younger children and boys

TABLE 8.6
RELATION OF SALIENT BACKGROUND AND OTHER INDEPENDENT VARIABLES TO VERBAL, NONVERBAL, AND TOTAL DEVIATION IQ SCORES FOR WHITE, BLACK, AND PUERTO RICAN CHILDREN, TIMES I-II

Variable[a]	White Verbal IQ	White Nonverbal IQ	White Total IQ	Black Verbal IQ	Black Nonverbal IQ	Black Total IQ	Puerto Rican Verbal IQ	Puerto Rican Nonverbal IQ	Puerto Rican Total IQ
					(standardized regression coefficients)				
1. DEV-IQ-I	.82***	.73***	.68***	.66***	.49***	.56***	.52***	.61***	.68***
2. AGE	.18	.19	.06	.16	.09	.23*	.04	.16	.07
3. SEX	.22	.35*	-.11	.03	-.09	.14	-.11	-.01	.00
4. AGE-SEX	-.26	-.49**	-.04	-.17	-.13	-.32**	.11	-.08	-.02
5. SES	-.08	-.09	.06	-.02	.03	-.01	-.03	-.07	.00
6. WEDLOCK	-.13	.01	.01	.03	.06	.02	.04	.08	.04
7. REASON-1	.02	-.05	-.03	-.13	-.08	-.12	-.13	.02	-.09
8. REASON-2	-.08	-.02	-.16*	.13	.03	-.05	.09	.16*	.09
9. REASON-3	.10	.11	.08	-.03	-.07	-.12	-.15	-.04	-.10
10. EVAL-MO	-.01	-.16*	-.07	-.01	-.02	-.02	-.01	-.10	-.01
11. CARELOG	.05	.13	.07	.16	.13	.12	.23**	.18*	.22***
12. VISITING	.09	.14	.07	.10	.07	.03	-.10	.10	.02
13. CASEWORK	-.04	-.12	-.19*	.02	.01	.06	-.07	.04	-.03
Multiple R	.84	.80	.75	.69	.58	.63	.66	.67	.73
Multiple R²	.70	.63	.56	.47	.33	.40	.43	.45	.53
No. of cases	88	88	116	144	144	207	143	143	167

*p < .05   **p < .01   ***p < .001

[a] Identification of independent variables: (1) deviation IQ—Time I, (2) age of child, (3) sex of child, (4) age–sex interaction, (5) socioeconomic status, (6) birth status, (7) reason for placement: child behavior, (8) reason for placement: abandonment, (9) reason for placement: neglect or abuse, (10) evaluation of mother, (11) log of days in care, (12) parental visiting pattern, (13) log of total casework contact rate.

TABLE 8.7

RELATION OF SALIENT BACKGROUND AND OTHER INDEPENDENT VARIABLES TO VERBAL, NONVERBAL, AND TOTAL DEVIATION IQ SCORES FOR WHITE, BLACK, AND PUERTO RICAN CHILDREN, TIMES II–III

Variable[a]	White			Black			Puerto Rican		
	Verbal IQ	Nonverbal IQ	Total IQ	Verbal IQ	Nonverbal IQ	Total IQ	Verbal IQ	Nonverbal IQ	Total IQ
	(standardized regression coefficients)								
1. DEV-IQ-II	.81***	.99***	.71***	.73***	.57***	.57***	.73***	.65***	.69***
2. AGE	-.07	-.36***	.09	-.05	-.01	.08	.00	-.14	-.12
3. SEX	.03	-.19**	.09	.12	.02	-.06	-.04	-.14	-.12
4. AGE–SEX	-.06	.35***	-.10	-.06	-.03	-.04	-.06	.11	.07
5. SES	-.05	.03	-.02	.06	.11	.11	.02	.06	.00
6. WEDLOCK	.11	.27***	.03	-.09	-.13	-.10	-.01	.12	.07
7. REASON-1	.22	.56***	.29*	-.10	-.03	-.13	.02	.07	.04
8. REASON-2	.12	.20***	.12	.03	.03	.06	-.05	-.21**	-.14*
9. REASON-3	-.10	.01	-.10	-.08	-.08	-.07	.06	.13*	.09
10. EVAL-MO	.08	.09	.11	.10	.05	.12	.13	.00	.00
11. CARELOG	-.25	-.38***	-.18	.05	.20**	.17**	.01	-.03	.04
12. VISITING	-.09	-.54***	-.23	-.02	.09	.03	-.01	-.03	-.03
13. CASEWORK	.11	.09	.03	.10	.10	.11	-.07	-.05	-.01
Multiple R	.80	.93	.74	.75	.68	.67	.74	.69	.71
Multiple R^2	.64	.87	.56	.57	.46	.46	.55	.47	.51
No. of cases	59	59	83	115	115	171	124	124	150

*$p < .05$ **$p < .01$ ***$p < .001$.
[a]Identification of independent variables as in table 8.6, except variable 1 is deviation IQ at Time II.

have fared better. However, older girls have fared better than younger boys when the interaction effect is examined.

Reason for placement is a significant predictor for children who have come into foster care because of their own behavioral difficulty or because they were abandoned; they show significant IQ non-verbal gains. For the former, the finding would seem indicative of some responsiveness to the treatment they have received with respect to their emotional disorders.

It is again of interest to observe that for the white children taken as a group, length of time in care is inversely associated with IQ gain; that is, longer tenure in care is associated with decline in nonverbal IQ. We also find that frequently visited white children show a decline in nonverbal IQ in this second half of the longitudinal time span. This runs counter to our theory that visiting of parents will show beneficial consequences for children.

Black children. Only one independent variable shows significance when we consider the performance of the black children; namely, length of time in care. We find that the longer the black children have been in care the more apt they are to show enhancement in their nonverbal and total IQ testing. We thus note that significant change comes to the fore during the second half of the study, whereas this was not true for the first half. We also observe the change to be a positive one for the black children in contrast with their white counterparts, who show a decline in nonverbal IQ scores.

Puerto Rican children. Other than the Time II premeasures, we find little source of explanation of IQ change among the independent variables when we analyze the performance of Puerto Rican children. Only abandonment and neglect or abuse as reasons for placement show significance as predictors. Abandoned Puerto Rican children lose ground over the final two-and-one-half-year period in nonverbal and total IQ scores. On the other hand, neglected or abused children in this ethnic group show significant gains in nonverbal IQ. It is noteworthy that length of time in care proves trivial as an explanatory variable for this time period.

Times I–III IQ Change

Predicting IQ change over a five-year time span is a more formidable task. Nevertheless, we find a number of significant predictors among our independent variables when we look at the performance of each ethnic group (Table 8.8).

White children. Other than the premeasure (Time I IQ score), none of the independent variables significantly predicts verbal IQ change. On the other hand, eight independent variables show significance when nonverbal IQ change is considered. Boys do better than girls, and younger children do better than older children in this regard. There is also a significant contribution of the age–sex interaction variable, indicating a group of older girls who have fared better than a group of younger boys. Two reason-for-placement dummy variables also emerge as significant predictors; children who came into care because of behavior problems and those who have been abused or neglected show significant gains in nonverbal IQ.

For the five-year period covering Times I–III, the longer a white child has been in care, the more likely he is to show loss in nonverbal and total IQ. The beta coefficients are significant in this regard. We also find a decline in nonverbal IQ associated with the visiting of parents and with indication of intensive casework attention.

Black children. As was the case with the white children, none of the independent variables (other than the Time I premeasure) proved to be significant predictors in assessing Times I–III verbal IQ change of black children. However, several variables showed significant beta weights when we looked at nonverbal and total IQ change. The most important variable is length of time in care. Unlike the findings we reported for the white children, the longer the black children were in care, the more likely was enhancement of their nonverbal and total IQs. One other variable is predictive of nonverbal IQ change; black children whose families were of higher socioeconomic status tended to show greater gains. This also held true with respect to total IQ scores.

We found one additional significant predictor related to reason for placement. Black children who entered care because of behavior difficulty tended to show a decline in total IQ; the opposite of this was found for the white children.

Puerto Rican children. As was the case with black children—but not with white children—length of time in care was a positive predictor of IQ change for the Puerto Rican children. However, unlike the black

TABLE 8.8
RELATION OF SALIENT BACKGROUND AND OTHER INDEPENDENT VARIABLES TO VERBAL, NONVERBAL, AND TOTAL DEVIATION IQ SCORES FOR WHITE, BLACK, AND PUERTO RICAN CHILDREN, TIMES I–III

Variable[a]	White			Black			Puerto Rican		
	Verbal IQ	Nonverbal IQ	Total IQ	Verbal IQ	Nonverbal IQ	Total IQ	Verbal IQ	Nonverbal IQ	Total IQ
				(standardized regression coefficients)					
1. DEV-IQ-I	.75***	.83***	.71***	.62***	.47***	.34***	.69***	.65***	.62***
2. AGE	.00	-.26*	.09	-.05	.04	.24	.04	-.03	-.04
3. SEX	.16	-.23*	.07	.02	-.08	.00	-.10	-.13	-.12
4. AGE-SEX	-.15	.23*	-.15	-.07	-.09	-.25	-.02	.03	.04
5. SES	-.07	.08	.05	.08	.14*	.15*	-.03	.01	-.02
6. WEDLOCK	-.02	.17	.07	-.06	-.11	-.12	-.03	.19**	.10
7. REASON-1	.17	.50***	.22	-.13	-.04	-.19*	-.12	-.03	-.07
8. REASON-2	.02	.03	-.05	.16	.07	.05	-.03	-.11	-.08
9. REASON-3	-.08	.25**	.03	-.09	-.11	-.11	.05	.14	.06
10. EVAL-MO	.16	.15	.06	.03	-.04	.06	.04	-.03	-.01
11. CARELOG	-.14	-.33***	-.22*	.11	.27***	.22**	.22***	.07	.21**
12. VISITING	.01	-.57***	-.29*	.05	.11	.07	.24**	.10	.12
13. CASEWORK	.03	-.19*	-.07	.14	.12	.10	-.09	-.05	-.02
Multiple R	.75	.82	.75	.66	.63	.53	.68	.66	.63
Multiple R^2	.56	.67	.56	.44	.39	.28	.46	.44	.40
No. of cases	56	56	83	100	100	169	124	124	149

*p < .05   **p < .01   ***p < .001

[a] Identification of independent variables as in table 8.6.

children, the significant change was in the verbal rather than the nonverbal measure. The variable also proved to be significant in the analysis of total IQ change. In addition, Table 8.8 shows that frequency of parental visiting, unlike what was reported for the white children, is a positive predictor of change. Why Puerto Rican children should show positive effects while white youngsters the reverse is not readily explainable.

One other variable proves to be a significant predictor for Puerto Rican children: children born in wedlock tended to show enhanced nonverbal IQ compared with those born out of wedlock.

In considering the analyses presented in Tables 8.6–8.8 we note that there is much better prediction from premeasures to post-measures for the white children than for the black or Puerto Rican children for all three time spans presented. This is another way of saying that the tests produce more stable results for the white children; sometimes there is as much as 20 percentage points of difference in variance accounted for between the groups.

The important finding that emerges from the analyses of IQ change undertaken separately for the three ethnic groups concerns the role of length of time in care. White children show significant decline over the second two-and-one-half-year period associated with remaining in care, while this was not the case during the first time span (Times I–II). For the whole five-year period, extended time in care is associated with loss of IQ. Minority children show significant gains in IQ over the five-year span associated with remaining in care. Black children show gains particularly for the Times II–III period, and Puerto Rican children show gains particularly for the Times I–II period. Our sense of the meaning of these findings is that they can best be explained by the notion of relative deprivation. White children tend to do better in their own homes over time because they are more apt to have intact families living under better material circumstances. The black and Puerto Rican children tend to come from single-parent households where the physical and material resources are much less adequate. Foster care is likly to offer a better provisioned and more stable environment in contrast to what the minority children find when they return home.[10]

---

[10] This is not an argument for keeping the children in care; it makes more sense to take measures to bolster the homes to which the children are returning.

TESTING OTHER ASSOCIATIONS WITH IQ CHANGE

We have thus far looked at the contribution of a selected number of variables in accounting for IQ change. We would now like to go beyond these as sources of explanation. Two types of caretakers related to the foster care situation demand attention as potential sources of influence: (a) foster parents who have day-to-day contact with children mainly cared for in foster families and (b) institutional personnel who care for children who have been primarily cared for in congregate settings. In looking at these influences, we will be examining reduced samples of subjects, since exposure to foster family care or institutional care is treated as mutually exclusive and a substantial number of children who left care early in the study are not included in the analyses.

Foster Parents and IQ Change

As discussed in chapter 3, foster parents caring for the subjects in foster family care were rated on two occasions by the caseworkers who knew them best. The rating instrument, the Foster Parent Appraisal Form (FPAF), was adopted from a previous study of foster parents in Pittsburgh and had also been used in a study in Montreal. A similar factorial structure was revealed by an analysis of the caseworker's ratings in both cities. In the current New York City study, ratings were secured on two occasions. Time I (FPAF) assessments took place when the children had been in care for an average of 10.5 months. A repeat assessment of each child's foster parents took place about 30 months later. At both times, 152 foster families were rated, although there was not a complete overlap of families rated on the two occasions.

As described in chapter 3 in our discussion of the study methodology, a factor analysis was carried out in parallel for the Times I and II foster parent ratings, and the results were used as a guide to the construction of indexes. The indexes were shown to have fairly high internal reliabilities (as measured by Cronbach alpha coefficients). The correlations between Times I and II index scores for the foster parents who were assessed twice were statistically significant but not large. The FPAF indexes include the following:

1. Role competence—can be interpreted to measure how well the foster parents are able to meet the emotional needs of the child, how well they understand child behavior, and their ability to respond to normally active children.

2. Intellectual climate—assesses the climate of the foster family as it might influence the intellectual development of the child. On the positive pole of the index, the foster family is seen as intellectually stimulating to the child. Its use of discipline is intellectually oriented.

3. Democratic permissiveness—can be interpreted, on the positive side, to measure the degree to which a foster family avoids harsh, rigid discipline and physical punishment with concomitantly little stress on demands for social conformity.

4. Perseverance–altruism—describes, on one pole, foster parents who can cope with the care of the physically handicapped or mentally retarded child. They tend to be altruistic in permitting natural parents easy entry into their homes and are able to separate from foster children who are returned home. They tend to be religious in their overall orientation to life.

5. Response to infants, toddlers, and older children—these three indexes measure the degree to which preferences for foster children of specific ages have been manifested by the foster parents.

We identified 138 children who had received foster family care as their major placement experience and who had been tested on a repeated basis.[11] These subjects tended to be younger than the overall sample. Their mean age when entering foster care was 46.5 months (standard deviation = 38.1), while the mean age for the entire sample was 60.2 months (standard deviation = 47.3).

In Table 8.9 we present the partial correlations in which we link the assessments of foster parents (FPAF indexes as assessed at two occasions) to Times II and III IQ scores. We have partialed out the premeasure (Times I or II deviation IQ) and length of time in care (log transformed). The analysis has been performed separately for verbal, nonverbal, and total IQ scores.

When we examine the Times I–II span, we find that none of the indexes is significantly correlated with the Time II verbal IQ (with Time I partialed out). While intellectual climate shows a positive correlation, it is not significant for either the first or second foster

---

[11] The children were primarily those in foster family care when the foster parents were rated on two occasions and were also identified as being in foster family care when tested by our psychologists.

TABLE 8.9
CORRELATIONS BETWEEN FOSTER PARENT INDEXES AND DEVIATION IQ SCORES, PARTIALING OUT EARLIER IQ SCORES AND LOG OF TIME IN CARE[a]

A. Time II Scores, with Time I Scores and Log of Time Partialed Out

	Partial Correlation with:		
Foster Parent Appraisal Form (FPAF) Indexes	Time II Verbal IQ ($N = 58$)	Time II Nonverbal IQ ($N = 66$)	Time II Total IQ ($N = 128$)
FPAF Time I Indexes			
Role competence	.05	.14	−.13
Intellectual climate	.12	.18	.05
Democratic permissiveness	.16	.25*	−.13
Perseverance–altruism	−.11	.02	−.02
Response to infants	−.13	.11	−.09
Response to toddlers	−.06	.17	−.10
Response to older children	−.16	−.19	−.12
FPAF Time II Indexes			
Role competence	−.08	−.08	−.18
Intellectual climate	.16	.07	.02
Democratic permissivenesss	.07	.14	−.13
Perseverance–altruism	−.01	−.21	.10
Response to infants	−.12	−.23	−.14
Response to toddlers	−.10	−.07	−.19*
Response to older children	−.20	.02	−.04

B. Time III Scores, with Time II Scores and Log of Time Partialed Out

	Partial Correlation with:		
Foster Parent Appraisal Form (FPAF) Indexes	Time III Verbal IQ ($N = 69$)	Time III Nonverbal IQ ($N = 69$)	Time III Total IQ ($N = 115$)
FPAF Time I Indexes			
Role competence	.11	.19	.16
Intellectual climate	.05	.09	.06
Democratic permissiveness	.18	.37**	.27**
Perseverance–altruism	−.07	.00	−.07
Response to infants	−.20	−.10	−.10
Response to toddlers	.04	−.04	.07
Response to older children	−.05	−.07	.04
FPAF Time II Indexes			
Role competence	.02	−.04	.01
Intellectual climate	.20	.09	.09
Democratic permissiveness	.09	.03	.13
Perseverance–altruism	.01	−.23	−.20*
Response to infants	−.18	−.17	−.17
Response to toddlers	−.11	−.18	−.11
Response to older children	−.19	−.25*	−.19*

TABLE 8.9. (Cont.)

C. Time III Scores, with Time I Scores and Log of Time Partialed Out

Partial Correlation with:

Foster Parent Appraisal Form (FPAF) Indexes	Time III Verbal IQ (N = 58)	Time III Nonverbal IQ (N = 58)	Time III Total IQ (N = 116)
FPAF Time I Indexes			
Role competence	.05	.26*	.12
Intellectual climate	.12	.20	.11
Democratic permissiveness	.16	.41**	.17
Perseverance–altruism	−.11	−.10	−.16
Response to infants	−.13	−.01	−.08
Response to toddlers	−.06	−.05	.10
Response to older children	−.16	−.23	.03
FPAF Time II Indexes			
Role competence	−.08	−.11	−.06
Intellectual climate	.16	.09	.10
Democratic permissiveness	.07	.12	.07
Perseverance–altruism	−.01	−.34**	−.26**
Response to infants	−.12	−.30*	−.22*
Response to toddlers	−.10	−.22	−.15
Response to older children	−.20	−.15	−.24**

*$p < .05$ **$p < .01$.

[a]This analysis is restricted to children whose experience in foster care was primarily in foster family homes.

parent assessment. For the nonverbal IQ, however, we do find one index that is associated with an enhancement in IQ, namely, democratic permissiveness (first assessment). The partial correlation (.25) suggests that children placed with more permissive foster parents tend to show more improvement in their nonverbal scores than those children placed with foster parents who are assessed as being strict disciplinarians. For the total IQ, we find only the variable assessing the response of foster parents to toddlers being significantly linked to IQ change. Children placed with foster parents who specifically sought out toddlers tended to show decline in total IQ on second testing ($r = −.19$).

In examining the Times II–III span, we note a repetition of our earlier finding, specifically, that none of the indexes is significantly linked to verbal IQ change. However, when we consider nonverbal IQ we again find that democratic permissiveness (first assessment) is significantly associated with IQ change ($r = .37$); it is also significantly linked to total IQ change ($r = .27$). One index is negatively linked to nonverbal and total IQ change, namely, response to older children.

Of interest is the fact that the index called perseverance–altruism (second assessment) is predictive of decline in IQ ($r = -.20$).

For the time span covering Times I–III, we confirm what has previously been learned; the qualities of foster parents secured from the two assessments do not show significant associations with verbal IQ change. However, four measures show statistically significant association with nonverbal IQ change. Democratic permissiveness shows a quite firm correlation ($r = .41$), and there is also a significant association between role competence and IQ change ($r = .26$). Of interest is the fact that perseverance–altruism again emerges as a negative indicator for nonverbal IQ change ($r = -.34$) and total IQ change ($r = -.26$). The tendency to have a strong age preference (either infants or older children) is linked to decline in nonverbal and total IQ.

Some comments are in order about these findings. First, the qualities of substitute caretakers as assessed by us do not seem to have significant influence on verbal IQ. This holds true even with respect to the index measuring the intellectual climate of the home. On the other hand, a permissive foster family environment is linked to cognitive growth as assessed by the performance (that is, nonverbal) components of the intelligence tests. This suggests that placement of children in a relaxed home environment can be conducive to cognitive growth. Such an atmosphere may be particularly salutary for children who have suffered traumatic experiences in homes rife with violence and severe intrafamilial discord.

One additional piece of analysis should be introduced at this point. We were interested in determining whether the infants in our study—who had entered foster care with relative parity when we analyzed their IQs by ethnicity (Puerto Rican, black, and white)—had changed over time to reflect the differentiation found among the older children when the latter had entered care. A multiple regression analysis of IQ change, in which the ethnic identification of the infants was entered into the analysis as a predictor variable after a string of demographic and foster parent assessment variables, failed to show a significant increment of explained variance attributable to ethnicity.[12] While black Protestant infants were about five points lower than the white infants at the final round of testing (Time III), the difference was not statistically significant. The failure to develop more pronounced differentiation causes us to wonder whether the experience in foster care has tended to provide more similar environments for cognitive growth than takes place for children living in the community at large.

Institutional Care

For analytic purposes, we identified 130 children who were residing in long-term institutional settings when psychological tests were administered at Time II.[13] In our effort to account for IQ change, we did not have available to us assessment instruments as elaborate as those used to describe foster parents. Instead, we relied on three agency study measures relevant to the institutional environments in which the children were placed: (a) a variable describing the experience of the institutional staff (years of employment in institutional work of the child-care counselor most actively involved with the child), (b) a single rating constituting an evaluation of the counselor by the child's caseworker (coded as *acceptable, valued,* or *highly valued*), and (c) a variable describing the school setting (indicating whether the child attends school on institutional grounds or in the community).

Table 8.10 shows the correlations between the three institutional measures and the deviation IQ's of the institutionalized children, partialing out three variables: (a) the child's earlier test scores (Times I or II), (b) the length of time the child spent in foster care, and (c) the child's age at the time of testing. Looking at IQ

[12] We do not provide tabular material here in the interest of saving space.
[13] Only 64 children were still residing in an institutional setting and tested during the final round (Time III) of psychological testing.

TABLE 8.10

CORRELATIONS BETWEEN INSTITUTIONAL CARE VARIABLES AND DEVIATION IQ, PARTIALING OUT EARLIER IQ SCORES, LOG OF TIME IN CARE, AND AGE OF CHILD[a]

A. Time II Scores, with Time I Scores, Log of Time, and Age Partialed Out

Partial Correlations with:

Index	Time II Verbal IQ (N = 122)	Time II Nonverbal IQ (N = 122)	Time II Total IQ (N = 130)
Institutional staff experience (low; HIGH)	.10	−.01	.13
Evaluation of institutional counselor (low; HIGH)	.09	−.19	−.03
School setting (institution; COMMUNITY)	−.05	−.09	−.12

B. Time III Scores, with Time II Scores, Log of Time, and Age Partialed Out

Partial Correlations with:

Index	Time III Verbal IQ (N = 64)	Time III Nonverbal IQ (N = 64)	Time III Total IQ (N = 64)
Institutional staff experience (low; HIGH)	−.36*	−.22	−.36*
Evaluation of institutional counselor (low; HIGH)	.02	−.17	−.10
School setting (institution; COMMUNITY)	−.12	−.21	−.21

C. Time III Scores, with Time I Scores, Log of Time, and Age Partialed Out

Partial Correlations with:

Index	Time III Verbal IQ (N = 64)	Time III Nonverbal IQ (N = 64)	Time III Total IQ (N = 64)
Institutional staff experience (low; HIGH)	−.29	−.24	−.37*
Evaluation of institutional counselor (low; HIGH)	.25	−.09	.07
School setting (institution; COMMUNITY)	−.03	−.42**	−.22

$*p < .05$ $**p < .01$

[a] Analysis is restricted to children whose experience in foster care was primarily in an institutional setting and who were tested at least twice.

change for the Times I–II span, we note that none of the institutional variables shows a significant partial correlation with the Time II score; this was true for verbal, nonverbal, and total IQ scores.

We find a different state of affairs when we examine the data in Table 8.10 for the Times II–III span. There is a statistically significant partial correlation linking the institutional staff experience of the counselor having major contact with the child and the Time III verbal IQ (partial $r = -.36$) and the total IQ (partial $r = -.36$). None of the other measures show statistically significant associations. It would appear that the inexperienced child care counselors to whom the subjects were exposed were a source of stimulation to them while seasoned counselors were less so; at least the association suggests this. It is our impression that contact with youthful persons who take on institutional employment on a time-limited basis has special value for foster children. They are often college-trained individuals who enter institutional work as a transitional career choice. They bring an intellectual freshness and liveliness that is intellectually stimulating to children.

When we examine the partial correlations covering Times I–III IQ change, we again observe a significant partial correlation (partial $r = -.37$) linking improvement in scores with care by inexperienced workers.

Table 8.10 also shows an association between a child's attending school on the institution's grounds—as opposed to attending a community-based school—and an improvement in IQ scores over a five-year span. The association is statistically significant for the nonverbal scores (partial $r = -.42$). We are not in a position to interpret this finding with any certainty. It suggests the possibility that attendance at school on institutional grounds is a more secure experience for the foster child and thereby possibly more conducive for cognitive growth.

Additional Analyses

We do not have space for details about our additional analyses related to IQ change. However, we briefly comment on findings related to artifacts of the test-taking situation that may have contributed "static and noise" in our analysis of IQ change in our subjects.

We have found evidence of an "examiner effect" in our data. Earlier analysis showed that children examined by one of our testers at Time I tended to show significantly lower mean IQ scores than those tested by the remaining two examiners. The phenomenon we were witnessing seemed to indicate either a tendency for lower achievement by the children of this examiner or enhancement in testing shown by the other children related to the quality of the interaction between the psychologists and the children.[14] The situation appeared to have particular impact on the black Protestant children. As we assessed changes in IQ scores over time, the gains achieved by these children when tested by different psychologists almost achieved statistical significance (when information about the identity of the examining psychologist was inserted into a multiple regression analysis of IQ change). We are thus concerned that an "examiner effect" be accounted for in studies of deprived children as one source of explained variance in outcomes of repeated testing.

There is evidence in our study of what might be called a "practice effect." It turned out that at Time I, while we were administering the WISC to older children in our sample, 99 of these subjects had been administered the same test by the agencies in whose care they were residing either before or after we had administered the test. These test scores were made available to us by the agencies. Examination of the performance of the children exposed to repeated testing at Time I showed a gain of almost five points in the later round of testing. Other investigators have reported similar findings.[15] However, analysis of our data at Time III showed that this practice effect was largely eliminated by the end of the five-year period.

We gathered a substantial amount of information covering the psychologists' impressions of the test-taking behavior of the subjects at each round of testing. Our analysis of these data reveals a significant differentiation among the children, by ethnicity, for a number of ratings. The findings point to the greater vulnerability of black children to emotional factors that interfere with their ability to perform satisfactorily in these standardized tests. They are reported

[14] We had received two inquiries from agencies about the failure of this psychologist to allow the children adequate "warm-up time" before testing.

[15] Anne Anastasi, *Psychological Testing*, 2nd ed. (New York: Macmillan, 1961), pp. 56–57.

to show greater lack of self-confidence, more shyness, and greater distractability than the other children. Despite their possible language handicap as bilingual children, the Puerto Rican subjects do not emerge as handicapped in the test-taking situation in this way.

One other piece of analysis should be briefly commented on here. We sought to determine whether a set of maternal care variables might contribute to an understanding of IQ change. We included information about the stability of care the child had received before placement (i.e., frequency of change in caretakers), the identification of the primary child caring person (i.e., whether the natural mother or not), the caseworker's evaluation of the mother, and the frequency of the mother's visiting. As a set, and as individual variables, this information contributed only trivially to an explanation of IQ change in the subjects for the three time-spans covered.[16]

SUMMARY COMMENTS

We have provided considerable information about what has happened to the cognitive abilities of a large sample of foster children as measured by standardized intelligence tests. Having examined the children at three points over a five-year period, and having extended our research to include youngsters who returned home as well as those remaining in care, we have sought to illuminate the influences at play which may account for IQ change. Among the variables we have been able to introduce into our analyses are: (a) demographic, (b) maternal care, (c) parent and foster parent assessments, and (d) the characteristics of institutions in which some of the children have been housed.

Our most important finding concerns the role of length of time in foster care as a predictor of IQ change. We have found that extended tenure in care is not associated with loss of IQ points for our sample taken as a whole. On the contrary, our evidence suggests that some benefits have accrued to the children remaining in care when their IQ scores are compared with those who have returned

---

[16] Our analysis focused on verbal, nonverbal, and total IQ change.

home. We do not necessarily see this as calling for plaudits for the foster care system, since we are mindful that these results may stem from the fact that discharged children are likely to have returned to homes that are problem-ridden and crisis-prone. In some ways, the foster care experience may came as a relief to some children, and their cognitive growth might well reflect this. Therefore, to present data indicating that children in care show some superiority over those who have returned home may not be an outcome that calls for complete reassurance. We may be comparing children who in either circumstance are living under less than optimal conditions for healthy growth.[17]

Our findings would indicate that extended tenure in care is associated with IQ gain according to ethnicity. White children actually tend to show a decline in IQ (particularly, verbal IQ) if they remain in care beyond two-and-one-half-years. Black children tend to show gains in IQ associated with tenure in care, over the full five years of the study; their gains are mainly in the nonverbal (performance) aspects of the tests. Puerto Rican children show gains associated with being in care, but this is largely a phenomenon associated with the first two-and-one-half-years of the period covered by the study.

We have provided some evidence in this chapter that characteristics of caretakers are linked to IQ gain; this, again, is particularly manifested with respect to performance rather than verbal subtests. Democratic permissiveness of foster parents has been linked to IQ gain of foster children. We have also demonstrated that children cared for by inexperienced counselors in institutions tend to show greater gains than those cared for by seasoned staff.

[17] In studying the families of these children, Jenkins and Norman found that financially the situations of the mothers appear to have somewhat worsened over the five years of the study. See Shirley Jenkins and Elaine Norman, *Beyond Placement: Mothers View Foster Care* (New York: Columbia University Press, 1975), p. 20.

NINE

THE
STUDY CHILD
IN SCHOOL

A major part of the life of any child over age five years is spent in attending school. Within the context of the educational system, each child is expected to progress at a pace defined by a norm that allows little accommodation for such roadblocks as a chronic illness, an emotionally disturbing home life, language handicap, or other such factors that can have a deleterious effect on the ability to learn. The expected level of performance and progress of a child in school presumes good health and a supportive home environment that minimizes both the physical and emotional impediments to learning, if not also an environment that aids learning by reinforcement and motivation.

Given the demands of the school situation, one might wonder how children fare when their home lives have been disrupted by placement in long-term foster care. Having experienced the turmoil of a problematic family situation that has culminated in separation, foster children can reasonably be seen as being vulnerable to impaired performance in school. They obviously carry burdens that do not afflict their classmates who have been reared in their own homes.

One can regard the relationships of foster children to their school situations from another perspective, however. It is conceivable that foster care offers some children respite from the anxieties of troubled and unpredictable environments, with concomitant improvement in school performance. Many of the children in our study came from homes that had known violence, disorganization, and malignant interpersonal relationships. For them, a secure foster home or stable institutional placement might constitute relief from intolerable living circumstances. The freeing of the child's cognitive resources might well be the fruit of the cessation of anxiety.

The issue of whether experience in foster care is detrimental to the school performance of children attracted our attention early in our research planning. Our review of the literature showed very little research data on the school performance of foster children, which was somewhat surprising since the foster care system is given the task of attending to the child's educational needs. One of the important barometers of how well the substitute living arrangement of a given child is working out is provided by the picture of his overall school adjustment.

Our longitudinal study of foster children offered an opportunity to include as part of its research an investigation of the foster child's performance in school. The principal objectives were to determine:

1. The level of school performance of children entering foster care.

2. The trend in performance over time (e.g., after five years of foster care, whether exposure to foster care generally has a beneficial or detrimental effect on the foster child's school performance).

3. How foster children remaining in care for five years compare in school performance with children in care for shorter periods.

4. Other variables predictive of the school performance of foster children.

METHODOLOGY
FOR STUDYING SCHOOL PERFORMANCE

The school performance of the subjects was appraised on three occasions over the five-year span of the study. A school report questionnaire was constructed for the purpose of gathering relevant data. The first round of school data collection took place during the academic year following entry into foster care; data were also collected during alternate years that followed. The initial record of school performance was collected during the fall 1966 and spring 1967 semesters and constituted the baseline for interpreting the child's level of school achievement at the point of entering foster care. The collection of Time I school data came somewhat later than the first round of psychological testing of the children; earlier collection of data was not possible because teachers had not had sufficient time to adequately know the child and his level of performance. The second survey was conducted during the spring of 1969 and the third (final) assessment of school performance, during the spring semester of 1971, some five years after the children's entry into foster care.

The principal reporter of the current school performance of the children was the teacher of each child. Teachers also provided information about the child's past school history (i.e., past grades) although in a substantial number of cases this information was completed by a school clerk.

The school report consisted of five major sections covering:

1. Characteristics of the child's current school enrollment— number of schools attended, type of school, attendance (full or part time), whether the child was in regular or special classes, and special educational needs not being met.
2. Child's school performance—number of classes ahead or behind grade for age, grade level for all individual subjects taught, quality of school work, grades given in all subjects, and class year.
3. Factors affecting child's school performance—impact of specific problems influencing school performance, whether treatment had been required at school guidance clinic, and frequency of attendance in classes.
4. Child's attitude toward school—child's general attitude and aspects of school which child liked best and least.
5. Child's relationships in school—with teacher and classmates.

INDEX OF ACHIEVEMENT

We focused on achievement as the major variable of interest. It was initially operationalized as a measure in two forms. The decision to have alternative measures stemmed from our concern with the "softness" in the situation inherent in the fact that we depended on teacher's reports for data in this area rather than administering achievement tests directly to the children.[1] One index was

[1] Although we had opportunity to administer achievement tests as part of our psychological testing program, we concluded that extending the testing session from two hours to three or four hours was not feasible, given the limited tolerance of many of our subjects.

developed from teacher's descriptions of the performance of the children for 11 basic subjects taught in class. It was our view that developing a summary measure on the basis of all subjects would likely lead to a more valid indication of the child's achievement level in school than would be the case if we focused on single subjects. The basis for computing this index was the number of years the child was advanced, within normal range, or behind the age-appropriate norm for each school subject. The teacher's rating of the child's status was based on his actual performance on a standarized achievement test or on the teacher's reported judgment. In the majority of cases, teachers indicated that the basis of their reports was the child's performance on tests administered by the school.

We constructed a second index using the letter–numerical report-card grades given for each class subject. A grade-point average was computed as a summary measure of performance. Analysis, however, revealed this index to provide less precision in distinguishing between subgroups of the study children when compared with the overall achievement-level index. Since the distribution of grades was skewed in the direction of more satisfactory levels of performance, we felt that the report cards may have been used to serve a purpose other than reflection of actual performance and therefore decided not to use this index.

For the achievement index used, the subjects taught in the classroom were classified for research purposes as either "basic" subjects reflecting the fundamental "three R's," science, and social studies, or "secondary" subjects, such as health education, art, and music. It was hypothesized and later confirmed that many children did not perform in a consistent manner across subjects.

Schools differed with respect to the variety of subjects they offered. The 11 subjects previously referred to were taken collectively by the majority of the study children; therefore, the index score was based on only these 11 subjects. Initially, the 11 subjects were arbitrarily classified into the categories cited, namely, *basic* or *secondary*. However, after data were collected, the classification was tested empirically by intercorrelations of grades and achievement levels for these subjects.[2] Only one reassignment of a subject

[2] The level of achievement for each of the eleven subjects was intercorrelated with every other subject. The intercorrelations among the basic subjects were found to be higher within

was necessary; one secondary subject actually correlated highly with other basic subjects and less with secondary subjects. Based on this criterion, social studies (including history and geography) were switched from inclusion among the secondary subjects to those classified as basic.[3]

After we analyzed our data using the three different combinations of subjects—basic, secondary, and all subjects combined—we discovered that the correlation between the achievement level for the basic subjects and all 11 subjects was high. The effect of including the secondary subjects was merely to always increase the achievement-level index score of each child by a few points. We therefore decided that rather than burden the reader with a replication of all tables for the three different combinations, we would describe results only from the perspective of all 11 subjects combined, with the result that our figures would slightly overrate the level of performance in the basic subjects.

In order to combine the 11 subjects into a summary measure, a number of different procedures were tested as ways of assigning a value indicative of a child's performance. Despite the efforts expended, the end result of the various methods of developing composite measures was the decision to use: (a) simple mean scores of the sums of items (i.e., years advanced or behind in each subject), without assigning weights to the items, and (b) an age-adjusted relative achievement score. A brief description of the index construction methods chosen, as well as those discarded, is offered for those readers interested in the methodological issues involved; others might wish to proceed to the discussion on the groups of children studied (p. 235).

Mean Achievement Level Score (Eleven Subject Index)

One method initially used for constructing an index of school achievement from the data available was an average score which assigned greater weight to performance in basic subjects. The fol-

---

these subjects than between any of the basic and secondary subjects. Likewise, the intercorrelations among the secondary subjects were found to be higher than those prevailing between the basic and secondary subjects.

[3] The classification scheme and labels do not reflect performance measures used by the school system; the scheme was established only for our own research purposes.

lowing formula was used:

$$\text{Mean AL} = \frac{\sum_{i=1}^{n} W_b AL_b + \sum_{i=1}^{n} W_s AL_s}{n_b + n_s}$$

where:

AL = achievement level = (actual grade minus normal grade + 10) multiplied by 10. Normal age-appropriate grade-level score = 100^4;
b = basic subjects;
s = secondary subjects;
W = weighting factor;
n_b = number of basic subjects;
n_s = number of secondary subjects

The ratings by the child's teacher as to the number of years advanced or behind in each subject were weighted by the type of subject, and an overall average of the weighted scores was computed. The appropriate weight to use was approached empirically. Experimentation with all variations was tried, from a weighted procedure whereby basic and secondary subjects were given equal weight to one in which basic subjects were given double weight. The results made it apparent that despite the variation in weights, the total AL scores were almost perfectly correlated with the simple average.[5] Furthermore, the different weighted and simple average index scores were correlated with several key independent variables in similar fashion. Correlation coefficients never varied by more than .02 between the extremes of the weighted scores. Similar results were obtained when the same weighting and testing process was applied to the child's grade-point averages. Given this experience in testing alternative approaches to compositing indexes, we felt justified in using the simple arithmetic mean of the 11 subjects (in terms of years ahead or behind in each subject) as our major measure of school achievement.

[4] The index is referred to as the *mean achievement level index* because it is an average of 11 subjects taken by most of the children. In those cases where less than the 11 subjects were taken or reports by teachers were not given for all subjects, the missing information was plugged in with the mean of the available subjects.

[5] The product moment correlation between the simple average and each of the various weighted scores was .99.

Age-adjusted Achievement-level Index Score

It was necessary to take into account the fact that as the child's age increases, it is possible for him to be increasingly further behind in school. In other words, it is possible for a six-year-old first-grader to be one year behind his peers, while a 16-year-old tenth grader can be 10 years behind. A group's average achievement level based on number of years behind or advanced is thus directly influenced by the number of children at various age levels in the group. It is obvious that two groups of children not precisely matched by age could not be compared without some form of age standardization.

Compounding this problem was also a substantive age factor. Since other measures of school performance and problems in school were found to be correlated with age, it was desirable to eliminate the age effects in order to explicate the true relationship between performance and problems. Our experience showed that the severity and range of problems children could show increase with age; more simply stated, older children have greater opportunity to get into difficulty. As we moved from one data-gathering occasion to the next, it was important to take into account whether increased difficulty in school simply reflected the broader repertoire of difficulties older children can experience, or was related to other substantive concerns, such as length of tenure in foster care.

Three methods of eliminating the spurious age influences were considered: (a) age-specific standard scores, (b) regression residuals, and (c) relative scores. We selected the method of relative scores.

The method of age-specific standard scores involved computing each child's achievement level as a measure of his deviation from the mean achievement level (AL) score for his own age group based on the standard deviation for all AL scores among his age peers. However, the small numbers of children of some specific age groups posed problems for computing a stable standard deviation base.

The method of regression residuals was also examined, as it would preserve the fluctuation of age groups as well as eliminate the overall trend of spurious age effects. Residual scores to be used as an index of the child's achievement were derived from a multiple regression equation in which age and data time lapse were the independent variables with the raw simple AL score used as the dependent variable.[6] The effectiveness of the regression technique was tested using analysis of variance. The ratio of variance between age groups to the variance within age groups (*F*-test) was decreased substantially.[7] The fact that a decrease in *F* ratio occurred because of the decrease in variation between the age groups confirms the fact that the undesired variation due to age effects was reduced.

We selected the relative score primarily because of its ease of computation and because its interpretation and meaning might be more easily comprehended by a general audience. The relative score is computed by taking the child's achievement level as a percentage of the expected (normal) age-appropriate grade level. Age effects are thus neutralized by transformation of the achievement level index into a relative proportion reflecting the degree to which a child is advanced or behind his age-appropriate grade level for all subjects combined rather than by the absolute count of the number of years advanced or behind. For example, a 10-year-old child performing at the third rather than fourth-grade level would have a relative score of 75.0—the same as for a 14-year-old child performing at the sixth- rather than the eighth-grade level. Both children's score would be 75.0 even though the 10-year-old was only one year behind and the 14-year-old was two years behind. In the special instance where a child began school a year later than his contemporaries, this was treated as being a year behind in school.

To recapitulate, we made the decision to use two measures of school performance, both of which would be based upon the teacher's assessment of the child's achievement in 11 subjects. One measure (achievement level score) summarizes a child's achieve-

6 "Time lapse" refers to the amount of time between the date the child entered foster care and the date the school data were recorded. The variable was included because of our concern over a delay of several months for some children in obtaining school reports in the initial school year following entrance into foster care. The time lapse could have had the effect of enhancing school performance if foster care was beneficial or hindering performance if foster care was detrimental for children whose school reports were received late in the school year.

7 For example, at Time I, the *F* ratio for the raw score achievement level in basic subjects was 2.43 (df 7/127) for the group assessed (1967), as compared to .77 (df 7/127) for the scores after standardization by regression analysis. The same pattern prevailed for the analysis of secondary subjects and for all subjects combined. Since the decrease in the *F* ratio occurred because of the decrease in variation between the age groups, it confirms that the undesired variation due to age effects was reduced.

ment in absolute terms whereas a second (relative score) is the same summary measure corrected to take into account the age factor.

CHILDREN STUDIED ON THREE OCCASIONS

In keeping with our longitudinal design, we placed special emphasis on the analysis of change in achievement scores for those subjects assessed on a repeated basis. The reader should remember that children added to the study of school performance had recently entered school and had not been included earlier because they were too young to attend. We thus wound up with cross-sectional groups reflecting the three data-gathering occasions. The groups contained some overlap of subjects who could be studied for changes occurring over time.

Variability in group membership was introduced over time by both the addition (as cited above) and the loss of subjects at Times II and III. We could not locate certain children discharged from care and also experienced lack of cooperation by certain schools or teachers who refused to provide the requested information.[8] It is our judgment, however, that despite the problems and obstacles we encountered in data collection, the returns have provided useful data that allow us to analyze trends in school performance over time with emphasis on the factors related to the foster care experience.

At the time of the initial study in 1967, 256 children in our sample were of school age. We received school reports concerning 157 children (61 percent). By 1969 there were 372 study children of school age, and school report forms were received for 267 of them (72 percent). The third and final survey took place in 1971; 223 out of 477 study children of school age (47 percent) were covered by returned forms. In this Time III phase, questionnaires were returned for 140 (85 percent) of the children remaining in foster care and for 83 (27 percent) of the discharged children.

---

[8] During the 1971 survey there was substantial public concern over protecting the rights of privacy of pupils. It became necessary to develop a special form to send to parents for their signatures which could then be sent to the schools with the school report form.

Characteristics of the Subjects

The demographic characteristics of children included in the school survey at Times I–III are displayed in Table 9.1. The groups have almost equal proportions of boys and girls. The mean age of the children at each data-gathering occasion is 9.5, 9.9, and 10.2 years, respectively (Times I–III). Puerto Rican children were over-represented and black children underrepresented at Time I. At each time, black and Puerto Rican children made up a large majority of the subjects (about 75 percent at Times I and III, and 66 percent at Time II).

Of concern in any survey with less than 100 percent participation is the possibility that the nonrespondents reflect a process of self-selection, which can bias the findings. In Table 9.1 there does not appear to be a marked deviation between the nonresponse group and the children assessed, with respect to age, sex, and ethnicity. The major source of disparity when we examined other variables with respect to participants and nonparticipants was the fact that the discharged children were markedly underrepresented. It was easier to obtain school reports for children still in care since their social workers were available to facilitate this matter; this was particularly true if the child went to a school on an agency's institutional grounds.

Selected family characteristics of the subjects for Times I–III are shown in Table 9.2. The distribution of children according to the socioeconomic status of the household in which they resided for the majority of the six-month period prior to entering foster care reflects the same pattern on each of the data-gathering occasions as prevailed for the full sample of 624 subjects. The majority of children on each occasion came from families where the main source of income was public assistance. A high proportion of the children (37–43 percent) were born out of wedlock. One out of four children of each cross-sectional group entered foster care by order of the Family Court, reflecting a neglect or abuse situation.

The distribution of children in each group (Times I–III) by grade in school is shown in Table 9.3. Since children selected for inclusion in the study were under age 13 years at the time of entry into foster care, the progression depicted in the table reflects the increase in age over the five years of longitudinal investigation.

TABLE 9.1

CHARACTERISTICS OF STUDY CHILDREN IN SCHOOL ASSESSMENT STUDY AND
COMPARISON TO NONPARTICIPANT CHILDREN

	Time I		Time II		Time III	
Characteristics	Study Children	Non-participants	Study Children	Non-participants	Study Children	Non-participants
			(percentages)			
Sex						
Male	52	48	49	50	50	51
Female	48	52	51	50	50	49
Age at time of assessment						
Under 6 yr.						
6–7	20	34	22	28	23	23
8–9	29	30	22	14	23	15
10–11	29	21	23	20	19	12
12–13	20	15	18	22	17	18
14–15	—	—	13	15	12	17
16–17	—	—	(a)	—	6	14
18–19	—	—	—	—	—	(a)
Ethnicity						
White	22	32	28	21	21	28
Black	49	38	33	41	40	37
Puerto Rican	49	30	39	38	39	35
No. of cases	157	122	267	105	223	254

a Less than 1 percent.

TABLE 9.2
SELECTED FAMILY CHARACTERISTICS
OF SCHOOL STUDY CHILDREN

Selected Characteristics	Time I	Time II	Time III
	(percentages)		
Socioeconomic status			
Lower	32.5	32.2	30.0
Middle	29.9	29.9	36.0
Higher	37.6	37.9	34.0
Public assistance status			
Mother on public assistance	30.6	34.9	38.6
Household, not mother	24.8	20.2	20.6
None	44.6	44.9	40.8
Birth status			
In wedlock	61.8	61.0	55.2
Out of wedlock	36.9	37.5	42.6
Unknown	1.3	1.5	2.2
Jurisdiction			
Bureau of Child Welfare	73.9	74.2	75.8
Family Court	26.1	25.8	24.2
No. of cases	157	267	223

Noteworthy are the variations within each grade, which support the need for use of age-adjusted achievement scores in order to make both inter- and intra-group comparisons.

The school status of the study children at the time of each survey is shown in Table 9.4. A higher proportion of children were attending public school as opposed to parochial school in the final year of the study. By 1971, many of the children were either in their own homes or had been transferred to foster family homes and were attending neighborhood schools. By this time, 87 percent of the children were attending community-based schools rather than institutional schools. At Time I, as reflected in Table 9.4, a high proportion of the children were in institutional placements; many were in congregate shelter care. They mainly attended special schools within the institutions, usually under public auspices. Five years later, few children were attending special schools or special classes.

TABLE 9.3
GRADE IN SCHOOL AT TIME OF STUDY

Grade in School	Time I Number	Time I Percent	Time II Number	Time II Percent	Time III Number	Time III Percent
1st	20	12.7	63	23.6	13	5.8
2nd	23	14.6	32	12.0	31	13.9
3rd	30	19.2	45	16.9	31	13.9
4th	16	10.2	23	8.6	25	11.2
5th	20	12.7	14	5.2	20	9.0
6th	20	12.7	20	7.5	19	8.5
7th	18	11.5	21	8.1	14	6.3
8th	5	3.2	30	11.2	13	5.8
9th	—	—	6	2.3	16	7.2
10th	—	—	2	.7	13	5.8
11th	—	—	—	—	6	2.7
12th	—	—	—	—	4	1.8
Ungraded[a]	5	3.2	9	3.4	16	7.2
Not reported	—	—	1	.4	2	.9
Total	157	100.0	266	100.0	223	100.0
Mean grade	3.99		3.93		5.23	

[a] Ungraded classes for exceptional children.

SCHOOL PERFORMANCE

Analysis of the overall achievement (11-subject achievement index) in school following entry into foster care and the ensuing five years revealed that at each assessment occasion (Times I, II, and III), the majority of children were performing at a level below the normal for their age (see Table 9.5). At Time I, reflecting the situation shortly after the arrival of the children in care, 59 percent were functioning below their age-appropriate grade level, including 11 percent whose overall functioning was three to five years below normal. At Time II, 55 percent of the children were below their age-appropriate grade achievement level, including 13 percent who were three to seven years behind. At Time III, 52 percent of the children were performing

TABLE 9.4
CHARACTERISTICS OF SCHOOLS ATTENDED
BY STUDY CHILDREN

Characteristics of School	Time I	Time II	Time III
	(percentages)		
Auspices of school			
Public	77.6	83.5	91.5
Parochial	22.4	16.5	8.5
Type of school			
Regular	17.2	63.5	83.4
Special	82.8	36.5	16.6
Location of school			
Community	22.7	80.1	87.4
Institution	77.3	19.9	12.6
Type classes			
Regular	31.2	59.9	81.6
Special class	7.6	13.1	10.3
Special classes (all)	61.2	27.0	8.1
No. of cases	156	267	223

below their age-appropriate achievement level, with 11 percent standing out as two to seven years behind.

The evidence we present, that many of the children in foster care (and those returned home) are behind their appropriate levels of achievement, should evoke concern. Coming from most deprived circumstances and with a heavy minority representation, these children seem destined to follow their parents on a path of failure in important life functions.

Yet the phenomenon of school failure is obviously not unique to foster children. These figures depict a situation that coincides with the findings of other studies of school performance that show urban children from minority groups and white children from deprived families to perform at a level below normal for their age. For example, the National Health Survey of the National Center for Health Statistics conducted a nationwide study of school achievement of children aged six to 11 years during July 1963 to

TABLE 9.5
DISTRIBUTION OF STUDY CHILDREN BY NUMBER OF YEARS ADVANCED
OR BEHIND AGE-APPROPRIATE OVERALL ACHIEVEMENT LEVEL[a]

Years Advanced or Behind	Time I		Time II		Time III	
	Number	Percent	Number	Percent	Number	Percent
2–3 years advanced	1	0.7	—	—	—	—
1–2 years advanced	1	0.7	3	1.2	2	1.0
0–1 year advanced	1	0.7	2	0.8	2	1.0
Normal	54	38.8	110	43.0	94	46.0
0–1 year behind	34	24.5	67	26.1	47	22.9
1–2 years behind	33	23.7	40	15.5	37	18.1
2–3 years behind	9	6.5	23	9.0	7	3.5
3–4 years behind	3	2.2	5	2.0	9	4.5
4–5 years behind	3	2.2	4	1.6	5	2.5
5–6 years behind	—	—	1	0.4	—	—
6–7 years behind	—	—	1	0.4	1	0.5
Total	139	100.0	250	100.0	205	100.0

[a] Years advanced or behind was calculated from school teacher reports based on standard achievement tests wherever possible or by teacher estimates by averaging the number of years advanced or behind in each of up to 11 school subjects.

December 1965—a period just prior to the initiation of our longitudinal study. The findings from this source indicated that on both reading and arithmetic scores on the Wide Range Achievement Test, black children scored significantly lower than white children of a given age and their scores fluctuated considerably more from one year of age to another.[9] Black children were found to be only slightly below whites on reading scores at age six, but the differences increased at each age-year through age 11 to a difference of 2.1 grade levels. The same pattern prevailed with respect to arithmetic except that the difference at age 11 was 1.5 grade levels. The Health Survey further concluded that school achievement scores were more strongly associated with the socioeconomic status of the children's families than with race. The Health Survey inves-

[9] Health Service and Mental Health Administration, P.H.S., U.S. Dept. of Health, Education, and Welfare, *School Achievement of Children by Demographic and Socioeconomic Factors, United States* (November, 1971), p. 6.

tigators compared their findings with those reported by Coleman. Having transformed their own and Coleman's data into standard score units that would permit direct comparisons of data between the two studies, they concluded that the findings in both studies regarding school achievement levels of black and white children were remarkably similar.[10]

Variation by Subjects
The proportion of children performing below their age-appropriate achievement level varied according to each of the 11 subjects included in the overall index. At the time of entering foster care, a higher proportion of children were behind in the three basic "R's": (a) reading (70 percent behind), (b) arithmetic (62 percent behind), and (c) written expression (61 percent behind). In other basic subjects such as oral expression, spelling, social studies, and science, about 40 percent of the children were behind one year or more (see Table 9.6). It was only in the secondary subjects such as health education, music, and art that the majority of children came within the normal achievement level for their age. At most, only 12 percent of the children functioned below normal for their age in these subjects.

The actual number of years behind for the three "R's" for all three assessment occasions is shown in Table 9.7. Clearly evident from the data is the proportion of children, regardless of data-gathering occasion (i.e., Times I, II, or III), who were behind in their age-appropriate achievement levels. About 33 percent of the children were more than two years behind in their reading ability on all three occasions. The proportion of children functioning at a normal or advanced reading performance level was 30–39 percent. With respect to written expression the proportion of normally functioning children was 39–49 percent, and for arithmetic, 38–47 percent. Some modest improvement in performance in all three subjects was shown over the five-year period. Whether this was related to the better performance of children for whom we had repeated assessments or changes in the composition of the groups being assessed is discussed in chapter 10.

[10]Ibid., p. 27.

TABLE 9.6
PROPORTION OF TIME I STUDY CHILDREN ADVANCED OR BEHIND
AGE-APPROPRIATE ACHIEVEMENT LEVEL, BY SPECIFIC SUBJECTS

Subject	Level of School Performance: Time I			Total Number
	Behind	Normal	Advanced	
	(percentaged across)			
Language Arts				
Reading	70.4	20.7	8.9	135
Oral expression	39.5	56.6	3.9	129
Written expression	61.2	36.4	2.4	129
Spelling	46.8	46.0	7.2	126
Handwriting	33.9	64.6	1.5	130
Social studies	40.4	56.7	33.9	104
Arithmetic	61.8	35.1	3.1	131
Science	39.1	59.1	1.8	110
Health education	12.2	86.9	1.9	107
Music	9.1	90.9	—	110
Art	10.6	86.7	3.7	113
Overall	59.0	38.9	2.1	157

The findings we have reported here should be viewed in the light of information revealed by a New York citywide test of reading skills conducted in 1971 by the Board of Education, which showed that two-thirds of pupils in the second through ninth grades were below their appropriate grades in reading.[11] This figure is close to those in our study.

CORRELATES OF ACHIEVEMENT LEVEL

One of the basic objectives in our research was to determine which characteristics of the child, family, and foster care situation are associated with overall school achievement. Two approaches were used to gain some understanding about the variation in achievement

[11] See Leonard Buder, "Scribner Asks for Improved Instruction in Reading," *New York Times* (February 20, 1972).

TABLE 9.7
DISTRIBUTION OF STUDY CHILDREN BY NUMBER OF YEARS ADVANCED
OR BEHIND AGE-APPROPRIATE GRADE LEVEL IN READING, WRITTEN
EXPRESSION, AND ARITHMETIC

Number of Years Advanced or Behind	Reading			Written expression			Arithmetic		
	Time			Time			Time		
	I	*II*	*III*	*I*	*II*	*III*	*I*	*II*	*III*
				(percentages)					
2–3 years advanced	5.2	2.8	2.0	1.6	1.4	—	—	0.4	1.0
1–2 years advanced	3.0	4.0	1.5	0.8	1.4	1.1	0.8	1.7	1.6
0–1 year advanced	0.7	1.2	2.9	—	0.5	2.8	2.3	0.4	1.6
Normal	20.7	30.0	31.6	36.4	41.9	44.7	35.1	41.5	42.8
0–1 year behind	6.7	10.8	24.3	1.6	6.5	21.2	3.8	6.8	25.8
1–2 years behind	29.6	21.6	21.4	23.3	20.3	19.6	27.5	23.3	17.0
2–3 years behind	20.0	13.6	7.8	24.0	12.0	5.6	19.9	12.3	4.6
3–4 years behind	8.9	9.2	4.9	7.8	11.5	2.2	8.4	11.4	3.1
4–5 years behind	3.7	4.4	1.9	2.3	3.7	2.2	0.8	1.3	2.1
5–6 years behind	0.7	0.4	1.5	1.6	0.9	—	—	0.9	—
6–7 years behind	—	0.4	—	—	—	—	1.5	—	—
7+ years behind	0.7	0.4	0.5	0.8	—	0.6	—	—	0.5
No. of cases	135	250	206	129	217	172	131	236	194

in school: (a) comparison of subgroup achieved scores (correlated with sex, ethnicity, etc.) and (b) regression analyses to ascertain which factors are most predictive of school achievement in terms of their contributions to explain variance in the overall performance measure.

School Achievement by Sex of Child

On all three assessment occasions, the female subjects showed somewhat higher mean overall achievement index scores (11-subject index), although the differences were not statistically significant. We observe in Table 9.8 that both boys and girls showed substantially higher index scores on the third assessment occasion than previously. On the whole, while the performance of the girls was consistently superior, the differences were fairly small. The findings

TABLE 9.8
MEAN AGE-ADJUSTED SCHOOL ACHIEVEMENT INDEX SCORE OF
STUDY CHILDREN, BY SEX

	Mean Age-adjusted School Achievement[a]					
	Time I[b]		Time II[b]		Time III[b]	
Sex	Mean	S.D.	Mean	S.D.	Mean	S.D.
Male (67/122/105)[c]	76.6	27.1	78.0	28.6	87.9	25.6
Female (70/130/106)	81.8	36.7	80.1	31.2	91.4	15.4
Total (137/251/211)	79.2	32.4	79.1	30.0	89.7	21.2

[a] Child's age-adjusted score is the complement of the relative proportion advanced or behind normal age-appropriate grade level (100.0), e.g., 75.0 = school achievement 25 percent below age-appropriate grade level, regardless of age.
[b] The results are not statistically significant, by the t-test.
[c] Data in parentheses give the number of children included at Times I, II, and III.

we report with respect to sex differences correspond to the information provided in the National Health Survey of school achievement. This nationwide study indicated that "girls consistently scored higher than boys on the average among both Negro and white children."[12]

School Achievement by Child's Ethnicity

Puerto Rican children performed somewhat lower than black children at Time I, and both of these groups showed overall index scores that portrayed their functioning as substantially below that of the white children. The mean scores were 72.6 for the Puerto Rican, 79.0 for the black, and 94.2 for the white children. This difference was statistically significant when tested by the one-way analysis of variance ($p = .008$). At Time II the disparities between the minority children and the white children were essentially the same, and we again found a statistically significant difference ($p = .005$). At Time III all children showed higher mean scores than at Time II. For the

[12] *School Achievement of Children by Demographic and Socioeconomic Factors*, p. 6.

minority children, the higher overall achievement scores were quite noteworthy, with increments of 11 points for the black children and 17 points for the Puerto Rican children. On the other hand, the white children had a mean that was only three points higher than the previous assessment occasion. We of course do not imply here that the children necessarily showed gains in scores, because of the different composition of the assessment groups on the three occasions (see chapter 10). We believe it noteworthy, however, that the difference in the mean index scores between the three groups at Time III was not statistically significant (Table 9.9).

School Achievement Level by Age
One of the difficulties inherent in using age as the base for establishing a norm of school performance is that not all children start school at the same age. However, according to the findings in the

TABLE 9.9
MEAN AGE-ADJUSTED SCHOOL ACHIEVEMENT INDEX SCORE
OF STUDY CHILDREN, BY ETHNICITY

	Mean Age-adjusted School Achievement[a]					
	Time I		*Time II*		*Time III*	
Ethnicity	*Mean*	*SD*	*Mean*	*SD*	*Mean*	*SD*
White (32/72/42)[b]	94.2	27.4	88.7	24.9	91.3	19.1
Black (34/81/86)	79.0	23.2	75.5	31.9	86.1	22.6
Puerto Rican (71/99/83)	72.6	35.9	75.0	30.1	92.5	22.1
Total (137/252/211)	79.2	32.4	79.1	30.0	89.7	21.2
Significance[c]	.008		.005		NS	

[a] Child's age-adjusted score is the complement of the relative proportion advanced or behind normal age-appropriate grade level (100.0), e.g., 75.0 = school achievement 25 percent below age-appropriate grade level, regardless of age.
[b] Data in parentheses give the number of children tested at Times I, II, and III.
[c] One-way analysis of variance.

National Health Survey regarding behavioral patterns of youth, 75 percent of the children studied began school in the first grade level when they were six years old,[13] and 20 percent of the children in the nationwide survey began school at five years of age. Given these proportions, it would seem acceptable from an operational stance to consider the age-appropriate grade for a first grade child at six years, a second grade child at seven years, and so on.

At the time the study children entered foster care, a substantial proportion were actually attending classes in a grade lower than their age-appropriate level (see Table 9.10). Moreover, the proportion of children attending a lower grade was substantially higher than the national average (five percent) starting school one year late (at age seven). In the absence of other explanations, we wonder whether the assignment of the children to grades below those expected for their age reflects a condition of impaired performance. By age nine years, our study children were already spread over a range of four different grades. The 10-year-olds were spread over six different grades, including one child still in the first grade and two children advanced into the sixth and seventh grades. In the main, the direction of spread is toward the grade levels below the age-appropriate grades. The spread of the study children of a given age over several grades is not atypical of other children throughout the United States. According to the National Health Survey of school achievement, children of any age between six and nine years are generally spread over four grades, children 10 years of age spread over five grades, and children 11 years of age spread over six grades (second through seventh grades).[14]

The overall non-age-adjusted mean school-achievement-level scores as shown in Table 9.10 can be used to interpret the extent to which children below or above their age-appropriate achievement level are functioning at a level commensurate with their assigned classroom grade. To clarify for the reader, we reiterate that the overall achievement level index (including all 11 subjects) is such that a score of 90 represents functioning at a level commensurate

[13] Health Resources Administration, National Center for Health Statistics, U.S. Dept. of Health, Education, and Welfare, *Parents Ratings of Behavior Patterns of Youths 12–17 Years: United States* (Vital and Health Statistics Series 11, No. 137, May 1974), p. 20.
[14] National Health Survey of School Achievement, pp. 80–81.

TABLE 9.10
MEAN SCHOOL ACHIEVEMENT INDEX SCORES[a] OF STUDY CHILDREN AT TIME I, BY AGE AND GRADE IN SCHOOL

Age (Years)	Grade in School									No. of Cases
	1st	2nd	3rd	4th	5th	6th	7th	8th	9th	
6	94.8[b]	100.0[c]								10
7	99.9	95.5								18
8		89.7	94.5							18
9		73.3	89.2	95.7						21
10	84.0[c]		87.0[c]	89.4	96.0					19
11				76.5[c]	96.6	108.0[c]	123.0[c]			18
12					90.2	90.7	90.6	93.0[c]		21
13					90.5[c]	83.7	85.4	93.3[c]		10
14					80.0[c]	70.0[c]		84.0[c]		1
No. of cases	17	21	24	14	18	20	17	5	0	136

[a] Key to index: age-appropriate grade level performance = 100.0; each deviation of 10 points = 1 grade level above or below normal.
[b] Italics represent appropriate grade for age.
[c] Mean for age and grade group are subject to instability: mean computed on less than five children.

with one grade below the age-appropriate level, a score of 80 is two grades below, a score of 110 is one grade level above, and so on. Given this index, one can see from the mean achievement level scores in Table 9.10 that most younger children in a grade below their age-appropriate classroom level were functioning fairly close to the norm for the grade in which they were placed. However, the older children (aged nine and above) were generally performing below par even for the lower grades in which they were placed. For example, nine-year-olds in the second grade should, on the average, have shown an achievement level score of 80.0 but in actuality had a score of 73.3, reflecting performance almost another full grade behind. The 12-and 13-year-old children who were placed one year behind their age-appropriate classroom level also showed mean achievement levels below par for the grade in which they were placed—83.7 and 85.4, respectively, compared to 90.0 as the expected level. This performance lag was not present five years later when the children were assessed at Time III (see Table 9.11).

Our interpretation of the mean scores achieved by the children in the age-appropriate class grades is that the younger children came closer to performing at a level one would expect for them. Their mean scores were close to the norm (100.0). We did find that children aged nine through 12 achieved at a noticeably lower level of performance, while the 13- and 14-year-olds showed an enhanced level of functioning. Looking at 15- to 17-year-old children, we again saw a drop in achievement levels. We cannot interpret here the nonlinearity of the trend but examine, in chapter 11, the variable of age in reference to change in achievement level of the same children over time, which may be a more meaningful way of looking at the age variable.

Another question of interest is how the school achievements of children reared in foster care during the preschool years compare to those of children reared in their own homes. A partial answer to this question can be constructed by drawing a comparison between the six-, seven-, or eight-year-old children assessed at Time I whose preschool years were spent at home prior to entering foster care, and the six-, seven-, and eight-year-old children assessed at Time III who entered foster care at the ages of one, two, or three.

The children reared in foster care for at least two years prior to

TABLE 9.11
MEAN SCHOOL ACHIEVEMENT INDEX SCORES[a] OF STUDY CHILDREN AT TIME III, BY AGE AND GRADE IN SCHOOL

Age (Years)	Grade in School												No. of Cases
	1st	2nd	3rd	4th	5th	6th	7th	8th	9th	10th	11th	12th	
6	98.1[b]	96.2											19
7	100.0[c]	99.2	98.8										26
8		99.8	99.3	98.2									31
9			95.0[c]	96.4	92.5[c]								17
10			89.0[c]	92.4	94.3	100.5[c]							20
11			98.0[c]		88.8	94.7	84.0[c]						17
12					93.5[c]	96.0	98.0[c]						15
13						94.0[c]	94.4	104.0					15
14							87.7[c]	96.0[c]	86.0[c]	93.0[c]	98.5[c]		14
15								96.0[c]	101.1	93.6	100.0[c]		10
16									96.0[c]	92.3[c]	82.5[c]	97.3[c]	10
17									45.0[c]		50.0[c]	65.0[c]	2
No. of cases	11	31	31	25	20	19	12	13	14	10	6	4	196

[a] Key to index: age-appropriate grade level performance = 100.0; each deviation of 10 points = 1 grade level above or below normal.
[b] Italics represent appropriate grade for age.
[c] Mean for age and grade group are subject to instability: mean computed on less than five children.

entering school showed better performance in school compared to their age counterparts reared at home. As may be seen in Table 9.12, among the six-year-old children reared at home, overall achievement-level index scores showed a mean of 94.8, whereas children reared in foster care had a mean of 98.1. For seven-year-olds, the mean was 95.5, compared to 99.2 for the children reared at home. Moreover, among those children reared in foster care, seven out of 18 subjects were in the first grade—already one grade behind their age-appropriate class levels (although these seven children also had a high mean achievement score, 99.9). Among the eight-year-old children reared at home, the average achievement score was 94.5, again several points behind the children reared in foster care who had a mean of 99.3. Noteworthy also in the contrast between the two groups of children is the fact that only one child (2.5 percent) was advanced among those reared at home compared to 30.3 percent of the children reared in foster care. We also note that the latter showed only 7.9 percent who were one grade below the age-appropriate grade level, compared to 28.3 percent of the children reared at home.

School Achievement by Ethnicity and Age
Ethnic group comparisons for each age year, using non-age-adjusted achievement level scores (raw scores) as displayed in Table 9.13 reveal that white children were generally less behind than either the black or the Puerto Rican children. At the time of entering foster care, the Puerto Rican subjects were performing at levels below both the black and the white children at each age level. However, with the passage of years we note that the Puerto Rican children at Time III showed a level of achievement above that of the black children for each age year except ages 10, 11, and 16. The Puerto Rican children also showed a level of achievement above that of the white children aged eight, nine, 12, and 13.

The decline in achievement level as age increases is depicted graphically in Figure 9.1. Among the children assessed at Time I, the general downward slope as age increases indicates the poorer performance of the older compared to the younger children just beginning school; this is especially true for the Puerto Rican children. We also see in Figure 9.1 that at Time I the achievement levels of the

TABLE 9.12
COMPARISON OF MEAN SCHOOL ACHIEVEMENT INDEX SCORES[a] OF CHILDREN REARED AT HOME, IMMEDIATELY PRIOR TO ENTRY INTO SCHOOL, AND CHILDREN REARED AT LEAST TWO YEARS IN FOSTER CARE[b]

		Reared at Home					Reared in Foster Care			
Age	N	First Grade	Second Grade	Third Grade		N	First Grade	Second Grade	Third Grade	Fourth Grade
6	10	94.8[c]	100.0[d]			19	98.1	96.2		
7	18	99.9	95.5			26	100.0[d]	99.2	98.8	
8	18		89.7	94.5		31		99.8	99.3	98.2

[a] Key to index: age-appropriate grade level performance = 100.0; each deviation of 10 points = 1 grade level above or below normal.

[b] Reared at Home refers to study subjects' Time I scores; they entered foster care at ages 6, 7, 8, and began school prior to entering care. "Reared in foster care" refers to children of ages 6, 7, and 8 who entered foster care at ages 1, 2, and 3 and were reared two to four years in foster care prior to entering school; their scores were obtained at Time III.

[c] Italics represent appropriate grade for age.

[d] Mean for age and grade group are subject to instability: mean computed on less than five children.

TABLE 9.13
MEAN SCHOOL ACHIEVEMENT INDEX SCORES OF STUDY CHILDREN, BY AGE AND ETHNICITY[a]

							Age (Years)					
Ethnicity	*6*	*7*	*8*	*9*	*10*	*11*	*12*	*13*	*14*	*15*	*16*	*17*
Time I												
White	100.0[b]	107.3[b]	94.7[b]	93.0	99.2	94.4	86.8	99.0[b]				
Black	98.7[b]	94.1	96.3[b]	86.7	89.3	88.0[b]	94.6	94.5[b]				
Puerto Rican	92.8	96.0	91.6	89.6	88.6	86.6	86.4	81.3	84.0[b]			
Time II												
White	98.1	96.7	96.0	98.0	94.5	91.6	100.3	94.3	92.9	77.0[b]		
Black	98.9	97.0	97.4	86.5	89.7	83.9	84.4	76.8	92.4	100.0[b]		
Puerto Rican	97.3	97.9	93.3	93.0	87.4	90.1	77.8	87.1	81.0	79.2	78.0[b]	
Time III												
White	99.8[b]	94.8	97.7[b]	90.5[b]	95.3[b]	95.3[b]	91.0[b]	101.5[b]	99.8	97.3[b]	99.5[b]	
Black	95.6	98.6	97.7	92.8	93.6	91.3	87.6	88.0	94.0[b]	92.0[b]	96.0[b]	
Puerto Rican	98.0[b]	98.6	100.7	93.2	90.3	89.5	94.9	106.5	98.0	94.7	82.9	57.5[b]

[a]Key to index: age-appropriate grade level performance = 100.0; each deviation of 10 points = 1 grade level above or below normal.
[b]Mean subject to instability: mean computed on less than five children.

black and Puerto Rican children between the ages of six and 11 years are quite similar; they are performing at a level noticeably lower than that of the white children. When we examine the performance of the children assessed at Time III, we notice shifts in the mean scores so that the age differentiation based on ethnicity for children aged six through 12 has been reduced considerably. It is noteworthy that for any given age grouping the discrepancies in achievement levels between ethnic groups were smaller than prevailing at Time I. Moreover, the slope displaying the decline in performance with increasing age is somewhat less steep at Time III.

School Achievement and Socioeconomic Status
In previous studies of school achievement, socioeconomic status had been found to be associated with school performance.[15] The

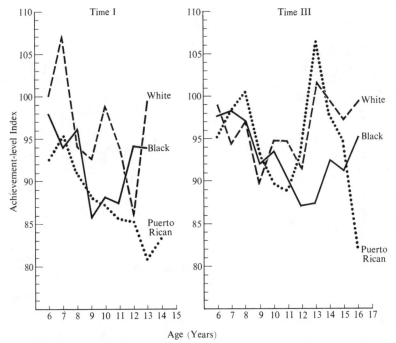

Age (Years)

FIGURE 9.1.

MEAN SCHOOL ACHIEVEMENT OF STUDY CHILDREN, BY AGE AND ETHNICITY.

[15] *School Achievement of Children by Demographic and Socioeconomic Factors*, p. 6.

mean age-adjusted overall achievement-level index scores (11 subjects) are displayed in Table 9.14 according to the socioeconomic status of the families of the children. This status is presented as lower, middle, and higher. We again remind the reader that this index was specifically prepared for a population of families largely living in poverty and is not a socioeconomic status index typically found in the social science literature. Examining our findings, we can report no statistically significant difference in mean scores by socioeconomic status characteristics on each of the three assessment occasions. However, at Time I the spread between the lower and the higher status groups was almost 10 points, and at Time II it was about seven points. The differentiation was only modest at Time III. We interpret these data to signify that there is some influence of socioeconomic status at play but it is moderated by the greater homogeneity in economic circumstances of our study population compared to the typical study of achievement found in the literature.

TABLE 9.14
MEAN AGE-ADJUSTED SCHOOL ACHIEVEMENT INDEX SCORES
OF STUDY CHILDREN,[a] BY SOCIOECONOMIC STATUS

	Mean Age-adjusted School Achievement					
	Time I[b]		Time II[b]		Time III[b]	
Socioeconomic Status	Mean	SD	Mean	SD	Mean	SD
Lower (45/80/65)[c]	74.4	24.4	74.1	31.0	87.8	18.5
Middle (43/76/76)	79.8	23.2	81.8	22.3	89.5	20.1
Higher (49/96/70)	83.2	43.4	81.0	33.6	91.6	24.3
Total (137/252/211)	79.2	32.4	79.1	30.0	89.7	21.2

[a] Child's age-adjusted score is the complement of the relative proportion advanced or behind normal age-appropriate grade level (100.0), e.g., 75.0 = school achievement 25 percent below age-appropriate grade level, regardless of age.
[b] The results are not statistically significant, by one-way analysis of variance.
[c] Data in parentheses give the number of children tested at Times I, II, and III.

DISCHARGE VERSUS REMAINING IN FOSTER CARE

Another objective of our research was to determine whether foster care has a positive influence on the school performance of children in placement. Within the constraints of relatively small numbers, our study does provide for the first time an opportunity to examine this question. School achievement of children who entered foster care and remained for 90 days but were discharged after one or two years was compared with that of children remaining in care for the entire five years of our longitudinal effort. We have calculated that the mean age-adjusted achievement level score for all ages of children who remained in foster care the entire five years is 89.1; this would indicate that, on the average, children in care were about 10 percent below their age-appropriate grade level. The discharged children who had by the end of five years as much as four or five years of schooling while living at home after their experience in foster care were functioning at a slightly higher (but not statistically significant) level; their mean score was 90.8.

The reader will see displayed in Table 9.15 the mean school-achievement index scores (raw scores not adjusted for age) according to whether the children had been discharged during each of the five years after entry into care or whether they were still in care at the end of the study. An analysis of difference between the discharged children and those remaining in foster care within each age group does not show a clear pattern of differentiation between the two groups with respect to performance. Children of ages six through nine who were discharged from care through four years show nearly normal achievement-level scores that were slightly better than those of the six- to nine-year-olds who remained in foster care. The older children who were discharged within three years of entering foster care showed slightly lower achievement scores than children of the same age remaining in care except for the 16- and 17-year-olds. Caution must be exercised in comparing groups because of the very small number of participating children in particular age categories discharged in each of the five years. Minimally, we can state that these data do not support any notion that remaining in foster care is a markedly depriving experience for children. For all of the children remaining in care, taken by

TABLE 9.15
MEAN SCHOOL ACHIEVEMENT INDEX SCORES OF STUDY CHILDREN, BY STATUS FIVE YEARS AFTER ENTRY INTO FOSTER CARE

Foster Care Status, Time III[b]	Mean School Achievement Index Score[a] Age (Years)												Total	N
	6	7	8	9	10	11	12	13	14	15	16	17		
Discharged[b]														
1st year	98.0	98.0	99.0	98.5	91.0	85.0	91.0	—	93.0	—	93.0	—	95.6	34
2nd year	—	99.0	101.0	102.0	70.0	80.0	98.5	116.7	98.0	—	—	—	98.1	14
3rd year	—	—	—	69.0	84.0	98.0	77.0	89.5	107.0	92.0	100.0	—	92.7	12
4th year	96.0	98.0	95.5	85.5	95.5	—	—	76.5	90.0	—	92.0	—	90.7	13
5th year	—	99.0	99.0	97.0	99.0	100.0	—	100.0	97.0	96.0	—	65.0	94.7	10
In care	96.6	97.7	99.5	93.3	94.2	93.9	92.0	95.5	98.8	95.5	82.3	50.0	94.9	140

[a] Key to index: age-appropriate grade level performance = 100; each deviation of 10 points = 1 grade level above or below normal.
[b] Mean scores for discharged groups by age and year discharged are unstable due to small number of cases; figures should be used with caution.

individual age segments, there are only a few points differentiating them from the children who have returned home.

Discharged Status and Ethnicity

In Table 9.16 we examine the school achievement measures with respect to the child's being in care or discharged, controlling for whether the subjects are white, black, or Puerto Rican. The data are presented for Times II and III assessments only, since at Time I the children had not yet had an experience in foster care. For the white children, we find that those in care had a somewhat superior achievement score, some five points greater than the discharged children. By Time III, however, the latter showed somewhat superior scores, about two points higher than those still in care. For the black children, the situation was reversed, in that at Time II the discharged children were somewhat superior to those still in care, while at Time III, the situation was turned around. However, we should note that the differences are quite small. For the Puerto

TABLE 9.16

MEAN AGE-ADJUSTED SCHOOL ACHIEVEMENT INDEX SCORE FOR STUDY CHILDREN, BY ETHNICITY AND FOSTER CARE STATUS FIVE YEARS AFTER ENTRY INTO FOSTER CARE

	Mean Age-Adjusted School Achievement[a]			
	Time II		Time III	
	Children	Mean	Children	Mean
White				
In care	51	90.1	21	90.2
Discharged	21	85.5	21	92.5
Black				
In care	61	74.8	62	86.8
Discharged	20	77.8	24	84.2
Puerto Rican				
In care	71	73.5	57	91.2
Discharged	28	78.8	26	95.4

[a]Child's age-adjusted score is the complement of the relative proportion advanced or behind normal age-appropriate grade level (100.0), e.g., 75.0 = school achievement 25 percent below age-appropriate grade level, regardless of age.

Rican children, we observe that at both Times II and III the discharged children have higher mean achievement scores. One might speculate that the Puerto Rican children experienced the conditions of learning at home as being somewhat superior to that which they experienced in care. However, the findings are very modest, and an analysis of variance of these data fails to show any significant main effects or a significant interaction effect between ethnicity and whether a child was in care or discharged.

PROBLEMS SHOWN IN SCHOOL

Teachers were asked to report on the behavior of the child in the classroom from a variety of perspectives. These are categorized in Table 9.17. Essentially they are various indicators of whether the child was coping adequately with the requirements of the school situation. For each item the teacher was asked to indicate whether the child had either major, minor, or no difficulty in the area. The table presents the observations of the teachers for each of the three assessment occasions. Overall, 66 percent of the children assessed at Time I, 73 percent at Time II, and 76 percent at Time III had at least one problem that was considered by the teacher to have major influence on the child's school performance. Getting into specific items, about one in four children were seen to be problematic with respect to their intellectual capacity at each assessment occasion and about a third were said to have difficulties in comprehension. At least 30 percent of the children on all three occasions were said to show little motivation to learn.

Behavior difficulty in the form of anxiety or acting out was observed in about 32 percent, and about 25 percent were assessed as being unable to follow class routines and to be excessively demanding of attention. The largest category of disability was related to poor work-study habits, with about 33 percent of the children characterized as having major problems in this area at Time I and about 43 percent said to have major problems at Times II and III. Overall, a fairly substantial proportion of the children appear to be disabled in their general orientation to class routines and the tasks required of them as students. The characterization of these

TABLE 9.17
PROBLEMS REPORTED BY SCHOOLTEACHERS
TO AFFECT STUDY CHILDREN'S SCHOOL PERFORMANCE

Problem and Degree	Time I	Time II	Time III
		(percentages)	
Inadequate intellectual capacity			
Major	24.2	22.9	27.4
Minor	19.8	19.5	14.4
No problem	56.0	57.6	58.2
Difficulties in comprehension			
Major	32.5	29.6	34.9
Minor	16.6	18.0	11.8
No problem	50.9	52.4	53.3
Little motivation to learn			
Major	28.0	30.7	36.3
Minor	15.9	15.4	16.0
No problem	56.1	53.9	47.7
Behavior problem (anxiety, acting out)			
Major	31.2	34.1	30.8
Minor	11.5	13.9	15.9
No problem	57.3	52.0	53.3
Inability to follow class routines			
Major	21.0	26.2	25.3
Minor	15.3	14.2	16.6
No problem	63.7	59.6	58.1
Poor work-study habits			
Major	33.8	42.7	43.7
Minor	12.1	13.1	12.1
No problem	54.1	47.2	44.2
Excessively demands attention			
Major	23.6	31.1	27.2
Minor	14.7	13.1	16.9
No problem	61.7	55.8	55.9
Problem in relationship with teacher			
Major	10.0	14.2	17.2
Minor	14.0	10.1	14.4
No problem	75.8	75.7	68.4
Problem in relationship with peers			
Major	19.8	21.4	26.8
Minor	18.5	13.5	15.0
No problem	61.7	65.1	58.2
No. of cases	157	267	215

children by the teachers suggests that educational problems loom fairly large on all three testing occasions, with about 25–33 percent of the children showing major problems in any one area and only about 25 percent of the children being entirely free of a major problem. This is a rather sobering perspective on the school problems of these children.

In 1971, when the survey was conducted as a final round of data collection, teachers were asked to complete an additional form, "Rating Scale for Pupil Adjustment", (RSPA) developed in 1950 and revised in 1953 by the Michigan Department of Mental Health.[16] Ratings were secured on 5-point scales of the following type:

Social Maturity:
(Definition: Ability to deal with social responsibilities in school, in the community, and at home appropriate to his age.)
A. Very superior social maturity
B. Slightly superior maturity
C. Average social maturity
D. Slightly inferior social maturity
E. Very inferior social maturity

Ratings were obtained for 206 of the 233 children assessed at Time III. As may be seen in Table 9.18, teachers reported a majority of the children (51 percent) as showing inferior levels of school achievement. A substantial proportion (45.2 percent) of the children were also seen by their teachers as being socially immature. About 33 percent were reported to be poorly adjusted, introverted, emotionally insecure, unstable in mood, and moderately to extremely irritable. Some 28 percent of the children were judged by their teachers to represent a troublesome disciplinary problem.

In Table 9.19 we present analyses of the teachers' responses for the five summary measures contained in the Rating Scale for Pupil Adjustment. The data are organized to show the percentage of children with problems, comparing children still in foster care at the end of five years and those children who had been discharged home. With respect to overall emotional adjustment, the discharged children were seen to present a somewhat higher degree of problems

---

[16] The Rating Scale for Pupil Adjustment is currently published by Science Research Associates, Inc., 259 East Erie Street, Chicago, Illinois 60611.

TABLE 9.18
DISTRIBUTIONS OF TEACHER RATINGS OF STUDY CHILDREN
ON SCALES FOR PUPIL ADJUSTMENT AT TIME III[a]
(N = 206)

Scale	Positive Rating[b]	Average Rating	Negative Rating
		(percentaged across)	
Overall emotional adjustment	36.4	33.0	30.6
Social maturity	16.5	38.3	45.2
Tendency toward depression	49.7	32.0	18.3
Tendency toward aggressive behavior	72.7	16.1	11.3
Extroversion–introversion	27.8	38.5	33.6
Emotional security	43.8	21.7	34.5
Motor control and stability	69.1	20.9	10.0
Impulsiveness	27.8	40.6	31.7
Emotional irritability	35.0	34.5	30.5
School achievement	15.4	33.7	51.0
School conduct	25.0	47.1	27.9

[a] Data obtained as ratings from teachers on "Rating Scale for Pupil Adjustment" published by Science Research Associates.

[b] An original 5-point response scale was collapsed by combining the two responses reflecting above average or positive ratings, retaining the central or average rating, and combining the two below average or negative ratings.

although the difference is quite small (four percentage points). However, there is a distinct difference between the children in foster care and those discharged with respect to social maturity; 53 percent of the discharged children were rated negatively as compared to 41 percent of the children still in foster care. The most marked difference between the children was on the issue of extroversion–introversion, with 49 percent of the discharged children categorized as introverted in contrast with 26 percent of those in foster care. This difference would seem to indicate that the children who returned home are under strain in their current living arrangements. This is further confirmed by the finding that 41 percent of the children at home were assessed as insecure with respect to their emotional security in contrast with only 30 percent of those in foster care. Both sets of children were seen in similar fashion with respect to the stability of mood; about 33 percent of each were seen as "moody."

The one area in which discharged children were rated in distinctively more positive fashion was with respect to the domain of emotional irritability, with 34 percent of the children in foster care being rated to indicate frequent irritability, in contrast with only 11 percent of the children discharged. Why children in foster care should be more labile in their emotional behavior is not clear to us. On the whole, we are impressed that in many areas the discharged children are more disabled, while at the same time it may be that continued status in foster care can create a source of discontent for the children so affected.

It should be pointed out to the reader that we will subsequently establish that the teachers' ratings of the children showed fairly strong correlations with caseworkers' assessments of the behavior of the children on the CBC form, indicating some degree of concurrent validity of the school reports.

TABLE 9.19
**PERCENT OF STUDY CHILDREN WITH BELOW AVERAGE RATINGS
BY SCHOOLTEACHERS ON FIVE SUMMARY MEASURES DEVELOPED
FROM SCALE OF PUPIL ADJUSTMENT, BY FOSTER CARE
STATUS AT TIME III**

	Percentage below average		
Scale	Total	In Foster Care	Discharged
Overall emotional adjustment (poor)	30	29	33
Social maturity (inferior)	45	41	53
Extroversion–introversion (introverted)	34	26	49
Emotional security (insecure)	35	30	41
Stability of moods (moody)	32	32	30
Emotional irritability (irritable)	31	34	11
No. of cases	206	136	70

FACTORS PREDICTIVE OF SCHOOL ACHIEVEMENT

We were interested in determining the nature of the influence of various characteristics of the children and their family backgrounds in predicting their overall achievement level. We were aware that there might be considerable overlap among variables in terms of their contributions of explained variance in the summary measures developed for the three assessment occasions. In Table 9.20 we display the results of a multiple regression analysis in which we have sought to "explain" the variance in the overall achievement summary measure that we have used as our major outcome variable with respect to school performance. We have looked at the influence of age, sex, age–sex interaction, reason for placement (child behavior versus all others), length of time in care, number of placements, and a series of measures dealing with parental visitation

TABLE 9.20
RELATION OF SELECTED VARIABLES IN ACCOUNTING
FOR VARIANCE IN PREDICTING SCHOOL ACHIEVEMENT LEVEL

Selected Variables	Time I	Time II	Time III
	(standardized regression coefficients)		
Age at entry	−.22*	−.33***	−.37***
Sex	−.08	−.07	−.39*
Age–sex interaction	−.02	−.01	.46**
Child's behavior[a]	−.16	.05	−.05
Length of placement[b]	−.07	.12	−.03
Number of placements	.13	.05	.12
Frequency parental visiting	.02	−.18*	−.04
Evaluation of mother	.02	−.10	−.04
Visiting behavior, early	.03	−.02	.02
Visiting behavior, later	.09	.02	.03
Visiting pattern	−.05	−.02	−.03
Ethnicity (black)	−.17	−.30***	.17
Ethnicity (Puerto Rican)	−.34**	−.27***	−.08
Multiple R	.45	.46	.31
Multiple R^2	.20	.21	.09
No. of cases	137	255	211

*$p < .05$ **$p < .01$ ***$p < .001$

[a] Reason for placement was child's own behavior problem versus all other reasons.
[b] Length of placement was transformed using logarithms.

patterns and evaluation of the mother of the child. We have also included two ethnicity variables in dummy-variable form.

Readers will note that the amount of explained variance at the three assessment occasions is relatively modest and is, in fact, quite low at Time III. Twenty and 21 percent of the variance is explained at Times I and II and only 9 percent at Time III. Thus, we must be aware that there are other factors operating in the situation to influence the child's achievement level and much is yet to be learned about what accounts for variation in these summary measures. The table shows that at Time I, the child's age at entry is a significant predictor; younger children show significantly higher achievement levels relative to their age in comparison with the older children. This finding is replicated at Times II and III. We also observe that at Time II, frequent parental visiting is not associated with a higher achievement score, rather, the reverse is true. While the percentage of variance explained by this visiting variable is very small, we are nevertheless surprised at the direction of the association. Other findings in this study have indicated a positive effect of parental visiting, but at Time II this emerges in reverse fashion. Some child care workers have noted that certain children react to parental visiting with renewed concern about their situation in foster care, and this may have some effect on stability of the child in the school situation. We note that in the description of teacher ratings, the children in foster care were considered to be more irritable than those who had returned home.

At Time III we find that age, sex, and age–sex interaction show significance, which again indicate that younger children are assessed in superior fashion and also that the girls in the sample were performing better than the boys. The age–sex interaction is the equivalent of a second-order interaction in analysis of variance. It would indicate that there are older girls in the sample who were performing in superior fashion at Time III and younger boys who were doing less well.

The dummy variables with respect to ethnicity confirm what has already been reported in the analysis of ethnicity, namely, that the black and Puerto Rican children had lower overall achievement index scores than the white children at Times I and II but this difference is no longer significant at Time III.

In the main, we are impressed with the modest yield from these regression analyses. In chapter 10 we examine the phenomenon of change in IQ scores achieved by the children on repeated testing as this relates to change in school achievement scores. We can anticipate for the reader that the explained variance in achievement is increased as a result.

SUMMARY

The school performance of our study children was investigated on three occasions in the five-year longitudinal study. Because many of our children were not of school age when they entered foster care and there was some loss of subjects over time, the children assessed on the three occasions do not completely overlap. There were 256 subjects where school reports were received for at least two assessment occasions, and these children become the object of special analysis in chapter 10.

We report findings indicating that a majority of the children at each assessment occasion were performing below their age-appropriate grade level. Fifty-nine percent of the children studied following entry into foster care were functioning below their age level, including 11 percent who were three to five years below the level that would be expected on the basis of their age. In the second assessment in 1969, 55 percent of the children were operating below their age-appropriate level and in 1971, the final year of the study, 52 percent were performing below their age-appropriate level. However, using an age-adjusted achievement index summarizing the degree to which a child was advanced or behind in each of 11 school subjects, we found that the children assessed at Time III were doing much better, on the average, than was found at the Time I assessment.

As was also found by the National Health Survey of school achievement for children on a nationwide basis, we observed that girls had higher achievement levels than boys, and that the white children in the sample were performing at a slightly higher level of achievement than their black or Puerto Rican peers. Among six- to nine-year-olds, children who were reared in foster care during their preschool years showed a tendency toward higher achievement than children reared at home. No major differences in school performance were found between children remaining in foster care for five years, compared to children discharged from care for a period from three to five years. An analysis to identify those factors predictive of better school achievement indicated that age and sex were better predictors than ethnicity, reason for placement, length of placement, number of placements, evaluation of the mother, or visitation patterns. However, none of these factors—individually or together—could account for more than a very minor amount of variance in school achievement.

We now proceed to an examination of changes in school achievement for those children for whom we were able to obtain repeated assessments over the course of the longitudinal study.

TEN

ANALYSIS
OF CHANGE
IN SCHOOL
ACHIEVEMENT

In this chapter we report the findings on change in school achievement among our study subjects during the five-year period of our
research. Similar to the procedure in the earlier chapter on IQ
change, we analyzed change in school achievement for three different time periods. This enabled us to assess the points in their
careers as foster children at which the subjects made greater
progress. The three time periods for which we provide change data
are Time I (entry) to Time II (two-and-one-half-years later), Times
II–III (five years after entry), and Times I–III.

In chapter 9, we reported the status of our subjects at each of
the three assessment occasions (Times I, II, and III). We could not
discuss change with any confidence because each cross-sectional
assessment represented somewhat different groups of children, and
the comparison of mean scores for each occasion could be
influenced by the loss or addition of subjects from one time to the
next. The analysis reported in this chapter, however, is based on
repeated assessments for the *same* children. The Times I–II panel
comprised 123 children, the Times II–III, 133, and the Times
I–III, 76.

Similar to our treatment of IQ change, our method of analyzing
change in school achievement was to partial out the effects of the
earlier level of school achievement as a covariate and then to
regress a series of predictor variables on the remaining residual. The

latter reflects the amount of change in school achievement during the period between the two assessment occasions under study. Standardized regression coefficients, after all predictor variables had been entered into the regression, were examined to establish the relative importance of a variable in influencing change in school achievement.

In all analyses reported in this chapter we use the relative score index of school achievement, which we developed as a means for adjusting a child's raw score of school achievement for the effects of age.[1] This adjustment was necessary owing to the variation in the numbers of children of each age year in any given analytical group.

In searching for factors that might explain improvement or deterioration in school achievement, we decided to explore three domains: (a) personal characteristics of the child, (b) characteristics of the foster care experience, and (c) nature of contact with parent(s). Among the personal characteristics of the child that we felt might be associated with school achievement were: (a) the child's age on entering foster care, (b) IQ, (c) sex, (d) ethnicity, (e) early developmental and health problems, (f) emotional stability, (g) birth status, and (h) socioeconomic status of family. The characteristics of the foster care experience that we included for analysis were: (a) length of placement (transformed into logarithmic form), (b) reason for entering care, (c) number of placements while in care, and (d) the casework or other treatment received by the child while in care (represented by logarithmic transformation of the number of treatment contacts). The nature of the parental contact with the child during placement was included for analysis by a measure of the visiting pattern of the child's mother, in terms of frequency of visits, and also an evaluation of the mother's capabilities as assessed by caseworker ratings. These variables coincide with those used to study IQ change.

AN OVERVIEW OF CHANGE

Before we provide results of our analysis of the factors associated with change in school achievement, it may be helpful for the reader

[1]See Chapter 9, pp. 233–35.

to have a general picture of the amount and direction of change in school achievement that occurred among the study children.

As shown in Table 10.1, the average level of school achievement for all 123 children assessed on Times I and II declined. Forty-seven percent of the children showed a gain in their school achievement, while 46 percent experienced decline. Although more children showed gain than loss, the amount of decline was sizable for many children, so that the overall net result for the entire group reflected a decline in school achievement.

The pattern of change was markedly different between Times II and III. During this period, extending to five years after entry into foster care, a majority (58 percent) of the children showed substantial gains in school achievement. Not only was there an average gain of 10 relative score index points (from 81 to 91), but the figures indicate that the group of study children had improved to within nine percent of their age-appropriate grade levels. In this period, only 28.5 percent of the children were doing less well in school (see Table 10.1).

The pattern of change over the full span of five years for the 76 children assessed on both Times I and III indicates that the majority of children (58 percent) improved in their school achievement. Approximately 32 percent showed a decline in school achievement over the five years.

To determine whether the amount of change in school performance shown by each child was significant, we used the matched-t statistical test to compare the actual with the probable amount of change that could have been expected.[2] Table 10.2 shows the results of this analysis. The distribution of changes in the study children's school achievement scores between Times I and II did not exceed what could have occurred by chance alone. However, changes in school performance between Times II and III, as well as those for the entire five-year span, were sufficiently large to exceed that which could have occurred by chance alone.[3]

---

[2] Allen L. Edwards, *Statistical Methods for the Behavioral Sciences* (New York: Holt, Rinehart, and Winston, 1963), pp. 278–82.

[3] Matched t-test: Times I–II, $p = .50$; Times II–III, $p = .001$; Times I–III, $p = .02$.

TABLE 10.1

DISTRIBUTION OF CHANGE SCORES AMONG STUDY CHILDREN, BY TIME PERIODS BETWEEN THREE TESTING OCCASIONS

Difference in Achievement-level Index Scores	Period Between Testing Occasions, and Number of Children					
	Time II minus Time I		Time III minus Time II		Time III minus Time I	
	Number	Percent	Number	Percent	Number	Percent
Declined:	50	45.9	35	28.5	19	31.7
−50 or more	4	3.7	3	2.4	1	1.7
−49 to −25	10	9.2	4	3.2	3	5.0
−24 to −1	36	33.0	28	22.7	15	25.0
No change: 0	8	7.3	17	13.8	6	10.0
Improved:	51	46.8	71	57.7	35	58.3
1–5	15	13.7	14	11.4	8	13.3
6–10	9	8.3	13	10.6	6	10.0
11–15	9	8.3	5	4.7	3	5.0
16–20	4	3.7	8	6.5	6	10.0
21–25	3	2.7	8	6.5	2	3.3
26–30	3	2.7	6	4.9	1	1.7
31–35	1	0.9	1	0.8	—	—
36–40	1	0.9	5	4.1	2	3.3
41–45	—	—	3	2.4	1	1.7
46–50	3	2.7	1	0.8	1	1.7
51–55	2	1.8	—	—	4	6.7
56–60	1	0.9	7	5.7	1	1.7
Number	109	100.0	123	100.0	60	100.0
Mean change score	−1.3		10.6		7.8	

AMOUNT AND DIRECTION
OF CHANGE FOR ETHNIC GROUPS

The amount and direction of change in school achievement when analyzed by ethnic groups revealed interesting results (see Table 10.2). White children declined in their school achievement between Times I and II, although the amount of change was not statistically significant. During Times II–III the white children as a group showed a small but not significant degree of improvement in school achievement. The black children in the study also showed a decline in school achievement between Times I and II, but their decline was only a third of the decline shown by the white children. Between Times II and III occasions, as well as over the entire five-year period, black children showed substantial improvement in school, exceeding what could be expected by chance alone. The Puerto Rican children improved in school regardless of the period of study, although the only period reflecting a statistically significant gain was during Times II–III.

Achievement Levels by Ethnicity and Sex

In Table 10.3 we present the achievement levels for the same children assessed at two different times, with a breakdown by ethnicity and sex. This mode of data tabulation enables us to compare mean scores for groups without consideration of loss or gain of subjects. We first observe that despite all gains made, every grouping of children (except a very small group of white females) was functioning in school at a level below the age-appropriate grade, regardless of the assessment occasion.[4]

During the period of two and one-half to three years following entry into foster care, the group of white male children showed a slight improvement in school achievement while the black and Puerto Rican males were declining in achievement, especially the black children, whose achievement index dropped from 75.6 to 64.6. The pattern of change for the females during this study period was exactly the reverse of that for the boys. White female children were doing less well three years after entry, while both the black and the Puerto Rican girls improved in school achievement.

---

[4] A mean of 100.0 reflects the age-appropriate grade level of subjects.

TABLE 10.2
DIRECTION AND AMOUNT OF CHANGE IN SCHOOL ACHIEVEMENT,
BY TESTING PERIOD AND ETHNICITY

Testing Period and Ethnicity	Mean Difference in School Achievement Index[a]	Standard Error	Degrees of Freedom $(N-1)$	t Statistic[b]	Probability
Times I–II					
Total ($N=109$)	−1.31	2.3	108	−.56	> .50
White (29)	−4.45	4.0	28	−1.10	.28
Black (29)	−1.60	5.5	28	−.29	> .50
Puerto Rican (51)	.65	3.2	50	.20	> .50
Times II–III					
Total ($N=123$)	10.56	2.7	122	3.86	.001***
White (28)	2.34	3.2	27	.73	.47
Black (43)	10.25	4.6	42	2.26	.03**
Puerto Rican (52)	15.24	4.9	51	3.10	.004**
Times I–III					
Total ($N=60$)	7.84	3.3	59	2.37	.02**
White (15)	1.03	6.4	14	.16	> .50
Black (12)	15.58	6.2	11	2.51	.03**
Puerto Rican (33)	8.11	4.7	32	1.72	.09

$**p < .01$ $***p < .001$

[a]Units are percentage points of advancement or decline relative to age-appropriate grade level.   [b]Matched t-test.

TABLE 10.3
MEAN RELATIVE SCHOOL ACHIEVEMENT-LEVEL INDEX SCORES FOR
THREE STUDY GROUPS OF CHILDREN AT EACH ASSESSMENT OCCASION,
BY SEX AND ETHNICITY[a]

| | | Mean Relative School Achievement Index | | |
| | | Time I | Time II | Time III |
Group	N	Mean	Mean	Mean
Times I–II		(b,c)		
Male				
White	18	86.6	87.2	
Black	15	75.6	64.6	
Puerto Rican	27	69.5	68.2	
Female				
White	12	106.0	95.1	
Black	20	82.6	88.8	
Puerto Rican	28	79.0	81.6	
Times II–III				
Male				
White	20		89.6	94.3
Black	15		88.4	87.0
Puerto Rican	26		76.1	88.0
Female				
White	13		90.0	92.7
Black	30		75.5	90.4
Puerto Rican	29		76.2	94.9
Times I–III			(c)	
Male				
White	10	82.2	84.6	97.7
Black	9	75.0	79.3	88.9
Puerto Rican	19	77.5	72.8	92.3
Female				
White	8	104.9	98.6	98.2
Black	9	85.1	91.2	94.1
Puerto Rican	19	85.3	84.4	91.2

[a] Age-appropriate grade-level school achievement = 100.0.
[b] Ethnic group differences are statistically different; one-way analysis of variance.
[c] Sex group differences are statistically different; t-test.

In the period between three and five years after entering foster care, the only children who failed to show a net improvement were the black male group, although the amount of their decline was quite small (1 index point). All of the other ethnic groups of both sexes showed improved school achievement. The gains made by the black and Puerto Rican girls were substantial—from about 75 on the school achievement index in the third year to over 90 by the fifth year. As may be seen in Table 10.3, these same general patterns of improvement in school achievement are reflected among the group of children assessed over the entire five-year period by assessments at Times I and III.

EXPLAINING CHANGE
IN SCHOOL ACHIEVEMENT DURING TIMES I–II

The relative influence of the selected characteristics of the child, parent, and agency service as factors accounting for *change* in school achievement within the first three years following entry into foster care is shown in Table 10.4. Since different levels of change in verbal and nonverbal intelligence were found among our study children, as reported in earlier chapters, we decided to analyze school change using each measure of intelligence separately, hence the three sets of figures shown in Table 10.4 for each assessment period. Specifically, we were seeking to determine whether gains achieved by children in either verbal or nonverbal IQ showed different results in explaining school change.

In searching for those variables that significantly influence improvement in school achievement, we found that only two variables account for a significant proportion of explained variance; (a) the child's sex (being female) and (b) the lack of any health problems prior to entering foster care. When verbal, rather than performance, IQ was used as a variable, age–sex interaction (young females) also constituted a significant factor influencing change in school achievement.

Noteworthy are those factors which were expected but not found to be influential in improving school achievement within a three-year period following entry into foster care. For example, the

TABLE 10.4
RELATION OF SALIENT BACKGROUND AND OTHER VARIABLES
TO DIRECTION AND AMOUNT OF CHANGE IN SCHOOL ACHIEVEMENT,
BY CHILD'S IQ AND TESTING OCCASION

	Times I–II		
Variable[a]	Verbal IQ	Nonverbal IQ	Total IQ
1. ACHVMT LVL	.35***	.39***	.35***
2. AGE	.22	.17	.17
3. CARELOG	.02	.05	.02
4. IQ T1 (or T2)	.07	.11	.14
5. IQ T2 (or T3)	.16	.04	.08
6. SEX	.96**	.84*	.86*
7. AGE–SEX	−.75*	−.64	−.64
8. SES	−.12	−.09	−.10
9. WEDLOCK	−.01	.01	.01
10. BLACK	−.19	−.17	−.17
11. PUERTO RICAN	−.10	−.14	−.11
12. REASON-1	.01	−.02	−.01
13. REASON-2	−.07	−.06	−.07
14. REASON-3	−.06	−.09	−.07
15. EVAL-MO	−.08	−.08	−.08
16. VISITING	−.12	−.10	−.10
17. CONTACT	.09	.12	.10
18. EMOT PROB	.04	.04	.03
19. DEVEL PROB	.05	.06	.06
20. HEALTH PROB	−.22*	−.23*	−.22*
21. NO. PLACEMTS	.07	.08	.08
Multiple R	.70	.69	.70
Multiple R^2	.49	.48	.49
No. of cases	123	123	123

$*p < .05$ $**p < .01$ $**p < .001$

child's age, ethnicity, lack of emotional problems, and change in intelligence did not account for a significant amount of variance in the change (improvement or deterioration) of a child's achievement in school. Such factors as the length of time in placement, number of placements, reason for placement, casework service, parental

TABLE 10.4 (*cont.*)

	Times II–III			Times I–III	
Verbal IQ	Nonverbal IQ	Total IQ	Verbal IQ	Nonverbal IQ	Total IQ
(standardized regression coefficients)					
.10	.14	.06	−.07	−.01	−.10
.19	.18	.21	.17	.09	.13
−.12	−.10	−.14	−.23	−.21	−.23
.01	.09	−.17	.13	.35	.31
.56***	.55***	.76***	.08	−.24	−.08
.67**	.73***	.67***	1.06	.83	1.04
−.51*	−.57**	−.50*	−1.02	−.82	−1.00
.08	.17	.11	.21	.20	.19
.05	−.00	.03	−.05	−.09	−.09
.09	−.00	.06	−.12	−.09	−.11
.18	−.05	.01	.01	−.02	.00
.08	.02	.01	−.17	−.20	−.17
.01	.01	.03	−.08	−.04	−.08
.03	−.03	.03	−.27	−.29*	−.29*
.15	.18*	.15*	−.01	.02	.02
.10	−.07	−.06	−.14	−.15	−.15
.00	.02	.01	.11	.08	.11
.02	−.07	.02	.17	.17	.14
−.15	−.17*	−.16*	−.35*	−.33*	−.36*
.11	.19*	.18*	.06	.05	.08
.11	.16	.14	.19	.15	.18
.71	.67	.74	.65	.67	.66
.50	.45	.55	.43	.45	.44
139	139	139	76	76	76

[a] Identification of variables: (1) achievement level at earlier testing occasion, (2) age of child, (3) log of days in care, (4) deviation IQ—Time I, (5) deviation IQ—Time II, (6) sex of child, (7) age–sex interaction, (8) socioeconomic status, (9) birth status, (10 black children, (11) Puerto Rican children, (12) reason for placement: child's behavior, (13) reason for placement: abandonment, (14) reason for placement: neglect or abuse; (15) evaluation of mother, (16) parental visiting pattern, (17) log of total casework contact rate, (18) emotional problem index, (19) developmental problem index, (20) health problem index, (21) number of placements.

visiting, and the caseworker's rating of the mother were also found not to be significantly associated with changes in school performance.

CHANGE IN SCHOOL ACHIEVEMENT DURING TIMES II–III

As indicated earlier, the increase in school achievement for most subjects was greater during the latter half of our study than in the earlier half. When we examined the predictors of change in school achievement for the Times II–III period, we found several significant explanatory variables. A significant proportion of variance in school achievement change was explained by the following variables, with their relative importance reflected by the standardized regression coefficient:

Change in IQ	.76
Sex (females)	.67
Age–sex interaction (younger female)	.50
Physical health problems in early development	.18
Lack of early developmental problems	.16
Evaluation of mother (positive)	.15

On a common-sense basis, it is not surprising that improved cognitive functioning, as measured by IQ change, is predictive of enhanced school performance over time. As far as we know, however, this has not been established in previously reported studies.

The finding that younger females improve more in school than either older females or males is in accord with our earlier findings. We are not in a position to explain the finding; future research might well focus on this phenomenon to determine whether the younger female child receives preferential treatment.

It is interesting to note that preplacement physical health and developmental histories of the children are identified as significant predictors of school achievement change. Evidently, children improved in school who had not suffered from earlier developmental problems (e.g., eating, walking, talking, and coordination) despite the fact that they may have had some physical problems at birth (e.g., premature birth or an early childhood illness). Contrary to what might be expected, early childhood behavior reflecting emotional problems was not found to be a significant factor.

The caseworker's positive evaluation of the mother during the third to fifth years was found to be a significant factor related to school change. This finding suggests that a more capable and interested mother can make a difference in the child's ability to increase his school achievement. How this influence affects the child's performance in school is not clear to us and could well be the subject of further research.

It is again noteworthy that predictor variables dealing with the institution of foster care are not significant factors in contributing to our understanding of improvement in school. The reason why a child entered foster care, the number of placements while in foster care, the amount of casework services received, and the length of stay were all found to be nonsignificant predictors of school change.

CHANGE IN SCHOOL ACHIEVEMENT DURING TIMES I–III

For the group of 76 children available for assessment at the time of entering foster care and again five years later, change in school achievement tends to be accounted for by age and sex (younger females), lack of early developmental problems, and having entered foster care for reasons other than neglect or abuse (i.e., not by a Family Court decision). However, only the latter two of these variables were statistically significant predictors (see Table 10.4). We observe that IQ change was not a significant predictor of change in school performance for the five-year span. Because of the smaller size of the group on which this Times I–III analysis is based, we feel that the findings for both two-and-one-half-year periods are of more substantive value in determining the factors accounting for change in school achievement.

CHANGE IN SCHOOL ACHIEVEMENT
WITHIN ETHNIC GROUPS

In Table 10.5 we present the findings regarding those variables that account for significant proportions of variance in school achievement for each ethnic group analyzed separately except for the white children. It was our judgment that the number of white children was too small to obtain valid results from a regression analysis using such an extensive list of independent (predictor) variables.

Black Children

Change in school achievement for black children in the more critical period during Times II–III appears to be influenced by several factors. Statistically significant amounts of variance are explained by the black child's sex, amount of IQ change (verbal, nonverbal, and total), family's socioeconomic status, level of emotional problems, and reason for placement. Age, although not contributing to a statistically significant gain in explained variance, also appears to be a relatively important variable.

Our interpretation of these findings is that among black children, improvement in school achievement was more likely to occur when the child was a female who showed an increase in IQ during the same period. Improvement in school performance by the black child was not deterred by having entered foster care through a decision by the Family Court for reason of neglect or abuse, when the child had a history of early childhood emotional problems, or when the child's family was below the study-group average in socioeconomic status. For black children, then, it appears that the effects of early childhood problems and other socioeconomic disadvantages prior to entering foster care are overcome during care to the extent that the child can perform in school. Moreover, our findings may suggest that black children with early emotional problems and from disadvantaged homes who were removed for reason of neglect or abuse were further behind at time of entering school but were then able to show significant and above-average gains in school achievement in the period of three to five years following entry into foster care.

The low standardized regression coefficients for such indepen-

TABLE 10.5
RELATION OF SALIENT BACKGROUND AND OTHER VARIABLES TO
DIRECTION AND AMOUNT OF CHANGE IN SCHOOL ACHIEVEMENT OF
BLACK OR PUERTO RICAN CHILDREN AT TIME III, BY IQ

	Black			Puerto Rican		
Variable[a]	Verbal IQ	Nonverbal IQ	Total IQ	Verbal IQ	Nonverbal IQ	Total IQ
	(standardized regression coefficients)					
1. ACHVMT LVL	.59**	.45*	.39*	−.16	.03	−.07
2. AGE	.57	.56	.55	.26	.16	.24
3. CARELOG	−.02	−.25	−.09	−.36*	−.23	−.32*
4. IQ T2	.16	.33	−.11	.02	−.01	.01
5. IQ T3	.51*	.48*	.70**	.69**	.40	.57*
6. SEX	1.25	1.65**	1.33*	.87*	.84*	.88*
7. AGE–SEX	−1.12	−1.27*	−1.12	−.65	−.74	−.71
8. SES	−.38*	−.60***	−.39*	.08	.18	.12
9. WEDLOCK	.09	.27	.13	.24	.03	.11
10. REASON-1	−.02	−.15	−.05	−.00	−.04	−.04
11. REASON-2	.21	.11	.20	.16	−.11	−.12
12. REASON-3	.25	.23	.26*	.11	−.14	−.03
13. EVAL-MO	−.04	.09	−.00	.11	.13	.10
14. VISITING	.13	.04	.07	.11	.08	.13
15. CONTACT	.03	.13	.04	−.20	−.11	−.17
16. EMOT PROB	.39*	.43**	.34*	.01	−.20	.11
17. DEVEL PROB	−.17	−.12	−.22	−.22	−.28	−.28
18. HEALTH PROB	.00	.12	.10	.26	.26	.29
19. NO. PLACEMTS	.10	.20	.10	.29	.22	.25
Multiple R	.85	.89	.88	.79	.72	.78
Multiple R²	.71	.79	.78	.63	.52	.61
No. of cases	44	44	44	53	53	53

*p < .05   **p < .01   ***p < .001

[a]Identification of variables: (1) achievement level—Time II, (2) age of child, (3) log of days in care, (4) deviation IQ—Time II, (5) deviation IQ—Time III, (6) sex of child, (7) age–sex interaction, (8) socioeconomic status, (9) birth status, (10) reason for placement: child's behavior, (11) reason for placement: abandonment, (12) reason for placement: neglect or abuse, (13) evaluation of mother–Time III, (14) parental visitation pattern—Time III, (15) log total casework contact rate, (16) emotional problem index, (17) developmental problems index, (18) health problems index, (19) number of placements.

dent variables as length of time in care, number of placements, caseworker contact rate, or the parental strengths and visiting pattern indicate that these predictors are not as highly relevant in accounting for change in school achievement as the factors mentioned earlier.

Puerto Rican Children
Among the predictor variables we included, only change in IQ (verbal and total), sex of child, and length of time spent in foster care were found to be significant predictors of change in school achievement among the Puerto Rican children. Thus change in our dependent variable was accounted for among Puerto Rican children primarily by females whose IQ had also increased during the same period, especially if the length of stay in foster care was less than the average for all Puerto Rican children in the study. Although not found to be statistically significant, the standardized regression coefficient for the age–sex interaction variable was quite high, relative to the others; this fact tends to indicate that among the females, it was the younger child that improved most.

Our findings also indicate that among Puerto Rican children gains in IQ are not only important for improving school achievement, but that the type of IQ gain is of significance. For Puerto Rican children, change in verbal IQ rather than nonverbal skill appears to be more important to improving school achievement. This finding may be important because the distinction is not characteristic of the black and other children. It may indicate that Puerto Rican children begin school with an English language skill handicap deriving from their bilingual situation, which takes several years to overcome.

As for the black children, change in school achievement does not appear to be significantly associated with the characteristics of the family we have included in our analysis or with such foster-care system factors as the number of placements or rate of casework contact.

White Children
Because of the small number of white children (35) in the Times II–III study group, comparable regression analyses to those com-

pleted for the black or Puerto Rican children were not possible. However, review of the correlations between the same set of predictor variables and school achievement as assessed at Time III give a clue about the differences and similarities that might prevail (see Table 10.6). Among the white children it would appear that,

TABLE 10.6
CORRELATION OF SELECTED VARIABLES WITH AGE-ADJUSTED SCHOOL ACHIEVEMENT SCORES—TIME III, BY ETHNICITY
(Group: Times II–III)

Variable[a]	Ethnicity		
	White	Black	Puerto Rican
1. ACHVMT LVL	.56*	.53***	.21
2. AGE	.27	.02	−.30*
3. CARELOG	.16	.07	−.16
4. DEV IQ-T2: TOTAL	.47*	.35*	.28
VERB	.53**	.34**	.32*
N-VERB	.25	.35*	.15
5. DEV IQ-T3: TOTAL	.75***	.63***	.50***
VERB	.77***	.56***	.52***
N-VERB	.52**	.58***	.34*
6. SEX	−.05	.11	.20
7. AGE–SEX	−.02	.07	−.03
8. SES	.26	−.12	.21
9. WEDLOCK	.00	−.27	.09
10. REASON-1	.26	−.08	−.06
11. REASON-2	−.04	−.09	−.09
12. REASON-3	−.57***	.15	−.14
13. EVAL-MO	.39*	.11	.17
14. VISITING	−.11	.02	−.07
15. CONTACT	.32	−.24	−.04
16. EMOT PROB	.22	−.03	−.18
17. DEVEL PROB	.10	−.35*	−.16
18. HEALTH PROBL	.22	−.20	−.00
19. NO. PLACEMTS	.03	.26	.15
No. of cases	35	47	57

*$p < .05$ **$p < .01$ ***$p < .001$
[a] Identification of variables, see Table 5.

unlike the black or Puerto Rican children, older children do some-what better in school. The higher correlations for white children on variables such as entering placement for reasons of the child's own problematic behavior, being from families with higher socio-economic status, evidence of greater or more positive strengths in the mother with more frequent visiting, and a greater rate of casework contact suggest that these factors might have favored the white child's school achievement.

CORRELATION BETWEEN IQ AND SCHOOL ACHIEVEMENT

The association between IQ and school achievement for each ethnic group is also indicated by the data given in Table 10.6. At Time II the correlation of IQ to school achievement was rather low for each of the three groups of children. Moreover, the correlation of non-verbal IQ to school achievement was lower than the correlation of verbal IQ. By Time III, five years following entry into foster care, the correlations between IQ and school achievement were much higher, and all correlations were statistically significant. For black children, the nonverbal IQ was slightly more highly correlated with school achievement than the verbal IQ measure. School achieve-ment and IQ were more highly correlated for the white children and least highly correlated for the Puerto Rican children.

SUMMARY

Our data indicate that the study children, as a group, show sig-nificant gains in school achievement over a five-year time span subsequent to entering foster care, however, the gains are more pronounced during the latter two and one-half years than during the earlier period. Although 47 percent of the children showed im-provement in school during the first two and one-half to three years, the decline among the remaining children was sufficiently large to account for a net decline for all children together. The picture was quite different during the period of two and one-half to five years following entry into foster care. Although only 58 percent of the children assessed showed gains in school achievement, each child's gain tended to be more substantial so that the net result for the group as a whole was fairly marked improvement (to within 9 percent below the children's respective age-appropriate grade levels). In other words, we can say that most of the study children were still performing below their age-appropriate grade level but the gap had been reduced substantially.

The general pattern of decline in the period following entry into foster care prevailed for both white and black children, especially the white children. Puerto Rican children were the only group to show a net increase in school achievement during this period. Black and Puerto Rican children showed substantial improvement in school performance between the third and fifth years of our investigation, whereas white children showed only modest improvement. Girls of all ethnic groups showed improvement in school that surpassed the gains made by the boys.

In our explorations of factors that account for change in school achievement, we found several variables emerging as more important contributors to explaining gains in school performance. Gains in IQ during the same period and being a young female are two such variables. The lack of early childhood developmental problems was also a significant factor, as was having a mother who was seen by the caseworker as being interested and involved.

It is noteworthy that many variables expected to have a positive influence on school achievement were found to be rather inconsequential. For example, such variables as the length of placement, number of placements, or rate of a caseworker's contact with the child and family were not significant contributors to explained variance in school change. In addition, the family's socioeconomic status and visiting pattern were not found to be significant factors.

With regard to ethnic factors, two facts emerged. For black children, it appears that any detrimental effects of early childhood problems and other socioeconomic family disadvantages prior to entering foster care are overcome between three to five years following placement so that the child improves in school achievement. Also, among the black girls, our data suggest that increases in nonverbal cognitive skill play a more important role in improving school achievement than verbal skill (IQ).

Among the Puerto Rican children in our study, gains in school achievement were made throughout the five-year period. Puerto Rican children made slightly less gain overall compared to the black children but markedly greater gain than the white children. For the Puerto Rican children, change in verbal, rather than nonverbal, IQ was the more critical factor. This finding may indicate that Puerto Rican children enter school with a linguistic handicap imposed by demands that they be English-speaking, which takes several years to overcome.

In conclusion, our findings suggest that with time, children from broken homes, after having experienced foster care for sustained periods, can do better in school and begin to close the gap between their own level of school performance and their age-appropriate grade level. However, we question why improvement for a substantial proportion of all children is delayed for approximately three years. Perhaps more emphasis on casework services *earlier* in the foster care experience would enhance the child's performance and achievement in school.

Since IQ change was found to be significantly linked to change in school achievement, it would appear that a potential solution to improving school performance is a program of service directed toward increasing the cognitive skills of the foster child. The success reported by Feuerstein in Israel suggests approaches that might be pursued experimentally.[5] For future research and program planning, we recommend exploration and experimentation with various alternative program models for accomplishing the objective of overcoming cognitive deprivation to enable these disadvantaged children to function more adequately in the classroom and learn at a pace closer to their age-appropriate norm.

---

[5] Reuven Feuerstein, "The Redevelopment of the Socio-Culturally Disadvantaged Adolescent in Group Care," in Martin Wolins and Meir Gottesmann, eds., *Group Care: An Israeli Approach* (New York: Gordon and Breach, 1971), pp. 232–45.

ELEVEN

CLINICAL ASSESSMENT OF THE CHILDREN THROUGH PSYCHOLOGICAL TESTING

Appraisal of the emotional condition of the study children associated with tenure in foster care was an important component of our study. We were mindful of Maas and Engler's finding that children who remain in foster care tend to show increasing emotional disturbance with the passage of time.[1] A typical finding was noted in one community; "Children who returned home were less likely to give evidence of psychological symptoms."[2] Such a report came as no surprise, since the earlier synthesis of research findings on the consequences of maternal deprivation published by John Bowlby had alerted professionals to the potential deleterious effects of separation from the parent.[3] Particular caution was expressed about the potential for developing a syndrome of "affectionless psychopathy." Bowlby cited confirmation of his concern in the reports of a number of investigators in the United States and Great Britain:

> With monotonous regularity each put his finger on the child's inability to make relationships as being the central feature from which all the other disturbances sprang, and on the history of institutionalization or ... of the child's being shifted about from one foster mother to another as being its cause. So similar are the observations and

---

[1] Henry S. Maas and Richard E. Engler, Jr., *Children in Need of Parents* (New York: Columbia University Press, 1959); David Fanshel and Henry S. Maas, "Factorial Dimensions of Characteristics of Children in Placement and Their Families," *Child Development* 33 (1962): 123–44.

[2] Henry S. Maas and Richard E. Engler, Jr., *Children in Need of Parents*, p. 348.

[3] John Bowlby, *Maternal Care and Mental Health* (Geneva: World Health Organization, 1952).

conclusions—even the very words—that each might have written the others' papers. (p. 31)

We particularly valued being able to administer psychological tests to the children through use of our own testing staff. This provided for uniform assessment procedures over the course of our longitudinal investigation. As previously mentioned, the fact that our psychologists were able to test the children who had returned home as well as those remaining in foster care was especially advantageous. This permitted analysis of the issue of whether extended time spent in care was linked to evidence of increased emotional disturbance in the children. As the reader will note in chapter 12, such comparative analysis was not possible when we used the assessments of caseworkers as the source of data about the children's adjustment. When a child returned home, it was the more usual experience that his case was closed shortly thereafter and he was no longer seen by the agency caseworker. Professional ratings of the children were thus available only for those subjects who remained in care.

The amount of time spent by our psychologists in the testing sessions of school-aged subjects was limited to about two hours. At least one hour was devoted to the administration of the age-appropriate intelligence test. To appraise the personal adjustment of the children, we used procedures recommended to us on the basis of a review of the test literature.[4] The children were given modifications of the Goodenough Draw-A-Man Test as revised and extended by Harris.[5] They were asked to draw a person and then one of the opposite sex. They were also asked to draw a family. The particular measures developed in the form of rating scales were based on modifications of those developed by Machover for use with adults.[6] A series of indicators was available for each scale as a guide to those rating the drawings.

---

[4] Consultation on the use of tests was provided by Dr. Leonard S. Kogan of the City University of New York.

[5] Dale B. Harris, *Children's Drawings as Measures of Intellectual Maturity* (New York: Harcourt, Brace, and World, 1963).

[6] Karen Machover, *Personality Projections in the Drawing of the Human Figure* (Springfield, Illinois: Thomas, 1949); idem, "Human Figure Drawings of Children," *Journal of Projective Techniques*, 17 (1953): 85–91.

We also utilized the Michigan Picture Test, a projective test much like the TAT and the CAT.[7] The figure drawing tests were administered to children four years and older, while the Michigan Picture Test was given to youngsters aged eight years and over.[8] Our analysis has been restricted to children aged eight and over. At Time I the mean age of the subjects was 10.5 years (standard deviation = 1.6) and at Time II it was 11.4 years (standard deviation = 2.0).

These tests were administered at Time I (at least 90 days after the children had entered care) and again at Time II (approximately two and one-half years after entry). They were not administered at Time III because we believed that repeated inclusion of tests of this sort in the test battery would not be warranted. A third use of the tests would bring into play problems of practice effect and furthermore, the measures seemed insufficiently rigorous to warrant use over such an extended time span.

To supplement data obtained from the performance of the subjects on the two projective tests, we asked our examining psychologists to carefully observe the behavior of the children during each of the three testing occasions and to provide a clinical judgement of their overall emotional adjustment. They were asked to rate each subject, on the basis of the behavior displayed, as "normal," "suspect," or "abnormal." This provided a global clinical judgment for all children tested. In this chapter we examine the results of our analyses of the use of the projective tests and the global assessments by the examiners.

FIGURE DRAWING TESTS

There has been substantial interest in human figure drawing as a research and clinical tool in the psychological literature for over two decades. In a thorough review, Swensen has analyzed the strengths and weaknesses of the test and suggested that it be used as a rough

---

[7] Gwenn Andrew, Samuel W. Hartwell, Max L. Hutt, and Ralph E. Walton, *The Michigan Picture Test* (Chicago: Science Research Associates, 1953).

[8] Consultations were held with Lawrence Berkowitz to discuss the Michigan Picture Test and with Karen Machover to discuss the figure drawing tests.

screening device or as an indicator of "level of adjustment."[9] He is careful to caution potential users of the test that it may not provide enough data for diagnosing the various factors or aspects of personality dynamics in the individual case. However, he indicates that it may be useful as a device for "screening large groups of people or as a rough gauge of how well the individual patient is functioning." He cites several studies that have reported significant differences between groups of subjects previously diagnosed as normal, neurotic, psychotic, or brain-damaged. In a later review, Swensen has updated the information available about figure-drawing tests and has introduced an even more positive note about the usefulness of the test. He feels there has been substantial increase in empirical justification for its use as a research tool.[10] He suggests, however, that since global ratings include all of the drawing behavior contained in a given test performance, such ratings are the most reliable and therefore constitute the most useful aspect of the test.

Under the procedures we established to test the children, one examining psychologist tested the children while another made "blind" ratings of the drawings. A series of judgment scales was used to rate the drawings, based on consultation with Machover. The scales and the frequencies of ratings associated with them for both testing occasions are shown in Table 11.1. The table shows only minor differences in the distributions of ratings for Times I and II.

Examination of the ratings reveals that few of the subjects were viewed as displaying signs of instability in their sex-role orientation but about 32 percent showed evidence of considerable internal conflict and about 51 percent were rated as being strikingly low in their sense of self-confidence. Signs of considerable repression were shown in 32 percent, and a similar proportion were rated as showing immaturity in their drawings.

Twenty percent were seen as being poorly related socially. However, most subjects were rated as showing some sense of

[9] Clifford H. Swensen, Jr., "Empirical Evaluations of Human Figure Drawings," in Bernard I. Murstein, ed., *Handbook of Projective Techniques* (New York: Basic Books, 1965), p. 647.

[10] Clifford H. Swensen, "Empirical Evaluations of Human Figure Drawings 1957–1966," *Psychological Bulletin* no. 70 (1968): 20–44.

TABLE 11.1
FREQUENCY DISTRIBUTIONS OF FIGURE DRAWING RATING SCALES
ASSIGNED CHILDREN FOR TIMES I AND II TESTING OCCASIONS

Scale	Time I (N = 183)	Time II (N = 212)
	(percentages)	
Stability of sex role		
Unstable	7.1	5.7
Marginal	18.0	31.1
Stable	74.9	63.2
Internal conflict		
Much	32.2	29.7
Some	52.5	57.1
Little	15.3	13.2
Self-confidence		
Little	50.8	45.8
Average	42.6	51.4
Much	6.6	2.8
Avoidance of repression		
Much	31.7	33.0
Some	57.9	49.1
Little	10.4	17.9
Maturity		
Immature	31.7	35.9
Average	63.4	56.1
Unusually mature	4.9	8.0
Social relatedness		
Poorly related	19.7	18.4
Somewhat related	52.5	59.9
Well related	27.8	21.7
Sense of family cohesion		
None	13.2	11.1
Some	72.5	67.6
Much	14.3	21.3
Family deprivation		
Feels homeless	12.2	13.0
Marginal	56.1	38.2
Feels he has a family	31.7	48.8
Life energy		
Little	5.5	14.9
Some	65.0	65.4
Much	29.5	19.7

PSYCHOLOGICAL TESTING

family cohesion. Of interest is the fact that at Time I only 32 percent were viewed as being sure of having a family but this was true for 49 percent of the subjects at Time II. Most children were seen as displaying some or much life energy.

To test the reliability of the ratings, 35 test protocols were selected from the Time II ratings and rated independently on six of the scales by two of the research psychologists. Their ratings were correlated as well as the original ratings assigned. The results shown in Table 11.2 reveal moderate reliability (averaging close to .6) for five of the six scales tested. These included: (a) stability of sex role, (b) self-confidence, (c) avoidance of repression, (d) social related-ness, and (e) internal conflict. The latter scale (e) showed quite a poor level of reliability. In the main, the reliabilities achieved here are smaller than those reported in the literature.

It is of interest to observe that when the children were asked to indicate which family was represented in their drawing, only 31 percent at Time I and 24 percent at Time II specified their own families. They much more often drew fantasy families and almost never drew their foster families. The latter finding is somewhat surprising since by Time II a substantial number of the children had experienced two to three years of continuous residence in foster

TABLE 11.2
RELIABILITY OF SELECTED FIGURE DRAWING RATING SCALES USING
THREE INDEPENDENT CLINICAL RATINGS[a]

Scale	Correlation between Raters A and B (N = 35)	Correlation between Raters A and C (N = 35)	Correlation between Raters B and C (N = 35)
Stability of sex role	.68	.57	.57
Internal conflict	.45	.23	.17
Self-confidence	.82	.50	.41
Avoidance of repression	.72	.67	.68
Maturity	.92	.70	.62
Social relatedness	.69	.56	.61

[a]The "A" ratings reflect those of the original "blind" rater. The "B" and "C" ratings were assigned by psychologist B and psychologist C in the special reliability check.

homes. There is clear indication here of the avoidance of the foster family as an object of fantasy and, for two-thirds of the children on each testing occasion, the failure to utilize their own families as well.

REASON FOR PLACEMENT: A VALIDITY CHECK

We postulated that if the tests we employed were valid, youngsters who entered foster care primarily because of their own emotional and behavioral difficulties would more significantly show signs of emotional maladjustment in their figure drawings than would those whose reasons for being in care stemmed from parental failure.

Our approach to the task of validation is similar to the "known groups" procedure used by Manis and others to test measures created from survey data.[11] They attempted to assay the mental health status of their subjects from responses to questionnaire items and validated their measurement scale by securing responses from subjects of known mental health status (e.g., hospitalized patients, persons receiving out-patient treatment, and untreated persons).

In Table 11.3 we compare mean Time I figure drawing scale scores for children entering foster care because of their own behavior problems with those who had experienced parental neglect, abuse, or desertion. We have included all residual children in a fourth group to complete the comparisons.

Examination of Table 11.3 shows that, indeed, children who entered foster care because of their own problems showed the lowest average scores (i.e., were most maladjusted) among the groups compared on all Time I figure drawing scales. For three of the scales, and for a summary emotional assessment measure, the differences were statistically significant.[12] The most outstanding difference was revealed for the scale of internal conflict ($F = 5.831$;

---

[11] Jerome G. Manis, Melton J. Brawer, Chester L. Hunt, and Leonard C. Kercher, "Validation of a Mental Health Scale," *American Sociological Review* 28 (1963): 108–16.

[12] A summary measure of the ratings assigned a child's drawings was developed by summing the scales shown in Table 11.1 except for "Stability of sex role." Cronbach's coefficient alpha was calculated as an internal consistency reliability coefficient for each testing occasion. For the Time I summary measure the alpha was .82 and for Time II, .77.

TABLE 11.3
MEAN FIGURE DRAWING SCALE SCORES ACCORDING TO SELECTED
REASONS FOR PLACEMENT, TIME I
(N = 183)

Reason for Placement	Stability of Sex Role	Internal Conflict	Self- confidence	Avoidance of Repression
Child Behavior (63)[a]				
Mean	2.64	1.64	1.46	1.67
SD	0.65	0.63	0.59	0.67
Neglect or Abuse (20)				
Mean	2.75	2.10	1.80	1.80
SD	0.43	0.77	0.68	0.51
Abandonment or Desertion (9)				
Mean	3.00	2.44	1.56	1.89
SD	0.00	0.69	0.50	0.31
Residual Cases[b] (91)				
Mean	2.66	1.85	1.57	1.86
SD	0.62	0.61	0.61	0.60
F-test	1.091	5.831	1.584	1.293
Significance	NS	***	NS	NS

$p = .001$). The children entering care because of their own problems apparently displayed more inner turmoil in their drawings than the other groups. They also showed problems with respect to sociability as measured by the scale of social relatedness ($F = 3.746$; $p = .01$), and gave evidence of a greater sense of family deprivation ($F = 3.486$; $p = .05$). On the overall measure based on the summation of eight of the scales, children entering care because of their own problems showed average scores considerably lower (i.e., were more maladjusted) than those assigned the other children ($F = 4.340$; $p = .01$). The overall results of this analysis would appear to constitute a fairly firm validation of the scores.

At Time II the differentiation among the four groups of children observed for Time I is no longer evident. Examination of Table 11.4 fails to show any scale where significant differences are manifested

TABLE 11.3 (*cont.*)

Maturity	Social Relatedness	Family Cohesion	Family Deprivation	Life Energy	Summary Measure: Emotional Assessment
1.68	1.92	1.90	2.03	2.14	1.80
0.56	0.70	0.59	0.63	0.53	0.42
1.85	2.20	2.05	2.50	2.50	2.10
0.57	0.75	0.50	0.50	0.50	0.39
1.67	2.67	2.00	2.44	2.33	2.13
0.47	0.47	0.47	0.69	0.47	0.18
1.75	2.10	2.08	2.21	2.42	1.96
0.53	0.64	0.47	0.63	0.54	0.38
0.550	3.746	1.394	3.486	2.35	4.340
NS	**	NS	*	NS	**

$*p < .05$ $**p < .01$ $***p < .001$

[a] Number of cases shown in parentheses.

[b] Category includes all children not covered by the three reasons for placement shown.

between the children who entered care because of their own problems and the other categories of children. The same lack of significant differentiation holds true for the overall summary measure.

How to interpret these findings? One possibility is that after two to three years in placement, the children who entered care because of their own disturbance were sufficiently improved to be a relatively undifferentiated from the other foster children. It is also possible that the latter have become more disturbed and their scores reflect an adverse reaction to being in care. We must also keep in mind the possibility that deterioration in the validity of the test measures is reflected here.

TABLE 11.4
MEAN FIGURE DRAWING SCALE SCORES ACCORDING TO SELECTED
REASONS FOR PLACEMENT, TIME II
(N = 212)

Reason for Placement	Stability of Sex Role	Internal Conflict	Self-confidence	Avoidance of Repression
Child Behavior (49)[a]				
Mean	2.59	1.74	1.57	1.92
SD	0.64	0.63	0.57	0.75
Neglect or Abuse (33)				
Mean	2.52	2.00	1.49	1.76
SD	0.66	0.60	0.50	0.65
Abandonment or Desertion (18)				
Mean	2.67	2.06	1.56	2.00
SD	0.47	0.62	0.60	0.67
Residual Cases (112)				
Mean	2.57	1.78	1.60	1.82
SD	0.58	0.63	0.54	0.68
F-test	0.261	2.051	0.362	0.683
Significance	NS	NS	NS	NS

An additional procedure for probing the validity of the figure drawing scores was available to us. The clinical rating by the examining psychologist (*abnormal/suspect/normal*) reflected the overall impression gleaned from testing the child in a two-hour session. It provided a somewhat soft test of concurrent validity. We use the term "soft" because the measures were not truly independent, since they derived from the same testing situation. While the ratings of the drawings were made "blind," the examiner obviously had access to the material. At the same time, we were aware that the measures based on the projective tests were related to specific responses of the subject to the test situation and permitted relatively objective scoring. The overall clinical rating was based on the child's general behavior in the test situation.

In Table 11.5 we present the correlations between the figure

TABLE 11.4 (*cont.*)

Maturity	Social Relatedness	Family Cohesion	Family Deprivation	Life Energy	Summary Measure: Emotional Assessment
1.76	1.98	2.00	2.33	2.00	1.90
0.69	0.62	0.55	0.69	0.55	0.39
1.73	1.94	2.00	2.47	1.94	1.91
0.51	0.60	0.56	0.75	0.56	0.41
1.78	2.06	2.12	2.18	2.12	2.00
0.53	0.71	0.68	0.71	0.58	0.47
1.70	2.08	2.17	2.37	2.09	1.95
0.60	0.63	0.53	0.68	0.61	0.36
0.167	0.568	1.414	0.677	0.742	0.410
NS	NS	NS	NS	NS	NS

[a] Number of cases shown in parentheses.

drawing scores and the clinical ratings for Times I and II. The associations are in the anticipated direction for each testing occasion and, although generally modest in size, achieve statistical significance within the context of the sample sizes involved. The strongest correlations emerge for the summary measure based on the summation of eight figure drawing scales.[13] On each occasion, the correlation was .39 ($p < .001$). Among the stronger associations at Time I are those involving internal conflict, social relatedness, maturity, and family cohesion. At Time II, internal conflict shows a somewhat stronger correlation than the other figure drawing scales.

One additional mode of assessment of the validity of figure

[13] The stability of sex-role scale was excluded from the summary measure because its content was more ambiguous with reference to adjustment.

TABLE 11.5
CORRELATIONS BETWEEN FIGURE DRAWING SCALE SCORES
AND ASSESSMENT BY EXAMINING PSYCHOLOGIST
OF EMOTIONAL CONDITION OF CHILD[a]

Variable	Time I[b] (N = 183)	Time II (N = 212)
Stability of sex role	.28***	.11
Internal conflict	.36***	.33***
Self-confidence	.17*	.28***
Avoidance of repression	.23**	.28***
Maturity	.30***	.22**
Social relatedness	.35***	.25***
Family cohesion	.30***	.21**
Family deprivation	.28***	.20**
Life energy	.10	.16*
Summary measure:		
Emotional Assessment[c]	.39***	.39***

$*p < .05$　　$**p < .01$　　$***p < .001$

[a] The examining psychologist was asked to rate the child as abnormal, suspect, or normal.
[b] The correlations represent scales and ratings generated at the same points in time.
[c] Summary measure reflects summation of the eight figure-drawing scales (not including stability of sex role).

drawing tests in another domain, intelligence, was available to us. Harris, in consultation with Goodenough, had developed a scoring procedure for determining a child's IQ based on the figure drawings for the "Draw a Man" test (73 items) and "Draw a Woman" test (71 items).[14] These scoring procedures were employed in connection with the Time II drawings of our subjects. Correlating these scores with the IQs resulting from the administration of the standardized intelligence tests—the WISC in the case of children six years or older—resulted in the following correlations:

　　1. The male figure drawing IQ showed a correlation of .40 with the verbal IQ, .51 with the performance, and .50 with the full-scale IQ.
　　2. The female figure drawing IQ showed a correlation of .23 with the verbal IQ, .46 with the performance, and .38 with the full-scale IQ.

[14] Dale B. Harris, *Children's Drawings as Measures of Intellectual Maturity*, pp. 68–107.

3. The total figure drawing IQ (averaging male and female scores) showed a correlation of .39 with the verbal IQ, .55 with the performance, and .52 with the full-scale IQ.

These results are encouraging and consistent with a number of validity studies using the WISC, reported by Harris.[15] For the subjects tested in the study reported here it would appear that the "Draw a Man" and "Draw a Woman" tests are more allied with performance than with verbal abilities. The associations were somewhat stronger when the child drew a male figure rather than a female figure.

FIGURE DRAWING SCORES AND ETHNICITY

We were interested in determining whether the scale scores assigned the children on the basis of their figure drawing productions would vary according to their ethnicity and/or religious backgrounds. We have stressed throughout this volume that we regard such differences in background as highly important social data. We provide in Table 11.6 the mean figure drawing scale scores achieved by the subjects at the Time I testing, and in Table 11.7 we set forth the results of the Time II testing.

We find statistically significant differences in means achieved by the five groups identified by ethnicity–religion for six of the nine figure-drawing scales and for the summary measure of emotional adjustment as well. The three scales where there was no significant differentiation were: (a) stability of sex role, (b) internal conflict, and (c) avoidance of repression. The Puerto Rican subjects tended to be assigned higher ratings on self-confidence than the children in the other four groups. They also appeared outstanding on the measures of social relatedness and family deprivation; this was also true for the consolidated summary measure. The overall impression one gains from reviewing the results of the figure drawing tests is that the Puerto Rican children appear to be in quite good emotional condition at Time I in comparison with the other children tested.

The white Catholic and Protestant children came closest to the

[15] Dale B. Harris, *Children's Drawings as Measures of Intellectual Maturity*, p. 97.

TABLE 11.6
MEAN FIGURE DRAWING SCALE SCORES ACCORDING TO
ETHNICITY–RELIGION, TIME I
($N = 183$)

	Stability of Sex Role	Internal Conflict	Self-confidence	Avoidance of Repression
White Catholic and Protestant (31)[a]				
Mean	2.58	1.94	1.52	1.81
SD	0.61	0.62	0.50	0.47
Jewish (20)				
Mean	2.40	1.65	1.50	1.70
SD	0.80	0.57	0.50	0.64
Black Catholic (13)				
Mean	2.69	1.77	1.39	1.77
SD	0.46	0.58	0.49	0.70
Black Protestant (42)				
Mean	2.67	1.76	1.21	1.74
SD	0.64	0.57	0.47	0.62
Puerto Rican (77)				
Mean	2.79	1.88	1.81	1.83
SD	0.49	0.76	0.67	0.63
F-test	2.010	0.805	7.682	0.272
Significance	NS	NS	***	NS

Puerto Rican subjects in the average positive scale scores achieved. This was true for the following scales: (a) self-confidence, (b) maturity, (c) family cohesion, (d) family deprivation, and (e) the overall summary measure. On the other hand, the black Protestant children showed the least positive assessments with respect to emotional adjustment. They achieved decidedly low average scores on the following scales: (a) self-confidence, (b) social relatedness, (c) family cohesion, (d) family deprivation, and (e) life energy. The overall summary measure reflected these tendencies. Black Catholic children were somewhat less marked as impaired although they achieved the lowest average score on the scale measuring maturity.

TABLE 11.6 (*cont.*)

Maturity	Social Relatedness	Family Cohesion	Family Deprivation	Life Energy	Summary Measure: Emotional Assessment
1.84	2.07	2.10	2.23	2.26	1.97[b]
0.45	0.62	0.47	0.61	0.51	0.31
1.55	2.10	1.95	2.17	2.40	1.87
0.50	0.70	0.61	0.69	0.49	0.39
1.54	1.85	2.00	2.00	2.00	1.79
0.50	0.66	0.39	0.56	0.56	0.39
1.57	1.71	1.81	1.88	2.00	1.71
0.50	0.63	0.45	0.59	0.44	0.34
1.86	2.33	2.10	2.39	2.36	2.07
0.58	0.63	0.55	0.59	0.56	0.41
3.368	6.514	2.503	5.127	4.461	6.827
*	***	*	***	**	***

$*p < .05$ $**p < .01$ $***p < .001$

[a] Number of cases shown in parentheses.

[b] Summary measure reflects summation of eight of scales presented. A high score reflects an overall positive assessment of the child's emotional condition.

Jewish children fell in the middle on a number of scales. They scored highest on life energy and fairly high on social relatedness. An indication that many of the Jewish children entered foster care because of their own emotional difficulties is their quite low average scores on the following scales: (a) maturity, (b) stability of sex role, (c) internal conflict, and (d) family cohesion. On the overall summary measure they scored a somewhat better average than the black

TABLE 11.7
MEAN FIGURE DRAWING SCALE SCORES ACCORDING TO
ETHNICITY–RELIGION, TIME II
($N = 212$)

Ethnicity–Religion	Stability of Sex Role	Internal Conflict	Self-confidence	Avoidance of Repression
White Catholic and Protestant (32)[a]				
Mean	2.53	1.72	1.50	1.69
SD	0.56	0.57	0.56	0.63
Jewish (18)				
Mean	2.89	1.44	1.39	1.94
SD	0.31	0.50	0.49	0.78
Black Catholic (15)				
Mean	2.60	1.67	1.53	1.67
SD	0.61	0.47	0.50	0.60
Black Protestant (55)				
Mean	2.42	1.75	1.47	1.73
SD	0.59	0.58	0.50	0.67
Puerto Rican (92)				
Mean	2.62	2.03	1.70	1.99
SD	0.62	0.67	0.57	0.70
F-test	2.415	5.094	2.317	2.152
Significance	*	***	NS	NS

Catholic and black Protestant children and lower than the Puerto Rican and the white Catholic and white Protestant children.

When the children were tested again some two-and-one-half years later the ethnic differentiation for the somewhat larger group of subjects was less pronounced. Statistically significant differences emerged for only two scales: (a) stability of sex role and (b) internal conflict. On this occasion, the Jewish children showed the highest average score on the former scale and the lowest score on the latter. The evidence for a high degree of internal conflict among the Jewish subjects is revealed by their scores. The Puerto Rican children again showed the most positive average score on the summary

TABLE 11.7 (*cont.*)

Maturity	Social Relatedness	Family Cohesion	Family Deprivation	Life Energy	Summary Measure: Emotional Assessment
1.63	1.97	2.09	2.31	1.94	1.86
0.60	0.59	0.68	0.73	0.61	0.38
1.78	1.89	2.06	2.29	2.24	1.86
0.79	0.57	0.43	0.57	0.64	0.38
1.80	1.87	2.14	2.43	2.07	1.88
0.54	0.50	0.52	0.62	0.59	0.32
1.55	2.00	1.96	2.28	1.89	1.82
0.57	0.69	0.47	0.76	0.57	0.36
1.84	2.13	2.19	2.42	2.14	2.06
0.56	0.63	0.57	0.68	0.55	0.39
2.388	1.157	1.399	0.414	2.362	4.157
NS	NS	NS	NS	NS	**

*$p < .05$ **$p < .01$ ***$p < .001$
  ^{a} Number of cases shown in parentheses.

measure of emotional condition based on the summation of the eight scale scores. The other ethnic groups were relatively undifferentiated on this measure.

It is difficult to interpret the underlying reasons for the ethnic differences with any sense of certainty. A major finding is that the Puerto Rican children appear to be in significantly better emotional shape on both testing occasions than their counterparts in the study. This is particularly indicated by their average scores on the summary measure that combines eight of the figure drawing scales. We should point out, in this connection, that twice as many of the white children entered foster care because of their own behavioral problems as did black and Puerto Rican children.[16]

ANALYSIS OF CHANGE IN SUMMARY
FIGURE DRAWING MEASURE

We were interested in determining the saliency of selected variables in accounting for change in performance on the figure drawing tests. The results of a multiple regression analysis of the Time II summary measure are shown in Table 11.8. We first entered the Time I measure so that the remainder of the analysis would be focused on *change*. We then entered selected demographic variables followed by measures reflecting an evaluation of the mother, parental visiting, logarithm of days in care, and the logarithm of the total casework contact rate. The zero-order correlations showed four variables with significant associations with the Time II summary measure: (a) the Time I summary measure ($r = .39$), (b) sex of the child ($r = .17$), (c) age–sex interaction ($r = .20$), and (d) the frequency of parental visiting ($r = .22$). The Times I–II association indicates modest stability in the overall score for the 144 children who were tested twice. The findings about sex and age–sex interaction indicate that girls tended to receive higher scores than boys and older girls were particularly well rated. Finally, high parental visiting was linked to more favorable ratings of drawings ($r = .19$).

The multiple regression analysis shown in Table 11.8 yielded only two variables that significantly contributed to explained variance: (a) the Time I summary measure, which accounted for about 12 percent of unique explained variance, and (b) the parental visiting variable, which explained about 4 percent. The latter is an interesting finding and lends support to the notion of the salutary impact of parental visiting, reported by other investigators.[17]

It is noteworthy that the amount of time spent in care made

---

[16] See Table 2.10.
[17] See Eugene A. Weinstein, *The Self-Image of the Foster Child* (New York: Russell Sage Foundation, 1960), p. 69; M. L. Kellmer Pringle and L. Clifford, "Conditions Associated with Emotional Maladjustment Among Children in Care," *Educational Review* 14 (1962): 112–23.

TABLE 11.8
RELATION OF SELECTED BACKGROUND AND OTHER INDEPENDENT
VARIABLES TO CHANGE IN FIGURE DRAWING SUMMARY MEASURE OF
EMOTIONAL ASSESSMENT (TIME II)[a]
(N = 212)

Independent Variables	Zero-Order Correlation	Standardized Regression Coefficient[b]	Percentage Unique Variance Explained
Figure-drawing summary measure (Time I)	.39***	.39***	12.30
Child's age at placement	.10	−.04	0.10
Sex of child (M: 1/F: 2)	.17*	−.22	0.20
Age–sex interaction	.20**	.33***	0.50
Socioeconomic status of family	−.06	−.01	0.00
Birth status (OW/IW)	−.03	−.10	0.80
Reason for placement: child behavior	−.06	.03	0.10
Preplacement developmental problems:			
Emotional problems index	.01	.05	0.20
Developmental problems index	−.02	.00	0.00
Health problems index	−.02	−.08	0.40
Evaluation of the mother— Time II	.05	.02	0.00
Parental visiting frequency— Time II	.19*	.22**	3.90
Log of days in care	−.03	.05	0.20
Log of total casework contact rate—Time II	−.02	−.06	0.30
Multiple R		.47	
Multiple R²		.23	

*p < .05   **p < .01   ***p < .001
[a] Summary measure reflects the sum of eight figure drawing scales.
[b] Italic coefficients are greater than twice their standard error.

only a trivial contribution to explained variance, thus supporting the inference that sustained exposure to foster care was not deleterious. That is, children who returned home did not receive more positive ratings based on their drawings than children remaining in care. We also observe that the caseworker's evaluation of the mother and the amount of casework time invested in the case proved insignificant in explaining variance in the summary measure.

In general, the amount of variance explained by all of the variables included in the analysis is fairly limited and indicates that there are important influences at play which are yet to be accounted for.

MICHIGAN PICTURE TEST

The Michigan Picture Test was administered to children eight years and older. As explained in chapter 3, the test had been included in the study because of the scoring system, which is relatively objective in nature and yields measures of interpersonal relationships and kinds and amounts of tension experienced by children. It has been described as the most carefully constructed variant of the Thematic Apperception Test, and Shneidman has observed that "the manual is, in many ways, the best manual for a projective technique to date.... It is well organized and clearly expressed."[18] Others, such as Shaffer, have referred positively to the effort that went into standardization and validation of the test.[19]

The Michigan Picture Test is a picture-story type of test in which each picture represents a kind of semistructured, social-emotional situation. It was developed through seven years of research by the Michigan Department of Mental Health. The pictures cover a number of common social and emotional conflict situations. Because a child can often talk about himself in the third person when he invents stories about pictures, it is anticipated that he may reveal many aspects of his needs and conflicts that would otherwise not emerge in a direct interviewing confrontation. In a study of children who had experienced separation from their parents, such as the subjects of this study, it was anticipated that pictures of family scenes, and parental figures in particular, would

[18] Edwin S. Shneidman (book review of the Michigan Picture Test), *Journal of Projective Techniques* 19 (1955): 192–93.
[19] Laurence F. Shaffer (book review of the Michigan Picture Test). *Journal of Consulting Psychology* 18 (1954): 475–76.

provide opportunity for the child to project quite profound reflections of the inner turmoil created by such experiences.

In codifying the responses of the foster children reported here, we were guided by the procedures reported by the constructers of the test. The responses of the subjects during the examination were tape recorded, and a number of objective scores were developed based on codification of responses reflecting four primary psychological needs: (a) love (or the need for affection), (b) extrapunitiveness (including oral, physical, or psychological aggression), (c) submission (as indicated by deference or passivity), and (d) personal adequacy (either physical or psychological). The sum of these scores produces a summary measure, "total needs." According to the test constructers, the greater the number of needs expressed, the stronger the indication of psychological maladjustment.

In addition to the tabulation of needs expressed, part of the scoring of the Michigan Picture Test includes an index of self-reference by counting first- and second- or third-person pronouns in the stories. Self-reference is considered a sign of better self-acceptance. The difference between the "well-adjusted" and "poorly adjusted" children was not significant in the original normative study.

The Michigan Picture Test also includes measures of the extent to which subjects use past, present, and future time references. It is assumed that a disproportionate emphasis on past tense tends to indicate avoidance of a current conflict situation, evidence of a regressive trend as a major mechanism of defense, schizoid character structure, and/or submissiveness or isolation. In the normative study it was found that the poorly adjusted children tended to use more past references. Emphasis upon present tense in the stories was generally associated with a good adjustment, although exclusive reliance on the present might indicate an attempt to deal with conflict situations by compulsivity. Heavy reliance on future tense was seen as possibly representing an attempt to deal with current anxiety-provoking situations.

For the 182 children tested with the Michigan Picture Test at Time I, the mean number of total needs expressed was 21.9. This compares with a mean of only 4.2 for the "well-adjusted" third-grade children reported by the test constructers and 6.8 for the "poorly adjusted" subjects. This disparity would make it appear that the foster children were displaying massive signs of maladjustment. However, the finding is difficult to accept at face value. The number of needs expressed closely approximates that reported in a study of 40 families on public assistance in the East Harlem district of New York City, where child subjects averaged 18.9 needs expressed on the Michigan Picture Test.[20] The fact that the authors of the test had suggested four or more needs as the cutting point in distinguishing between well and poorly adjusted children, while two studies in the New York City area show such high average numbers of needs expressed, raised for us question as to the validity of the test measures. The differences in results were of such an order as to challenge credulity.

One way of assessing the validity of the findings was to use the approach previously described in connection with the figure drawing tests, namely, to compare the average needs measures of children categorized by selected reason for placement. The assumption is that children entering care because of their own disturbance should be differentiated in their scores from the other children.

In Tables 11.9–10 we show results of the Michigan Picture test for Times I and II. We compare mean scores of children who came into care primarily because of their own behavioral problems with those who were placed because of neglect or abuse, abandonment, or for residual reasons. For none of the need scores at Time I do we find children who entered care because of their own behavioral problems showing significantly different means than the other categories of children. As a matter of fact, they showed the lowest mean of total needs expressed of the four categories of children and were decidedly lower in number in this regard than children entering care because of neglect or abuse. The same finding holds true for the means of love needs and submission needs. We also failed to find significant differentiation by reason for placement for the Time II measures. The validity of the measures of need is thus brought heavily into doubt.

With regard to verb tense and use of first-person pronouns, we

---

[20] Alice R. McCabe et al., "*Forty Forgotten Families: A Study of Young AFDC Families*" (New York: Community Service Society, 1965, p. 107. (mineographed.)

TABLE 11.9
MEAN SCORES ON MICHIGAN PICTURE TEST ACCORDING TO REASON FOR PLACEMENT AT TIME I
(N = 182)

Reason for Placement	Total Needs	Love-needs Ratio	Extrapunitive-needs Ratio	Submission-needs Ratio	Personal Adequacy-needs Ratio	Past-tense Ratio	Present-tense Ratio	Future-tense Ratio	First-person Pronoun Ratio
Child behavior (65)									
Mean	19.85	32.40	22.79	4.77	40.60	27.72	67.79	4.83	12.79
SD	20.45	24.18	20.21	8.12	28.56	27.88	27.66	6.53	21.13
Neglect or abuse (19)									
Mean	31.21	38.32	27.79	11.16	29.68	36.00	58.79	5.11	13.68
SD	23.74	22.26	23.83	20.20	21.66	33.24	30.66	6.88	15.91
Abandonment or desertion (9)									
Mean	28.78	35.44	20.00	9.56	35.67	31.89	62.79	5.33	9.44
SD	28.39	7.97	8.78	9.36	18.56	26.98	26.27	5.44	9.97
Residual cases (89)									
Mean	20.69	36.54	20.35	6.85	31.47	23.29	70.98	6.66	13.65
SD	18.01	19.90	17.27	12.54	18.70	21.86	22.26	9.63	18.88
F-Test	1.986	0.609	0.878	1.539	2.269	1.469	1.331	0.674	0.143
Significance	NS	NS	NS	NS	NS	NS	NS	NS	NS

TABLE 11.10
MEAN SCORES ON MICHIGAN PICTURE TEST ACCORDING TO REASON FOR PLACEMENT AT TIME II
(N = 204)

Reason for Placement	Total Needs	Love-needs Ratio	Extrapunitive-needs Ratio	Submission-needs Ratio	Personal Adequacy-needs Ratio	Past-tense Ratio	Present-tense Ratio	Future-tense Ratio	First-person Pronoun Ratio
Child behavior (47)									
Mean	9.45	36.04	24.38	3.67	31.64	22.09	71.02	6.68	22.40
SD	6.02	26.74	21.29	6.71	22.04	21.99	22.58	9.64	29.05
Neglect or abuse (32)									
Mean	8.53	42.06	25.53	1.91	30.47	25.16	67.94	6.59	21.63
SD	6.60	30.38	26.21	4.73	24.25	24.63	26.98	9.12	24.96
Abandonment or desertion (18)									
Mean	8.44	47.11	14.22	2.61	30.44	20.56	74.06	5.39	16.33
SD	8.13	27.63	16.85	6.89	24.21	19.68	20.76	6.66	18.09
Residual cases (107)									
Mean	10.79	38.83	26.08	3.22	29.95	22.07	71.90	6.17	17.93
SD	12.17	25.00	24.13	6.73	25.33	22.54	23.71	8.23	23.83
F-Test	0.640	0.863	1.328	0.513	0.051	0.207	0.312	0.116	0.520
Significance	NS	NS	NS	NS	NS	NS	NS	NS	NS

again find a lack of validating support for the measures. The children who entered foster care because of their own behavioral difficulty demonstrated a tendency to avoid use of the present tense or first-person pronouns in no greater proportion than the other categories of children with whom they were compared.

As was the case with the figure drawing scores, a further test of the validity of the Michigan Picture Test was available through the clinical assessments of the emotional condition of the subjects made by the examining psychologists. The product–moment correlations for Time I and Time II are displayed in Table 11.11. They show, again, a lack of validation of the Michigan Picture Test scores. At Time I the score representing the total needs of the subject is significantly correlated with the clinical assessment but in a direction opposite to what one would expect on the basis of the test rationale. The more needs expressed by the child the more likely he was to be assessed as normal $(r = .18)$. Frequent use of past tense,

TABLE 11.11

ZERO-ORDER CORRELATIONS BETWEEN MICHIGAN PICTURE TEST
SCORES AND EXAMINING PSYCHOLOGIST'S ASSESSMENT
OF CHILD'S EMOTIONAL CONDITION AT TIMES I AND II[a]

Variable	Time I (N = 182)	Time II (N = 211)
Total needs	.18*	.06
Love-needs ratio	.04	−.16*
Extrapunitive-needs ratio	.13	.10
Submission-needs ratio	.09	.04
Personal-adequacy-needs ratio	−.14	.13
Love plus personal-adequacy-needs ratio	−.15*	−.03
Extrapunitive plus submission-needs ratio	.17*	.10
Past-tense ratio	.28***	.04
Present-tense ratio	−.31***	−.02
Future-tense ratio	.09	−.03
1st person pronoun—percent of total	−.22**	−.24***
2nd–3rd person pronoun—percent of total	.24**	.26***

$*p < .05$ $**p < .01$ $***p < .001$
[a]The correlations shown for Time I involve only Time I data, and only Time II data are shown for Time II (i.e., we have not shown correlations for Time I Michigan Picture Test scores and Time II clinical assessments).

contrary to expectations, was significantly linked to a positive assessment ($r = .28$). The same reversal in expected findings held true for use of first-person pronouns ($r = -.22$ at Time I and $r = -.24$ at Time II).

Further evidence that brought into question the validity of the Michigan Picture Test scores emerged when they were correlated with the figure drawing scores derived from the same testing occasions. At Time I many of the correlations were in a direction opposite to that which was predicted, and many of the associations were statistically significant (but in the reverse direction). Thus, the total needs score was positively correlated with the figure drawing summary measure ($r = .39$, $p < .001$), indicating that better-adjusted children were expressing more needs. Indeed, review of our data suggests that the open expression of needs may be a sign of better emotional health, at least as manifested by subjects who have experienced foster care.[21]

We also observe here that the Jewish subjects, with the highest quota of children coming into care because of emotional problems, were among those expressing the lowest number of needs. On the other hand, the Puerto Rican children, previously described as appearing in the best condition on the figure drawing tests, showed an average of total needs expressed far above the other ethnic groups at Times I and II.

By way of summary comment, we observe that the findings from the Michigan Picture Test, if accepted as valid, would indicate a very widespread condition of maladjustment among these subjects. While children having suffered separation from their parents for more than 90 days may well display more pathology than children from so-called normal populations, the evidence of invalidity of the measures we have provided is too strong to accept such an interpretation.

CLINICAL ASSESSMENT

As a final section of this chapter, we provide further analysis of a measure already discussed, namely, the examining psychologist's

---

[21] We do not present the data in tabular form in the interest of saving space.

assessment of the child's emotional condition on the three testing occasions (abnormal/suspect/normal). We were interested in the patterns that emerged for the three assessments (Times I–III). That is, we sought to determine whether the children remained stable in their emotional adjustment, as reflected in the clinical assessments, or showed change over time, either regressing or improving in the course of the five-year study.

The distribution of assessment patterns is shown in Table 11.12. We note that 52 percent of the children were always rated as being normal in their emotional adjustment on the occasions when they were tested.[22] Another 18 percent of the sample showed patterns that reflected a shift from suspect or abnormal to normal (SUSP-ABN → NORM), thus indicating some improvement in their situation.

About 7 percent of the subjects (40 children) showed a pattern of assessment as normal when they entered care, then as

TABLE 11.12
PATTERNS OF EMOTIONAL ASSESSMENT OF SUBJECTS
BY EXAMINING PSYCHOLOGISTS OVER FIVE-YEAR PERIOD[a]

Pattern of Assessment	Number	Percentage
Always normal (NORM)	303	51.9
Shift from suspect or abnormal to normal (SUSP-ABN → NORM)	103	17.7
Shift from normal to suspect to normal (NORM → SUSP → NORM)	40	6.9
Shift from suspect to normal to suspect (SUSP → NORM → SUSP)	14	2.4
Shift from normal to suspect or abnormal (NORM → SUSP-ABN)	55	9.4
Always suspect or abnormal (SUSP-ABN)	68	11.7
Total	583	100.0

[a] Forty-one cases (6.6 percent) are not included in this table; the children were never given psychological tests.

[22] Not all of the children were examined on all three testing occasions. As indicated in chapter 7, 62.8 percent of the subjects were tested on all three occasions, 16.5 percent on two occasions, and 12.8 percent once. In the patterns of assessment displayed in Table 11.12, if a child was seen only once and rated normal, he was included in the pattern "always normal". Similar treatment was accorded other subjects seen on less than all occasions.

suspect (or abnormal) at Time II, and normal again at Time III (NORM→SUSP→NORM). The "dip" at Time II could reflect a regression that had taken place at the midpoint of the study. It is also possible, of course, that it reflects measurement error.

The remaining three patterns contain 23.5 percent of the study subjects. One in four children were seen as reflecting emotional maladjustment by the examining psychologists.

An issue that constantly confronts social planners about the foster care system concerns the proportion of emotionally disturbed children being cared for. The amount of fiscal support required to operate the system is very much linked to this matter. The data we present here suggest a parameter for such planners; about one in four children who experience care for at least 90 days will tend to show a pervasive pattern of emotional disturbance over a five-year period.

Age

In Table 11.13 we present the patterns of assessment of subjects according to age at time of entering foster care. We had anticipated that signs of emotional disturbance would be strongly linked to this variable since behavioral problems tend to expand with age as a child's behavioral repertoire broadens. Table 11.13 tends to support this notion but only in modest fashion. Thus, only 42 percent of the children over six years of age were consistently rated as normal, compared to 61 percent who entered care before two years of age, and 57 percent, at two to five years. However, some 24 percent of the older children showed a shift from ratings of suspect or abnormal to normal (SUSP-ABN→NORM); this was almost twice the proportion of children in the two younger groups. One might conjecture that the shift shown by the older children is in response to treatment.

Of considerable interest is the fact that almost 25 percent of the children who entered foster care under two years of age and 20 percent of those who entered at two to five years show patterns that indicated consistent or emerging maladjustment as reflected in the psychologists' assessments. The children who entered care at age six or over showed 25 percent classified in this manner; they are thus relatively undifferentiated from the younger children on this

TABLE 11.13
PATTERNS OF EMOTIONAL ASSESSMENT OF SUBJECTS
BY EXAMINING PSYCHOLOGISTS OVER FIVE-YEAR PERIOD,
BY AGE OF CHILDREN AT ENTRY INTO FOSTER CARE
(N = 583)

Pattern of Assessment	Under Two Years	Two to Five Years	Six Years or Older
	(percentages)		
Always normal (NORM)	60.9	57.4	42.2
Shift from suspect or abnormal to normal (SUSP–ABN → NORM)	11.2	14.2	24.2
Shift from normal to suspect to normal (NORM → SUSP → NORM)	3.5	8.3	8.2
Shift from suspect to normal to suspect (SUSP → NORM → SUSP)	4.1	0.6	2.9
Shift from normal to suspect or abnormal (NORM → SUSP–ABN)	12.4	7.1	9.0
Always suspect or abnormal (SUSP–ABN)	8.2	12.4	13.5
No. of cases	170	169	244

$\chi^2 = 32.215$, df = 10, $p < .001$

score. If the findings are valid, the implications are important. They indicate a sizable reservoir of disturbed children in the younger ranks, many of whom will require care for quite a few years.

Reason for Placement

Another perspective on the assessments of the psychologists can be obtained by examining the patterns according to reason for placement. In Table 11.14 we segregate the children entering foster care primarily because of their own behavioral problems from all of the other children. The differences in patterns are fairly pronounced but not overwhelming in their decisiveness. Thus, 42 percent of the behavioral-problem children show a pattern of consistent or emergent maladjustment, compared to 21 percent of the remaining children. Twenty-four percent of the former showed a shift from a suspect or abnormal assessment to normal over the course of the

TABLE 11.14
PATTERNS OF EMOTIONAL ASSESSMENT OF SUBJECTS
BY EXAMINING PSYCHOLOGISTS OVER FIVE-YEAR PERIOD,
BY REASON FOR PLACEMENT

Pattern of Assessment	Child Behavior	Other Reasons
Always normal (NORM)	26.8	55.5
Shift from suspect or abnormal to normal (SUSP–ABN → NORM)	23.9	16.6
Shift from normal to suspect to normal (NORM → SUSP → NORM)	7.0	6.8
Shift from suspect to normal to suspect (SUSP → NORM → SUSP)	1.4	2.7
Shift from normal to suspect or abnormal (NORM → SUSP–ABN)	14.1	8.8
Always suspect or abnormal (SUSP–ABN)	26.8	9.6
No. of cases	71	512

$\chi^2 = 29.889$,   df = 5, $p < .001$

five years (SUSP-ABN → NORM), and this was true of 17 percent of the remaining children.

Twenty-seven percent of the behavioral-problem children were consistently rated normal, compared to 56 percent of the remaining children. While the differences are clear, the validity of the assessments is not firmly established. The measurement issues involved here are complex. Obviously, children who enter care primarily because of parent-related reasons may, nevertheless, be severely maladjusted because of the mishandling to which they have been exposed. It is also possible that children placed because of behavioral difficulties may not reflect this maladjustment when relieved of intimate interaction with their parents and the environments that have fostered their disturbance.

Ethnicity

When the patterns of assessment were examined according to ethnicity using the familiar five-way ethnic break, the Jewish children appeared to represent the highest proportion of children consistently seen as being maladjusted. This was true of 52 percent of the Jewish subjects but only about 20 percent of each of the remaining groups. Aside from the Jewish group's obvious preponderance of emotionally disturbed children, the differences in frequency of assessment patterns among the remaining four groups are trivial. While the Puerto Rican group stood out most positively among the ethnic groups when the figure drawing measures were examined, such differentiation is not apparent with respect to the general clinical ratings (Table 11.15).

Discharge Status

When we compared the patterns of assessment of discharged children with those of children remaining in care at the end of five years, we found some small differences (Table 11.16). Fifty-four percent of the discharged children had consistently been rated as normal while this was true of 46 percent of the children remaining in care. Twenty-three percent of the latter showed a shift from a rating of suspect or abnormal, compared to about 15 percent of the discharged children. Almost 21 percent of the children in care reflected consistent or emergent maladjustment patterns, compared to 27 percent of the discharged children. The differences are modest but certainly do not reflect a process whereby the most maladjusted children are being committed to foster care on a long-term basis. All but two of the 19 adopted children were rated as normal, and one child was rated so after first being assessed as suspect.

In Table 11.17 we examine consolidated patterns of assessment according to ethnicity while controlling for discharge status. For white Catholic or Protestant children and Puerto Rican children we find little difference in the patterns of assessment for discharged subjects as opposed to those still in care. About 80 percent of such children received assessments of normal (or shifts to normal) regardless of whether they were discharged or remained in care. The same was true for black Catholic or black Protestant children who remained in care; about 80 percent received the positive assessments. However, only about 70 percent of the black children who returned home were rated positively. The Jewish children still in care were too few to make the discharge/in-care comparison meaningful.

TABLE 11.15
PATTERNS OF EMOTIONAL ASSESSMENT OF SUBJECTS
BY EXAMINING PSYCHOLOGISTS OVER FIVE-YEAR PERIOD,
BY ETHNICITY–RELIGION

Pattern of Assessment	White Catholic and Protestant	Jewish	Black Catholic	Black Protestant	Puerto Rican	Total
			(percentages)			
Always normal (NORM)	59.1	17.2	48.4	49.6	56.1	52.0
Shift from suspect or abnormal to normal (SUSP–ABN→NORM)	14.8	20.7	17.2	19.0	17.9	17.6
Shift from normal to suspect to normal (NORM→SUSP→NORM)	6.1	10.3	10.9	7.3	5.1	6.9
Shift from suspect to normal to suspect (SUSP→NORM→SUSP)	—	—	1.6	2.8	4.1	2.4
Shift from normal to suspect or abnormal (NORM→SUSP–ABN)	8.7	17.2	12.5	10.1	7.1	9.4
Always suspect or abnormal (SUSP–ABN)	11.3	34.6	9.4	11.2	9.7	11.7
No. of cases	115	29	64	179	196	583

$\chi^2 = 36.555$,   df $= 20$, $p < .05$

TABLE 11.16
PATTERNS OF EMOTIONAL ASSESSMENT OF SUBJECTS
BY EXAMINING PSYCHOLOGISTS OVER FIVE-YEAR
PERIOD BY DISCHARGE STATUS AT END OF STUDY

Pattern of Assessment	Remaining in care	Discharged	Adopted
	(percentages)		
Always normal (NORM)	45.7	54.1	89.4
Shift from suspect or abnormal to normal (SUSP–ABN → NORM)	23.0	14.5	5.3
Shift from normal to suspect to normal (NORM → SUSP → NORM)	10.6	4.7	—
Shift from suspect to normal to suspect (SUSP → NORM → SUSP)	4.4	1.5	—
Shift from normal to suspect or abnormal (NORM → SUSP–ABN)	8.8	10.1	5.3
Always suspect or abnormal (SUSP–ABN)	7.5	15.1	—
No. of cases	226	338	19

CHANGE IN CLINICAL ASSESSMENT

In Table 11.18 we show the results of a multiple regression analysis of the changes in the emotional assessments of the subjects made by the examining psychologists during Times I–II, Times II–III, and Times I–III. The regressor variables we used should be familiar to the reader by now. They include demographic variables such as age, sex, and ethnicity, and foster care–related variables such as reason for placement, log of days in care, frequency of parental visiting, casework contacts, and the caseworker's evaluation of the child's mother. We also included the child's developmental history as measured by the three indexes described in chapter 3.

When we examine the Times I–II change in clinical assessments, we find—as might be expected—that the Time I measure is a significant predictor of the later assessment. It is the strongest predictor among the regressor variables; the raw correlation between Time I and Time II assessments is .34 ($p < .001$). Another

TABLE 11.17
PATTERNS OF EMOTIONAL ASSESSMENT BY EXAMINING PSYCHOLOGISTS (CONSOLIDATED), BY ETHNICITY–RELIGION, CONTROLLING FOR DISCHARGE STATUS AT END OF FIVE YEARS

Consolidated Patterns	White Catholic and Protestant	Jewish	Black Catholic	Black Protestant	Puerto Rican
A. Still in Care					
Always normal or shift to normal[a]	81.3	25.0	82.2	79.7	79.5
Always suspect or abnormal or shift to suspect or abnormal[b]	18.7	75.0	17.8	20.3	20.5
No. of cases	32	4	28	84	78
B. Discharged					
Always normal or shift to normal	78.1	52.0	69.7	71.1	77.8
Always suspect or abnormal or shift to suspect or abnormal	21.9	48.0	30.3	28.9	22.2
No. of cases	73	25	33	90	117

[a] Includes patterns: (NORM), (SUSP–ABN→NORM), and (NORM→SUSP→NORM).
[b] Includes patterns: (SUSP→NORM→SUSP), (NORM→SUSP–ABN), and (SUSP–ABN).

TABLE 11.18
THE RELATION OF SALIENT BACKGROUND AND OTHER INDEPENDENT VARIABLES TO CHANGES IN THE ASSESSMENT OF THE EMOTIONAL CONDITION OF THE SUBJECTS

Independent Variables	Time II Assessment (Change from Time I)	Time III Assessment (Change from Time II)	Time III Assessment (Change from Time I)
	(standardized regression coefficients)		
Earlier assessment (Time I or Time II)	.26***	.26***	.17***
Child's age at placement	−.08	.19*	.19*
Sex of child	.05	.11	.11
Age–sex interaction	−.08	−.03	−.08
Socioeconomic status of family	−.02	−.01	.00
Ethnicity:[a]			
Black	−.08	−.01	−.04
Puerto Rican	.08	−.05	−.07
Reason for placement:[b]			
Child behavior	−.16**	−.06	−.09
Neglect or abuse	.02	−.08	−.06
Abandonment	.03	−.02	−.01
Developmental history indexes:			
Emotional problems index	.03	.04	.03
Developmental problems index	−.17***	−.10	−.13*
Health problems index	.02	−.05	−.02
Log of days in care	−.06	.03	.05
Parental visiting pattern	−.06	−.06	−.07
Log of total casework contact rate	.02	−.01	.05
Worker skill index	−.02	.10*	.12*
Evaluation of mother	.05	.07	.05
Multiple R	.47	.35	.32
Multiple R^2	.22	.12	.10
No. of cases	490	404	404

*$p < .05$ **$p < .01$ ***$p < .001$
[a] Referenced to white children.
[b] Referenced to all other children.

significant predictor is child behavior as a reason for placement; children who came into care because of this reason tended to show a decline in assessments over the two testing occasions. The only other significant predictor was the index indicating that the child had suffered from developmental problems prior to entering care (based on information secured from the mothers during field interviews).

Looking at changes in ratings during Times II–III, we again find the earlier assessment is a significant predictor; the Times II–III correlation is .25 ($p < .001$). Age is also a significant predictor, with older children showing gains in assessment. One final predictor proved to be significant, namely, the index measuring the skill of the caseworker assigned to the child. The index is based on two items: (a) education of the worker with respect to social work training and (b) years of experience (in logarithmic form). It would appear that children exposed to more skilled caseworkers showed gains in assessments over the final two and one half years of the study.

For the full expanse of the study (Times I–III), there were four significant predictors: (a) the earlier assessment, (b) the child's age, (c) report of earlier developmental problems, and (d) caseworker skill.[23]

We observe that the amount of variance accounted for in predicting the Time III assessments from the vantage points of Time I and Time II is very low (12 percent and 10 percent, respectively). We also point out that length of time in care, parental visiting, casework contact rate, and evaluation of the mother fail to contribute significantly to the explanation of change in ratings.

SUMMARY COMMENTS

We have reported in some detail our efforts to appraise the emotional condition of our subjects through psychological testing. The availability of such data for both discharged children and those remaining in care made such testing valuable to our purposes. We are of course aware that when we assessed the quality of the data,

---

[23] The product-moment correlation between the Time I and Time III assessments is .18 ($p < .001$).

we came up with mixed results. The figure drawing scales showed moderate reliability and the validity checks were within an acceptable range for this kind of study. On the other hand, the Michigan picture test results did not hold up under validity checks, and the results are thus dubious. The overall clinical assessments by the psychologists for the three testing occasions, together with the figure-drawing scores, appear to be more useful for our purposes. Among the findings reported here, the following stand out:

1. On the figure drawing tests almost a third of the subjects showed high internal conflict, a similar proportion appeared immature, and almost half seemed lacking in self-confidence as reflected in rating scales for the two testing occasions. Less than 15 percent produced drawings reflecting a total lack of family cohesion and signs of feeling homeless.

2. The children appeared significantly differentiated in their drawings at Time I with respect to reason for placement. Children who entered foster care primarily because of their own behavior problems showed more signs of maladjustment on four measures than the children with whom they were compared. Such differentiation failed to emerge at Time II.

3. The Puerto Rican children in the study appeared to show better adjustment than the other subjects as reflected in the figure drawing results. This differentiation was not manifested when the psychologists' global assessment of the emotional condition of the children was analyzed.

4. In the regression analysis of change in the summary measure based on the sum of eight figure drawing scales, high degree of parental visiting was predictive of positive change. This did not emerge in the analysis of change in the psychologists' global ratings.

5. The Michigan Picture Test showed a lack of positive results when its validity was tested, and its usefulness in explaining change in the condition of the children over time was thereby brought into question.

6. The patterns of emotional assessment by the examining psychologists covered three testing occasions over the five-year time span of the study. Consistently normal ratings were obtained for 52 percent of the subjects, and another 25 percent progressed to normal over the course of the study. This left almost 24 percent of the subjects who had always been rated as suspect or abnormal or whose ratings had shifted in this direction over the course of the study.

7. Almost 25 percent of the younger children were in the suspect or abnormal categories at the end of five years.

8. Casework skill proved to be a significant predictor of positive change in clinical assessment of the children.

9. The length of time children spent in foster care failed to emerge as a significant predictor of change with respect to both figure drawing scores and the global assessments by the psychologists.

TWELVE

CHILD
BEHAVIOR
CHARACTERISTICS
OF FOSTER CHILDREN

The Child Behavior Characteristics (CBC) form provided an opportunity for caseworkers to rate the behavior of children known to them, using an adjective checklist.[1] The rating instrument was developed on the basis of a number of prior studies of children, and considerable effort was invested in the selection of items and the development of scoring procedures. The work covering the instrument construction phase has been described in an earlier publication.[2]

As pointed out in chapter 3, the use of the behavioral rating instrument was based on the need to chart the course of a child's development over time through use of a constant set of descriptive categories. It was particularly suited to the requirements of a longitudinal study covering a broad age span of children, since

[1] Originally, three forms were made up, on an age-related basis (Form 1—up to two years, Form 2—two to six years, and Form 3—seven to 17 or more years). These were subsequently consolidated into a General Research Form containing 109 items.

[2] Edgar F. Borgatta and David Fanshel, "The Child Behavior Characteristics (CBC) Form: Revised Age-Specific Forms," *Multivariate Behavioral Research* 5 (1970): 49–82. For earlier efforts, see David Fanshel, Lydia Hylton, and Edgar F. Borgatta, "A Study of Behavior Disorders in Children in Residential Treatment Centers," *Journal of Psychological Studies* 14 (1963): 1–24; Edgar F. Borgatta and David Fanshel, *Behavioral Characteristics of Children Known to Psychiatric Out-Patient Clinics* (New York: Child Welfare League of America, 1965); Edgar F. Borgatta and Patricia Cautely, "Behavior Characteristics of Children: Replication Studies with Foster Children," *Multivariate Behavioral Research* 1 (1966): 399–424.

behavioral items were keyed to age. No items were retained for younger children that were phrased in a way that prevented their application to the older age groups. As children became older during the study, the number of items on which they could be rated was expanded to include behaviors that are more clearly part of the behavioral repertoire of older children. The specific cluster of items and component CBC scores have been described in chapter 3.

As we pointed out, the major limitation inherent in the use of the rating instrument is the fact that we could only secure ratings for children who remained in foster care. Those who were discharged were usually no longer in contact with their caseworkers after a relatively short period of time. The data in this chapter are therefore restricted to children who remained in care, and for whom we were able to chart behavioral change over the full course of the five-year study. Despite the truncation of our sample, we consider the analysis of the behavioral characteristics of our subjects a worthwhile undertaking since children who have spent many years in foster care have been identified in the professional literature as highly vulnerable to emotional disorders.[3] The developmental progress of children who remain in foster care many years is an appropriate concern for students of the foster care system.

We secured forms for each of the three data-gathering periods as follows:

Time	Number of Forms Received	Percentage of Eligible Children
I	560	90
II	350	94
III	226	93

[3] There is evidence that the foster care system has many children who spend large proportions of their childhood years in care. A recent analysis of data in a new computerized information system in New York City showed that 56 percent of the children had been in foster care for five years or more. See David Fanshel and John Grundy, *Computerized Data for Children in Foster Care: First Analyses from a Management Information System in New York City* (New York: Child Welfare Information Services, 1975).

By and large, the many agencies participating in the study were cooperative in returning the forms, and the yield of usable forms received was impressive since all data-gathering transactions were handled by mail (with follow-up by telephone when required).

MEAN SCORES AND CHANGES OVER TIME

In Table 12.1 we present the means and standard deviations of the CBC composite scores assigned our subjects on the three occasions on which they were rated by the social workers who knew them. In Table 12.2 we go on to examine changes in the scores assigned the same individuals on repeated assessments; we use the matched t-test as a measure of the significance of differences in scores.[4] For children who were six years of age or over at the time of their entry into care, a complete set of 16 composite scores was available for examination of individual change when rated on successive occasions over time.

The overall picture that emerges portrays behavior difficulty of the subjects to generally increase with age and time spent in foster care. Thus, when we examine the Times I–II differences in mean scores, the perceptions of the social workers filling out the questionnaires significantly change in the direction of seeing the children as less agreeable, more defiant, less likable, more withdrawn, and more emotional and tense. Some of this perceived behavioral change may well be related to the age maturation of the children and would be in accord with the assumption that children are capable of becoming more aggressive and hostile as they get older. It is also possible that the behavioral change is related to the foster care experience. We shall subsequently analyze in this chapter the contribution of a number of variables, including some related to the foster care experience, to explaining behavioral change.

We observe that there are significant changes in scores related to sexual precociousness and sexual inhibition. It would appear that the social workers are witnessing more sexual play and sexual precocity while also detecting increased fear in sexual matters.

[4] Ralph H. Kolstoe, *Introduction to Statistics for the Behavioral Sciences* (Homewood, Ill: Dorsey Press, 1973), pp. 221–29.

TABLE 12.1
MEAN CBC COMPOSITE SCORES AND STANDARD DEVIATIONS
FOR THREE DATA-GATHERING OCCASIONS

	Time I (N = 560)[a]		Time II (N = 350)		Time III (N = 226)	
	Mean	SD	Mean	SD	Mean	SD
Alertness–attention (IA)	17.58	4.55	17.91	4.32	17.25	4.42
Intelligence (IB)	4.81	4.21	8.19	2.28	7.67	2.56
Alertness–intelligence (I)	22.08	6.42	25.90	6.26	24.91	6.58
Learning difficulty (II)	7.17	2.77	7.18	2.87	7.02	2.71
Responsibility (III)	5.86	5.19	9.90	2.78	9.69	2.96
Unmotivated–laziness (IV)	4.09	3.38	5.47	2.69	5.41	2.51
Agreeableness (V)	25.69	6.06	24.29	5.92	24.26	6.14
Defiance (VIB)	4.30	2.47	5.36	2.16	5.02	2.11
Hostile–unsocialized (VIB)	6.61	7.37	11.44	5.85	11.57	6.72
Defiance–hostility– unsocialized (VI)	10.77	8.92	16.57	7.55	16.59	8.31
Likability (VII)	29.57	6.04	28.94	5.89	25.81	3.52
Emotionality–tension (VIII)	15.94	7.20	12.98	4.28	18.36	7.04
Infantilism (IX)	4.20	4.11	6.79	2.92	6.98	3.12
Withdrawal B (XA)	5.40	2.84	6.20	2.79	6.13	2.85
Withdrawal C (XB)	4.61	5.01	7.33	4.57	7.47	4.33
Withdrawal (X)	9.71	6.74	13.30	6.79	13.61	6.72
Appetite (XI)	6.54	1.62	6.57	1.59	6.55	1.57
Sex precociousness (XII)	1.24	2.17	3.15	2.61	3.17	2.72
Overcleanliness (XIII)	3.13	3.02	5.10	2.27	4.85	2.55
Sex inhibition (XIV)	1.10	1.45	1.97	1.36	2.03	1.42
Activity (XV)	6.17	1.77	6.55	1.53	6.16	1.66
Assertiveness (XVI)	4.64	4.31	8.08	3.80	7.05	2.81

[a]The N values reflect the maximum numbers of subjects rated, i.e., for scores appropriate for all age groups.

For the period Times II–III, there is significant decline in alertness and intelligence; this was not the case for the Times I–II time span. Again, the subjects are seen as significantly more hostile and defiant, less likable, less agreeable, and more withdrawn. They are also seen as less active and more assertive but not more emotional or tense.

For the full five-year span we find significant changes in the direction of the subjects being less agreeable, more defiant, less likable, and more withdrawn. They are also seen as being more sexually precocious as well as inhibited.

For children aged two to five years at the time of entry there is a reduced set of behavioral items that are age-appropriate. We show the changes for nine composite scores based on these items and four concerning the physical development of the child (see section B of Table 12.2). For the Times I–II period, there are two significant changes. The subjects tend to show more emotionality and tension and are more active. They also show better coordination and appear more robust and sturdy. For the second time span (Times II–III) there are significant changes in two composite scores: (a) likability (VII) and (b) activity (XV). By the end of the five-year span, the children are perceived as less likable and less active. They are also seen as less clumsy.

For the full five-year span, the children who entered foster care between two and five years of age show significant change for two composite scores: (a) learning difficulty (II) and (b) likability (VII). They show less learning difficulty but are perceived as less likable over the course of five years. They are also perceived as showing better coordination.

For the children who entered care under the age of two, we are able to use four composite scores that are age-appropriate and four items dealing with the children's physical condition. They show increased alertness and attention and better coordination for the Times I–II comparison. There is a negative turn for the Times II–III span, with a significant decrease in alertness and attention and activity. They also are perceived as less likable. For the full five-year span, the subjects have significant lowering of scores, indicating that they are perceived as less agreeable and less likable.

We observe for the three age groups that there is some evidence of behavior unfolding of a more aggressive and less likable character. This may be related to increase in age and/or factors related to the foster care experience. We shall examine this matter further as we proceed.

Stability of Scores

Five years in the life of a child who has had a continuous living experience in foster care represents a relatively long time span. It

TABLE 12.2

MEAN CHANGES IN CBC COMPONENT SCORES ON REPEATED ASSESSMENTS FOR THREE TIME PERIODS

A. For Children Six Years or over (mean, 9.2 years) at Entry into Care

CBC Composite Scores	Change, Times I–II (N = 138)			Change, Times II–III (N = 76)			Change, Times I–III (N = 70)		
	Mean Difference	SD	t-value[a]	Mean Difference	SD	t-value	Mean Difference	SD	t-value
Alertness–attention (IA)	-0.17	4.86	-0.42	-1.30	4.26	-2.65**	-0.89	5.15	-1.43
Intelligence (IB)	-0.00	2.64	-0.00	-0.70	2.32	-2.61*	-0.33	2.60	-1.05
Alertness–intelligence (I)	-0.30	7.05	-0.49	-1.78	6.20	-2.48*	-1.16	7.32	-1.31
Learning difficulty (II)	0.11	3.06	0.42	-0.32	2.48	-1.10	-0.24	3.44	-0.59
Responsibility (III)	-0.21	3.26	-0.76	-0.61	3.61	-1.45	-0.81	3.93	-1.72
Unmotivated–laziness (IV)	0.19	3.53	0.62	0.08	3.00	0.23	-0.04	4.02	-0.09
Agreeableness (V)	-2.28	6.49	-4.12***	-2.21	6.13	-3.12**	-3.37	7.08	-3.97***
Defiance (VIB)	1.09	2.51	5.08***	0.46	2.48	1.61	1.20	2.88	3.47***
Hostile–unsocialized (VIB)	0.97	7.19	1.58	2.32	7.28	2.76**	2.67	8.21	2.70
Defiance–hostility (VI)	1.93	9.16	2.46*	2.99	8.99	2.88**	3.91	10.36	3.14**
Likability (VII)	-1.87	7.22	-3.03**	-3.40	6.19	-4.75***	-3.97	7.26	-4.54***
Emotionality–tension (VIII)	2.23	7.99	3.26***	0.42	7.52	0.49	1.71	7.86	1.81
Infantilism (IX)	0.49	3.50	1.62	0.37	3.58	0.89	0.37	3.75	0.82
Withdrawal B (XA)	0.85	3.18	3.13**	0.50	2.59	1.67	0.67	3.37	1.66
Withdrawal C (XB)	0.94	5.37	2.05*	1.40	4.77	2.53*	1.50	5.71	2.18*
Withdrawal (X)	1.62	7.81	2.42*	2.13	6.64	2.78**	2.24	8.59	2.17*
Appetite (XI)	0.20	2.08	1.14	-0.00	2.00	-0.00	0.10	1.94	0.43
Sex precociousness (XII)	1.64	3.22	5.95***	0.78	3.44	1.95	2.07	3.43	5.02***
Overcleanliness (XIII)	-0.05	2.69	-0.22	0.33	3.01	0.95	-0.13	2.82	-0.38
Sex inhibition (XIV)	0.41	1.61	3.01**	0.18	1.42	1.12	0.54	1.72	2.62*
Activity (XV)	0.12	2.00	0.68	-0.80	1.84	-3.79***	-0.31	2.05	-1.27
Assertiveness (XVI)	0.20	3.26	0.70	-0.74	0.34	-2.15*	-0.36	3.25	-0.91

B. For Children Two to Five Years (mean, 3.7 years) at Entry into Care

	Change, Times I–II (N = 89)			Change, Times II–III (N = 59)			Change, Times I–III (N = 58)		
Alertness–attention (IA)	0.89	4.91	1.70	0.31	3.99	0.58	0.62	5.58	0.84
Learning difficulty (II)	-0.11	3.45	-0.31	-0.70	2.77	-1.91	-1.16	3.12	-2.79**
Agreeableness (V)	-0.21	7.01	-0.29	-0.36	5.75	-0.47	-0.02	5.99	-0.02
Defiance (VIB)	0.24	2.94	0.75	-0.19	2.17	-0.65	-0.17	3.27	-0.40
Likability (VII)	1.12	7.17	1.47	-3.75	4.60	-6.20***	-2.47	7.34	-2.54*
Emotionality–tension (VIII)	2.92	8.42	3.25**	-1.53	7.21	-1.61	1.72	9.02	1.44
Withdrawal B (XA)	-0.00	4.01	0.00	0.27	3.63	0.57	0.29	2.99	0.74
Appetite (XI)	0.33	2.02	1.52	0.27	2.18	0.95	0.50	2.03	1.86
Activity (XV)	0.65	2.26	2.71**	-0.54	1.47	-2.82**	-0.03	2.41	-0.11
Physical items									
Physical development	-0.02	0.81	-0.15	-0.03	0.58	-0.44	0.00	0.97	0.00
Awkward or clumsy	0.06	0.78	0.61	-0.34	0.65	-3.95***	-0.11	0.73	-1.00
Coordination	0.31	0.83	3.39***	-0.02	0.82	-0.16	0.31	0.99	2.29*
Robust and sturdy	0.38	0.85	4.04***	-0.21	0.83	-1.89	0.23	0.99	1.72

C. For Children Under Two Years (mean, 0.7 years) at Entry into Care

	Change, Times I–II (N = 97)			Change, Times II–III (N = 77)			Change, Times I–III (N = 77)		
Alertness–attention (IA)	0.92	4.36	2.06*	-2.01	4.74	-3.70***	-1.29	6.18	-1.82
Agreeableness (V)	-2.06	6.62	-3.05	-0.35	6.81	-0.45	-1.94	7.56	-2.23*
Likability (VII)	-0.65	6.07	-1.05	-4.68	5.51	-7.40***	-5.27	6.19	-7.43***
Activity (XV)	0.47	1.55	3.00**	-0.69	1.65	-3.65***	-0.09	2.15	-0.37
Physical items									
Physical development	0.13	0.83	1.42	-0.11	0.53	-1.73	-0.00	0.82	-0.00
Awkward or clumsy	0.12	0.63	1.68	-0.08	0.46	-1.51	0.04	0.65	0.55
Coordination	0.19	0.75	2.42*	-0.16	0.75	-1.84	0.04	0.92	0.38
Robust and sturdy	0.08	0.93	0.87	-0.14	0.69	-1.69	-0.06	0.89	-0.52

*p < .05 **p < .01 ***p < .001   aMatched t-test for repeated observation of the same subjects.

would not be surprising to find quite wide fluctuations in behavioral profiles over this period. Such changes in the child could well reflect the influence of maturation, the stability and kind of caretaker arrangements made available by the agency, the kind of interest shown by the child's parents, and the extent and quality of casework or psychiatric attention provided. One might also consider the influence of siblings and peers, environmental factors in the neighborhood of residence, and the role played by the school system. Our sense of the fluctuating nature of behavioral scores was reinforced by prior longitudinal studies of children raised by their own parents; these have shown a broad range in the correlations between repeated measures of behavior.[5]

In Table 12.3 we show the zero-order correlations between earlier and later scores achieved by the subjects who were rated by the caseworkers on the CBC forms on three occasions. These provide another perspective of the stability of scores from that provided through the examinations of "change" in the preceding section. It is clear that there is greater stability of scores over the shorter two-and-one-half-year time segments (Times I–II and Times II–III) than those shown for the full five-year time span (Times I–III). We also observe that the correlations spanning the second half of the study are somewhat stronger than those based on the Times I–II comparisons. Thus the correlation for alertness–intelligence (CBC IA + B) is .47 for the Times II–III comparison, .24 for Times I–II, and only .12 for Times I–III. Similarly, the correlations reflecting repeated measurements for distractibility–learning difficulty (CBC IIB) are .42 for the second half of the study period, .39 for the first half, and .24 for the full five-year time span.

Several of the CBC scores stand out as being the most stable: (a) agreeableness (CBC VB), (b) defiance (CBC VIA), (c) defiance–hostile–unsocialized (CBC VIA + B), (d) emotionality–tension (CBC VIII), (e) withdrawal B–Withdrawal C (CBC XA + B), and (f) sexual inhibition (CBC XIV). These composite scores show statistically

[5] See Wanda C. Bronson, "Central Orientations: A Study of Behavior Organization from Childhood to Adolescence" in Mary Cover Jones, Nancy Bayley, Jean Walker Macfarlane, and Marjorie Pyles Honzik, eds., *The Course of Human Development* (Waltham, Mass.: Xerox College Publishing, 1971), pp. 201–15.

TABLE 12.3
ZERO-ORDER CORRELATIONS BETWEEN CBC SCORES
ASSIGNED CWRP SUBJECTS ON REPEATED ASSESSMENT

CBC	Correlation Times I–II (N = 324)[a]	Correlation Times II–III (N = 212)	Correlation Times I–III (N = 205)
Alertness–attention (IA)	.40***	.44***	.17*
Intelligence (IB)	.04	.44***	.10
Alertness–intelligence (IA + B)	.24***	.47***	.12
Distractibility–learning difficulty (IIB)	.39***	.42***	.24***
Responsibility (IIIB)	.12*	.29***	.08
Unmotivated–laziness (IVB)	.36***	.32***	.14*
Agreeableness (VB)	.33***	.41***	.29***
Defiance (VIA)	.28***	.33***	.14*
Hostile–unsocialized (VIB)	.30***	.41***	.33***
Defiance–hostile– unsocialized (VIA + B)	.33***	.43***	.36***
Likability–less gloomy– sourness (VII)	.30***	.26***	.09
Emotionality–tension (VIII)	.36***	.43***	.23***
Infantilism (IX)	.26***	.35***	.01
Withdrawal B (XA)	.15**	.30***	.08
Withdrawal C (XB)	.31***	.32***	.24***
Withdrawal B – withdrawal C (XA + B)	.29***	.34***	.18**
Appetite (XI)	.20***	.08	.04
Sex precociousness (XII)	.22***	.23***	.29***
Overcleanliness (XIII)	−.01	.14*	.13
Sex inhibition (XIV)	.30***	.21**	.25***
Activity (XV)	.26***	.39***	.11
Assertiveness (XVI)	.08	.14*	.17*
Physical development	.12*	.44***	.11
Awkward or clumsy	.23***	.36***	.24**
Coordination	.21***	.24***	.06
Robust and sturdy	.19***	.39***	.24**

*$p < .05$ **$p < .01$ ***$p < .001$

[a]The sample sizes represent the maximum for behavior scores suitable for all ages of children. They are somewhat reduced for those not suitable for young children (see chapter 3).

significant correlations for the five-year comparisons as well as for the shorter time segments (Times I–II and Times I–III).

Statistically significant correlations are to be found for the shorter time segments, but not for the full five-year span, for the following: (a) responsibility (CBC IIB), (b) likability–less gloomy–sourness (CBC VII), (c) infantilism (IX), and (d) activity (XV).

Lack of stability of scores may reflect measurement error or actual changes in behavior. In this chapter we examine through simple multiple regression analysis the degree to which variables theoretically associated with behavioral change account for variance in change in CBC scores.

ASSESSMENT OF THE VALIDITY
OF THE BEHAVIORAL SCORES

As was the case with the measures originating from the psychological tests (as discussed in chapter 11), we were interested in probing the CBC measures for their validity. We were mindful that the behavioral ratings were made by social workers of varying educational backgrounds, whose contacts with the children ranged from intense and frequent involvements to sporadic encounters. We have, therefore, conducted the following analyses:

    1. A test of the difference in behavioral scores according to the reason for placement, with the assumption that children who enter care because of their own emotional problems will tend to show different scores than children who enter care because of family reasons.

    2. A correlational analysis of the association of CBC scores with other related measures as a reflection of concurrent validity.

These measures include the IQ scores achieved by the children on the standardized intelligence tests, the figure drawing scores, and assessments of the emotional condition of the children based on the psychological tests, and the ratings of the adjustment of the children by their teachers. Such analyses should provide the reader with needed perspective about the behavioral measures employed.

Reason for Placement

In Table 12.4 we compare the Time I composite CBC scores for six groups of children, all of whom had entered foster care at six years of age or older. The groups were organized according to the following reasons for placement:

1. Group 1—mental illness of child caring person.
2. Group 2—behavior of child.
3. Group 3—hospitalization for physical illness of child caring person.
4. Group 4—neglect, abuse, or abandonment.
5. Group 5—unwillingness of child caring person to continue care.
6. Group 6—all other children.

For most of the 16 composite scores displayed in Table 12.4 there are significant differences between the groups (as tested by the one-way analysis of variance). In all instances, the children entering care because of their own behavioral difficulty show scores which would identify them as the most problematic among those entering care. They are perceived as being less alert and intelligent, showing problems in learning, less responsible, and more unmotivated in their behavior. They are also less agreeable, less likable, and more defiant and hostile. Such children are more tense and more withdrawn than the other children. They also appear to be more sexually precocious.

In the pairwise comparisons, the children entering care because of behavioral difficulty were significantly more problematic in their behavior, compared to children entering care because of the mental illness of the child caring person, with respect to: (a) (learning difficulty), (b) CBC III (responsibility), (c) CBC IV (unmotivated–laziness), (d) CBC V (agreeableness), (e) CBC VI (defiance–hostility–unsocialized), and (f) CBC XII (sexual precociousness). They were significantly higher (more problematic) on CBC IV (unmotivated–laziness) than children entering care because of neglect, abuse, or abandonment and significantly higher (more problematic) on CBC VIII (emotionality–tension) than children entering care because of the physical illness of the child-caring person. We are aware that a number of the pairwise comparisons failed to show significant differences between the children entering care because of

TABLE 12.4
MEAN CBC COMPOSITE SCORES (TIME I) FOR SUBJECTS SIX YEARS OR OVER AT ENTRY INTO CARE, BY REASON FOR PLACEMENT
(N = 227)

CBC Composite Scores (Time I)		Reason for Placement[a]						
	Group 1 (N = 44)	Group 2 (N = 64)	Group 3 (N = 24)	Group 4 (N = 44)	Group 5 (N = 25)	Group 6 (N = 26)	F-test (significance)
Alertness–intelligence (I)							
Mean	25.77	21.97	23.08	23.68	25.92	25.65	2.800*
SD	6.86	6.16	7.02	5.70	7.84	5.05	(p = .018)
Learning difficulty (II)							
Mean	6.73	8.45	7.13	7.39	6.88	7.19	2.553*
SD	3.12	2.59	3.30	2.33	2.79	2.63	(p = .029)
	(Paired comparisons: group 1 significantly less than group 2)						
Responsibility (III)							
Mean	10.68	8.41	9.58	9.68	9.44	10.04	3.180**
SD	3.46	2.66	2.94	2.93	3.35	2.77	(p = .009)
	(Paired comparisons: group 1 significantly higher than group 2)						
Unmotivated–laziness (IV)							
Mean	5.68	7.77	6.38	6.09	6.00	6.12	3.593**
SD	3.25	2.97	2.88	2.17	3.11	2.52	(p = .004)
	(Paired comparisons: group 1 significantly less than group 2; group 2 significantly higher than group 4)						

Agreeableness (V)							
Mean	25.86	22.31	25.50	25.43	24.16	24.92	2.479*
SD	6.88	5.07	5.27	5.89	7.24	5.95	(p = .033)
	(Paired comparisons: group 1 significantly higher than group 2)						
Defiance–hostility– unsocialized (VI)							
Mean	14.14	19.47	15.08	15.89	16.72	17.15	2.400*
SD	9.32	6.83	7.70	8.80	9.46	9.36	(p = .039)
	(Paired comparisons: group 1 significantly less than group 2)						
Likability (VII)							
Mean	29.50	26.27	30.04	28.32	27.92	29.00	2.300*
SD	5.51	5.34	5.25	5.83	7.50	6.91	(p = .046)
	(Paired comparisons: group 1 significantly higher than group 2)						
Emotionality–tension (VIII)							
Mean	18.89	20.70	15.42	17.27	17.56	18.27	2.295*
SD	7.39	6.91	6.30	6.70	7.98	9.32	(p = .047)
Infantilism (IX)							
Mean	6.77	7.61	6.13	6.52	5.52	6.42	1.978
SD	3.31	3.11	3.69	2.59	3.14	3.10	(p = .083)
Withdrawal (X)							
Mean	12.30	15.97	13.08	13.89	11.96	13.19	2.589*
SD	5.79	6.73	5.35	5.89	6.64	6.11	(p = .027)
Appetite (XI)							
Mean	6.27	6.11	6.46	6.25	6.52	6.19	0.318
SD	1.71	1.39	1.38	1.75	1.75	1.71	(p > .500)

TABLE 12.4 (cont.)

Reason for Placement[a]

CBC Composite Scores (Time I)	Group 1 (N = 44)	Group 2 N = 64)	Group 3 (N = 24)	Group 4 (N = 44)	Group 5 (N = 25)	Group 6 (N = 26)	F-test (significance)
Sex precociousness (XII)							
Mean	1.68	3.38	2.13	1.86	2.20	1.42	3.694**
SD	1.98	3.17	2.20	2.21	2.83	1.86	(p = .004)
	(Paired comparisons: group 1 significantly less than group 2)						
Overcleanliness (XIII)							
Mean	5.16	5.14	5.25	4.91	5.60	5.12	0.332
SD	1.98	2.16	1.83	2.30	1.70	2.71	(p > .500)
Sex inhibition (XIV)							
Mean	1.75	2.25	2.00	2.02	1.96	1.85	0.684
SD	1.49	1.59	1.12	1.27	1.46	1.59	(p > .500)
Activity (XV)							
Mean	5.84	5.53	5.68	5.86	6.08	6.27	0.829
SD	1.61	1.86	1.62	1.80	1.74	1.65	(p > .500)
Assertiveness (XVI)							
Mean	8.02	7.41	7.79	7.16	8.64	8.35	1.238
SD	2.71	2.82	3.16	3.38	2.51	3.04	(p = .293)

*p < .05   **p < .01   ***p < .001

[a] Group 1 = mental illness of child-caring person; Group 2 = behavior of child; Group 3 = hospitalization of child-caring person for physical illness; Group 4 = neglect, abuse, or abandonment; Group 5 = caretaker unwilling to continue care; Group 6 = all other cases.

behavioral difficulty and those entering for other reasons for placement, although their behavior was always the most problematic. We view the data set forth in Table 12.4 as constituting modest evidence of the validity of the CBC measures.

Correlations with Standardized Intelligence Tests

A fairly firm test of the concurrent validity of the CBC scores was available to us in the form of standardized intelligence tests. The first major concept measured by the behavioral rating instrument was related to alertness and intelligence. Six items were used in rating all children, including infants, on: (a) alertness and (b) attention–curiosity (CBC score IA). In a longitudinal study entailing repeated measurement from infancy to later childhood, CBC score IA represents the general concept through time, holding the items constant. The component score IB, Intelligence, is composed of three items and involves notions of rationality and reasoning; it is not seen as applicable to infancy. The two scores are combined into a nine-item composite score CBC I (IA + IB) alertness–intelligence.

In Table 12.5 we present the correlations of deviation IQ scores (verbal, nonverbal, and total) with the CBC composite scores dealing with alertness and intelligence. All correlations are statistically significant at the .001 level and average between .3 and .4. The strongest correlation is between the Time III deviation verbal IQ and CBC IB (intelligence); the correlation is .50. In general, the later the time period under study, the higher the correlations between the caseworker's ratings and the IQ scores. One possible interpretation of this is that the caseworkers have attained firmer perceptions of the children's intelligence on the basis of longer periods of contact. We also find that of the three composite scores, ratings of intelligence (CBC IB) show the highest correlations with the intelligence test scores; this is to be expected on conceptual grounds.

Although the correlations reported are not very large, we are not inclined to construe the findings as reflecting massive doubt about the validity of the CBC scores. It is our view that when linkage is sought between two such diverse data-gathering instruments as an intelligence test and an adjective checklist filled out by social workers of varied backgrounds, correlations on the order of .3 or .4 (significant at .001 level) reflect the kind of association which

TABLE 12.5

ZERO-ORDER CORRELATIONS BETWEEN CBC ALERTNESS-INTELLIGENCE COMPOSITE SCORES AND DEVIATION IQ'S ACHIEVED BY SUBJECTS[a]

CBC Composite Scores[b]	Time I			Time II			Time III		
	Verbal IQ	Nonverbal IQ	Total IQ	Verbal IQ	Nonverbal IQ	Total IQ	Verbal IQ	Nonverbal IQ	Total IQ
Alertness-attention-curiosity (IA)	.31***	.25***	.28***	.41***	.31***	.31***	.39***	.30***	.38***
Intelligence (IB)	.23***	.20***	.14***	.39***	.32***	.33***	.50***	.38***	.49***
Alertness-intelligence (IA + IB)	.32***	.27***	.29***	.43***	.33***	.33***	.45***	.35***	.45***

***$p < .001$.

[a]For CBC IA, $N = 522$ (Time I), 323 (Time II), 283 (Time III).
For CBC IB and IA + IB, $N = 360$ (Time I), 323 (Time II), 283 (Time III).

[b]The correlations are always calculated for data collected at the same time. For example, the IQ test scores of the Time I testing are correlated with the Time I CBC scores, and so forth.

one can optimally expect from such an effort. We are mindful that the less than perfect interrater reliability of the CBC scores serves to attenuate the validity coefficients. A correction for attenuation would bring the reported correlations closer to .5.[6]

CBC Scores and Psychological Assessments

As indicated, another approach available to us for testing the concurrent validity of the CBC scores was to correlate them with the measures developed from the administration of the figure drawing tests to the older subjects and the ratings of the emotional condition of all subjects by the examining psychologists.[7] It is our impression that the independence of the data-gathering procedures was well maintained during the study, and the validity check we introduce here is therefore a fairly stringent one.

The reader should bear in mind that the content domains assayed by the psychological testing session and the CBC rating procedures were different although clearly related to a notion of personal adjustment. For instance, a high CBC VI rating (defiance–hostility) would presumably indicate an emotional condition deviating from that of normal or average children. There is no basis for expecting correlations that can approach unity, but some concordance between the two sets of measures would be theoretically expected.

Table 12.6 correlates the CBC scores with the figure drawing summary measure of emotional assessment (based on all scales except stability of sex role). The correlations between the two sets of measures are provided concurrently for Times I and II. The results indicate significant correlations for quite a few of the CBC measures for both time occasions, but the magnitudes of the associations are not very large. The validation effort has yielded only modest results.

<hr/>

[6] In the early trial use of the CBC, the between-rater correlation of CBC I alertness–intelligence for 83 pairs of raters responding for subjects two to six years of age was .65, and it was .56 for 165 pairs of raters responding for children age seven years and older. See Edgar F. Borgatta and David Fanshel, "The Child Behavior Characteristics (CBC) Form," p. 73.

[7] In chapter 11 we show that the Michigan picture-test scores appeared to be seriously lacking in validity. We do not present the data here for lack of space, but calculation of the correlations between the total needs scores achieved by our subjects on this test and the CBC scores again produced results that showed this absence of validity.

TABLE 12.6
ZERO-ORDER CORRELATIONS BETWEEN CBC SCORES AND FIGURE
DRAWING TEST SUMMARY MEASURES OF EMOTIONAL ASSESSMENT FOR
TIMES I AND II

CBC Score[a]	Time I Figure-Drawing Summary Measure (N = 164)	Time II Figure-Drawing Summary Measure (N = 149)
Alertness–intelligence (IA + B)	.32***	.15*
Learning difficulty (IIB)	−.29***	−.31***
Responsibility (IIIB)	.24**	.17*
Unmotivated–laziness (IVB)	−.24**	−.16*
Agreeableness (VB)	.19*	.13
Defiance–hostility (VIA + B)	−.17*	−.16*
Likability (VIIA)	.15	.13
Emotionality–tension (VIIIA)	−.20*	−.22*
Infantilism (IXC)	−.21*	−.20*
Withdrawal C (XB)	−.16*	−.10
Appetite (XIB)	−.08	.04
Sex precociousness (XIIC)	−.17*	−.13
Overcleanliness (XIIIC)	.09	.02
Sex inhibition (XIVC)	−.03	−.02
Activity (XVA)	.03	.01
Assertiveness (XVIB)	.07	.05

*$p < .05$ **$p < .01$ ***$p < .001$.

[a] Time I CBC scores are correlated with Time I figure-drawing measures, and Time II CBC scores are correlated with Time II figure-drawing measures.

[b] Figure-drawing summary measure is an index based on the sum of eight scales described in chapter 11.

The CBC measures that appear related to adjustment and are significantly correlated with the figure-drawing summary measures at both Times I and II include: (a) CBC III (responsibility), (b) CBC IV (unmotivated–laziness), (c) CBC VI (defiance–hostility), (d) CBC VIII (emotionality–tension), and (e) CBC IX (infantilism). The following CBC measures were significantly correlated with the figure drawing scores for Time I only: (a) CBC V (agreeableness), (b) CBC X (withdrawal), and (c) CBC XII (sexual precociousness). There were no significant associations for either occasion for: (a) CBC VII (likability), (b) CBC XI (appetite), (c) CBC XIII (overcleanliness), (d) CBC XIV (sexual inhibition, (e) CBC XV (activity), and (f) CBC XVI (assertiveness).

In Table 12.7 we set forth the correlations between the CBC scores and the examining psychologists' assessments of the emotional condition of the subjects at three testing occasions over the five years of longitudinal investigation. The two sets of measures derive from concurrent time periods. The firmest associations are evidenced for Time II, followed by Time III. In the early period of a child's placement (Time I), the knowledge of the child seems most tenuous and the correlations appear relatively low.

Overall, it is our impression that these data reflect only moderate support for the notion that valid assessments of the children have been made. None of the correlation coefficients is higher than .36. Even with corrections for attenuation due to the limited reliabilities of the measures, the associations only suggest a fair degree of validity. Nevertheless, it should be pointed out that the magnitude of these associations is consistent with findings reported in several other studies attempting to link assessments of the same children from independent observers.[8] We consider our findings to reflect the general "softness" of procedures now available for the measurement of personality and behavioral dimensions of childhood.

Teacher Ratings

Another test of the concurrent validity of the CBC scores was made possible through the availability of teacher ratings of subjects at Time III. For this purpose, we had used the scales provided on a rating instrument developed by the Michigan Department of Mental

[8] See Norman A. Polansky, Robert D. Borgman, and Christine De Saix, *Roots of Futility* (San Francisco: Jossey Bass, 1972), pp. 136–37; Sister Mary Paul Janchill, "Differential Perception of the Behavior Characteristics of Adolescent Girls in Residential Treatment Centers by Caseworkers, Child Care Workers, and Teachers" (doctoral dissertation, Columbia University School of Social Work, 1975); and David Fanshel, Lydia Hylton, and Edgar F. Borgatta, "A Study of Behavior Disorders of Children in Residential Treatment Centers," *Journal of Psychological Studies* 14 (1963): 1–23.

TABLE 12.7
ZERO-ORDER CORRELATIONS BETWEEN CBC SCORES
AND ASSESSMENT OF EMOTIONAL CONDITION
OF CWRP SUBJECTS AT TIMES I, II, AND III[a]

CBC Composite Scores	Correlation Time I Assessment and CBC I (N = 521)	Correlation Time II Assessment and CBC II (N = 323)	Correlation Time III Assessment and CBC III (N = 214)
Alertness–intelligence (IA)	.18***	.29***	.27***
Intelligence (IB)	−.05	.33***	.36***
Alertness–intelligence (IA + B)	.10*	.32***	.32***
Distractibility–learning difficulty (IIB)	−.24***	−.34***	−.27***
Responsibility (IIIB)	−.07	.29***	.27***
Unmotivated–laziness (IVB)	−.20***	−.28***	−.21*
Agreeableness (VB)	.15***	.27***	.19*
Defiance (VIA)	−.13**	−.26***	−.15*
Hostile–unsocialized (VIB)	−.22***	−.25***	−.07
Defiance–hostile– unsocialized (VIA + B)	−.21***	−.27***	−.10
Likability–less gloomy– sourness (VII)	.14**	.24***	.06
Emotional–tension (VIII)	−.19***	−.32***	−.21**
Infantilism (IX)	−.25***	.32***	−.28***
Withdrawal B (XA)	−.07	−.14*	−.04
Withdrawal C (XB)	−.22***	−.24***	−.06
Withdrawal B–withdrawal C (XA + B)	−.18***	−.22***	−.06
Appetite (XI)	.07	−.05	−.03
Sex precociousness (XII)	−.17***	−.15**	−.01
Overcleanliness (XIII)	−.11*	.18**	.21**
Sex inhibition (XIV)	−.13**	−.13*	.10
Activity (XV)	.07	.14**	.05
Assertiveness (XVI)	−.11*	.06	.17*
Physical development	−.09	−.20***	−.07
Awkward or clumsy	−.16***	−.24***	−.26***
Coordination	.08	.27***	.29***
Robust and sturdy	.07	.19***	.17*
Physical defects	−.04	—[b]	−.24***

*p < .05   **p < .01   ***p < .001

[a] The examining psychologist was required to rate the emotional condition of the subject on a scale so that 1 = abnormal, 2 = suspect, 3 = normal.

[b] Not calculated.

Health.[9] The instrument was filled out by teachers for 213 subjects in our study. While the content domains covered by the ratings do not exactly match those included in the CBC, they are nevertheless sufficiently similar to indicate linkage between the two types of measures. We view the teacher ratings as providing a partial basis for validation of the CBC composite scores. In Table 12.8 we provide the zero-order correlations between the Time III CBC scores and the teacher ratings. The number of children represented by the correlations ranges from 123 to 130.[10]

Ratings of teachers related to the emotional adjustment of subjects are significantly correlated with CBC composite scores with domains of similar content. The correlations for a number of these are of the order of .3, .4, and .5. Thus the pupil adjustment scale, "overall emotional adjustment," is positively correlated with CBC III, responsibility ($r = -.48$), and CBC VIII, emotionality-tension ($r = -.37$). Similar associations are to be found with the pupil adjustment scales labeled: (a) social maturity, (b) tends to aggressive behavior, (c) emotional security, and (d) impulsiveness.

We observe that the pupil rating scale called "school achievement" correlates positively with CBC IB, intelligence ($r = .45$), and with CBC IA + IB, alertness–intellignce ($r = .45$). The pupil-rating scale called "school conduct" correlates positively with CBC III, responsibility ($r = .47$).

The manual of instructions for the Rating Scale for Pupil Adjustment (RSPA) suggests combining items for three summary measures. The "total emotional adjustment score" is a summation of ratings for: (a) overall emotional adjustment, (b) social maturity, (c) emotional security, and (d) impulsiveness. This summary measure correlates positively with the scores of CBC III, responsibility ($r = .46$), and CBC V, agreeableness ($r = .50$), and negatively with CBC VI, defiance–hostility ($r = -.52$), and CBC VIII, emotionality–tension ($r = -.43$).

The summary measure of "aggressive behavior" is developed

[9] The *Rating Scale for Pupil Adjustment* is published with normative data by Science Research Associates, 259 East Erie Street, Chicago, Illinois 60611. It was developed as part of the research for the Michigan picture test.

[10] While teacher-rating forms were received for 213 subjects, the CBC forms were, as previously noted, only available for the reduced number of children remaining in care.

TABLE 12.8

ZERO-ORDER CORRELATIONS BETWEEN TEACHER RATINGS OF SUBJECTS ON PUPIL ADJUSTMENT FORM AND CASEWORKERS' RATINGS ON CBC FORM FIVE YEARS AFTER ENTRY INTO FOSTER CARE[a]

CBC Scores (Time III)	Pupil Adjustment Scores[b]							
	1	2	3	4	5	6	7	8
Alertness–attention (IA)	.27***	.30***	.14	.07	.05	.25**	.11	.26**
Intelligence (IB)	.36***	.36***	.36	.19*	-.06	.26**	.20	.36***
Alertness–intelligence (IA + B)	.32***	.34***	.16	.12	.01	.27**	.15	.31***
Learning difficulty (II)	-.37***	-.41***	-.13	-.13	.03	-.21*	-.30***	-.30***
Responsibility (III)	.45***	.42***	.23**	.32***	-.08	.30***	.20*	.38***
Unmotivated–laziness (IV)	-.26**	-.30***	-.07	.01	-.16	-.24**	-.11	-.15
Agreeableness (V)	.52***	.41***	.24**	.43***	-.10	.38***	.18*	.36***
Defiance (VIA)	-.41***	-.35***	-.27**	-.27**	.05	-.35***	-.08	-.26**
Hostile–unsocialized (VIB)	-.47***	-.42***	-.29***	-.45***	.13	-.40***	-.19*	-.38***
Defiance–hostile–unsocialized (VIA + B)	-.48***	-.43***	-.31***	-.43***	.12	-.42***	-.18*	-.38***
Likability–less gloomy–sourness (VII)	.16	.15	.17	.14	.14	.26**	-.09	.12
Emotionality–tension (VIII)	-.37***	-.31***	-.20*	-.30***	.01	-.36***	-.22*	-.32***
Infantilism (IX)	-.25**	-.24**	-.14	.05	-.11	-.11	-.26**	-.24**
Withdrawal B (XA)	-.07	-.02	-.17	.06	-.25**	-.23	.07	.01
Withdrawal C (XB)	-.21*	-.18*	-.20*	-.08	-.21	-.27**	-.00	-.11

Withdrawal (XA + B)	-.17	-.13	-.20*	-.02	-.24**	-.27**	.03	-.07
Appetite (XI)	.08	.10	.10	-.05	.07	.14	-.00	.10
Sex precociousness (XII)	-.23**	-.14	-.09	-.12	.04	-.23**	.01	-.29**
Overcleanliness (XIII)	.05	.05	-.08	.11	-.13	-.08	-.08	-.03
Sex inhibition (XIV)	-.09	-.04	-.17	-.04	-.06	-.17	.01	-.06
Activity (XV)	.06	.03	.09	-.11	.16	.24**	-.06	-.02
Assertiveness (XVI)	-.04	-.05	-.06	-.20*	.16	-.14	.05	-.05
Physical development	.03	-.02	.13	-.06	.12	.10	-.17	-.00
Awkward or clumsy	.01	-.02	.13	.05	.02	.10	-.34***	-.00
Coordination	-.01	-.02	-.20*	-.03	.00	-.02	.14	-.06
Robust and sturdy	.15	.20*	.08	.01	-.10	.19*	.21*	.15
Physical/mental defects	-.01	-.14	.04	-.07	-.07	-.02	-.30***	.11

Pupil Adjustment Scores

CBC Scores (Time III)	9	10	11	12	13	14	15
Alertness–attention (IA)	.25**	.42***	.29***	-.11	.31***	.23**	.26**
Intelligence (IB)	.39***	.45***	.36***	-.06	.39***	.37***	.38***
Alertness-intelligence (IA + B)	.32***	.45***	.34***	-.11	.36***	.30***	.32***
Learning difficulty (II)	-.27***	-.49***	-.34***	.05	-.39***	-.32***	-.44***
Responsibility (III)	.40***	.43***	.47***	-.12	.46***	.46***	.47***
Unmotivated-laziness (IV)	-.14	-.27**	-.22*	-.12	-.28**	-.15	-.21*
Agreeableness (V)	.48***	.31***	.44***	.05	.50***	.50***	.44***
Defiance (VIA)	-.40***	-.27**	-.32***	-.07	-.41***	-.37***	-.33***
Hostile–unsocialized (VIB)	-.48***	-.29***	-.41***	-.18	-.51***	-.51***	-.45***
Defiance–hostile-unsocialized (VIA + B)	-.49***	-.30***	-.42***	-.17	-.52***	-.51***	-.45***

TABLE 12.8 (cont.)

	Pupil Adjustment Scores[b]						
CBC Scores (Time III)	9	10	11	12	13	14	15
Likability–less gloomy-sourness (VII)	.26**	.12	.11	-.00	.22**	.16	.04
Emotionality–tension (VIII)	-.33***	-.19*	-.29***	-.00	-.43***	-.39***	-.40***
Infantilism (IX)	-.12	-.28**	-.15	-.22	-.27**	-.15	-.34***
Withdrawal B (XA)	.01	-.11	-.00	-.17	-.10	.06	.02
Withdrawal C (XB)	-.15	-.11	-.11	-.27	-.25**	-.12	-.12
Withdrawal (XA + B)	-.09	-.11	-.07	-.25	-.20*	-.05	-.07
Appetite (XI)	.10	.06	-.06	-.41	.12	.02	.03
Sex precociousness (XII)	-.24**	-.08	-.23**	-.08	-.25**	-.24**	-.22*
Overcleanliness (XIII)	.03	.01	.09	-.05	-.01	.05	.03
Sex inhibition (XIV)	-.18*	.00	-.09	-.21	-.11	-.09	-.09
Activity (XV)	-.01	.08	-.08	.11	.10	-.08	-.07
Assertiveness (XVI)	-.18*	.12	-.02	-.07	-.10	.18*	-.04
Physical development	.02	.08	.01	.02	.02	-.00	-.16
Awkward or clumsy	.09	-.05	.06	-.15	.05	.07	-.18
Coordination	-.14	.01	-.07	.14	-.04	-.08	.05
Robust and sturdy	.11	.20*	.16	.16	.21*	.10	.27**
Physical/mental defects	-.01	-.16	-.06	.40*	.08	-.06	-.25**

$*p < .05$ $**p < .01$ $***p < .001$.

[a] The N for the correlations ranges from 123 to 130 except for correlations with pupil adjustment score 12, where $N = 34$.

[b] The pupil adjustment scores include the following: (1) overall emotional adjustment, (2) social maturity, (3) tends to depression, (4) tends to aggressive behavior, (5) extroversion–introversion, (6) emotional security, (7) motor control and stability, (8) impulsiveness, (9) emotional irritability, (10) school achievement, (11) school conduct, (12) physical ailments, (13) emotional adjustment score (total), (14) aggressive behavior score, (15) inhibitory control score.

from four teacher-rating scales: (a) tends to aggressive behavior, (b) impulsiveness, (c) emotional irritability, and (d) school conduct. The summary measures correlate positively with CBC III, responsibility ($r = .47$), and CBC V, agreeableness ($r = .44$), and negatively with CBC VI, defiance–hostility ($r = -.45$), and CBC VIII, emotionality-tension ($r = -.40$).[11]

The summary measure of "inhibitory control" was created by combining three teacher ratings: (a) motor control and stability, (b) impulsiveness, and (c) school conduct. It correlated positively with CBC III, responsibility ($r = .47$), and CBC V, agreeableness ($r = .44$), and negatively with CBC II, learning difficulty ($r = -.44$), CBC VI, defiance–hostility ($r = -.45$), and CBC VIII, emotionality–tension ($r = -.40$).

Considering the very different contexts within which teachers and caseworkers have access to the children and the varied opportunities they have to perceive them, the degree of association between ratings demonstrated here should be seen in a positive light. There is some demonstrated tendency to see the same qualities in a child even though the amount of shared variance is limited.

ANALYSIS OF CHANGE
IN BEHAVIORAL RATINGS

We were interested in analyzing the contribution of a number of predictor variables to change in behavioral scores over the five years of investigation. We list these variables in the note to Table 12.9. We included in our analysis demographic variables, developmental history indexes, parental assessments, measures of parental visiting, and number of placements, as well as other variables. In each analysis of change in a CBC score, we included the child's earlier score (Times I or II) so that unique variances attributed to other variables would essentially represent contributions to "understanding" the later CBC measures with the earlier scores partialed out.

[11] The direction of the summary measure combining teacher ratings was arranged so that high scores would reflect better adjustment.

In the interest of economy, we chose to analyze only seven CBC composite scores that seemed to be most pertinent to our purpose of assessing adjustment. The results of the 21 separate multiple regressions we ran cannot be shown in detail due to lack of space, so we present our findings in summary fashion and report only those variables that significantly contribute to explained variance in the measure being treated as the criterion.

Times I–II Change

Our first analysis focuses on the changes during Times I–II, spanning the first two-and-one-half years the children spent in care. Five variables made significant contributions to change in CBC III (responsibility) scores: (a) the earlier CBC score, (b) the child's age at entry, (c) the stability of his preplacement care, (d) the caseworker's evaluation of his mother, and (e) the frequency of parental visiting. We interpret the data to indicate that a child showed increased responsible behavior if he entered care at a relatively younger age, had previously been in the care of an agency rather than being afforded care by his own parents, had a mother who was evaluated more positively, and had frequent visits from his parents.

The analysis of change in CBC IV (unmotivated–laziness) shows two variables, in addition to the earlier CBC IV measure, that significantly contribute in accounting for variance in the Time II measure.

1. Older children entering care tended to be rated as more unmotivated with the passage of time.
2. Children whose parents reported preplacement health or developmental problems tended to be perceived as showing increasingly unmotivated behavior.

Three variables made significant contributions to explained variance in the later CBC V (agreeableness) score: (a) the earlier CBC measure, (b) the child's age at entry, and (c) the frequency of parental visiting. Children who entered foster care when younger and those visited more frequently by their parents tended to be perceived as being more agreeable in their behavioral manifestations with the passage of time.

For some composite scores, none of the independent variables contributed significantly to explaining the later scores. For CBC VI (defiance–hostility) and CBC VIII (emotionality–tension), only the earlier measures of the same composite scores made significant contributions. For CBC X (withdrawal), no independent variables showed significance. For CBC VII (likability), the earlier CBC score and the age of the child proved to be significant predictors. The younger the child at entry, the more likely he was to be increasingly described as likable with the passage of time.

Our overall impression of the Times I–II analysis is that two variables stand out as important: (a) age at entry and (b) parental visiting. The findings suggest that younger children settle into the foster care situation more easily and that visited children are more at peace with themselves.

Times II–III Change

Measuring the change from Time II to Time III, we observe a marked increase in the magnitude of the multiple correlations and the amount of variance accounted for in contrast to the assessment of change for the first two-and-one-half years of placement.

For the measure CBC III (responsibility), only one significant predictor emerged, namely, jurisdiction at intake. Children admitted on a voluntary basis rather than through court procedure were perceived as increasingly responsible in their behavior over time.

For CBC IV (unmotivated–laziness) we find three significant regressor variables: (a) the earlier (Time II) CBC measure, (b) evaluation of the mother, and (c) ethnicity (the child being Puerto Rican). The data can be interpreted as indicating that children whose mothers have been assessed (at Time II) as less adequate tend to be perceived as increasingly unmotivated over time. It also appears that Puerto Rican children were rated as showing more positive change in this domain than the other children.

The measure CBC V (agreeableness) proved to have four significant predictors: (a) the earlier CBC score, (b) age–sex interaction,[12] (c) identification of the preplacement parental figure, and (d) the number of children in the child's family. The direction of the

---

[12] Age–sex interaction is a contrived variable; it is the product of age and sex. It is identical with the first-order interaction effect of analysis of variance.

associations involved indicates that younger girls were increasingly perceived as agreeable, as opposed to older boys, and children originating from larger groups of siblings were likewise positively regarded. We also observe that children raised by persons other than their mothers showed significantly more gain in scores.

The CBC VI (defiance–hostility) score has two significant predictors: (a) the earlier Time II measure and (b) the frequency of parental visiting. We interpret the latter to indicate that children who tend to be unvisited become more defiant and hostile with the passage of three to five years after entry into foster care.

The analysis of change in CBC VII (likability) reveals three significant predictors: (a) the earlier (Time II) measure (b) age–sex interaction, and (c) an indication that the child's family received public assistance. The second indicates that younger girls are viewed more benignly than older boys. The fact that a family is on public assistance is more difficult to connect with the tendency of the caseworkers to see such children as less likable during the second half of the longitudinal study period. Are the children perhaps reflecting greater stresses experienced by their families? Are the raters influenced in their perceptions by the status of the children's families?

The four significant predictors for CBC VIII (emotionality–tension) are: (a) the earlier CBC score, (b) number of children in the family, (c) indication that a child's mother was a drug abuser, and (d) frequency of parental visiting. Again we find that children who originate from large family groups are rated more positively over time, that is, they are seen as less tense and emotionally strained than single children remaining in foster care. It is not clear why children of drug abusers are rated as being under greater strain.[13] That children who are less frequently visited by their parents appear to be increasingly under emotional strain is consonant with our previous findings linking more negative ratings to this phenomenon.

For the CBC X score (withdrawal) we observe that the earlier

---

[13] In a previously published report from this study, we have indicated that other than in the area of school performance, children of drug-abusing mothers in our sample did not appear to have more adjustment problems than the other subjects. See David Fanshel, "Parental Failure and Consequences for Children: The Drug-Abusing Mother Whose Children Are in Foster Care," *American Journal of Public Health* 65 (1975): 604–12.

measure is a significant predictor of the Time III measure and, again, that Puerto Rican children are positively perceived in this regard, that is, that they appear less withdrawn over time compared to the other subjects

Times I–III Change

Trying to find significant predictors of behavioral change over the full five years of the study would appear to be a hazardous venture because of the relatively long time span involved. Yet, inspection of Table 12.9 shows that a number of interesting predictors of behavior change have emerged from the multiple regression analyses.

For CBC III (responsibility), the only significant predictor of change over five years is the caseworker's evaluation of the mother. The more positive the evaluation, the more likely is the child to be perceived as showing an enhanced sense of responsibility in his behavior over time.

For CBC IV (unmotivated–laziness), there are two significant predictor variables: (a) evaluation of the mother and (b) ethnicity (Puerto Rican vs. other). These results coincide with those reported for the Times II–III analysis. Children whose mothers are evaluated positively are perceived as changing in the direction of being more highly motivated over the five years of study. The same holds true for the Puerto Rican children.

We again find parental characteristics to be salient when we examine the analysis of behavioral change for CBC V (agreeableness). Positive evaluation of the mother and a high level of parental visiting are predictive of a greater tendency to rate the child as agreeable over the five-year period. In addition, we find the earlier CBC score (Time I) is significantly predictive of the later measure (Time III). The CBC VI (defiance–hostility) and CBC VIII (emotionality–tension) scores both show parental visiting to be salient. The higher the level of parental visiting over the five years, the more the child is likely to be seen as less defiant over time and less tense.

For CBC VII (likability), we find only one significant predictor of change, namely, jurisdiction at intake. Children coming into care on a voluntary rather than court-ordered basis, are more apt to have

TABLE 12.9
SUMMARY OF MULTIPLE REGRESSION ANALYSES OF CHANGE
IN SELECTED CBC COMPOSITE SCORES FOR ALL CHILDREN IN CARE[a]

CBC Composite Score	Mult. R	Mult. R²	Independent Variables Making Significant Contribution to Explained Variance
			A. Change from Time I to Time II
CBC III (Time II) Responsibility (N = 235)	.47	.22	1. Earlier CBC score (Time I) beta weight = .35*** unique variance = 4.8% 2. Age at entry beta weight = −.47*** unique variance = 4.8% 13. Stability of care preplacement beta weight = −.22* unique variance = 2.0% 20. Evaluation of mother (Time II) beta weight = .16* unique variance = 1.5% 21. Parental visiting pattern (Time I) beta weight = .18* unique variance = 2.1%
CBC IV (Time II) Unmotivated–laziness (N = 249)	.49	.24	2. Age at entry beta weight = .22* unique variance = 1.3% 5. Preplacement problems: health beta weight = .22* unique variance = 1.3% 7. Preplacement problems: developmental beta weight = .16* unique variance = 2.2%
CBC V (Time II) Agreeableness (N = 249)	.48	.23	1. Earlier CBC score (Time I) beta weight = .26*** unique variance = 5.4% 2. Age at entry beta weight = −.30** unique variance = 3.1% 21. Parental visiting pattern (Time I) beta weight = .18* unique variance = 2.0%
CBC VI (Time II) Defiance–hostility (N = 249)	.43	.19	1. Earlier CBC score (Time I) beta weight = .26*** unique variance = 4.1%

TABLE 9 (cont.)

CBC Composite Score as Criterion	Mult. R	Mult. R²	Independent Variables Making Significant Contribution to Explained Variance
CBC VII (Time II) Likability (N = 249)	.50	.25	1. Earlier CBC score (Time I) beta weight = .19** unique variance = 3.0% 2. Age at entry beta weight = −.30** unique variance = 3.1%
CBC VIII (Time II) Emotionality–tension (N = 249)	.46	.21	1. Earlier CBC score (Time I) beta weight = .26*** unique variance = 5.1%
CBC X (Time II) Withdrawal (N = 235)	.45	.21	—

B. Change from Time II to Time III

CBC III (Time III) Responsibility (N = 161)	.51	.26	14. Jurisdiction at intake beta weight = .17* unique variance = 2.3%
CBC IV (Time III) Unmotivated–laziness (N = 161)	.49	.24	1. Earlier CBC score (Time II) beta weight = .21* unique variance = 3.3% 20. Evaluation of mother (Time II) beta weight = −.26* unique variance = 3.5% 25. Ethnicity: Puerto Rican beta weight = .37** unique variance = 5.1%
CBC V (Time III) Agreeableness (N = 161)	.67	.45	1. Earlier CBC score (Time II) beta weight = .48*** unique variance = 19.9% 4. Age–sex interaction beta weight = −.43* unique variance = 3.4% 9. Number of children in family beta weight = .17* unique variance = 2.1% 10. Principal preplacement person beta weight = −.24* unique variance = 1.8%

TABLE 12.9 (*cont.*)

CBC Composite Score as Criterion	Mult. R	Mult. R²	Independent Variables Making Significant Contribution to Explained Variance
CBC VI (Time III) Defiance–hostility (*N* = 161)	.67	.45	1. Earlier CBC score (Time II) beta weight = .46*** unique variance = 18.3% 21. Parental visiting pattern (Time I) beta weight = −.20* unique variance = 2.2%
CBC VII (Time III) Likability (*N* = 161)	.50	.25	1. Earlier CBC score (Time II) beta weight = .18* unique variance = 2.5% 4. Age–sex interaction beta weight = −.40* unique variance = 2.8% 11. Public assistance status beta weight = .17* unique variance = 2.3%
CBC VIII (Time III) Emotionality–tension (*N* = 161)	.62	.39	1. Earlier CBC score (Time II) beta weight = .43*** unique variance = 15.0% 9. Number of children in family beta weight = −.20* unique variance = 3.1% 10. Drug abusing mother beta weight = −.19* unique variance = 2.4% 21. Parental visiting pattern (Time I) beta weight = −.23* unique variance = 3.0%
CBC X (Time III) Withdrawal (*N* = 161)	.52	.27	1. Earlier CBC score (Time II) beta weight = .35*** unique variance = 9.5% 25. Ethnicity: Puerto Rican beta weight = .33* unique variance = 3.8%

C. Change from Time I to Time III

CBC III (Time III) Responsibility (*N* = 147)	.47	.22	20. Evaluation of mother (Time II) beta weight = .32** unique variance = 5.6%
CBC IV (Time III) Unmotivated–laziness (*N* = 155)	.47	.22	20. Evaluation of mother (Time II) beta weight = −.28** unique variance = 4.4% 25. Ethnicity: Puerto Rican beta weight = .35** unique variance = 4.7%

TABLE 12.9 (*cont.*)

CBC Composite Score as Criterion	Mult. R	Mult. R²	Independent Variables Making Significant Contribution to Explained Variance
CBC V (Time III) Agreeableness (N = 155)	.59	.34	1. Earlier CBC score (Time I) beta weight = .28*** unique variance = 6.2% 20. Evaluation of mother (Time II) beta weight = .23* unique variance = 2.9% 21. Parental visiting pattern (Time I) beta weight = .24* unique variance = 3.0%
CBC VI (Time III) Defiance–hostility (N = 155)	.57	.33	1. Earlier CBC score (Time I) beta weight = .27** unique variance = 4.3% 21. Parental visiting pattern (Time I) beta weight = −.24* unique variance = 3.0%
CBC VII (Time III) Likability (N = 155)	.47	.23	14. Jurisdiction at intake beta weight = .19* unique variance = 2.6%
CBC VIII (Time III) Emotionality–tension (N = 155)	.52	.27	21. Parental visiting pattern (Time I) beta weight = −.30** unique variance = 4.8%
CBC X (Time III) Withdrawal (N = 147)	.44	.19	—

*p < .05   **p < .01   ***p < .001.

Predictor Variables: (1) earlier CBC score (Times I or II), (2) age at entry, (3) sex of child, (4) age–sex interaction, (5) preplacement developmental problems—health, (6) preplacement developmental problems—emotional, (7) preplacement developmental problems—developmental, (8) birth status, (9) number of children in family, (10) drug-abusing mothers vs. others, (11) public assistance status of family, (12) principal preplacement child-care person, (13) stability of care before placement, (14) jurisdiction at intake (court vs. voluntary), (15) reason for placement—child behavior, (16) log of days in care over five years, (17) number of placements while in care, (18) visiting stability of parents assessed (yes/no), (19) evaluation of mother (Time I), (20) evaluation of mother (Time II), (21) parental visiting pattern (Time I), (22) parental visiting pattern (Time II), (23) parental visiting stability (Time II), (24) ethnicity: black, (25) ethnicity: Puerto Rican.

enhanced ratings of likability. For CBC X (withdrawal), there are no significant predictors of change over the five-year time period.

Regarding the information contained in Table 12.9, we are impressed with the fact that parental indicators in the form of evaluation of the mothers and frequency of parental visiting emerge as being predictive of change over a five-year period for five out of the seven CBC composite scores subjected to analysis. Such findings lend support for the notion that continued parental involvement in the lives of foster children through visitation is potentially salutary. This is in accord with the findings of previous investigators.[14] We also observe that the more positive the evaluation of the parent, the more likely is the child to change in a positive direction on several CBC scores.

The reader might well ponder with us about the full implications of these findings. We must keep in mind the fact that, as reported in chapter 4, 57 percent of the parents were not visiting the children remaining in foster care at the end of the five years of follow-up. Our data suggest that the disappearance of parents from the lives of their children is associated with negative behavioral developments in the children. It would seem prudent for agencies to invest in strenuous efforts to recapture the interest of parents as a way of mitigating the injury to the personalities of the children created by the awareness that their parents have no interest in them.

We find ourselves also pondering about the parents who are unable to take their children home after five years of foster care but who nevertheless maintain contact with them. The fact that positive evaluation of the mothers in these cases is associated with enhanced behavioral functioning of their children suggests that "half a loaf is better than none." However, we need to know more about how the children cope with having contact with both their own parents and foster parents (or institutional personnel). How do they reconcile the fact that their parents do not take them home and yet continue to maintain an interest in them? In chapter 13, we show that the

---

[14] See Eugene A. Weinstein, *The Self-Image of the Foster Child* (New York: Russell Sage Foundation, 1960), pp. 68–9; and M.L. Kellmer Pringle and L. Clifford, "Conditions Associated with Emotional Maladjustment Among Children in Care," *Education Review* 14 (1962): 112–23.

children appear to suffer from noticeable strain because of the conflicting pulls they experience.

CHILDREN IN FOSTER FAMILY CARE

In chapter 8 we analyzed the contribution of indexes based on ratings of the qualities of foster parents (as assessed through use of the FPAF) to changes in IQ scores of children who had received foster family care as their primary placement experience. We found that children who had been cared for in homes rated high in qualities that we labeled as "democratic permissiveness" tended to improve in the nonverbal aspects of the IQ test; this held true for all time periods analyzed (Times I–II, Times II–III, and Times I–III). We now proceed to examine possible foster parent influences in accounting for change in the CBC scores assigned to subjects in foster family care over the five years of study. However, we first introduce the cautionary note, that the CBC ratings and the appraisals of foster parents came from the same source. The associations we find may reflect this fact, and our conclusions must be more tentatively held than in the case of our investigation of IQ change, where the dependent and independent variables derived from different sources.

We constructed a set of simple multiple regressions for the seven CBC composite scores previously utilized; these were performed separately for the Times II and III scores as the dependent variables. The earlier score (Time I or II) was included among the regressor variables, followed by: (a) the age of the child at entry, (b) the three preplacement developmental-history indexes (health, emotional, and developmental), (c) log days in care, (d) number of placements, and (d) four foster parent appraisal (FPAF) indexes (intellectual climate, democratic permissiveness, perseverance–altruism, and response to older children). The results of these multiple regression analyses are shown in Table 12.10.

Times I–II Change

We find that fewer significant effects of variables are manifested through the multiple regression analyses covering the first two and one-half years of the children's tenure in care as compared to the second two and one-half years. There are more substantial multiple correlations and amounts of variance accounted for in the latter period.

For Times I–II change in CBC III (responsibility), we observe that none of the independent variables show significant predictors. We also find that the amount of variance accounted for is quite low.

For CBC IV (unmotivated–laziness), there are four regressor variables where the coefficients show significant effects: (a) the earlier measure of the same composite score (Time I), (b) pre-placement developmental problems, (c) log days in care, and (d) the FPAF index of intellectual climate. We interpret the findings to indicate that children who had developmental problems before coming into care were perceived as showing more unmotivated behavior over time. It appears that these problems continue to influence the child's adjustment after placement. The length-of-time variable suggests that children who are in care longer tend to appear more unmotivated over time.[15] Of considerable interest is the fact that the intellectual climate index was the only foster parent measure to show a significant coefficient, and it accounted for 4.6 percent unique variance in the later CBC measure. The intellectual climate of the family appears related to a higher degree of motivated behavior shown by the foster child. We also find a similar result for CBC X (withdrawal), with the same FPAF index producing a significant coefficient and accounting for 4.2 percent of unique variance. The findings indicate that the more intellectually stimulating the family, the less withdrawn the child is apt to appear over the first half of the five-year period of investigation. No other regressor variable included in the regression analysis of withdrawal showed a significant effect.

For three CBC measures, the multiple regression analyses produced only one predictor variable with a significant beta weight; in each case, it was the earlier (Time I) version of the measure. These measures included CBC V (agreeableness), CBC VII (likability), and CBC VIII (emotionality–tension). For CBC VI

[15] We tend to take a guarded view of this variable since CBC scores were only available for children who were still in care or had recently left care. The limited variability available in this measure reflects the movement of some children out of care and their later return.

TABLE 12.10

ANALYSIS OF CHANGE IN SEVEN COMPOSITE CBC SCORES, FOR CHILDREN IN FOSTER FAMILY CARE ONLY

CBC Composite Score	Independent Variables[a]											Mult. R	Mult. R²
	1	2	3	4	5	6	7	8	9	10	11		
A. Times I–II Change (N = 120)													
CBC III, Responsibility													
Beta weight	.14	-.12	.05	-.09	.00	-.03	-.11	.22	.05	.08	-.02	.30	.09
Unique variance	0.6	0.3	0.2	0.6	0.0	0.0	1.1	3.3	0.2	0.5	0.0		
CBC IV, Unmotivated–laziness													
Beta weight	.23*	-.19	.09	-.05	.21*	.24*	.10	-.25**	.11	-.04	.04	.45	.20
Unique variance	3.0	1.3	0.7	0.2	3.8	2.9	0.9	4.6	1.2	0.2	0.1		
CBC V, Agreeableness													
Beta weight	.22*	.07	.04	-.04	.00	.03	-.06	.18	.10	.03	-.05	.32	.10
Unique variance	4.2	0.2	0.2	0.1	0.0	0.1	0.3	2.4	1.0	0.1	0.1		
CBC VI, Defiance–hostility													
Beta weight	.30*	-.32*	-.12	-.03	-.05	.05	.14	-.04	-.08	.02	-.04	.31	.09
Unique variance	4.6	3.7	1.2	0.0	0.2	0.1	1.7	0.1	0.6	0.0	0.1		
CBC VII, Likability													
Beta weight	.27**	.04	.04	-.05	.00	.02	-.03	.14	.06	.07	-.06	.32	.11
Unique variance	5.9	0.1	0.1	0.2	0.0	0.0	0.1	1.5	0.3	0.5	0.2		
CBC VIII, Emotionality–tension													
Beta weight	.24**	-.07	-.12	.06	-.07	.13	.17	-.07	-.04	-.09	.04	.38	.15
Unique variance	4.8	0.2	1.3	0.3	0.4	0.9	2.5	0.4	0.1	0.8	0.1		
CBC X, Withdrawal													
Beta weight	.13	-.22	-.02	-.02	.09	.06	.08	-.24*	.09	.01	-.12	.34	.12
Unique variance	0.9	1.8	0.1	0.0	0.6	0.2	0.5	4.2	0.7	0.0	0.1		

Independent Variables[a]

B. Times II–III Change (N = 98)

CBC Composite Score	1	2	3	4	5	6	7	8	9	10	11	Mult. R	Mult. R²
CBC III, Responsibility													
Beta weight	.31**	.07	-.10	.06	-.11	-.06	-.13	.36**	.11	.04	-.16	.55	.30
Unique variance	8.5	0.3	0.9	0.3	1.0	0.3	1.5	8.0	1.0	0.1	1.5		
CBC IV, Unmotivated–laziness													
Beta weight	.04	.11	.02	-.03	.07	.09	.33**	-.35**	.04	-.19	.16	.50	.25
Unique variance	0.2	0.9	0.0	0.1	0.3	0.8	8.9	7.2	0.1	3.2	1.6		
CBC V, Agreeableness													
Beta weight	.49***	-.10	-.07	-.01	.07	-.17	.01	.21	.10	.09	-.10	.60	.36
Unique variance	22.3	0.7	0.4	0.0	0.4	2.8	0.0	2.9	0.9	0.7	0.6		
CBC VI, Defiance–hostility													
Beta weight	.35**	.15	-.13	-.11	-.09	.16	-.02	-.08	-.20	-.04	.01	.53	.28
Unique variance	11.0	1.6	1.6	0.9	0.7	2.2	0.0	0.4	3.6	0.1	0.0		
CBC VII, Likability													
Beta weight	.23*	-.23*	-.03	-.06	.09	-.16	-.08	.37**	.01	.03	-.23	.45	.21
Unique variance	5.0	4.0	0.1	0.3	0.7	2.3	0.6	8.6	0.0	0.1	3.3		
CBC VIII, Emotionality–tension													
Beta weight	.37***	-.08	-.03	-.14	.14	.01	.04	-.06	-.10	-.13	-.09	.48	.24
Unique variance	12.8	0.5	0.1	1.6	1.6	0.0	0.2	0.2	0.8	1.5	0.5		
CBC X, Withdrawal													
Beta weight	.15	.27*	-.07	-.14	.06	.12	.20*	-.41***	-.07	-.07	.22	.53	.28
Unique variance	2.0	5.4	0.5	1.5	0.3	1.2	3.4	10.1	0.4	0.4	3.0		

C. Times I-III Change ($N = 84$)

	1	2	3	4	5	6	7	8	9	10	11	Multiple R	R^2
CBC III, Responsibility													
Beta weight	.15	.00	−.05	.02	−.11	−.03	−.24*	.46***	.16	.06	−.17	.53	.28
Unique variance	0.6	0.0	0.3	0.0	0.9	0.1	4.8	12.5	2.4	0.3	1.7		
CBC IV, Unmotivated–laziness													
Beta weight	.08	.01	.00	−.06	.09	.10	.39***	−.37**	.03	−.14	.14	.52	.27
Unique variance	0.4	0.0	0.0	0.3	0.6	0.8	12.5	8.8	0.1	1.7	1.1		
CBC V, Agreeableness													
Beta weight	.29**	.05	.04	.02	.02	−.13	−.01	.30*	.14	.08	−.06	.49	.24
Unique variance	7.1	0.2	0.1	0.0	0.0	1.5	0.0	5.9	1.7	0.6	0.2		
CBC VI, Defiance–hostility													
Beta weight	.19	−.02	−.24*	−.13	−.13	.17	.05	−.16	−.23*	−.02	.03	.48	.23
Unique variance	1.9	0.0	5.3	1.2	1.4	2.6	0.2	1.7	4.5	0.0	0.1		
CBC VII, Likability													
Beta weight	.02	−.12	−.03	−.10	.08	−.13	−.12	.38**	.04	.09	−.21	.40	.16
Unique variance	0.0	1.0	0.1	0.7	0.6	1.5	1.1	9.0	0.2	0.7	2.6		
CBC VIII, Emotionality–tension													
Beta weight	−.07	−.05	−.14	−.11	.10	.03	.09	−.09	−.12	−.13	−.05	.34	
Unique variance	0.5	0.2	1.8	1.0	0.9	0.1	0.6	0.5	1.2	1.4	0.1		
CBC X, Withdrawal													
Beta weight	−.06	.24	−.07	−.19	.08	.04	.33**	−.50***	−.50***	.01	.21	.51	.26
Unique variance	0.2	2.8	0.5	2.5	0.5	0.1	8.8	14.8	.02	0.0	2.6		

*$p < .05$ **$p < .01$ ***$p < .001$.

[a]Identification of independent variables: (1) earlier CBC composite score (Time I or II), (2) age of child at entry into care, (3) preplacement developmental problems: health, (4) preplacement developmental problems: emotional, (5) preplacement developmental problems: developmental, (6) log days in care, (7) number of placements, (8–11) foster parent appraisal form indexes: (8) intellectual climate, (9) democratic permissiveness, (10) perseverence–altruism, (11) response to older children.

(defiance–hostility), age at entry and the earlier CBC measure are the only significant predictors; children who entered care at an earlier age were seen as being less defiant over time.

Times II–III Change

Looking at section B of Table 12.10, we see that the most outstanding predictor of behavioral change for the final two and one-half years of the study is the foster parent qualities identified by the intellectual climate index. This FPAF index is shown to be a significant predictor for CBC III (responsibility), CBC IV (unmotivated–laziness), CBC VII (likability), and CBC X (withdrawal). We surmise from our analysis that children reared in homes where the overall environment produced by the foster parents is rated, by the social workers, as intellectually stimulating are more likely to be perceived as showing increased responsibility and to be more likable, less withdrawn, and to show more motivated behavior in the final years of the study. The unique variance accounted for by inclusion of the index in the analyses of change in the four behavioral measures is impressive (7–10 percent).

The remaining foster parent indexes fail to show any strength as predictors of behavioral change. Particularly noteworthy is the fact that the FPAF index of democratic permissiveness, which proved to be a significant predictor of IQ change, does not show any predictive strength with respect to behavioral change. The findings might strike the reader as being contrary to expectation, namely, that IQ changes would be related to intellectual climate and the behavioral changes to the quality of democratic permissiveness. Yet, it does not seem farfetched to construe an intellectually stimulating environment as one that encourages children to take more responsibility for their lives, to be more motivated in their behavior, and not to withdraw from those around them.

We observe that children who have experienced greater turnover in living arrangements (measured by the number of placements) are apt to be seen as more unmotivated (CBC IV) and withdrawn (CBC X) as one goes from Times II to III. The significant coefficients reported here suggest a negative consequence of such turnover. Finally, it should be noted that children who entered care at a younger age were apt to be perceived as more likable (CBC VII) over the course of time.

Times I-III Change

Covering the full five-year span of the study, we are even more impressed with the saliency of the FPAF index that we have entitled "intellectual climate." In addition to being a significant predictor of change in the four CBC measures previously cited for the Times II-III period, it is also a significant predictor for CBC V (agreeableness). Considering the time span covered (five years), it is quite striking to find this fairly persistent association. The finding should be of interest to practitioners. As far as we are aware, the selection of foster families by social agencies has not tended to be strongly influenced by the intellectual qualities exhibited by foster parent applicants.[16]

We observe that for one measure, CBC VI (defiance–hostility), the FPAF democratic permissiveness index shows a significant effect. Children placed with foster parents who particularly avoid harshness and severity in their disciplinary techniques tend to be perceived as less defiant and hostile over the five-year period.

As was the case for the Times II–III comparisons, we find that the number of placements experienced by the subjects is a significant predictor of changes in CBC IV (unmotivated–laziness) and CBC X (withdrawal). Children experiencing more moves are likely to be seen as increasingly unmotivated and withdrawn at the end of five years. They also show less evidence of responsible behavior. We should introduce a critical word of caution here, we cannot be sure whether the greater number of placements causes the deterioration in behavior or whether the behavior itself has influenced the tendency to move. It has not been possible to time-order the moves experienced by the children in clear relationship to behavioral tendencies, so this issue must be left moot at this point. Finally, we find that children who had preplacement developmental problems with respect to health tended to be seen as less defiant and hostile at Time III (CBC VI). Our overall impression based on these

---

[16] See Martin Wolins, *Selecting Foster Parents* (New York: Columbia University Press, 1963), pp. 89–92.

findings is the apparent saliency of the intellectual climate created by foster parents in their homes for understanding behavioral change.

CHILDREN IN INSTITUTIONS

In chapter 8 we examined factors predictive of IQ change for children whose primary foster experience was in institutions. In our analyses we included variables that were descriptive of the institutional setting. An interesting finding that emerged linked exposure of children to inexperienced child care workers with IQ gain over the second two-and-one-half-year period of the study (Times II–III). This was not a finding that had been anticipated but nevertheless it evoked interest.

We consider it useful to again segregate the cases of the institutionalized children. We wish to analyze behavioral change relative to several institutional variables. Since we are dealing with behavioral scores that require the presence of a social worker to make the ratings, we have available a group that is reduced in size, namely, only those remaining in care. Children who returned home prior to the rating occasions are not included in the analysis.[17] The independent variables entered into the simple regression analyses included: (a) the earlier CBC scores, (b) age of the child at entry, (c) the three preplacement developmental measures, (d) log days in care, (e) number of placements, and (f) three institutional measures [the routine of institutional care (routine vs. special attention), institutional staff experience (very little vs. three years plus), and the evaluation of the institutional counselor].[18]

Times I–II Change

Overall, we observe in Table 12.11 stronger results for the first two and one-half years in assessing behavioral change, as compared with the results obtained from the analysis of children in foster

---

[17] The study of IQ change in the institutionalized sample included more children because data were secured for those who returned home as well as for those remaining in care.

[18] For a description of these variables, see p. 78 in chapter 3.

TABLE 12.11

ANALYSIS OF CHANGE IN SEVEN COMPOSITE CBC SCORES, FOR CHILDREN IN INSTITUTIONS ONLY

CBC Composite Score	Independent Variables[a]										Mult. R	Mult. R²
	1	2	3	4	5	6	7	8	9	10		
	A. Times I–II Change (N = 96)											
CBC III, Responsibility												
Beta weight	.34**	-.25*	-.11	.13	-.14	.08	.12	-.04	-.01	-.08	.44	.20
Unique variance	9.0	4.6	1.1	1.2	1.6	0.6	1.2	0.1	0.0	0.5		
CBC IV, Unmotivated–laziness												
Beta weight	.06	.27*	.14	-.31**	.12	.04	-.09	.22*	-.20	-.01	.46	.21
Unique variance	0.3	5.9	1.9	7.2	1.3	0.2	0.7	4.4	3.5	0.0		
CBC V, Agreeableness												
Beta weight	.35***	-.23*	-.01	.02	-.10	.08	.08	-.06	-.02	-.05	.46	.21
Unique variance	11.1	4.4	0.0	0.0	1.0	0.5	0.5	0.3	0.0	0.3		
CBC VI, Defiance–hostility												
Beta weight	.38****	.16	.15	-.07	.04	-.16	-.05	.10	-.09	.09	.48	.23
Unique variance	12.7	2.1	2.0	0.4	0.1	2.2	0.2	1.0	0.7	0.7		
CBC VII, Likability												
Beta weight	.26*	-.31**	.06	.06	.03	-.10	.03	-.15	.11	-.08	.45	.21
Unique variance	6.2	8.0	0.3	0.3	0.1	0.9	0.1	2.0	1.1	0.5		
CBC VIII, Emotionality–tension												
Beta weight	.31**	.08	.12	.05	.14	-.09	-.04	.28**	.09	.02	.51	.26
Unique variance	8.4	0.5	1.3	0.2	1.8	0.7	0.1	7.6	0.8	0.0		
CBC X, Withdrawal												
Beta weight	.18	.19	-.15	-.03	.05	.11	.05	.09	-.02	-.01	.37	.14
Unique variance	2.5	2.9	1.9	0.1	0.2	1.0	0.2	0.7	0.0	0.0		

TABLE 12.11 (*cont.*)

Independent Variables[a]

B. Times II–III Change ($N = 57$)

CBC Composite Score	1	2	3	4	5	6	7	8	9	10	Mult. R	Mult. R^2
CBC III, Responsibility												
Beta weight	.28*	-.16	.28*	-.28	-.06	-.04	.11	.03	-.39**	.53	.61	.37
Unique variance	6.1	1.8	5.7	5.1	0.2	0.1	0.8	0.0	11.6	0.4		
CBC IV, Unmotivated-laziness												
Beta weight	.35**	.05	-.11	.33*	-.20	.23	-.20	.08	.46***	.13	.67	.45
Unique variance	8.9	0.2	0.9	7.3	3.2	3.6	2.7	0.5	15.2	1.3		
CBC V, Agreeableness												
Beta weight	.37**	-.08	.20	-.13	-.11	-.24	.04	-.02	-.39**	-.18	.67	.45
Unique variance	11.3	0.4	2.8	1.1	0.9	4.0	0.1	0.0	11.2	2.6		
CBC VI, Defiance-hostility												
Beta weight	.61***	-.02	-.10	.23	.12	.20	-.09	-.01	.37**	.06	.71	.50
Unique variance	30.7	0.0	0.7	3.7	1.1	2.7	0.6	0.0	9.8	0.2		
CBC VII, Likability												
Beta weight	.19	-.16	.09	-.05	.13	.05	.15	.03	-.10	-.11	.43	.18
Unique variance	2.8	1.6	0.5	0.2	1.5	0.2	1.5	0.1	0.8	1.0		
CBC VIII, Emotionality-tension												
Beta weight	.49***	.10	-.10	.14	.22	.09	-.19	.02	.03	.14	.67	.45
Unique variance	20.5	0.7	0.8	1.4	4.0	0.5	2.3	0.0	0.1	1.6		
CBC X, Withdrawal												
Beta weight	.46***	.03	.21	.25	-.29*	.13	-.11	.17	.17	.09	.61	.37
Unique variance	17.5	0.0	3.0	4.4	6.9	1.2	0.8	2.0	2.2	0.7		

C. Times I-III Change (N = 52)

	(1)	(2)	(3)	(4)	(5)	(6)	(7)	(8)	(9)	(10)		
CBC III, Responsibility												
Beta weight	-.02	-.18	.25	-.18	-.12	-.03	.19	-.01	-.39*	-.01	.55	.31
Unique variance	0.0	2.0	4.1	1.9	1.2	0.1	2.8	0.0	11.0	0.0		
CBC IV, Unmotivated–laziness												
Beta weight	-.01	.24	.08	.11	-.21	.23	-.25	.03	.39*	.25	.59	.35
Unique variance	0.0	3.8	0.4	0.7	3.3	3.5	4.6	0.1	10.6	4.7		
CBC V, Agreeableness												
Beta weight	.23	-.18	.17	-.14	-.16	-.10	.16	.06	-.49**	-.24	.65	.43
Unique variance	4.6	2.4	2.0	1.3	1.9	0.7	2.0	0.2	16.6	4.5		
CBC VI, Defiance–hostility												
Beta weight	.34	-.07	-.11	.27	.19	.03	-.24	-.04	.38*	.09	.59	.34
Unique variance	9.8	0.3	0.9	4.6	2.8	0.1	4.2	0.1	10.1	0.6		
CBC VII, Likability												
Beta weight	.08	-.15	.11	-.09	.17	.07	.10	-.03	-.12	-.10	.37	.14
Unique variance	0.6	1.6	0.8	0.5	2.1	0.3	0.7	0.1	1.0	0.8		
CBC VIII, Emotionality–tension												
Beta weight	.50***	.07	-.02	.11	.16	-.10	-.39**	-.06	.13	.25*	.73	.53
Unique variance	19.4	0.4	0.0	0.7	1.9	0.7	10.9	0.2	1.3	4.9		
CBC X, Withdrawal												
Beta weight	.11	.09	.20	.18	-.35*	-.02	-.02	.07	.20	.11	.45	.20
Unique variance	0.9	0.6	2.7	2.1	10.1	0.0	0.0	0.3	2.7	0.9		

$*p < .05$ $**p < .01$ $***p < .001$

[a] Identification of independent variables: (1) earlier CBC composite score (Time I or II), (2) age of child at entry into care, (3) preplacement developmental problems: emotional, (4) preplacement developmental problems: health, (5) preplacement developmental problems: developmental, (6) log of days in care, (7) number of placements, (8–10) institutional measures: (8) routine of institutional care (routine, SPECIAL ATTENTION), (9) institutional staff experience (very little, THREE YEARS PLUS), (10) evaluation of institutional counselor (acceptable, HIGHLY VALUED).

family care. The multiple correlations are quite a bit stronger, albeit remaining on the modest side.

For CBC III (responsibility), CBC V (agreeableness), and CBC VII (likability), we find two variables with significant standardized regression coefficients: (a) the earlier CBC measure and (b) the age of the subject at entry. The role played by the latter would indicate that the younger the child at the time he entered care, the more likely would his behavior be viewed as showing an increased sense of responsibility. He is also likely to be perceived as more agreeable and likable by the rater. In contrast, the older children would appear to be perceived as increasingly problematic in their behavior. This view is reinforced by an examination of CBC IV (unmotivated–laziness), which again shows that younger children are more positive in their behavior over time.

For CBC IV (unmotivated–laziness), two variables in addition to age at entry showed significant coefficients: (a) a history of preplacement developmental problems in the emotional sphere and (b) an indication that the child was a recipient of special attention in the institution. The data are not easily interpreted. The meaning that suggests itself is that children with earlier emotional problems did not come across as being unmotivated (or lazy); such children would appear to be more active and motivated despite their inner turmoil. Nonroutine institutional attention may have been brought into play by the child's behavior, and we make note of the association as something worthy of further investigation. We observe that for CBC VIII (emotionality–tension), the indication of special attention is significantly predictive of increased tension in the child.

Times II–III Change
The major finding that emerges from the series of simple multiple regressions of Times II–III behavioral change is the fact that for four out of seven CBC measures, the identification of a relatively inexperienced child caring person as the major influence on the child is a significant predictor of change. Children exposed to these more youthful institutional personnel are perceived as showing an increased sense of responsibility and more motivated behavior. They also are perceived as more agreeable and less defiant or hostile, in contrast to the children exposed to more senior child care staff.

The preplacement developmental history indexes are significant predictors of behavior change for three CBC measures, but the meaning of the associations is difficult to interpret. With respect to CBC III (responsibility), children who had earlier health problems appeared to shift toward showing increased responsible behavior from Time II to Time III. This may perhaps be explained by the abatement of health problems while in foster care. On the other hand, children who had preplacement emotional problems showed increasing signs of unmotivated behavior (CBC IV). For CBCX (withdrawal), children who were free of earlier developmental problems nevertheless moved in the direction of increasingly withdrawn behavior.

Times I–III Change

For the full five-year time span, we again come up with the finding that, for a number of CBC measures, it appears to make a difference whether a child is exposed to relatively new child-care workers or to those who have been on the job at least three years. This variable is a significant predictor with CBC III (responsibility), CBC IV (unmotivated–laziness), CBC V (agreeableness), and CBC VI (defiance–hostility). We are impressed with the fact that unique variances accounted for are substantial (10–17 percent).

The institutional variable based on the evaluation of the counselor is a significant predictor in only one instance, namely, CBC VIII (emotionality–tension). The more highly evaluated staff persons appear to be caring for the most tense children.

SUMMARY COMMENTS

We have studied behavioral change as assessed by caseworkers who knew the children for three time spans. We would stress the following findings:

    1. Children tend to show somewhat more problematic behavior with passage of time in foster care, particularly those who enter at age six years or older.

    2. We have established a modest degree of concurrent validity of the composite behavior scores as reflected in correlations with IQ

scores, teacher ratings, and psychological assessments. Some validity coefficients went as high as .5, but some of the key associations were on the order of .3.

3. In assessing the contribution of a number of independent variables in accounting for behavioral change, we were impressed with the saliency of age of the child at entry and parental visiting for Times I–II and with parental visiting, number of children in the family, and ethnicity (Puerto Rican vs. others) for Times II–III. Parental visiting was again a significant predictor of change for several CBC measures covering the full five years of longitudinal investigation.

4. For children in foster family care we cite the contribution of a FPAF index to explained variance in behavioral change. Children in the homes of foster parents perceived as providing an intellectually stimulating environment were rated as showing positive behavioral changes for the three time spans studied.

5. For children in institutional care, we found that those exposed to younger, less experienced counselors were seen as showing positive behavioral changes during the three time spans covered. The variable had been previously shown to make a significant contribution to an understanding of nonverbal IQ change.

THIRTEEN

THE CHILD'S ADAPTATION TO FOSTER CARE

It is commonly recognized that children entering foster care are faced with unusual demands for adaptation. Placement in a new environment can impose heavy burdens, and the experience may well constitute a threat to a child's emotional stability. Kline and Overstreet have graphically described the kind of dislocation experienced by foster children:

> Any aspect of the human and the nonhuman environment in which the child experienced continuity is lost when the child leaves it. The nuclear family as a unit, its ways, its customs, its dynamic system, of which he has been a part, have also been a part of him, his equilibrium, and his sense of identity. Each relationship within the family has had its place, whether primarily positive or negative, in his psychic equilibrium. Having a younger sibling to envy, tease, hug, or push around, or one close in age to play with, quarrel with, and use as a companion in mischief or in loneliness, or a big brother or sister to turn to for help or to envy, provoke, or emulate, or a younger child in the family to mother—all have their place in the child's inner life as well as in his social relationships.
>
> The familiarity of his home, the place he sleeps, his friends, his school, and the neighborhood to which he is accustomed have special meaning in the child's experiencing of his world and his place in it. The neighborhood may be deteriorated, the friends few and even undesirable, the educational opportunities inferior—but these are adult reactions. The child himself does not feel this way. To him they are known and familiar, and hold aspects of cherished intimacy which he has made privately his own. All of the small mysteries and rituals of a child and his absorbing feelings about these activities are a part of his life in a specific environment; they are his ways of gaining comfort and gratification, his ways of solving some of his problems of living.[1]

[1] Draza Kline and Helen-Mary Forbush Overstreet, *Foster Care of Children: Nurture and Treatment* (New York: Columbia University Press, 1972), p. 73.

We view the task of describing the child's *adaptation* to the foster care experience as being somewhat different from that of assessing his personality or describing his behavioral characteristics in a general way. We are concerned here with the matter of environmental mastery, that is, how the child meets the situational requirements imposed on him by being separated from his parents and cared for by nonrelated persons. How does he develop a sense of relationship with the strangers who have become his parent surrogates? What is the nature of his ongoing relationship with his own parents? How much stress does he encounter in assuming the status of a foster child? These are similar to the questions that were posed by Weinstein in his study of foster children in Chicago: "How well do foster children understand the placement situation? How do they view themselves in relation to the situation? With whom do they identify? What conditions in the placement situation ... tend to promote or attenuate the child's ability to function effectively in it?"[2]

In this chapter we report our efforts to assess the child's adaptation to his foster care situation throughout the period of time he remained in placement. Data on adaptation were obtained at each of the three assessment occasions (Times I, II, and III) by a questionnaire completed by the caseworker responsible for supervising the child's placement.[3] For the purposes of our investigation, we combined items into six indexes covering different domains related to our overall interest in adaptation. We describe the indexes and present findings related to our study population at successive assessment occasions. In keeping with our overall approach, we then analyze changes in index scores and focus on the Times II and III data reflecting adaptation at the midpoint of the study and at the end of five years.

We are aware that our decision to use the observations of

[2] Eugene A. Weinstein, *The Self-Image of the Foster Child* (New York: Russell Sage Foundation, 1960), p. 16.

[3] The questionnaire was developed to cover the following topics: reaction to separation, adaptation to foster care, relationships with adults, peers and family, capacity to cope with daily experiences, strains experienced in foster care, health status, and, behavioral reactions. Where possible, identical questions were included for each of the questionnaires used on the three data-gathering occasions. The rate of return of questionnaires was 76, 93, and 93 percent, respectively for Times I, II and III assessment occasions.

caseworkers as the source of our data is an approach to the measurement task that has its own inherent limitations. The qualities of adaptation we have sought to describe are complex, and there are obvious limits to the degree to which an external observer is able to capture the internal emotional states experienced by the children. Some of these states are subtle, and it is possible that children are too well defended to allow their emotions to come to the surface so that their reactions can be adequately rated. We view our effort in this area as the best approach available to us and recognize that ours is essentially an exploratory undertaking in which we are trying to chart new ground in the study of foster children. We are attempting to move beyond discussion based on clinical assessment of individual cases to analysis of aggregates of children.

The indexes we developed cover the following areas: (a) ability of the child to cope with being separated from home, (b) ability to cope with the foster care experience and environment, (c) the child's degree of entrenchment or feeling of belonging in his foster care situation (foster family or institution), (d) conflicts in identity, (e) degree of attachment to the natural family, and (f) ability to form satisfactory relationships to both adults and peers.

INITIAL REACTION
OF STUDY CHILDREN TO SEPARATION

We preface our description and analysis of the index scores with the overall perspective we obtained of the reactions of the study children to separation. Our findings suggest that the severe emotional trauma associated with the separation of a child from his own home and family that one would anticipate from reviewing the literature is not often apparent to those who are in a position to observe the children closely. When caseworkers were asked to rate the observable behavioral reactions of the children some 30 days after they entered care, the majority of the subjects were reported as showing little overt indication of inner turmoil or distress.[4] On a

---

[4] While the reports were received from the caseworkers, comments on their returns indicated frequent consultation with foster parents and institutional child care workers. Perspectives about a child's adaptation to foster care, therefore, often reflect the view point of more than one observer.

15-point rating scale covering a range from a very stressful and maladaptive reaction to placement (point 1 on the scale) to a highly adaptive response (point 15), the average rating[5] for all 308 children studied at the time was 10.6.

In 36 percent of the cases, the caseworkers and child-care workers reported the child was doing extremely well, appearing content in his new surroundings and being actively involved in activities, with little or no evidence of concern over living away from his own home. In another 42 percent of the cases, the children were seen as reacting quite positively despite their separation from home. Although these children were perceived as showing some initial degree of anxiety or sadness, they apparently had quickly settled into the living routines provided by substitute care. They showed a surface equanimity despite their sense of loss, accepted the demands of the living situation, made new friends, and began to explore their new environments with interest. Only 22 percent of the children were reported 30 days after entering care as showing a troubled reaction to being separated from home and being in placement.

We are aware that we are dealing with the surface behavior of the subjects as perceived by the child care workers. We are also aware that we cannot label a child's strong protest against the changes besetting him as "unhealthy." Indeed, protest may serve very useful purposes for the child, and some investigators would see the absence of protest as a cause for concern.[6]

[5] The 308 children assessed at this time were only 76 percent of our sample of children over the age of one year. The rate of return was low because the formal selection of the study sample was not completed until sixty days after this assessment. Caseworkers were being asked to complete forms on each entering child. Given the high volume of cases, workers were unable to complete forms for every entering child from the large group of admissions from which our sample was chosen.

[6] A recent investigation of the early experiences of children in foster care was stimulated by the following observation of the investigator working in institutional, foster home, and adoptive settings: "At various times colleagues remarked on the frequency with which children who showed signs of distress at the time of placement made a good adjustment while those who separated easily from their families and remained calm at placement later exhibited behaviors symptomatic of emotional or social disturbance. Their distress seemed to show a "sleeper" effect. With experience, workers learned to remain alert to late appearing signs of difficulty in 'easy' placements." Inez Lorraine Sperr, *On Becoming a Foster Child: An Ethological Study of the Behaviors of Children.* Unpublished doctoral dissertation, Columbia University School of Social Work, 1974, p. 9.

We were interested to find that the more a child was aware of the reasons for placement—was in tune with the troubles and calamities that had beset his family—the more he was perceived to show a troubled response ($r = .44$). Stated another way, children who were more emotionally removed from the preplacement difficulties seemed to settle into placement with greater ease. Our data also suggest that children who strongly felt that placement was to be temporary, a stay of only a few days, found continued tenure in care beyond 30 days to be a hardship, and they had much more difficulty "settling in."

Caseworkers responsible for supervising the study subjects were again surveyed by questionnaire approximately one year after the child entered care. Our scrutiny of the returns indicates that the large majority of children remaining in foster care for the year were seen by their caseworkers as displaying relatively few indications of emotional distress that could be construed as maladaptive or as indicating strong opposition to being in foster care. An attitude reflecting an overall acceptance of the placement situation was reported in 83 percent of the cases. Moreover, where changes in reaction were noted during the year, the greatest degree of shift was reported by caseworkers to be in the direction of improved adaptation, that is, better integration into their current living situations.

This view of the majority of children not being traumatized by being in care has its parallel in ratings of the child's degree of homesickness during the year and judgments about the extent to which he or she was pressing to return home. The caseworkers reported 41 percent of the children as showing no overt signs of homesickness, with another 27 percent showing only a slight reaction. Nine percent of the children were reported as being very homesick during the year following their entry into foster care. With respect to manifestations of a desire to return home, 43 percent of the children were reported as showing no substantial overt indication of a desire to return home; their behavior indicated that they were content to remain in foster care. An additional 18 percent of the children were reported as displaying only a slight, or occasional, desire to return home. For 40 percent there was some desire evidenced to return home; this was more likely to be true of the older children.

THE DEVELOPMENT OF INDEXES

Our experience with the assessments made by the caseworkers approximately one year after the children entered care led us to make several changes in the questionnaire used for the second and third assessments (two and one-half and five years after entry). However, many questions dealing with the child's adaptation were retained in identical form so that changes over the five-year span could be monitored.

Our approach to the task of index construction combined conceptual and empirical considerations. It was apparent from inspection of the correlations among items included in the questionnaire that there was similarity of content between several of the domains being assessed. Further analysis using a special computer program developed by project staff was undertaken to find clusters of questions with high internal reliability. Six indexes relating to concepts dealing with the child's adaptation to foster care were constructed.[7]

Capacity to Cope with Separation

The Index of Capacity to Cope with Separation provides a measure of the child's ability to overcome the trauma of separation from his own home and family. It is made up of ratings by caseworkers with respect to the following five items of inquiry:

1. Overall, how would you rate this child's present level of coping with his/her being separated from own family and home?
2. Is the continuing separation from own parent(s) and home having any ill effects on the child at the present time?

---

[7] While we factor analyzed the two waves of data (Time II and Time III) obtained from the caseworker-raters, and found some similarity between the factorial structures that emerged, we found we could not use factorial scores because the weights assigned items changed from one occasion to the next. We wanted indexes based upon raw scores that would reflect a constant approach to scores assigned subjects. We used the factor analyses as a guide to an item analysis procedure programmed for the computer by John Grundy and Carlos Stecher of our staff. The procedure employed starts with a complete correlation matrix and defines composites of items according to maximal item-criterion correlations (the correlation between each item and the remaining pool of items in the group in which it is included) and maximal internal consistency reliability coefficients (Cronbach's coefficient alpha). After abstracting the first set of items for the first index, the residual items were then subjected to the same search for the best composite.

3. To what degree has each of the following phenomena been a source of strain for this child while in foster care?

a. lack of parental visiting;
b. being separated from parent's home;
c. being separated from siblings.

Capacity to Cope with Foster Care Environment

The Index of Capacity to Cope with the Foster Care Environment provides a measure of the extent to which the child was able to adapt to the daily activities and demands of being in foster care. In many cases the foster care environment was different from that experienced by the child in his own home and required substantial readjustment. This index comprised eight items:

1. To what degree has each of the following phenomena been a source of strain for this child while in foster care?

a. living in a different environment;
b. following rules, expectations, and daily routines of foster care setting;
c. meeting peer demands in group living;
d. relating to many new adults;
e. having to share attention and affection with other children in setting;
f. type of placement (foster family vs. institution);
g. limitations on freedom and independence.

2. What is your prediction as to how capable this child will be in adjusting to or overcoming problems in his/her life's experiences while growing up?

Embedment in Foster Care Setting

The Index of Embedment in the Foster Care Setting provides a measure of the extent to which the child had become an integral part of the particular foster family or institutional setting. It was composed of responses to eight questions intended to capture the degree to which the child appeared to feel an integral part of and "belonging" to the family or institution. The items comprising this index are:

1. Is this child consciously aware that he/she is not living with own parent(s) or relatives who substitute as parents?

2. Please list the people in this child's life who appear to be most meaningful to him/her (from the child's point of view).

3. Does the child treat the child caring person as if she were the

TABLE 13.1
INDEX OF EMBEDMENT IN FOSTER CARE SETTING

Judgment	Time II (%)	Time III (%)
A. Is this child consciously aware that he/she is not living with own parents (or relatives who substitute as parents)?		
1. No	26	20
2. Yes	74	80
Number of cases	(341)	(227)
B. (If A is *no*.) Does the child treat the child-caring person as if he/she were the natural parent?		
1. Yes, in all respects	60	69
2. Yes, for the most part	22	21
3. Yes, to a slight degree	6	5
4. No	12	5
Number of cases	(116)	(42)
C. Please list the people in this child's life who appear to be most meaningful to him/her (from the child's point of view).		
1. Persons other than own parent	59	78
2. Own parent	41	22
Number of cases	(338)	(217)
D. Please check the category that best describes the child's present acceptance of being in foster care.		
1. Content to remain in foster care	42	57
2. Tolerates foster care	22	19
3. Mixed feelings	17	18
4. Prefers home	16	5
5. Intense dislike of foster care	3	1
Number of cases	(269)	(201)
E. What is child's expectation of his/her length of stay in foster care?		
1. Child does not really understand foster care	37	32
2. Expects to remain in care until grown up	13	39
3. Child expects to return home, but not in immediate future	34	21
4. Child expects to return home soon	16	8
Number of cases	(285)	(195)

TABLE 13.1 (*cont.*)

Judgment	Time II (%)	Time III (%)
F. Has the child become an integral part of the household, cottage, or institutional groups indicated by his/her "feeling at home," wanting to participate in activities, showing pride in living or "belonging" there, and accepting this as "home"?		
1. Yes, definitely	48	58
2. Yes, for the most part	33	35
3. Yes, but only to slight degree	10	5
4. No	9	2
Number of cases	(337)	(224)
G. (If F is *yes*.) Do you think this child would react to the separation by becoming emotionally upset over having to leave at some time in the future?		
1. Definitely yes	30	40
2. Probably yes	34	39
3. Probably not	27	17
4. Definitely not	9	4
Number of cases	(303)	(223)
H. How would you describe this child's emotional ties to the foster mother, counselor, or housemother(s) responsible for the child's care?		
1. Quite strong	42	52
2. Moderately strong	30	31
3. Slightly weak	15	14
4. Very weak	5	2
5. No emotional ties	8	1
Number of cases	(339)	(225)
Embedment in Foster Care Index:		
Mean	4.28	3.72
Standard deviation	1.79	1.35
Skewness	0.18	0.54
Kurtosis	−1.24	−0.42
Cronbach alpha	.90	.86
Number of cases	(345)	(228)

TABLE 13.1 (cont.)

Time III	A	B	C	D	E	F	G	H	Time II	Time III
			Intercorrelation Among Items						Item Criterion Correlations	
A	.43[b]	.70	.41	.37	.69	.43	.41	.38	.60	.37
B	.49	.19	.73	.67	.78	.76	.60	.63	.91	.79
C	.21	.46	.41	.56	.64	.44	.56	.48	.68	.57
D	.23	.69	.50	.37	.62	.59	.51	.53	.69	.72
E	.44	.60	.54	.61	.65	.49	.56	.47	.78	.68
F	.24	.43	.44	.61	.36	.40	.52	.64	.69	.63
G	.24	.56	.44	.58	.56	.58	.57	.57	.67	.67
H	.20	.73	.44	.54	.33	.65	.60	.44	.65	.65

[a] A low score indicates greatest embedment, and a high score, least embedment.
[b] Correlations between Times II and III ratings of the same item are shown in the diagonal cells (in italics). Time II intercorrelations are above the diagonal and Time III are below.

natural parent? (When child is unaware of substitute parent status.)

4. Please check the category which best describes this child's present acceptance of being in foster care (content to remain through intense dislike of foster care).

5. What is the child's expectation of his/her length of stay in foster care?

6. Has the child become an integral part of the household, cottage, or institutional group as indicated by his/her "feeling at home," wanting to participate in activities, showing pride in living or "belonging" there and accepting this as "home"?

7. Do you think this child would react to the separation by becoming emotionally upset over having to leave his/her foster care placement at some time in the future?

8. How would you describe this child's emotional tie (degree of affective involvement) to the foster mother, counselor, or housemother(s) responsible for child care?

While limited space does not permit us to display the details of all the indexes discussed in this chapter, we present item frequencies and intercorrelations for the embedment in foster care setting index, since we regard this as central to our conception of adaptation (see Table 13.1).

Attachment to Natural Parents

The Index of Attachment to Natural Parents provides a measure of the degree of emotional closeness between the child and parents, and attempts to determine how the child's present level of attachment to his/her natural mother and father would be rated. If the child doesn't know his mother or father, it specifies who the child considers as his mother and father and rates the degree of attachment to them.

Conflict in Identity

The Index of Conflict in Identity provides a measure of the extent to which the child evidences conflicted loyalty and concern about who he is or to whom he belongs—natural parents, foster parents, institution, or no person at all. The index consists of four items:

1. Does the child show any signs of feelings responsible and/or guilty for the situation that caused his/her placement?
2. Does the child show any signs of being confused about his/her familial identity?
3. To what degree has each of the following phenomena been a source of strain for this child while in foster care?
   a. developing conflict in loyalties for parent and child caring person;
   b. insecurity about his/her future.

Capacity to Relate to Others

The Index of Capacity to Relate to Others provides a measure of the emotional and social problems encountered by the child in relating to other people with whom he comes in daily contact. It deals with the child's capacity to form sustained and satisfying human relationships. The index consists of the following items:

1. How well does this child get along (relate) in his/her daily activities with other children and adults?
2. In general, what type of response does this child evoke from people?
3. Is the child often teased by other children as being odd, different, a poor sport, clumsy, dumb, tomboyish, a foster child, and so on?
4. To what extent has the child been difficult to care for while in placement?
5. Does the child pose any problems that concern you (case-

worker) or the child care person(s) with regard to his/her play, such as play behavior or choice of activities or playmates?

6. What is the child's present level of social development in each of the following areas?

a. developing social conscience;

b. social participation (engaging in social group activities);

c. self-control of own behavior (compliance, obedience).

As seen in Table 13.2, the internal reliability of each of the indexes (as measured by Cronbach's alpha coefficient) is quite high, indicating that each item appears to be a measure of the same concept as each other item within the scale.[8] For example, the Index of Embedment in Foster Care Placement, which, as we have indicated, measures an important concept dealing with the roots developed by a child while in foster care, shows the highest internal reliabilities (.90 at Time II and .86 at Time III).

In Table 13.2 we also show the product–moment correlations between index scores. Some of the associations are quite high. The lack of orthogonality in the relationship between measures no doubt reflects a limitation in our ability to clearly demarcate aspects of the adaptation of subjects and to develop appropriate operational indicators.[9] We are also aware that it is quite difficult to develop rating instruments where the individual items do not reflect a global orientation of the rater.

The child's capacity to cope with separation appears to be significantly correlated with his ability to cope with the foster care environment, deeper embedment in placement, lower conflict in identity, and fewer difficulties in relating to other people. Similar patterns of correlation also prevail with respect to the child's ability to cope with the foster care environment. Embedment in foster care

---

[8] Cronbach's alpha is measured by the formula:

$$\left(\frac{k}{k-1}\right)\left(1-\frac{\sum\limits_{}^{k} S_i^2}{S_x^2}\right)$$

where k stands for the number of items in the index, $\sum\limits_{}^{k} S_i^2$ for the sum of the item variances, and S_x^2 for the variance of the total score. This is a generalization of Kuder and Richardson's KR20 internal consistency reliability formula. See Lee J. Cronbach, "Coefficient Alpha and the Internal Structure of Tests, "*Psychometrika* 16 (1951), pp. 297–334.

[9] The lack of orthogonality displayed in Table 13.2 no doubt reflects our failure to use an approach to index construction more fully based upon solutions derived from factor analysis.

TABLE 13.2
INTERINDEX CORRELATIONS AND CRONBACH ALPHA MEASURE OF INTERNAL RELIABILITY FOR INDEXES FOR TIMES II and III

| | Correlations | | | | | | Cronbach alpha | |
| | Time III[a] (228) | | | | Time II[b] (345) | | | |
Index	A	B	C	E	E	F	Time II	Time III
Capacity to cope with separation	.45***[c]	.60***	.68***	−.01	.61***	.39***	.77	.77
Capacity to cope with foster care environment	.53***	.46***	.58***	.09	.64***	.65***	.87	.85
Embedment in foster care setting	.54***	.38***	.66***	−.10	.46***	.35***	.90	.86
Attachment to natural parents	.26***	.20**	.28***	.34***	.11*	.10	.70	.73
Conflict in identity	.57***	.59***	.30***	.28***	.48***	.51***	.76	.64
Capacity to relate to others	.36***	.63***	.18**	.16*	.42***	.39***	.84	.81

$*p < .05$ $**p < .01$ $***p < .001$.
[a] Time III correlations are below the diagonal.
[b] Time II correlations are above the diagonal.
[c] Italicized correlations are the intercorrelations of Time II with Time III.

and capacity to cope with separation are highly correlated ($r = .68$), indicating that a child who feels he belongs with the particular family or group simultaneously shows little difficulty in being separated from home. While in foster care, the child's ability to cope with the foster care environment appears to be highly correlated with whether he is able to relate to other children and adults ($r = .65$). As shown in Table 13.2, the intercorrelations for the indexes at Time III show patterns similar to those reported for Time II.

Assessment of Validity

We considered it useful to assess whether the perceptions of the caseworkers were in accord with those of other observers, namely, the examining psychologists and the children's teachers. We saw this as constituting a test of concurrent validity since the ratings of three observers covered similar domains of content and were secured in the same waves of data collection. We decided to correlate the scores assigned subjects on the index described in this chapter as "ability to relate to others" with the emotional assessments made by the examining psychologists and an index of "total emotional adjustment" based on a combination of four teacher ratings on the RSPA used at Time III.

The results of our validation effort are shown in Table 13.3. The correlations are modest but of an order one might expect in this kind of linkage between diverse measures. The Time II emotional assessment by the examining psychologist shows a correlation of $-.31$ ($p < .001$) with the Time II index of ability to relate to others and $-.36$ ($p < .001$) for the measure at Time III. The Time III emotional assessment by the examining psychologist shows a correlation of $.15$ ($p < .05$) with the Time II index of ability to relate and $.34$ ($p < .001$) with the Time III index.

The correlation between the composite of four teacher ratings from the RSPA and the Time III index of capacity to relate to others is $-.42$ ($p < .001$).[10]

[10] To develop a total emotional adjustment measure from the teacher ratings, we followed the recommendations of the RSPA manual and combined the rating scales labeled: (a) overall emotional adjustment, (b) social maturity, (c) emotional security, and (d) impulsiveness. The negative correlation we report is due to the fact that a high score on the teacher summary measure reflects a good adjustment while a high score on the index derived from the social worker ratings reflects poor adaptation.

TABLE 13.3
CORRELATIONS OF SCORES ASSIGNED SUBJECTS ON INDEX OF
CAPACITY TO RELATE TO OTHERS (BASED ON SOCIAL WORKER
RATINGS) AND RATINGS BY EXAMINING PSYCHOLOGISTS AND TEACHERS

| Social worker Rating[a] | Psychologist Rating[b] | | Teacher Rating[c] |
	Emotional Assessment Time II	Emotional Assessment Time III	Index of Total Emotional Adjustment Time III
Index, Time II	−.31***	−.15*	—
Index, Time III	−.36***	−.34***	−.42***

*p < .05   ***p < .001

[a] A high score on the index reflects more difficulty in relating to others.

[b] The rating of the emotional condition of the subject by the examining psychologist utilized the following scale: 1—abnormal, 2—suspect, 3—normal.

[c] Index consists of four items from the RSPA. A high score indicates better adjustment.

ADAPTATION AFTER THREE TO FIVE YEARS OF FOSTER CARE

The caseworker ratings applied only to children remaining in foster care. At Time II, approximately three years after entering foster care, 82 percent of the children were deemed by their caseworkers to be quite solidly entrenched in their foster care settings, with one child out of every four described as not being aware that the foster family with whom they were living was not their biological family. When we examined the situation as it prevailed after five years of placement, 21 percent of the children were apparently still uninformed about their status. The potential trauma to such children, which might occur if they were moved because of the appearance of a long-lost natural parent or if the agency decided to move the child for administrative reasons, is readily apparent.

It seems clear from inspection of the data related to the indexes for Times II and III that most of the subjects were perceived as being settled in their foster care situations and were able to form relationships that could serve to support their normal maturation. We shall subsequently provide data, however, which reveal variation in the adaptation of the children according to whether the natural parents were in the picture. We now present a summary of our findings for each scale showing the perceived adaptation of the children at both Times II and III.

The Child's Capacity to Cope with Separation

The distribution of index scores pertaining to coping with separation by the 345 study children assessed at Time II is shown in Table 13.4 The majority of children were reported by their caseworkers as showing a relatively good capacity to cope with separation from their natural parents. The mean index score was 35.3 and the median 34.0, within a possible range of 10–90 points (where a score of 10 represents a high capacity to cope and a score of 90, a low capacity). Less than 8 percent of the children received a score over 61. We note that for the 228 children still in care at the end of five years, their capacity to cope with separation was almost the same as described for Time II (see Table 13.5). The mean index score for the third assessment occasion was 34.7. The proportion of children having great difficulty (i.e., with a score over 60) had dropped to less than 4 percent.

We considered the age of the child to be quite critical with respect to the content covered by the six indexes. It seemed obvious that a child entering foster care at a very early age would experience the separation phenomenon quite differently from the way an older child would, particularly if the latter had experienced exclusive preplacement contact with his own parents. In Table 13.6 we display the mean Time II scores for each of the six indexes according to the age of the child at entry into care. We use three age categories: (a) under two years, (b) two to five years, and (c) six to 13 years. The same data aggregated for Time III are shown in Table 13.7.

As shown in Table 13.6, the capacity of the children to cope with separation is linearly related to age. For the index, a higher score reflects lower capacity to cope with the separation problem. For children who entered care under two years, the mean score was 22.5; for those who were two to five years at entry, the mean score was 35.9; and, for the oldest children, the mean score was 43.3. A one-way analysis of variance showed the differences to be statisti-

TABLE 13.4
DISTRIBUTION OF INDEX SCORES OF STUDY SUBJECTS AT TIME II (in percentages)

Index Score[a]	Capacity to Cope with Separation	Capacity to Cope: Foster Care Environment	Embedment in Foster Care	Attachment to Parents	Conflict in Identity	Capacity to Relate
10–15	3.2	6.4	—	29.4	19.8	—
16–20	20.3	9.1	12.8	6.4	15.9	1.2
21–25	7.8	12.9	9.0	—	7.8	8.7
26–30	9.9	11.7	12.5	18.5	9.3	17.7
31–35	10.7	10.8	9.0	—	9.6	20.3
36–40	11.0	10.2	6.4	5.2	6.3	11.3
41–45	5.5	8.2	3.5	—	5.7	7.2
46–50	9.3	10.2	6.1	15.5	7.2	7.8
51–55	4.1	5.6	10.7	—	3.6	7.0
56–60	4.9	5.6	11.6	6.1	5.7	9.3
61–65	4.3	3.2	6.7	—	1.2	3.8
66–70	1.7	3.5	6.4	8.2	5.1	4.3
71–75	.9	1.2	3.8	—	.6	1.4
76–80	.9	1.2	2.0	4.9	1.5	—
81–85	—	.3	.3	—	.3	—
86–90	—	—	—	6.1	.3	—
Mean	35.3	37.3	42.8	38.2	33.8	40.5
SD	15.6	16.0	17.9	25.5	18.3	13.7
Median	34.0	35.0	43.0	30.0	30.0	36.0
Number	345	342	345	330	333	345

[a] Key to scale: low index scores refer to: separation—highest capacity to cope; foster care environment—highest capacity to cope; embedment—deeper embedment; attachment—strong attachment to parents; identity—low conflict in identity; relating—minimal difficulties in ability to relate.

TABLE 13.5

DISTRIBUTION OF INDEX SCORES OF STUDY SUBJECTS AT TIME III (in percentages)

Index Score[a]	Capacity to Cope with Separation	Capacity to Cope: Foster Care Environment	Embedment in Foster Care	Attachment to Parents	Conflict in Identity	Capacity to Relate
10–15	3.9	6.1	—	24.3	16.2	—
16–20	19.3	8.8	13.2	6.4	18.0	2.6
21–25	9.2	16.2	3.5	—	10.5	11.8
26–30	16.7	11.0	21.1	17.4	9.6	11.4
31–35	6.7	13.2	14.0	—	9.6	19.7
36–40	10.5	11.8	13.2	8.7	9.2	14.5
41–45	10.5	9.2	7.5	—	7.5	8.3
46–50	8.3	8.8	8.8	14.2	7.5	11.8
51–55	5.7	4.8	8.3	—	2.2	6.1
56–60	5.3	5.3	4.8	7.8	3.9	8.3
61–65	1.3	2.6	2.6	—	3.1	1.7
66–70	1.3	1.3	2.2	10.6	1.8	2.6
71–75	0.4	—	.9	—	.4	.4
76–80	0.4	—	—	7.3	.4	.4
81–85	0.4	.4	—	—	—	—
86–90	—		—	3.2	—	—
Mean	34.7	35.2	37.2	40.4	32.0	39.2
SD	14.6	14.0	13.5	24.5	15.6	12.6
Median	32.0	34.0	34.0	40.0	29.0	37.5
Number	228	228	228	218	228	228

[a] Key to scale is same as that in Table 13.4.

TABLE 13.6
MEAN SCORES ON ADAPTATION TO FOSTER CARE INDEXES
FOR TIME II STUDY SUBJECTS, BY AGE

| Index and Age at Entry | Index Score | | Number | Significance[a] |
	Mean	SD		
Capacity to cope with separation	35.3	15.6	345	< .001
Under 2 years	22.5	9.7	98	
2–5 years	35.9	14.8	98	
6–13 years	43.3	13.6	149	
Capacity to cope with foster care				
environment	37.3	16.0	342	< .001
Under 2 years	27.3	13.4	96	
2–5 years	37.3	15.3	97	
6–13 years	43.8	14.5	149	
Embedment in foster care setting	42.8	17.9	345	< .001
Under 2 years	24.8	8.9	98	
2–5 years	40.4	13.3	98	
6–13 years	56.3	13.1	149	
Attachment to natural parents	38.2	25.5	330	.006
Under 2 years	35.1	31.5	90	
2–5 years	45.5	24.0	92	
6–13 years	35.6	20.9	148	
Conflict in identity	33.8	18.3	333	< .001
Under 2 years	21.3	11.8	91	
2–5 years	34.3	18.2	96	
6–13 years	41.3	17.4	146	
Capacity to relate to others	40.5	13.6	345	< .001
Under 2 years	35.9	12.0	98	
2–5 years	40.2	13.0	98	
6–13 years	43.9	14.0	149	

[a]One-way analysis of variance.

cally significant ($p < .001$). The mean index score of the oldest children is almost double that of the youngest group. It would appear from these data that children who entered foster care after the age of five years found it more difficult to accept being placed away from their own family, whereas the young toddler or infant experienced this with much less evidence of strain. The pattern of reaction according to age is again manifested at Time III. The

TABLE 13.7
MEAN SCORES ON ADAPTATION TO FOSTER CARE INDEXES
FOR TIME III STUDY SUBJECTS, BY AGE

| Index and Age at Entry | Index Score | | Number | Significance[a] |
	Mean	SD		
Capacity to cope with separation	34.7	14.6	228	<.001
Under 2 years	25.8	11.3	82	
2–5 years	38.0	12.7	64	
6–13 years	41.0	14.5	82	
Capacity to cope with foster care environment	35.2	14.0	228	<.001
Under 2 years	30.0	12.2	82	
2–5 years	36.8	14.6	64	
6–13 years	39.2	13.7	82	
Embedment in foster care setting	37.2	13.5	228	<.001
Under 2 years	27.0	8.5	82	
2–5 years	37.9	10.6	64	
6–13 years	46.8	12.2	82	
Attachment to natural parents	40.4	24.5	218	<.001
Under 2 years	26.1	24.1	76	
2–5 years	47.8	21.6	63	
6–13 years	48.2	20.5	79	
Conflict in identity	32.0	15.6	228	<.001
Under 2 years	25.0	13.9	82	
2–5 years	35.1	17.3	64	
6–13 years	36.7	13.1	82	
Capacity to relate to others	39.2	12.6	228	.010
Under 2 years	36.2	11.7	82	
2–5 years	39.5	12.9	64	
6–13 years	42.1	12.6	82	

[a]One-way analysis of variance.

differences between the three age groups is statistically significant (see Table 13.7).

With regard to ethnicity, black children were perceived as showing slightly better capacity to cope with separation than the Puerto Rican and white children for both assessment occasions (Times II and III). We present mean index scores for the three ethnic groups in Tables 13.8–9. Although the differences in index scores at Time II

TABLE 13.8
MEAN SCORES ON ADAPTATION TO FOSTER CARE INDEXES
FOR TIME II STUDY SUBJECTS, BY ETHNICITY

| Index and Ethnicity | Index Score | | Number | Significance[a] |
	Mean	SD		
Capacity to cope with separation	*35.3*	*15.6*	*345*	.04
White	37.4	15.1	85	
Black	32.8	16.0	147	
Puerto Rican	37.0	15.0	113	
Capacity to cope with foster care				
environment	*37.3*	*16.0*	*342*	.04
White	39.1	15.3	85	
Black	34.8	15.5	146	
Puerto Rican	39.3	16.7	111	
Embedment in foster care setting	*42.8*	*17.9*	*345*	(NS)
White	46.6	17.9	85	
Black	36.8	17.0	147	
Puerto Rican	47.9	16.6	113	
Attachment to natural parents	*38.2*	*25.5*	*330*	< .001
White	33.1	22.1	81	
Black	38.3	26.9	138	
Puerto Rican	41.9	25.2	111	
Conflict in identity	*33.8*	*18.9*	*333*	(NS)
White	36.5	18.9	85	
Black	31.9	18.2	140	
Puerto Rican	34.1	17.6	108	
Capacity to relate to others	*40.5*	*13.6*	*345*	(NS)
White	43.5	14.8	85	
Black	39.3	13.6	147	
Puerto Rican	39.8	12.1	113	

[a] One-way analysis of variance.

appear small, there was a statistically significant difference between the mean score of 32.8 for black children and 37.4 for white and 37.0 for Puerto Rican children ($p = .04$). At Time III, the differences in scores among the three ethnic groups is not statistically significant.

We were interested in the potential contribution of a number of independent variables in explaining the *changes* in index scores assigned to the subjects. The analysis was formulated as a multiple

TABLE 13.9
MEAN SCORES ON ADAPTATION TO FOSTER CARE INDEXES
FOR TIME III STUDY SUBJECTS, BY ETHNICITY

| Index and Ethnicity | Index Score | | Number | Significance[a] |
	Mean	SD		
Capacity to cope with separation	34.7	14.6	228	(NS)
White	35.5	17.6	42	
Black	32.6	13.1	111	
Puerto Rican	34.3	14.3	75	
Capacity to cope with foster care environment	35.2	14.0	228	(NS)
White	37.5	14.9	42	
Black	35.1	13.6	111	
Puerto Rican	34.1	13.9	75	
Embedment in foster care setting	37.2	13.5	228	.01
White	34.5	11.2	42	
Black	35.5	12.9	111	
Puerto Rican	41.3	14.6	75	
Attachment to natural parents	40.4	24.5	218	(NS)
White	40.5	23.8	41	
Black	39.1	26.0	104	
Puerto Rican	42.1	22.5	73	
Conflict in identity	32.0	15.6	228	(NS)
White	34.3	16.6	42	
Black	30.6	15.2	111	
Puerto Rican	32.9	15.4	75	
Capacity to relate to others	39.2	12.6	228	.04
White	43.5	14.5	42	
Black	37.7	12.1	111	
Puerto Rican	39.1	11.7	75	

[a] One-way analysis of variance.

regression procedure in which the Time III score was treated as the dependent variable to be analyzed and the Time II score was included as one of the regressor variables. By including the earlier index score as a covariate, the remaining residual (the amount of change) could become the datum to be explained by all other entering variables. Results for the analysis of the Capacity to Cope with Separation Index are shown in Table 13.10.

TABLE 13.10
RELATION OF SALIENT BACKGROUND AND OTHER INDEPENDENT
VARIABLES TO CHANGES IN CAPACITY TO COPE WITH SEPARATION
(TIME III)[a]
(N = 228)

Independent Variables	Zero-order Correlation	Standardized Regression Coefficient
Index of capacity to cope with separation (Time II)	.45***	.35***
Child's age at placement	.41***	.24**
Sex of child	−.09	−.08
Ethnicity[b]		
Black	.14*	.01
Puerto Rican	.13	.07
Reason for placement: child behavior vs. others	.16*	.01
Developmental history indexes		
Emotional problems index	.16*	−.02
Developmental problems index	−.03	−.04
Health problems index	.05	.02
Parental visiting pattern (Time I)	.15*	−.10
One or both parents visit (Time I)	−.03	−.09
Evaluation of mother (Time II)	−.04	−.05
Log of total casework contact (Time I)	.01	−.02
Worker skill index (Time I)	.10	−.06
Parental visiting pattern (Time II)	.27***	.23**
One or both parents visit (Time II)	.01	−.09
Evaluations of mother (Time II)	.02	−.07
Log of total casework contact (Time II)	.07	.00
Worker skill index (Time II)	.16*	.16*
Parental visiting pattern (Time III)	.17*	.07
One or both parents visit (Time III)	−.02	.06
Evaluation of mother (Time III)	.01	.02
Log of total casework contact (Time III)	.08	−.12
Worker skill index (Time III)	.09	.06
Multiple R	.59	
Multiple R²	.35[c]	

*$p < .05$ **$p < .01$ ***$p < .001$

[a] A high score on the index of capacity to cope with separation indicates lower capacity.
[b] Referenced to white children.
[c] Multiple R^2 corrected for degrees of freedom = .27.

A number of the variables showed significant standardized coefficients.[11] We observe that changes in the caseworker's interpretation of how well the child was able to cope with separation varied beyond chance according to such factors as the age of the child at entry, reason for placement (child behavior vs. other reasons), the visitation patterns of parents, and the level of caseworker skill. We note further that the correlation of age at entry with the Time III index score is .41, and the standardized regression coefficient is .24 ($p < .01$). This indicates that older children were perceived as reacting with greater difficulty to separation and that changes in their adaptation over time reflected poor capacity to cope.

It is of interest that parental visiting repeatedly shows significant correlations with the index scores for *each* of the three time occasions when such information was gathered. The Time II visiting data appear to be outstanding, however, in importance as predicting the child's perceived capacity to cope with separation. The direction of the variables involved leads us to interpret the findings as indicating that five years after entry into care, children still visited by their parents had a greater problem over time in coping with the separation problem than those whose parents had dropped out of the picture. The latter children appear to have made their peace with the absence of their parents; at least this is how their surface behavioral demeanor is interpreted by their caseworkers. We further observe that visited children had significantly changed for the worse in their capacity to cope with separation.

There is a certain common-sense appeal to the finding that visited children are more apt to be entangled in conflicting pulls than children who have been essentially abandoned. Yet we should note that elsewhere in this report, such as in assessing the emotional condition of the subjects through use of figure drawing tests, frequent parental visiting was linked to improvement in the condition of the children. We further analyze the role of parental visiting as we proceed with this chapter.

The association of the measure of the caseworker's skill with

---

[11] The *t*-test gives a significance level for testing the hypothesis that each coefficient is zero.

capacity to cope with separation reveals that high coping ability—
and improved capacity to cope—on the part of children is linked to
contact with inexperienced caseworkers. This finding is difficult to
interpret. We would conjecture that more trained and/or experienced caseworkers would tend to perceive greater underlying
difficulty in coping as a function of a more sophisticated view of the
child's adaptation. It is also possible that the workers with greater
experience would tend to seek more actively to engage the child in
consideration of feelings about separation from parents, hence stir-
ring up some of the underlying conflict, while less experienced
workers would be inclined to accept the surface adjustment of the
child without question. This is obviously only speculation on our
part and is an area that deserves further scrutiny. Change in coping
with separation was not found to vary with the sex of the child or
evaluation of the mother.

The Child's Capacity to Cope with Foster Care Environment
The demands placed on a child entering foster care to adapt to a
new environment can be quite trying, as described earlier. Despite
the potential problems, our analysis of caseworkers reports reflects
that after the passage of several years in foster care, the majority of
the study children were judged as not being particularly troubled by
their placement settings. At Time II the mean index score assigned
subjects was 37.3, and for Time III, 35.2 (see Tables 13.4–5). As
may be seen in the tables, the distributions of scale scores for the
children are skewed in the direction of coping well with the foster care
situation.

   With respect to the age of subjects, as with the previous index,
we find that older children were seen as having more difficulty
coping with the foster care environment at the Time II than their
younger counterparts. Furthermore, while the differences between
age groups were less pronounced at the end of five years, they were
nevertheless significant ($p < .001$) (see Table 13.6–7).

   At the time of the second assessment, black children were
viewed as coping slightly better than the Puerto Rican or white
children. The differences were statistically significant. At the final
assessment occasion these differences had become trivial (see
Tables 13.8–9).

TABLE 13.11
RELATION OF SALIENT BACKGROUND AND OTHER INDEPENDENT
VARIABLES TO CHANGES IN CAPACITY TO COPE WITH
FOSTER CARE ENVIRONMENT (TIME III)[a]
(N = 228)

Independent Variables	Zero-order Correlation	Standardized Regression Coefficient
Index of capacity to cope with foster care environment (Time II)	.46***	.43***
Child's age at placement	.26***	.14
Sex of child	−.14*	−.13*
Ethnicity[b]		
Black	−.01	−.02
Puerto Rican	−.06	−.08
Reason for placement: child behavior vs. others	.22***	.09
Developmental history indexes		
Emotional problems index	.16*	−.07
Developmental problems index	.12	.12
Health problems index	−.03	−.02
Parental visiting pattern (Time I)	.04	−.05
One or both parents visit (Time I)	−.09	−.07
Evaluation of mother (Time I)	−.12	−.10
Log of total casework contact (Time I)	−.02	−.08
Worker skill index (Time I)	.05	.00
Parental visiting pattern (Time II)	.11	.06
One or both parents visit (Time II)	.01	−.07
Evaluation of mother (Time II)	−.03	−.03
Log of total casework contact (Time II)	.09	−.05
Worker skill index (Time II)	.00	−.02
Parental visiting pattern (Time III)	.06	−.11
One or both parents visit (Time III)	−.02	.09
Evaluation of mother (Time III)	−.02	.08
Log of total casework contact (Time III)	.23***	.14*
Worker skill index (Time III)	.03	.00
Multiple R	.57	
Multiple R²	.33[c]	

*p < .05   ***p < .001

[a] A high score on the index of capacity to cope with foster care environment reflects a lower capacity to cope.

[b] Referenced to white children.

[c] Multiple R^2 corrected for degrees of freedom = .25.

In Table 13.11, the results of the regression analysis of the Time III index scores are displayed. As with the preceding index, the amount of variance explained is modest, some 33 percent (and only 25 percent when the multiple R^2 is corrected for degrees of freedom). The product–moment correlations with the Time III measure, as displayed in Table 13.11, show several predictor variables having significant associations: (a) the child's age and sex, (b) reason for placement, (c) history of prior emotional problems in his preplacement history, and (d) amount of casework attention received. We interpret these correlations as indicating that older children and boys were viewed as showing greater problems in coping as were those who entered care because of their own behavioral difficulties. We also find that more casework time is being invested in children who are perceived as having more problems in coping.

In Table 13.11, we find only two significant predictors of change in index scores: (a) the child's sex and (b) the amount of casework contact. The age of the child and reason for placement make no significant contribution to explaining change in coping capacity. That girls are seen as becoming more adaptive to being in foster care may reflect a surface accommodation in accord with cultural pressures and expectations that are sex-based.

The Child's Embedment in Foster Care
The extent to which the child had become rooted in the particular foster care setting is seen as a critical issue from several perspectives. Has he indeed become an integral part of the foster family or the institutional group? Has the substitute family become the "real" family for him, replacing the natural family as the center of his world?[12]

As may be seen in Table 13.4, our data show substantial

---

[12] Widespread attention and considerable acceptance have been accorded the view propounded by Goldstein, Freud, and Solnit that the *real* parent of a child is one who nurtures him totally. They indicate the following: "But once the prior tie has been broken, the foster or other temporary placements can no longer be considered temporary. They may develop into or substantially begin to become psychological parent-child relationships which in accord with the continuity guideline deserve recognition as a common-law adoption." Joseph Goldstein, Anna Freud, and Albert J. Solnit, *Beyond the Best Interests of the Child* (New York: Free Press, 1973), p. 39.

variation in the intensity of embedment for the subjects as displayed for Time II. However, this variation declined when the assessments were again made for children still remaining in care at the end of five years (see Table 13.5). The degree of embedment for the subjects at Time II was in the midrange, reflected by a mean score of 42.8. At Time III, the overall group mean was 37.2, indicating an increase in the proportion of children who had become more embedded in their placements.

These overall group averages mask an important facet of embedment—the variation that is accounted for by the age of the subjects. As shown in Tables 13.6–7, children who had entered care when very young were much more likely to become deeply embedded in their foster care situations than their older counterparts. Moreover, there is substantially less variation of this phenomenon in the youngest child group (as reflected in lower standard deviations), in contrast to those children over the age of two at the time of entry. Our data show a mean index score of 24.8 for those children entering foster care under two years of age, reflecting deep embedment, with a standard deviation of 8.9, in contrast to a mean of 56.3 and standard deviation of 13.1 for the children aged six to 13 years. The older children remaining in care for the full five years have a somewhat deeper embedment score than was found for the older group at Time II (means of 46.8 and 56.3, respectively).

With regard to ethnicity, we observe some greater tendency for black children to be entrenched in their foster care settings at Time II, but they are relatively undifferentiated from the white children at Time III. The Puerto Rican children show the least intensity of embedment in their settings (see Tables 13.8–9).

In Table 13.12 we show the results of the multiple regression analysis of the Time III scores. We first observe that considerably more variance is explained in this analysis than that reported for the prior two indexes. The multiple R^2 is 56 percent (and is reduced to 51 percent when corrected for degrees of freedom). As might be expected from our earlier findings, age is a major contributor to explained variance; the correlation of the child's age with the Time III index score is .62. Age is also an important predictor of change, with the younger children moving toward much deeper embedment in their placements.

TABLE 13.12
RELATION OF SALIENT BACKGROUND AND OTHER INDEPENDENT
VARIABLES TO CHANGES IN EMBEDMENT IN FOSTER CARE SETTING
(TIME III)ᵃ
(N = 228)

Independent Variables	Zero-order Correlation	Standardized Regression Coefficient
Index of embedment in foster care setting (Time II)	.65***	.41***
Child's age at placement	.62***	.34***
Sex of child	−.10	−.09
Ethnicityᵇ		
Black	−.13	−.16*
Puerto Rican	.21**	.16*
Reason for placement: child behavior vs. others	.33***	.04
Developmental history indexes		
Emotional problems index	.31***	−.05
Developmental problems index	−.07	−.13*
Health problems index	.06	.02
Parental visiting pattern (Time I)	.17**	−.12
One or both parents visit (Time I)	−.01	.00
Evaluation of mother (Time I)	.09	−.05
Log of total casework contact (Time I)	.09	.00
Worker skill index (Time I)	.17*	.12*
Parental visiting pattern (Time II)	.29**	.06
One or both parents visit (Time II)	.04	−.05
Evaluation of mother (Time II)	.20**	.06
Log of total casework contact (Time II)	.17**	.02
Worker skill index (Time II)	−.01	−.08
Parental visiting pattern (Time III)	.18**	.05
One or both parents visit (Time III)	−.13	−.11
Evaluation of mother (Time III)	.16*	.08
Log of total casework contact (Time III)	.19**	−.03
Worker skill index (Time III)	.02	−.03
Multiple R	.75	
Multiple R²	.56ᶜ	

*p < .05   **p < .01   ***p < .001
ᵃA low score on the index of embedment in foster care setting reflects a deeper or stronger degree of embedment.
ᵇReferenced to white children.
ᶜMultiple R² corrected for degrees of freedom = .51.

Ethnicity is also a significant predictor of change, with black children becoming more deeply embedded than Puerto Rican children. In addition to these variables, the presence of earlier developmental problems and the worker-skill index (Time I) are the only other variables to show significant beta weights. We observe that parental visiting for all three time occasions showed significant zero-order correlations with the Time III embedment index; but the influence of this variable as a measure of change is so intertwined with the others included in the regression analysis that the beta weights are not significant.

Because of our interest in the phenomenon of embedment, we analyzed the index scores further. While space does not permit us to present additional tables of data, we summarize our findings here:

1. At times II and III, there were no significant differences in mean index scores when boys and girls were compared.

2. There were no significant differences in mean index scores when children who entered care through the courts were compared with those who were placed on a voluntary basis.

3. Degree of embedment was found to be more intense for those children entering care as infants because their mothers were unwilling to assume care (mean index score = 22.4).

4. Degree of embedment was least in children in residential treatment centers receiving extended care because of their own behavior difficulties (mean index score = 61.3).

5. Among the other reasons for placement associated with less intense embedment of the children were hospitalization of the child caring person for physical or mental illness.

Attachment to Natural Parents

As can be seen in Tables 13.4–5, there is considerable variability in the scores assigned children on the Index of Attachment to Natural Parents. The standard deviations for Times II and III index scores are much higher than for the other five adaptation indexes discussed in this chapter. At Time II, the attachment of younger children (under two years at entry) was hardly differentiated from the older children; however, by the end of five years the youngest children are revealed to have the greatest level of attachment. The children who entered care under age two years showed a mean of 26.1, compared to 47.1 for those who entered care between two and five

TABLE 13.13
RELATION OF SALIENT BACKGROUND AND OTHER INDEPENDENT
VARIABLES TO CHANGES IN ATTACHMENT TO
NATURAL PARENTS (TIME III)[a]
(N = 228)

Independent Variables	Zero-order Correlation	Standardized Regression Coefficient
Index of attachment to natural parents (Time II)	.34***	.30***
Child's age at placement	.32***	.30***
Sex of child	−.11	−.15*
Ethnicity[b]		
Black	−.05	.11
Puerto Rican	.05	.02
Reason for placement: child behavior vs. others	.09	.00
Developmental history indexes		
Emotional problems index	.14	−.08
Developmental problems index	.00	.05
Health problems index	.02	−.03
Parental visiting pattern (Time I)	.18**	.05
One or both parents visit (Time I)	.18**	.14
Evaluation of mother (Time I)	−.05	−.09
Log of total casework contact (Time I)	.12	.02
Worker skill index (Time I)	.08	.12
Parental visiting pattern (Time II)	.18**	−.03
One or both parents visit (Time II)	.02	−.17*
Evaluation of mother (Time II)	.07	.00
Log of total casework contact (Time II)	.26**	.07
Worker skill index (Time II)	.07	−.11
Parental visiting pattern (Time III)	.15*	.06
One or both parents visit (Time III)	.13*	.06
Evaluation of mother (Time III)	.04	.10
Log of total casework contact (Time III)	.33***	.18*
Worker skill index (Time III)	−.01	−.06
Multiple R	.59	
Multiple R^2	.34[c]	

*$p < .05$ **$p < .01$ ***$p < .001$
   [a] A low score on the index of attachment to natural parents reflects a stronger attachment to parents.
   [b] Referenced to white children.
   [c] Multiple R^2 corrected for degrees of freedom = .26.

years and 48.2 for those who entered at age six years or older (see Tables 13.6–7). We were surprised by this finding since we assumed that very young children would feel less attached to their natural parents, having had less experience of direct care in their own homes. It is possible that the perceptions of the caseworkers reflect the fact that our information is restricted to children remaining in care and therefore to parents who are the most sorely troubled. It may well be that older children tend to disengage themselves from such parents after three to five years in care.

White children were perceived as significantly more attached to their parents at Time II. However, the ethnic differentiation in index scores by the time the children had been in care for five years was quite trivial (see Tables 13.8–9).

In Table 13.13 we present the product–moment correlations of the independent variables with the Time III attachment scores and also show the beta weights from the multiple regression analysis. We again note that the age of the children is significantly correlated with the level of attachment, younger children being more attached and increasingly so as we move from Time II to Time III. We also note that parental visiting is significantly associated with the index, but the direction of the association was surprising to us. Unvisited children seemed more attached to their parents than visited children.[13] This is a puzzle. It suggests that caseworkers perceived continued pining for parents even if they were no longer in the picture. Interestingly, the frequency of parental visiting is not a significant predictor of change in perceived attachment of the child.

The amount of casework attention is significantly correlated with the degree of attachment at Time III ($r = .33$), and is a significant predictor of change in attachment from Time II to Time III. Children who were recipients of more frequent casework attention were perceived as progressively less attached to their parents.

---

[13] Because of the surprising direction of the association between levels of parental visiting and the amount of parental attachment shown by the children, we carefully checked our data by retracing our coding procedures and reviewing our original research protocols. We confirmed that our findings had not resulted from an inadvertent coding or computer-analysis error. The following cross-tabulation shows the relation between parental visiting and the caseworkers' reports of level of attachment to the natural mother for data collected some five

Conflict in Identity

Another area we explored was the extent to which a child in foster care became caught up in conflicting emotions about his identity, wondering to whom he "belonged," and specifically, whether he experienced conflicts in loyalty to surrogate and natural parents.

Our data (Table 13.14) suggest that the majority of children did not manifest major problems with respect to the issues of identity. As shown in Tables 13.4–5, the mean score at the Time II assessment was 33.8 and at Time III, 32.0. However, we should point out that a minority of children were viewed as having rather severe conflicts over identity or loyalty to dual sets of parents.

Variations in the extent of the child's concern over identity were significantly associated with age for both the Time II and the Time III assessments. Whereas children who entered care under two years of age showed little manifestation of conflict (mean score of 21.3 at Time II), children aged two to five years showed more of a problem (mean score of 34.3), and children six to 13 years, the most conflict (mean score of 41.3). At Time III the same differentiation prevailed, although differences between the middle and older age groups were substantially decreased (see Tables 13.6–7).

As may be seen in Tables 13.8–9, the differentiation among mean

---

years after the child entered care:

Attachment	No Visiting	Minimum Visiting	Frequent Visiting	Maximum Visiting	Child Visits Home	Total
			(Percentages)			
Quite strong	40.1	17.6	—	20.6	21.4	31.2
Moderate	23.3	23.5	—	23.5	35.8	23.1
Slight, weak	18.3	35.4	20.0	29.5	21.4	22.1
Very weak	10.8	23.5	60.0	17.6	14.3	15.9
None	7.5	—	20.0	8.8	7.1	7.7
No. of cases	120	17	10	34	14	195

We observe that there is a large group of children no longer being visited by their parents but attached to their mothers.

TABLE 13.14
RELATION OF SALIENT BACKGROUND AND OTHER INDEPENDENT
VARIABLES TO CHANGES IN CONFLICT IN IDENTITY (TIME III)[a]
(N = 228)

Independent Variables	Zero-order Correlation	Standardized Regression Coefficient
Index of conflict in identity (Time II)	.48***	.40***
Child's age at placement	.28***	.10
Sex of child	−.10	−.11
Ethnicity[b]		
Black	−.09	−.06
Puerto Rican	.04	−.01
Reason for placement: child behavior vs. others	.18**	.02
Developmental history indexes		
Emotional problems index	.14	.05
Developmental problems index	.12	.14*
Health problems index	−.01	−.10
Parental visiting pattern (Time I)	.19**	.06
One or both parents visit (Time I)	.00	−.10
Evaluation of mother (Time I)	−.09	−.08
Log of total casework contact (Time I)	.09	.02
Worker skill index (Time I)	.13*	.03
Parental visiting pattern (Time II)	.22**	.01
One or both parents visit (Time II)	.14*	.03
Evaluation of mother (Time II)	.08	.01
Log of total casework contact (Time II)	.20**	.03
Worker skill index (Time II)	.07	−.01
Parental visiting pattern (Time III)	.19**	.06
One or both parents visit (Time III)	.02	.01
Evaluation of mother (Time III)	.01	.01
Log of total casework contact (Time III)	.20**	.03
Worker skill index (Time III)	.01	−.02
Multiple R	.55	
Multiple R^2	.30[c]	

*p < .05   **p < .01   ***p < .001

[a] A high score on the index of conflict of identity reflects high conflict or confusion over identity.

[b] Referenced to white children.

[c] Multiple R^2 corrected for degrees of freedom = .22.

scores when children are compared on the basis of ethnicity was not significant for either Time II or Time III.

When we examine the results of the regression analysis of the Time III index scores, we find only one variable showing a significant beta weight. Children who had suffered from developmental problems prior to entering care manifested greater conflict over the pulls to the two sets of parents over the course of their years in placement. We observe that significant product–moment correlations are shown for parental visiting; the influence of this phenomenon as a predictor, however, is markedly reduced when the other variables are considered simultaneously in the regression analysis. The same holds true for the amount of casework contact and the dummy variable indentifying the children who entered care because of their own behavioral difficulties.

Capacity to Relate to Others

The final concept that we developed from the ratings of the children made by caseworkers concerned the child's ability to relate to other people. We were mindful that each subject had experienced sustained separation from home and may have had reason to shy away from meaningful human relationships as a result. Indeed, we were aware that John Bowlby in his classic review of the problem of maternal deprivation, had voiced concern that children exposed to the loss of mother figures tended to display a syndrome he labeled as the "affectionless personality."[14]

Inspection of the distribution of scores in Tables 13.4–5 shows that they are relatively normally distributed, with most subjects concentrated in an area that indicates some moderate difficulty in relating to others. There is little change in the means of these scores between Times II (40.5) and III (39.2). When we examine the mean scores for the three age groups shown in Tables 13.6–7, we see that the phenomenon has a strong age-related quality. There are statistically significant differences for both rating occasions, with the very young children showing the most positive scores while the older children are perceived as exhibiting the least capacity to relate well to others.

---

[14] John Bowlby, *Maternal Care and Mental Health* (Geneva: World Health Organization, 1952), pp. 30–35.

TABLE 13.15
RELATION OF SALIENT BACKGROUND AND OTHER INDEPENDENT
VARIABLES TO CHANGES IN CAPACITY TO RELATE
TO OTHERS (TIME III)[a]
(N = 228)

Independent Variables	Zero-order Correlation	Standardized Regression Coefficient
Index of capacity to relate to others (Time II)	.39***	.35***
Child's age at placement	.20**	.06
Sex of child	−.11	−.09
Ethnicity[b]		
Black	−.12	−.16
Puerto Rican	−.01	−.04
Reason for placement: child behavior vs. others	.10	.01
Developmental history indexes		
Emotional problems index	.23**	.15*
Developmental problems index	.20**	.11
Health problems index	.03	−.06
Parental visiting pattern (Time I)	.00	−.13
One or both parents visit (Time I)	−.07	−.10
Evaluation of mother (Time I)	−.24***	−.15*
Log of total casework contact (Time I)	.00	−.02
Worker skill index (Time I)	−.05	−.11
Parental visiting pattern (Time II)	.08	.17*
One or both parents visit (Time II)	−.12	−.19
Evaluation of mother (Time II)	−.12	−.12
Log of total casework contact (Time II)	.15*	.13
Worker skill index (Time II)	−.03	.04
Parental visiting pattern (Time III)	.01	−.06
One or both parents visit (Time III)	.02	.18*
Evaluation of mother (Time III)	−.12	.01
Log of total casework contact (Time III)	.16*	−.01
Worker skill index (Time III)	.04	.04
Multiple R	.60	
Multiple R²	.35[c]	

*$p < .05$ **$p < .01$ ***$p < .001$

[a] A high score on the index of capacity to relate to others reflects more difficulty in relating.

[b] Referenced to white children.

[c] Multiple R^2 corrected for degrees of freedom = .27.

At both Time II and Time III, the white children are rated lower than the black and Puerto Rican children. The ethnic differences are statistically significant at Time III (see Tables 13.8–9).

In Table 13.15 we analyze change in the child's ability to relate to others. We observe that the child's age at placement, although correlating significantly with the Time III index score ($r = .20$; $p < .001$), fails to emerge as a significant predictor of change (from Time II to Time III). It is of course understood that older children were more likely to enter care because of behavioral difficulties, and this may well explain the correlation of age with index scores.

Four variables emerge as significant: (a) early emotional problems prior to entering care, (b) poor evaluation of the mother, (c) parental visiting at Time II, and (d) whether one or both parents visit. Children with identified preplacement emotional problems showed increased problematic orientation in their relationship with others. Their tenure in care was apparently not a factor in altering their lifetime pattern of maladaptive adjustment.

Change in ability to relate was associated with more frequent parental visiting, especially at a point about three years after entry when both parents visited. Implied in this finding is the view that children from intact families remaining in foster care have increased difficulty in establishing satisfactory human relations, especially when they maintain closer ties with their own family. The possibility emerges that they are caught in a web of relationships that may be difficult to fathom and not easily sorted out. Visitation by parents at Time III, five years after the child entered foster care, was still a significant predictor of change; however, the visitation pattern associated with change at this point was more among the single-parent cases.

Change in ability to relate was not found to be significantly predicted by such variables as the ethnicity or the sex of the child, the caseworker's skill, or the amount of casework contact.

Parental Visitation

In the series of regression analyses just reviewed, the quantity and nature of parental visiting has been a significant predictor of change in scores for several of the indexes we constructed to measure facets of the child's adaptation to foster care. We have viewed these

TABLE 13.16
DIFFERENCES IN ADAPTATION-INDEX SCORES OF CHILDREN
ACCORDING TO VISITATION PATTERNS OF PARENTS, TIMES II AND III

Adaptation Indexes[a]	Mean Scores		SE	df	t-Test Statistic
	Little or No Parental Visiting	Frequent Parental Visiting			
Time II					
Capacity to cope with separation	30.1	39.1	1.64	338	-5.46***
Capacity to cope with foster care environment	31.8	41.3	1.69	335	-5.68***
Embedment in foster care setting	31.4	50.8	1.64	338	-11.81***
Attachment to natural parents	39.5	37.7	2.87	323	0.64
Conflict in identity	28.5	37.7	1.99	327	-4.66***
Capacity to relate to others	38.4	42.1	1.48	338	-2.56*
Time III					
Capacity to cope with separation	33.4	38.0	2.12	208	-2.22*
Capacity to cope with foster care environment	34.3	37.7	2.09	208	-1.62
Embedment in foster care setting	34.8	43.7	1.94	208	-4.62***
Attachment to natural parents	37.7	44.6	3.68	198	-1.87
Conflict in identity	30.6	35.5	2.26	208	-2.16*
Capacity to relate to others	38.9	39.5	1.89	208	-0.31

*p < .05   **p < .01   ***p < .001

[a] Key to index scores: higher scores reflect lower capacity to cope with separation, lower capacity to cope with foster care environment, less deep embedment, weaker attachment to parents, more conflict in identity, and more problems in ability to relate to others.

data with considerable interest because, unlike some of the positive findings related to parental visiting reported in earlier chapters, the influence of parental visiting appears to have disturbing consequences with respect to certain aspects of the adaptation of the children. To clarify this, we have organized the data to reflect high and low parental visiting patterns for Times II and III (Table 13.16).

More frequently visited children show considerably less capacity to cope with separation at Time II. The differences are reduced somewhat at Time III but are nevertheless statistically significant ($p < .05$). A similar finding is revealed with respect to the capacity of the children to cope with the foster care environment. There are major differences in scores favoring the unvisited child at Time II ($p < .001$), but the differences are not significant at Time III. We observe similar findings with respect to conflict in identity; there are pronounced differences at Time II ($p < .001$) and somewhat reduced but significant differences at Time III ($p < .05$). While professional thinking strongly endorses the maintenance of relationships between foster children and their natural parents, it seems clear that after several years of placement, the presence of two sets of parental figures in the child's life can be a source of strain. Although parental visits may nevertheless have benefits with respect to a child's inner view of his own worth, such visiting is obviously not an unalloyed blessing.

As might be expected on a common-sense basis, children who are frequently visited are less embedded in their foster care placements. The differences between the visited and unvisited children is significant ($p < .001$) for both time occasions. When we examine the index measuring attachment of the children to their natural parents, we see that there is no significant difference in mean attachment scores for visited and unvisited children. At the end of five years, however, the frequently visited children are somewhat less attached (mean of 44.6) than the less visited children (mean of 37.7).

SUMMARY COMMENTS

Our findings about the children's ability to adapt to their experience in foster care point up several areas for further investigation that have strong implications for practice:

1. In the ratings by caseworkers, we find little evidence of massive emotional trauma experienced by children on entering foster care. Intense reactions to separation were apparently displayed by only a minority of the subjects.

2. Children who remain in foster care for several years are living away from their parents for a *long* period of time. Certainly five years in care can have the aura of a *lifetime* for these children. Continued involvement of the parents over such extended periods presents the child with tasks in adaptation that are not easy to carry off without strain. This is particularly true of the older children who have experienced prior parental care in their own homes. The very young children (under age two at time of entry) are more likely to become deeply entrenched in their foster home settings and to experience their living arrangements in foster care as equivalent to those in the home of their natural parents.

3. Casework intervention in these matters is, surprisingly, sometimes associated with increased problems in coping on the part of the child. We are unable at this juncture to determine whether the more troubled child tends to draw greater professional concern and attention or whether the impact of professional attention is such as to stir up disquieting feelings in the child. Further, we do not know whether it is more harmful for a child to openly struggle with the problem of conflicting loyalties to parents who visit, but are unable to take him home, as opposed to the situation of children who are unvisited and take the foster care situation as the "real" home. We need more information about the covert feelings in the latter type of adaptation.

4. We were not able to investigate the matter of how substitute parents and natural parents relate to each other when children are in care for several years or more. We do not know whether those serving as surrogate parents tend to displace the natural parents in the affections of the child, particularly when a child remains in care for as long as five years. We also do not know the extent to which the two sets of parent figures compete with each other.

5. It seems obvious that the best approach to sparing the child the experience of conflicting loyalties while in foster care is to seek, in as vigorous a manner as possible, to forestall long-term placements.

As a final note, we must stress the point that we regard our investigation of the children's adaptation as a first attempt to obtain systematic data in this area. Our approach to measuring the concepts involved in this chapter will likely strike the reader as quite soft. The reliability of the caseworkers' judgments is yet to be established. The limited test of the validity of the indexes has produced modest results. We are also quite conscious of the lack of orthogonality of the index scores. We see the indexes as obviously interrelated but not equivalent indicators of adaptation. Future efforts in this area might well focus on the task of sharpening concepts and improving the measurement procedures as a prelude to a deeper analysis of the situation facing the child in foster care.

FOURTEEN

BEHAVIOR
SYMPTOMS
AT END OF STUDY

In this chapter we develop a portrait of the children's adjustment at the end of the longitudinal study according to the behavioral symptoms of potential emotional problems ascribed to them by two kinds of reporters. Some five years after their entry into care, we requested the parents of subjects who had returned home to respond verbally to our inquiries about any symptomatic behavior their children might have displayed. The questions were asked by psychologists on our staff who visited the homes of the children in order to administer the final round of psychological tests.

For children still in foster care at the end of the study, we prepared a similar list of symptoms included in the same profile instrument described in chapter 13. The information was provided by the social worker who knew the child best and was returned to us by mail. The symptom lists used with the parents for the discharged children and with the social workers for those youngsters who were still in care were not exact duplicates but there was a fair amount of overlap. There were 22 items common to both instruments.[1]

We chose to employ symptom-description procedures as yet another mode of assessing the children, for several reasons. Certain investigators have demonstrated that symptom checklists are particularly useful in epidemiological studies of psychopathological

[1] The failure to create exactly identical instruments was due to the different times when the symptom lists were created. Our thinking about the relevance of items changed as we proceeded with the investigation.

disorders of children in the general population.[2] They have revealed high interrater reliabilities between parents and teachers and good test–retest reliability. They have also been shown to discriminate between known normal and emotionally disturbed children.

Furthermore, we were attracted to the use of a behavioral symptom list by the prior experience of one of the authors in a longitudinal study of adopted children in 15 states.[3] The earlier experience reinforced the impression that behavioral symptoms were easily observed and reported by persons of varying degrees of sophistication, such as parents, untrained social workers, teachers, child care workers, and foster parents. It was our view that indexes based on composites of individual items would be more useful in the long run, showing greater reliability and validity than a procedure calling for the designation of a single category from a breakdown such as "well," "moderately well," "moderately poorly," and "poorly," adjusted.

Another reason we were particularly interested in exploring the symptomatic behavior of our subjects, as described by parents and social workers of varying degrees of training, was the hope that such types of information might lend themselves to the child-description requirements of the computerized management information systems being developed to monitor the status of children in foster care.[4] The use of a list of symptoms commonly shown by children has appeal because it may obviate the possibility of diagnostic labels with connotations of psychiatric impairment being imposed on children by persons lacking the educational background for such judgments.

Before we proceed to examine the distribution of symptomatic behaviors among our subjects, an observation about missing cases is

[2] See Rema Lapouse and Mary A. Monk, "Behavior Deviations in a Representative Sample of Children: Variation by Sex, Age, Race, Social Class and Family Size," *American Journal of Orthopsychiatry* 36 (1964): 436–46; John S. Werry and Herbert C. Quay, "The Prevalence of Behavior Symptoms in Younger Elementary School Children," *American Journal of Orthopsychiatry* 41 (1971): 136–43.

[3] David Fanshel, *Far From the Reservation: The Transracial Adoption of American Indian Children* (Metuchen, N.J.: Scarecrow Press, 1972).

[4] One of the authors, David Fanshel, has recently tested the use of symptomatic behavior description, building upon the work described in this chapter, in five agencies in New York City for the computerized information system developed by Child Welfare Information Services, Inc.

in order. For the ratings of 227 children still in care at the end of five years, we were able to obtain 220 returned forms (97 percent). We thus had no problem about the representativeness of these children. However, we faced a different set of circumstances with respect to children who returned home. We were able to interview parents of 137 children; these were 78 percent of those tested in their own homes. The parents not seen were mainly those who were not at home when the child was tested.[5]

The 137 children represent only 39 percent of the discharged children; the modest nature of our yield reflects the fairly large group of children who were not tested at Time III. We therefore decided to compare the 137 subjects with the 233 discharged children for whom we had no symptomatic behavior information in order to determine how representative our group was. We performed a number of analyses and came up with the following information:

1. There were only trivial differences in composition between the two groups with respect to the sex of the child, age, and reason for placement.

2. We had a somewhat higher proportion of Puerto Rican children among those whose symptomatic behavior was reported; the white and black children were somewhat underrepresented. The differences were not statistically significant.

3. There were only trivial differences between the two groups on whom we did and did not have this information, with respect to the emotional assessment by the examining psychologists at Time I.

4. There were no significant differences between the two groups for the Time I total deviation IQ scores and the nonverbal IQ scores. However, the children for whom no reports were secured had significantly higher deviation verbal IQ scores (103.4, compared to 98.8).

5. There were no significant differences between most of the Time I CBC scores. The exceptions were: (a) responsibility, (b) unmotivated–laziness, (c) infantilism, and (d) withdrawal, with those children who were not covered by reports showing more problematic behaviors.

In the main, the differences between the reported group and the unreported group are not striking.

---

[5] For the 137 children, we received information from the following informants: mothers (80.3 percent), fathers (8.8 percent), and other relatives (10.9 percent).

PARENTS, REPORTS ON SYMPTOMATIC BEHAVIOR
OF SUBJECTS WHO RETURNED HOME

In Table 14.1 we present the percentage frequencies of the symptomatic behaviors reported by parents for the subjects who had returned home. We can give a sense of the picture obtained by noting the following items of information:

1. Some 16 percent of the children were described as very hard to raise and others (19 percent) as somewhat hard.

2. Almost seven percent of the children were described as usually not happy; another 34 percent showed a mixed pattern of sadness and happiness.

3. About eight percent of the children were often moody or depressed, and 36 percent were sometimes depressed.

4. Some 13 percent of the children were often under a strain; 19 percent were seen as quite nervous.

5. The children exhibited a variety of specific behavioral symptoms: 10 percent were thumbsuckers, 21 percent had disturbing dreams, 12 percent wet their beds at night, 3 percent were soilers, 19 percent had poor appetites, 14 percent showed nervous tics and mannerisms, and 25 percent were nail biters.

6. More than 18 percent of the parents indicated that the child was overdependent on them.

7. Some 38 percent of the parents indicated that the child "got on their nerves."

8. About 54 percent of the children were described as hypersensitive and too easily hurt.

An examination of the published research literature provides a few examples of parental reports of the symptomatic behavior of their children. These provide some basis for putting our findings into perspective.

A national Health Examination Survey was conducted in 1963/65, resulting in the selection of over 7,000 children six to 11 years of age who were representative of roughly 24 million children in this age grouping in the United States. In addition to physical examinations administered to the children, the parents (usually the mothers) were asked to provide ratings on their children's behavior. The findings of this survey have been published, and some of the

TABLE 14.1

FREQUENCY OF BEHAVIORAL SYMPTOMS REPORTED BY PARENTS FOR CHILDREN DISCHARGED FROM FOSTER CARE AND IN OWN HOMES AT TIME III

(in percentages; N = 137)

1. Has child been difficult to raise?	17.5 Very easy	24.8 Easy	22.6 Average	19.0 Somewhat hard	16.1 Very hard
2. Child's mood this past year?	59.1 Usually happy	34.3 Mixed	6.6 Usually not happy		
3. Is child excitable?	25.7 Very excitable	30.2 Somewhat excitable	44.1 Not excitable		
4. Has child been moody or depressed?	8.1 Often	36.0 Sometimes	55.9 Few times or never		
5. Child under strain this past year?	13.1 Often	19.0 Sometimes	67.9 Few times or never		
6. Considered a nervous child?	51.1 Not at all	29.9 Somewhat	19.0 Yes, quite so		
7. Sucks thumb?	89.8 No	10.2 Yes			
8. Has disturbing dreams?	78.8 No	21.2 Yes			

9. Masturbates, plays with self?	88.0 No	12.0 Yes	
10. Wets self in daytime?	96.3 No	3.3 Yes	
11. Wets bed at night?	88.3 No	11.7 Yes	
12. Soils self?	97.1 No	2.9 Yes	
13. Has poor appetite?	81.0 No	19.0 Yes	
14. Has nervous tics or mannerisms?	86.1 No	13.9 Yes	
15. Bites nails?	75.2 No	24.8 Yes	
16. Tends to cry a lot?	11.0 Lot	25.5 Sometimes	63.5 Little
17. Parent concerned about child telling lies?	19.0 Very much	33.5 Sometimes	47.5 No
18. Concerned about child taking things?	12.4 Very much	17.5 Sometimes	70.1 No
19. Concerned about child being destructive	9.6 Very much	16.2 Sometimes	74.3 No
20. Does child cling too much?	18.3 Very much	24.8 Sometimes	56.9 No

TABLE 14.1 (cont.)

21. Does child get on parent's nerves?	48.5 No	13.2 Minimal	38.3 Yes	
22. Child affectionate to parent?	55.5 Very much	35.0 Somewhat	9.5 Hardly	
23. How many friends does child have?	53.3 Many	11.7 Some	30.7 Few	4.3 None
24. Child excluded by other children?	85.9 No	12.6 Yes	1.5 Other	
25. Child afraid of other children?	78.8 No	21.2 Yes		
26. Plays too aggressively?	76.6 No	23.4 Yes		
27. Chooses "wrong" kind of children?	86.1 No	13.1 Yes	0.8 Other	
28. Child too serious for play?	75.7 No	23.5 Yes	0.8 Other	
29. Child too sensitive, easily hurt?	44.4 No	54.1 Yes	1.5 Other	
30. Child's health past year?	46.7 Very good	39.4 Good	11.0 Fair	2.9 Poor

items covered are comparable to those included in our survey of parents of returned foster children.[6]

1. Of the national study sample, 1.8 percent were reported to have frequent unpleasant dreams; an additional 41.8 percent were said to have this problem, but "not often." Among the former foster children, those under nine years of age were said to have disturbing dreams in 22.0 percent of the cases, and this was true of 26.7 percent of those aged nine to 11 years.

2. In the national study, 22.8 percent of the children were said to be either somewhat fussy about the kinds of food they would eat, or would not eat many kinds of foods. Among the former foster children, 14 percent under age nine were described as suffering from poor appetite, and this was true of 26.7 percent of those aged nine to 11 years.

3. In the national study, 37.4 percent of the children were said to have "only a few" friends. This was true of 32.0 percent of the former foster children under nine years and 33.3 percent of those aged nine to 11.

4. For the national sample, 10.0 percent of the children were described as thumbsuckers. This compares with 14.0 percent of the former foster children under age nine and 6.6 percent of those aged nine to 11.

5. For the national sample, 15.4 percent wet the bed at various levels of frequency. Among the former foster children, 16 percent of those under age nine were bedwetters, as were 6.7 percent of those aged nine to 11.

6. In the national study, 17.1 percent of the children were described as "rather high strung" and 27.5 percent as "moderately tense." Among the former foster children under age nine, 14.0 percent were described as "nervous" and 32.0 percent as "somewhat nervous." For the group aged nine to 11 years, 20.0 percent were described as "nervous" and 33.3 percent as "somewhat nervous."

On the whole, the former foster children appear to show a higher proportion with symptoms indicative, but not dramatically so, of problematic adjustment.

Another study that provides comparative data is a major study of childhood on the Isle of Wight in Great Britain.[7] Over 3,000

[6] Jean Roberts and James T. Baird, Jr., *Parent Ratings of Behavioral Patterns of Children*, Vital and Health Statistics, ser. 11, no. 108 (Washington, D.C.: U.S. Department of Health, Education and Welfare, November 1971).

[7] Michael Rutter, Jack Tizard, and Kingsley Whitmore, *Education, Health and Behavior* (New York: Wiley, 1970).

children aged 10 through 12 years were described by their parents and teachers. The following parental reports are of interest:

1. Thumbsucking—11.4 percent of the 10-year-olds, 9.9 percent of the 11-year-olds, and 7.2 percent of the 12-year-olds were thumb-suckers. This compares to 6.6 percent of the former foster children aged nine to 11 and 8.6 percent of those aged 12 to 14 years.

2. Bedwetting—4.1 percent of those 10 years old, 2.6 percent of the 11-year-olds, and 1.8 percent of the 12-year-olds were bedwetters. This was true of 6.7 percent of the former foster children aged nine to 11 years and 4.3 percent of those aged 12 to 14 years.

3. Eating difficulty (slight)—22.3 percent of the 10-year-olds, 20.3 percent of the 11-year-olds, and 16.5 percent of the 12-year-olds had some difficulty. This was true of 13.3 percent of the former foster children aged nine to 11 years and 14.3 percent of those aged 12 to 14 years.

On the whole, the former foster children showed somewhat greater proportions where problems of destructiveness, lying, and stealing were reported to be a problem, but not dramatically so. However, when we examined the reports of Lapouse and Monk (1964) and Werry and Quay (1971), cited in footnote 2, for common items, our former foster children appeared to be less afflicted with symptoms of maladjustment.

CASEWORKERS' REPORTS ON THE SYMPTOMATIC BEHAVIOR OF SUBJECTS STILL IN FOSTER CARE

In Table 14.2 we present the item percentage distribution for the ratings made by social workers for 220 children still in care at the end of five years. The distributions do not show a heavy pre-ponderance of serious symptomatic behaviors. The following are indicative of the findings:

1. Frequent immature behavior was seen in 18 percent of the children.

2. Almost 28 percent showed frequent demands for attention.

3. Only 2.3 percent had a daytime wetting problem and 6.5 percent had this problem at night.

4. Only 7 percent of the children were often seen as destructive.

5. Frequent tension was observed in 13 percent.

6. Frequent signs of insecurity were seen in 15 percent.

7. Only 4 percent of the children seemed often under strain.

On a number of items it was possible to report the same behavior for children in foster care and those who had returned home; we note the following:

1. Destructive behavior was of major concern for 7.0 percent of the children in care and for 9.6 percent of those who had returned home.
2. Disturbing dreams were described as a problem for 12.5 percent of the children in care. For children who had returned home, the parents reports showed that 21.2 percent had problems.
3. Moodiness was a frequent problem identified for 7.3 percent of the children in care and 8.1 percent of those who had returned home.
4. Frequent demand for attention was seen in 27.5 percent of the children in care, while 18.3 percent of the children at home tended to be overdependent.
5. Telling lies was a frequent problem for 12 percent of the children in care and 19 percent of those at home.

Inspecting the frequencies presented in Tables 14.1–2, we have a sense of some greater tendency for problems to be reported for the children who were at home as opposed to those in care.

PARENT-DERIVED INDEXES

The responses of parents were organized into indexes. A factor analysis was used as a guide to the inclusion of items, and adjustments were made based on a computer program maximizing item-criterion correlations and an overall measure of internal reliability (Cronbach's alpha coefficient). On this basis, five parent-derived indexes were organized.[8] Their identification and the items they contain are as follows:

1. General behavior index
   a. ease of raising child;
   b. mood during past year;
   c. child's excitability;
   d. tendency to be moody or depressed during past year;
   e. evidence that child is under strain;

(continued p. 427)

[8] The intercorrelation of items and the item-criterion correlations for the indexes can be obtained by writing to Dr. David Fanshel, Columbia University School of Social Work, 622 W. 113th Street, New York, N.Y., 10025.

TABLE 14.2
FREQUENCY OF BEHAVIORAL SYMPTOMS REPORTED BY SOCIAL
WORKERS FOR CHILDREN STILL IN FOSTER CARE AT TIME III
(in percentages; N = 220)

1. Child behavior is immature for his age	44.7 Sometimes	18.4 Frequently	36.9 Rarely
2. Child has disturbing dreams	12.5 Yes	87.5 No	
3. Child tells lies	32.4 Sometimes	12.0 Fairly often	55.6 Rarely or never
4. Child makes demands for attention	17.4 Rarely or never	55.0 Sometimes	27.5 Frequently
5. Child soils self	4.6 Yes	95.4 No	
6. Child has daytime wetting problems	2.3 Yes	97.7 No	
7. Child has nocturnal wetting problems	6.5 Yes	93.5 No	
8. Child shows fear of animals	12.1 Sometimes	1.4 Often	86.4 Rarely or never
9. Child is overactive	41.7 Rarely or never	40.4 Sometimes	17.9 Quite often
10. Child has fear of high places	0 Quite often	15.9 Sometimes	84.1 Rarely or never
11. Child is sensitive to scolding	18.2 Hardly ever	30.4 Frequently	51.4 Sometimes
12. Child's sleeping patterns	61.3 Soundly	32.3 Somewhat soundly	6.5 Somewhat unsoundly
13. Child's behavior is destructive	24.7 Sometimes	7.0 Fairly often	68.4 Rarely or never

TABLE 14.2 (*cont.*)

14. Child's appetite is poor	5.5 Yes	94.5 No	
15. Child has a speech problem	13.2 Yes	86.8 No	
16. Child has fear of thunderstorms	73.4 Hardly ever	2.4 Often	24.2 Sometimes
17. Child has fear of strangers	29.0 Sometimes	4.6 Often	66.4 Rarely or never
18. Child bites nails	14.2 Yes	85.8 No	
19. Child is finicky about what he eats	61.0 Hardly ever	34.7 Sometimes	4.2 Often
20. Child has unusual tics or mannerisms	7.9 Yes	92.1 No	
21. Child has upset stomach	1.4 Frequently	21.0 Sometimes	77.6 Rarely or never
22. Child sucks his thumb	4.6 Yes	95.4 No	
23. Child is shy	39.3 Hardly ever	53.0 Sometimes	7.8 Often
24. Child is destructive	68.5 Rarely or never	5.1 Often	26.4 Sometimes
25. Child is tense	42.7 Sometimes	13.3 Often	44.0 Rarely or never
26. Child has personality problems	32.1 Yes	67.9 No	

TABLE 14.2 (*contd.*)

27. Child shows signs of feeling insecure	39.3 Hardly ever	45.7 Sometimes	15.1 Often
28. Child has allergies or skin disorders	2.8 Often	10.1 Occasionally	87.1 Rarely or never
29. Child has colds or respiratory difficulties	6.9 Often	33.9 Occasionally	59.2 Rarely or never
30. Child has periods of moodiness	34.7 Rarely or never	58.0 Sometimes	7.3 Frequently
31. Child is usually avoided by other children	4.6 Yes	95.4 No	
32. Child is typically over or underweight	16.7 Yes	83.3 No	
33. Child is too sensitive, easily hurt by children	19.9 Yes	80.1 No	
34. Child is too serious for play	3.7 Yes	96.3 No	
35. Child worries	37.4 Rarely or never	7.8 Frequently	54.8 Sometimes
36. Child's disposition	54.6 Usually happy	43.6 In-between	1.8 Usually unhappy
37. Child seems upset or under strain	48.8 Hardly ever	47.0 Sometimes	4.1 Often

(continued from p. 423)
 f. view of child as nervous;
 g. parent concern regarding masturbation;
 h. parent concern regarding nervous tics and mannerisms;
 i. parent concern regarding nail biting;
 j. parent concern regarding other behaviors;
 k. child's tendency to cry;
 l. parent concern regarding telling lies;
 m. parent concern regarding taking things;
 n. child's tendency to be destructive;
 o. child's exclusion by other children;
 p. child's aggressiveness in play;
 q. child's preference for wrong kind of children;
 r. parent desire to change child.

(Cronbach alpha = .85)
Low score = most problems
High score = least problems

2. Health problems
 a. child's appetite;
 b. nature of child's health during past year;
 c. degree to which illness has limited activities;
 d. frequency of colds;
 e. frequency of headaches;
 f. frequency of stomach or intestinal disorders;
 g. frequency of allergies or skin disorders;
 h. frequency of respiratory difficulties;
 i. weight problem (overweight or underweight).

(Cronbach alpha = .69)
Low score = poor health
High score = excellent health

3. Security–sociability
 a. tendency to be overdependent on parent;
 b. number of friends;
 c. fears or shyness with children;
 d. ability to enjoy self in play;
 e. sensitivity or hurt feelings with other children.

(Cronbach alpha = .57)
Low score = insecure, unsociable
High score = sociable, confident

4. Toileting problems
 a. wetting self in daytime;
 b. wets bed at night;
 c. soils self.

(Cronbach alpha = .51)
Low score = most concerned
High score = no problem

5. Sleep problems
   a. disturbing dreams;
   b. sleep disorders.

(Cronbach alpha = .50)
Low score = shows problems
High score = no problems

In Table 14.3 we show the intercorrelations among the index scores. While the correlations displayed do not reflect a truly orthogonal character, they are relatively small and in line with past experience with ratings of this kind. The 18-item index of general behavior is significantly correlated at modest levels with the remaining four indexes. There is also a significant association between the indexes of health problems, security–sociability ($r = .36$), and sleep problems ($r = .23$).

As a way of assessing the validity of the symptomatic behavioral indexes, we were able to correlate the scores with two concurrent measures of child adjustment: (a) a summary measure derived from the ratings of the subjects by their teachers and (b) clinical assessments made by the examining psychologists in the final round of testing. The teacher ratings were made on the instrument RSPA discussed in chapter 3. We used nine of the 11 ratings to form a single summary measure of adjustment; this was based on our analysis of the dependency among ratings. The nine-item index showed strong item-criterion correlations, and the measure of internal reliability was high (Cronbach alpha = .91).

TABLE 14.3
INTERCORRELATIONS AMONG
PARENT-DERIVED SYMPTOM INDEX SCORES
($N = 137$)

	General Behavior	Health Problems	Security– Sociability	Toileting Problems	Sleep Problems
General behavior	1.00	.21*	.29***	.32***	.23***
Health problems		1.00	.36**	.06	.23**
Security–sociability			1.00	.15	.10
Toileting problems				1.00	.03
Sleep problems					1.00

*$p < .05$ **$p < .01$ ***$p < .001$.

We have shown in Table 14.4 that our 18-item index of general behavior, our closest approximation to an overall adjustment measure based on parent ratings, is significantly correlated with the summary pupil adjustment score ($r = .37$; $p < .01$). Thus, there is some noticeable tendency for the parents and the teachers to see the same qualities in the children. We likewise see that the rating made by the examining psychologist (abnormal/suspect/normal) is significantly associated with the index of general behavior ($r = .33$; $p < .001$). While these correlations do not provide cause for major claims about the validity of the parental ratings, it is our impression that we are doing well to establish this level of association, considering the primitive state of the art of child description. We are also mindful of the fact that the measures with which the general behavior index scores have been correlated are based on different items and different opportunities for observing the child.

It is noteworthy that none of the remaining parent-derived indexes is significantly correlated with the summary pupil-adjustment scores. This is not the case when we look at the associations with the clinical assessments made by the examining psychologists.

TABLE 14.4

CORRELATIONS OF BEHAVIORAL-SYMPTOM INDEX SCORES DERIVED FROM RATINGS OF DISCHARGED CHILDREN BY PARENTS WITH RATINGS BY TEACHERS AND EXAMINING PSYCHOLOGISTS (TIME III)

Parent-Derived Indexes (for Discharged Children)	Summary Pupil Adjustment Score[a] (N = 66)	Assessment by Examining Psychologist[b] (N = 135)
General behavior	.37**	.33***
Health problems	−.05	.14
Security–sociability	.03	.18*
Toileting problems	.02	−.21*
Sleep problems	.06	.20*

*$p < .05$ **$p < .01$ ***$p < .001$

[a] Summary measure of pupil adjustment based on nine teacher ratings. High score reflects good adjustment.

[b] Assessment of emotional condition of subject by examining psychologist at Time III testing (1 = abnormal, 2 = suspect, 3 = normal). High score reflects better adjustment.

Three indexes show significant correlations: (a) security–sociability ($r = .18$), (b) toileting problems ($r = -.21$), and sleep problems ($r = .20$).

Multiple Regression Analyses

In Table 14.5 we show the results of a series of multiple regression analyses in which we seek to "understand" the parent-derived behavioral symptom scores assigned children with respect to the contribution of the following regressor variables: (a) age and sex of child, (b) race–ethnicity, (c) child behavior as a reason for placement (treated as a dummy variable contrasting child behavior cases with all others), (d) the three preplacement developmental history indexes derived from interviews with the parents early in the study (emotional, developmental, and health problems), (e) the logarithm of length of time in foster care, (f) frequency of parental visiting, (g) an index based on the caseworker's evaluations of the child's mother, (h) frequency of caseworker contacts, (i) amount of training and experience of the caseworker, and (j) the number of placements experienced by the child over the five years covered by the study.

In contrast with some of the regression analyses presented in previous chapters, we are not concerned here with analyzing changes in scores; this is not possible because the information on symptomatic behavior was only gathered at the end of our study (Time III; see Table 14.5). However, the inclusion of the three preplacement developmental indexes does create something of a baseline from which to measure change.

General behavior. When we look at the analysis of the 18-item index of general behavior, we find only two independent variables to be significant predictors: (a) the preplacement developmental index of health problems and (b) the length of time spent in foster care. We interpret the findings to indicate that children free of health problems prior to entry tended to show better adjustment scores at the end of five years. This is difficult to comprehend, since we would logically have found that the absence of early emotional problems or developmental problems rather than problems of health predicted better adjustment. We can only note that being in excellent physical health predicts better child adjustment five years later.

It is of interest that children who spent less time in foster care

TABLE 14.5

RELATION OF SALIENT BACKGROUND AND OTHER INDEPENDENT VARIABLES TO BEHAVIORAL-SYMPTOM INDEX SCORES OF CHILDREN DERIVED FROM PARENT INTERVIEWS FOR CHILDREN DISCHARGED FROM CARE (TIME III)

Variable[a]	General Behavior	Health Problems	Security–Sociability	Toileting Problems	Sleep Problems
	(standardized regression coefficients)				
1. AGE	-.03	-.06	.08	.22*	.09
2. SEX	.01	-.04	-.02	-.16	.01
3. BLACK	.01	-.08	.04	-.15	.04
4. PUERTO RICAN	.08	-.29**	-.16	-.27**	.07
5. CH BEH	.08	-.01	-.04	-.03	-.19
6. EMOT PROB	-.20	-.00	-.11	-.08	.05
7. DEVEL PROB	.08	-.12	-.13	-.27**	-.03
8. HEALTH PROB	-.24**	-.24**	-.11	-.09	-.17
9. CARELOG	-.20*	.02	.11	.02	.01
10. VISITING	-.02	.07	.24**	-.15	-.06
11. EVAL-MO	.05	.05	.05	.19*	-.02
12. CONTACT	.01	.19*	-.06	.10	.03
13. SKILL	-.04	-.05	.01	.12	.00
14. NO. PLACEMENTS	.02	.05	-.14	.04	-.02
Multiple R	.38	.46	.39	.50	.27
Multiple R^2	.14	.21	.15	.25	.07
No. of cases	137	137	137	137	137

$*p < .05$ $**p < .01$

[a]Identification of Variables: (1) age of child at entry, (2) sex of child, (3) black children, (4) Puerto Rican children, (5) reason for placement: child's behavior, (6) emotional problem index, (7) developmental problem index, (8) health problem index, (9) log of days in care, (10) parental visiting pattern, (11) evaluation of mother, (12) log of total casework contact rate, (13) index of worker skill, (14) number of placements.

are described by their mothers in terms that suggest better adjustment by the end of the study. This is the only occasion, in the many analyses we have performed, where extended time in care emerges as a negative influence. Our analysis is of course restricted to children who have been discharged. The implication of the finding is that if children are to be discharged home, they are apt to be less afflicted with adjustment problems if their tenure in care has been limited rather than extended.

Health problems. We find three significant predictors of the index of health problems: (a) ethnicity, (b) an early history of health problems, and (c) amount of casework contact. It appears that Puerto Rican children had more health problems than the other children who had returned home. The fact that children who had been reported as being sickly at the beginning of the study showed more health problems than the other subjects at the end of the study occasions no surprise.

Children with health problems and their families apparently received more casework attention while in care. We would conjecture that their problems required more activities to be initiated, such as securing health services.

Security–sociability. Only one variable emerges as important in accounting for variance in the index score of security–sociability, namely, the frequency of parental visiting. Children who appeared to be more secure (i.e., less dependent, less shy with friends, and less sensitive) were those whose parents visited them more frequently while they were in care. Here, we thus find another indication that parental visiting is a beneficial phenomenon for the child.

Toileting problems. Four variables contribute significant amounts of explained variance to the index of toileting problems: (a) the age of the child, (b) ethnicity, (c) prior history of developmental problems, and (d) the caseworker's evaluation of the mother. Older children were relatively free of bedwetting, daytime wetting, and soiling problems; this is not a surprising finding. We again find that Puerto Rican children are more afflicted with wetting and soiling problems than the other children.

We find that a prior history of developmental difficulty helps explain toileting problems five years later. If we can assume the mothers were accurate in their earlier descriptions, it would appear that the child is a good predictor of himself in the sense that there is constancy of adjustment difficulty over time. It is of course possible that the finding merely reflects the constancy of the mother's orientation to the child and her mode of reporting his behavior.

One other source of explained variance is the index based on the caseworker's evaluation of the mother. The more positive the assessment, the less likely it is that toileting problems will be reported. It is possible that a circular process is at play, in that the caseworkers may have more negatively assessed the mothers when they discovered that the child had toileting problems.

Sleep problems. None of the variables proved to be significant in predicting sleep problems.

A final note is in order about our analyses of the symptomatic behaviors of the children based on the reports of the parents. The multiple correlations ranged from .27 to .50, and the greatest amount of variance accounted for was 25 percent. One must be impressed with the small size of the yield reported here.

SOCIAL WORKER–DERIVED INDEXES

As was the case with the responses of the parents, the social worker ratings of the children were factor analyzed and then organized into indexes reflecting the analysis in which item-criterion correlations and internal reliabilities were maximized. On this basis, five indexes were created.[9]

1. Emotional maturity
   a. evidence of personality problems;
   b. sensitivity and vulnerability to hurt by children;
   c. too serious for play;
   d. behavioral immaturity;
   e. propensity to tell lies;
   f. evidence of tension;
   g. demands for attention;
   h. feelings of insecurity;

[9] The intercorrelations among items in the index can be obtained from the senior author at the address given in note 8.

    i. periods of moodiness;
    j. evidence of strain;
    k. sensitivity to scolding;
    l. tendency to worry.

                             (Cronbach alpha = .84)
                             Low score = stable, mature
                             High score = unstable, immature

2. Body and bowel control
    a. sleeping patterns;
    b. disturbing dreams;
    c. soiling self;
    d. daytime wetting problems;
    e. nocturnal wetting problems.

                             (Cronbach alpha = .53)
                             Low score = excellent control
                             High score = poor control

3. Fears
    a. fear of high places (vertigo);
    b. upset stomach;
    c. biting of nails;
    d. thumbsucking;
    e. fear of animals;
    f. fear of strangers;
    g. shyness;
    h. fear of thunderstorms.

                             (Cronbach alpha = .63)
                             Low score = low fear
                             High score = high fear

4. Psychosomatic reactions
    a. evidence of allergies or skin disorders;
    b. tendency to colds or respiratory difficulties;
    c. appetite level;
    d. weight problem.
    e. food finickiness.

                             (Cronbach alpha = .49)
                             Low score = few symptoms
                             High score = many symptoms

5. Aggressiveness
    a. avoidance of child by other children;
    b. destructiveness of child's behavior;
    c. overactiveness of child.

                             (Cronbach alpha = .73)
                             Low score = not aggressive
                             High score = aggressive

TABLE 14.6
INTERCORRELATIONS AMONG SOCIAL WORKER–DERIVED SYMPTOM INDEX SCORES
(N = 228)

	Emotional Maturity	Body and Bowel Control	Fears	Psychosomatic Reactions	Aggressiveness
Emotional maturity	1.00	.25***	.36***	.06	.43***
Body and bowel control		1.00	.16*	-.02	.27***
Fears			1.00	.13*	.27***
Psychosomatic reactions				1.00	.15*
Aggressiveness					1.00

*p < .05   ***p < .001

In Table 14.6 we show the intercorrelations among the index scores derived from the social worker ratings. The picture we obtain is similar to that found for the parent-derived indexes. While the index scores are not clearly orthogonal, the correlations tend to be relatively modest. The indexes of emotional maturity and aggressiveness appear most closely associated ($r = .43$; $p < .001$). We also find that emotional maturity and fears are significantly related ($r = .36$; $p < .001$).

In Table 14.7 we display the correlations between the social worker–derived index scores we have just presented and the summary pupil adjustment scores and the assessments of the emotional condition of the children made by the examining psychologists. For the summary teacher ratings, the strongest associations are with the index of aggressiveness ($r = -.45$; $p < .001$) and emotional maturity ($r = -.39$; $p < .001$).[10] The associations with the psychologist ratings are much less firm. The correlation with the index of aggressiveness is $-.24$ ($p < .001$) and with the index of

TABLE 14.7
**CORRELATIONS OF BEHAVIORAL-SYMPTOM INDEX SCORES
DERIVED FROM RATINGS OF CHILDREN STILL IN FOSTER CARE
BY SOCIAL WORKERS WITH RATINGS BY TEACHERS
AND EXAMINING PSYCHOLOGISTS (TIME III)**

Social-worker–derived Indexes (for Children Remaining in Care)	Summary Pupil Adjustment Score[a] (N = 132)	Assessment by Examining Psychologist[b] (N = 217)
Emotional maturity	−.39***	−.17*
Body and bowel control	−.25**	−.23**
Fears	−.08	−.13
Psychosomatic reactions	−.07	−.01
Aggressiveness	−.45***	−.24***

$*p < .05$ $**p < .01$ $***p < .001$
[a] See note shown in Table 14.4.
[b] See note shown in Table 14.4.

[10] The negative correlations result from the fact that a high score on the behavioral symptom indexes indicates greater problematic behavior while the teacher ratings and the psychological assessment had a reverse orientation.

emotional maturity, it is $-.17$ ($p < .05$). The social workers and the teachers both had the benefit of more extensive contact with the subjects than did the examining psychologists; this may explain the difference in the magnitude of the correlations we observe.

Multiple Regression Analyses

We used the same set of independent variables in the multiple regression analyses of the social worker–derived indexes as in the analyses of the parent–derived indexes. The size of the multiple correlations and the variance accounted for in each index is lower than was true of the parent–derived indexes.

Emotional maturity. Only two significant predictors emerge from the regression analysis: (a) the age of the child and (b) the index summarizing the caseworker's evaluation of the mother. It is of interest that the older children are seen as showing more evidence of personality problems. The social workers see them as being under greater strain, showing more frequent periods of moodiness, and appearing to be more uncertain of themselves. We have had other indications that the children who entered foster care at a very young age have settled into their foster homes to the point where the foster parents have become, in effect, the psychological parents. It would appear that these younger children are relatively secure and more comfortable with the circumstances in which they find themselves.

The caseworker's evaluation of the mother tends to be in line with the qualities perceived in the child. Those children who are seen to be the most troubled have mothers who are also viewed as the most impaired. Such an association is easy to understand, since it is almost axiomatic among child welfare professionals that troubled people beget troubled children. However, the significant association we find may well be an artifact of the circumstance that ratings of both the child and the mother come from the same source.

It is of interest that children who came into foster care because of their own behavior difficulties were not viewed as more troubled at the end of five years than the other children remaining in care.

Body and bowel control. Only one variable stands out as contributing a significant piece of explained variance to this index—the sex of the child. Boys were more often described as having disturbing dreams, or having wetting or soiling problems.

Fears. No variable in the set entered into the regression equation makes a significant contribution to explaining variance in this index. The overall amount of variance accounted for is trivial.

Psychosomatic reactions. Two variables stand out when we look at the proneness of children to show allergic disorders, a tendency to catch colds, poor appetite, and so forth: (a) the sex of the child and (b) length of time spent in care. The girls in the study were more often seen as showing these symptoms than the boys. The role played by length of time in care would indicate that children with less tenure in care are less prone to psychosomatic reactions. However, since all of the children were in care at the end of the five-year period, the variability we report is related to the phenomenon of children who have been discharged in the past and have returned to care. These children are reported to show more psychosomatic reactions than their peers who have had uninterrupted tenure in care.

Aggressivness. Three variables are indentified in Table 14.8 as significant in the regression analysis: (a) the sex of the child, (b) a preplacement history of emotional problems, and (c) the case-worker's evaluation of the mother. As might be expected, boys are more likely to show problems of aggressive behavior than are girls. We also find that children who were described by their parents at the beginning of the study as having preplacement emotional problems in growing up were more likely to be seen as aggressive in their behavior five years later. As was the case with the index of emotional maturity, a negative evaluation of the mother was significantly linked to a higher aggressiveness score assigned to the child.

Additional analyses. We performed additional multiple regression analyses using a somewhat different set of predictors in addition to most of those shown here (birth status, the nature of the child's preplacement care, etc.). We do not have the space to report fully on this work but some findings are of interest:

1. With respect to the index of emotional maturity, children visited more frequently by their parents showed better adjustment scores.
2. With respect to the index of aggressiveness, more highly visited children and those whose mothers were more positively evaluated tended to show fewer symptoms of aggressiveness.

TABLE 14.8
RELATION OF SALIENT BACKGROUND AND OTHER INDEPENDENT VARIABLES TO BEHAVIORAL-SYMPTOM INDEX SCORES DERIVED FROM SOCIAL WORKER REPORTS FOR CHILDREN STILL IN FOSTER CARE (TIME III)

Variable[a]	Emotional Maturity	Body and Bowel Control	Fears	Psychosomatic Reactions	Aggressiveness
	(standardized regression coefficients)				
1. AGE	.20**	-.03	-.04	-.15	-.04
2. SEX	-.11	-.16*	.11	.14*	-.24***
3. BLACK	-.10	-.03	.04	-.11	-.09
4. PUERTO RICAN	-.05	-.12	-.01	-.05	-.06
5. CH BEH	-.07	-.06	.01	-.03	.02
6. EMOT PROB	.13	-.08	-.07	.04	.17*
7. DEVEL PROB	.08	.08	.06	.02	.06
8. HEALTH PROB	.02	.04	.03	.09	-.12
9. CARELOG	-.12	-.13	-.01	-.19*	-.02
10. VISITING	.02	-.07	.05	.02	-.06
11. EVAL-MO	-.23***	-.02	-.07	-.11	-.20**
12. CONTACT	-.04	.01	-.11	-.10	-.03
13. SKILL	.01	-.06	.09	.10	-.10
14. NO. PLACEMENTS	.06	.08	-.08	.11	-.10
Multiple R	.39	.27	.23	.32	.40
Multiple R^2	.15	.08	.05	.11	.16
No. of cases	228	228	228	228	228

*p < .05   **p < .01   ***p < .001

[a]Identification of variables is same as shown in footnote on Table 14.5.

3. When the analysis was performed for only children who entered care at age six years or over, parental visiting frequency and evaluation of the mother were again significant predictors of the index of emotional maturity. In addition, children seen by more skilled caseworkers and who suffered less turnover by their caseworkers appeared better adjusted.

4. For children in foster family care, placement in a foster home rated highly in qualities measured by the index of intellectual climate were relatively free of behavioral symptoms measured by the index of emotional maturity.

AN OVERALL PICTURE
OF SYMPTOMATIC BEHAVIOR

We have provided analyses of the symptomatic behaviors of the children, with our subjects separately treated according to their status at the end of the investigation. The division of our study into two separate efforts was dictated by the fact that we could no longer depend on caseworker reports on child symptoms for those subjects who had returned home. We thus relied on parental reports for discharged children and caseworker reports for those still in care. This approach provided some useful insights on the adjustment of the children but left us dissatisfied because of the compartmentalization involved. We therefore decided to enter into a third area of analysis in which we would examine all subjects for whom symptomatic behavior was reported, using a pool of 22 items where the content of both instruments (parent interview and social worker profile instrument) was identical or very similar.

In deciding to merge the data for discharged children with those still in care, we were aware that the procedure might be open to question because we cannot establish equivalent symptom-reporting tendencies for parents and social workers. We view our effort as exploratory, a further examination of the data in yet another form. We were encouraged to do this by the fact that the scores derived from both sources showed equivalent levels of validity when compared with teacher ratings. We placed high value on the latter because they derived from informants who, like the parents and social workers, had extensive contact with the children.

We chose the following 22 items as reflecting content common to both the parent– and social worker–derived reports on symptomatic behavior:

1. Disturbing dreams (yes/blank/no).
2. Tells lies (very much/some/no).
3. Soils self (yes/blank/no).
4. Wets self—daytime (yes/blank/no).
5. Wets self—night (yes/blank/no).
6. Sleep disorder (often/occasionally/rare).
7. Destructive (very much/some/no).
8. Poor appetite (yes/blank/no).
9. Bites nails (yes/blank/no).
10. Nervous tics (yes/blank/no).
11. Stomach disorders (often/occasionally/rare).
12. Sucks thumb (yes/blank/no).
13. Afraid or shy (yes/blank/no).
14. Allergy or skin disorder (often/occasionally/rare).
15. Colds (often/occasionally/rare).
16. Moody or depressed (often/sometimes/few/never).
17. Excluded by children (yes/blank/no).
18. Over or underweight (yes/blank/no).
19. Too sensitive (yes/blank/no).
20. Too serious (yes/blank/no).
21. Mood of child (sad/happy–sad/happy).
22. Under strain (often/sometimes/no).

A factor analysis of the data for 360 children for whom usable reports were available suggested that five indexes could best reflect the domains covered by the symptomatic reports. Again, using a special computer program to maximize item-criterion correlations and internal reliability of the indexes, we organized the following groupings of items;

1. Externalized behavior pathology
   a. tells lies;
   b. destructive;
   c. moody or depressed;
   d. mood of child;
   e. under strain.

(Cronbach alpha = .71)
Low score = poor adjustment
High score = good adjustment

2. Internalized behavior pathology:
   a. poor appetite;
   b. stomach disorders;
   c. allergies or skin disorders;
   d. colds;
   e. over- or underweight.

   (Cronbach alpha = .52)
   Low score = poor adjustment
   High score = good adjustment

3. Hypernervous behavior:
   a. bites nails;
   b. nervous tics;
   c. excluded by other children;
   d. too sensitive;
   e. too serious.

   (Cronbach alpha = .55)
   Low score = nervous behavior
   High score = free of problems

4. Enuretic pathology:
   a. soils self;
   b. wets self in daytime;
   c. wets self at night.

   (Cronbach alpha = .55)
   Low score = problem behavior
   High score = free of problems

5. Sleeping pathology:
   a. disturbing dreams;
   b. sleep disorders.

   (Cronbach alpha = .41)
   Low score = sleeping problems
   High score = free of problems

The intercorrelations among the index scores as shown in Table 14.9 tend to be quite small but statistically significant. The correlation of the index of externalized behavior pathology with the index of hypernervous behavior is .34 and with the index of sleeping pathology, .30. For the most part, however, the separate domains of symptomatic behavior are fairly well delimited.

When we look at the validity of the indexes by examining their correlations with the teacher ratings and the assessments of the examining psychologists at Time III, we find patterns of association similar to those reported earlier in this chapter. As shown in Table 14.10, the index of internalized behavior pathology shows a fairly

TABLE 14.9

INTERCORRELATIONS AMONG SYMPTOM INDEX SCORES DERIVED FROM COMMON PARENT AND SOCIAL WORKER ITEMS

$(N = 360)$

	Externalized Behavior Pathology	Internalized Behavior Pathology	Hypernervous Behavior	Enuretic Pathology	Sleeping Pathology
Externalized behavior pathology	1.00	.12*	.34***	.20***	.30***
Internalized behavior pathology		1.00	.23***	.04	.12*
Hypernervous behavior			1.00	.16**	.17**
Enuretic pathology				1.00	.16**
Sleeping pathology					1.00

*$p < .05$ **$p < .01$ ***$p < .001$

TABLE 14.10
CORRELATIONS OF BEHAVIORAL-SYMPTOM INDEX SCORES
DERIVED FROM COMMON ITEMS FROM PARENT AND SOCIAL WORKER
RATINGS OF CHILDREN WITH RATINGS BY TEACHERS
AND EXAMINING PSYCHOLOGISTS (TIME III)

Indexes Derived from Common Parent and Social-Worker Ratings	Summary Pupil Adjustment Score[a]		Assessment by Examining Psychologist[b]	
Externalized behavior pathology	.45***	(194)	.25***	(347)
Internalized behavior pathology	.05	(194)	.08	(347)
Hypernervous behavior	.22**	(193)	.09	(346)
Enuretic pathology	.19**	(193)	.17**	(346)
Sleeping pathology	.15*	(192)	.17**	(344)

*p < .05   **p < .01   ***p < .001
[a] See note shown in Table 14.4.
[b] See note shown in Table 14.4.
[c] Numbers in parentheses are numbers of cases.

strong correlation with the summary pupil adjustment score ($r = .45$; $p < .001$). The correlation of the same index with the assessment made by the examining psychologist is more modest ($r = .25$; $p < .001$). As previously mentioned, it is our impression that the teacher ratings show higher validity coefficients because, unlike the testing psychologists, the teachers had quite extensive contact with the children. The remaining symptomatic behavior indexes show relatively minor associations with the ratings of the teachers and the psychologists.

Multiple Regression Analyses

We have analyzed the five indexes based on the common set of items of parents and social workers, using the same independent variables included in the previous multiple regressions reported in this chapter. Our results are shown in Table 14.11.

Externalized behavior pathology. We find three significant regression coefficients: (a) the age of the child, (b) a history of emotional problems prior to entry into foster care, and (c) evaluation of the child's mother. Younger children were viewed as showing fewer signs of strain, being less moody or destructive. It is also apparent

TABLE 14.11
RELATION OF SALIENT BACKGROUND AND OTHER INDEPENDENT VARIABLES TO BEHAVIORAL-SYMPTOM INDEX SCORES DERIVED FROM COMMON ITEMS FROM PARENT INTERVIEWS AND SOCIAL WORKER REPORTS (TIME III)

Variable[a]	Externalized Behavior Pathology	Internalized Behavior Pathology	Hypernervous Behavior	Enuretic Pathology	Sleeping Pathology
	(standardized regression coefficients)				
1. AGE	-.20**	.06	-.09	.14*	.02
2. SEX	.14	-.11*	.03	.06	.02
3. BLACK	.05	.01	.03	-.08	.06
4. PUERTO RICAN	.03	-.11	-.03	-.06	.12
5. CH BEH	.09	.02	-.03	.02	-.07
6. EMOT PROB	-.16**	-.15*	-.14*	-.08	-.02
7. DEVEL PROB	.02	-.07	-.03	-.14*	-.08
8. HEALTH PROB	-.01	-.13*	-.10	-.05	-.09
9. CARELOG	-.07	.18**	.25***	.08	.02
10. VISITING	.00	-.04	.00	-.07	.07
11. EVAL-MO	.16**	.11*	.14**	.10	.06
12. CONTACT	.02	.09	.05	.06	.00
13. SKILL	-.02	-.05	.01	.09	.03
14. NO. PLACEMENTS	.02	.05	-.04	.01	-.05
Multiple R	.35	.36	.35	.28	.20
Multiple R^2	.12	.13	.12	.08	.04
No. of cases	360	359	359	359	357

*$p < .05$ **$p < .01$ ***$p < .001$

[a]Identification of variables same as shown in footnote of Table 14.5.

that children who were spared earlier developmental problems of an emotional nature tended to be relatively free of symptoms five years later. As indicated earlier, the preservation of differences among the children may reflect the stability of behavioral tendencies over time or the tendency of the parents to view their children in a consistent manner.

The evaluation of the mother is a significant predictor. Those mothers who were assessed as being impaired have children who display the most problematic behavior. We have previously commented that it is not possible to determine the extent to which the assessment of a mother is conditioned by the social worker's awareness of the problematic behavior of the child.

Internalized behavior pathology. The analysis has produced five significant predictors: (a) the sex of the child, (b) a prior history of emotional problems in development, (c) health problems, (d) length of time in care, and (e) evaluation of the mother. The girls in the sample were more likely to have symptoms reported, as were children who had early histories of emotional and/or health problems.

Children who returned home showed more problematic adjustment than those remaining in care. They were more apt to be reported as showing appetite or weight problems, colds, or allergies. Since the length of time in care is the variable most closely linked to the source of symptom description, its significance as a predictor must be regarded with tentativeness. It is possible that parents may have a greater readiness to report symptoms such as low appetite than social workers.

Evaluation of the mother is again significantly linked to the report of symptoms; the more negative assessments are associated with scores indicating a greater manifestation of problem symptoms.

Hypernervous behavior. We again find that an earlier history of emotional problems, shorter time in care, and negative assessments of the mothers are significantly linked to reports of more symptomatic behavior shown by the child.

Enuretic pathology. It probably occasions no surprise for the reader to be informed that children who were described as manifesting wetting or soiling problems tended to be younger and with history of developmental problems.

Sleeping pathology. None of the independent variables proved to be a significant predictor of sleeping problems of the child.

By way of summary comment, we observe that the amount of variance in the index scores accounted for by the independent variables we used is quite low. We were somewhat surprised that the number of placements experienced by a child and the reason for entry being his own behavior problems were not significant predictors of symptom scores. We note further that the amount of casework contact and the training of the social worker did not account for significant amounts of variance in the index scores.

TEACHER RATINGS

The ratings of subjects in the classroom provided an approach to child assessment that we particularly valued. The teachers had opportunity to observe the children over sustained periods of time, and their assessments were less likely to be colored by a view of the child's past history or his family circumstances. We have previously shown that a summary measure based on nine items taken from the Rating Scale for Pupil Adjustment (RSPA) correlated significantly with the parent-derived behavioral symptom measure, index of general behavior ($r = .37$; $p < .001$), the social worker –derived index of emotional maturity ($r = -.39$; $p < .001$), index of aggressiveness ($r = -.45$; $p < .001$), and the combined index of external behavior pathology ($r = .45$; $p < .001$).[11]

The summary measure of pupil adjustment is based on the following nine teacher ratings: (a) overall emotional adjustment, (b) social maturity, (c) tendency toward depression, (d) emotional security, (e) motor control, (f) stability, (g) impulsiveness, (h) emotional irritability, and (i) school conduct. Our decision to compact the nine items into a single index was based on an item analysis. The items show quite high item-criterion correlations and the Cronbach alpha measure of internal reliability is .91.

---

[11] The correlation between the summary pupil adjustment scores and the clinical assessments made by the examining psychologists at Time III was .16 ($p < .05$).

We decided to subject the teacher–derived summary measure to the same multiple regression procedure previously employed with the symptom measures discussed earlier. The results are shown in Table 14.12. Three variables show significant regression coefficients: (a) the sex of the child, (b) the report of preplacement health problems, and (c) the frequency of parental visiting. The adjustment of the girls was seen as better than that of the boys. Children with no history of health problems were also seen as showing fewer

TABLE 14.12
RELATION OF SALIENT BACKGROUND AND OTHER INDEPENDENT
VARIABLES TO SUMMARY PUPIL ADJUSTMENT SCORES
BASED ON TEACHER RATINGS[a]
(N = 213)

Independent Variables[b]	Zero-order Correlation	Standardized Regression Coefficient	Percent Unique Variance Explained
1. AGE	−.05	−.09	0.6
2. SEX	.22**	.23***	5.2
3. BLACK	−.05	.01	0.0
4. PUERTO RICAN	.07	.10	0.6
5. CH BEH	−.06	.01	0.0
6. EMOT PROB	−.13	−.11	0.8
7. DEVEL PROB	.04	.11	1.1
8. HEALTH PROB	−.15*	−.17*	2.5
9. CARELOG	−.01	.06	0.3
10. VISITING	.13	.20**	3.3
11. EVAL-MO	.06	.08	0.5
12. CONTACT	−.07	−.14	1.6
13. SKILL	.10	.13	1.5
14. NO. PLACEMENTS	−.05	−.04	0.1
Multiple R		.40	
Multiple R^2		.16	

$*p < .05$ $**p < .01$ $***p < .001$

[a] Summary measure of pupil adjustment is based on nine teacher ratings from RSPA (Science Research Associates, Chicago, Ill., 1953). The ratings include: (a) overall emotional adjustment, (b) social maturity, (c) tendency toward depression, (d) emotional security, (e) motor control and stability, (f) impulsiveness, (g) emotional irritability, and (h) school conduct.

[b] Independent variables are the same as described in the footnote shown in Table 14.5.

problems. Finally, children who were exposed to higher levels of parental visiting seemed to be better adjusted than those who had been essentially abandoned or visited infrequently. Thus, we again see the saliency of parental visiting as a key element in the welfare of the children.

SUMMARY COMMENTS

We have explored the symptomatic behavior of children who were discharged as well as those remaining in care at the end of five years. Our key summary measures were the indexes of general behavior (parent–derived), emotional maturity, and aggressiveness (both social worker–derived), and externalized behavior pathology (common items). They were all fairly well correlated with the summary measures based on teacher ratings and to a somewhat lesser degree with the clinical assessments of the examining psychologists. The validity of the measure is thus established on a somewhat modest level.

The age of the children emerged as a significant predictor for several indexes. It came as no surprise that enuretic problems were age-related; younger children were more prone to be bed-wetters or to soil themselves. On the other hand, analysis of two major adjustment measures showed that older children were subject to more strain, showed greater moodiness, and were more destructive. Older children show more symptomatic behavior in the social worker–derived index of emotional maturity and the index of externalized behavior pathology (based on common parent and social worker items). One source of explanation of this phenomenon is that the repertoire of behavioral symptoms defined as pathological expands as children get older. Older children have more ways of getting into trouble than younger children. This is no doubt a major factor in our findings. We do question, however, whether increased age invariably brings with it more problematic behavior. From our involvement in these data and other investigations, we feel that children who enter foster care as infants and live stable lives in the same settings emerge as teenagers who are relatively free of problems, compared to children who enter the system in latency or

early adolescence.[12] This requires study in more extended longitudinal perspective than was possible in the work we have reported here.

One expects more "acting out" behavior from boys than girls.
However, we found that sex as a variable was not important in the
analyses of the parent–derived index scores. However, when we
examined the indexes based on social worker reports, we found
that significantly more aggressive behavior was attributed to the
boys. We also found that the boys were more often described as
having disturbing dreams and wetting problems. Yet when we examined the indexes based on common items, we found that the girls
were more often rated as having poor appetites, colds, and allergies.
From our examination of teacher ratings, it would appear that the
girls in our study were making a better school adjustment than the
boys. More research on sex-related aspects of the experiences of
children in foster care is required to further elucidate these
phenomena.

Aside from the tendency of Puerto Rican parents to report
more health problems for their children, there is relatively little
differentiation in the symptom pictures developed by our index
scores on the basis of race or ethnicity. In other words, we do not
find that black children have more problems than white or Puerto
Rican children in our sample, or that Puerto Rican children have
more problems than white children. It is also *not* our impression—
based on various analyses we have undertaken—that this relative
similarity of symptom distribution among the children is due to the
attrition of our sample such that, for example, more problem-prone
black children have dropped out of the study.

Interestingly, we find no indication that child behavior problems
as a reason for placement are predictive of greater evidence of
behavioral difficulty five years after entry into foster care. Time in
care may have served to diminish the severity of behavioral disorder
in these children. It is also possible that relative parity has been
established because children who have entered care for other

---

[12] This observation reflects a recent study of symptomatic behaviors of 525 children in
foster care in New York City, conducted by David Fanshel and John Grundy for Child
Welfare Information Services, Inc. An instrument called the "Foster Child Appraisal Form" has
been used to secure ratings and is being further tested in ongoing research.

reasons may have become more disturbed. Inspection of our data (CBC scores and clinical ratings) suggests that the former statement is the more likely valid explanation of the state of parity. Children who enter foster care as disturbed children tend to show amelioration of symptoms over an extended period of time.

We have had several indications in our analyses that the child's early developmental history as garnered from interviews with parents (usually mothers) early in the study is predictive of reports of symptoms five years later. For the parent-derived indexes, a prior history of health problems is predictive of relatively more health problems five years later as well as overall behavioral difficulty. Early developmental problems are also predictive of greater reports of toileting problems later. For the social worker–derived index called "aggressiveness," we find that reports of preplacement developmental difficulties of an emotional nature presage relatively more aggressive symptomatic behavior some five years after the child's entry into care.

Three of the five indexes created from the items that were common to the inquiries of parents and social workers were linked with earlier histories of emotional problems. Children with preplacement emotional difficulties showed more negative scores five years later for the indexes of externalized behavior pathology, internalized behavior pathology, and hypernervous behavior. Children with higher scores on the index of enuretic pathology tended to have early histories of developmental difficulty. We also found that children who seemed relatively problem-free on the summary teacher measure had no history of health problems. The analyses support the view that some of a child's later adjustment can be predicted from earlier developmental patterns, even though he may have experienced profound changes in life circumstances through entrance into foster care. We emerge with the view that in many ways the child is the best predictor of himself.

We find a few indications that frequent parental visiting is linked with better adjustment. We are particularly impressed that the visiting variable is significantly predictive of the overall teacher assessment of the subjects. We also find that frequent parental visiting is linked to better scores on the parent-derived index of security–sociability.

Evaluation of the mother is significantly associated with symptom scores. The more favorable the assessment of the mother, the greater is the tendency to see the child as free of problems. As we said earlier, we cannot ascertain whether the evaluations of the mother are independent of the early assessments of the child.

With one exception, we find no significant association between the volume and quality of casework contacts (as measured by the skill of the social workers) and the symptom pictures we have measured. We also find no significant association between the number of placements experienced by children and the measures of symptoms.

FIFTEEN

THE CHILDREN AND
THEIR SOCIAL WORKERS
PERCEIVE FOSTER CARE

To flesh out the perspectives achieved from the many statistical analyses we have reported in the preceding chapters, we turn now to personal narratives secured by interviewing the children old enough to be interviewed at Time II, some two and one-half years after their entry into foster care. The children were at least seven years of age and were interviewed by our examining psychologists as part of the second round of longitudinal testing. To gain further insight into how they experienced placement, we also administered a sentence-completion test, which we prepared for our particular purposes.

To round out our qualitative analysis of the foster care phenomenon, we also present the overall perspectives secured from the social workers through use of the mailed profile form, which was the source of data for our reports in chapters 13 and 14. Several opportunities were provided them to assess the overall impact of the foster care experience on the child.

We believe that an added dimension of understanding is made possible by these narratives, and they provide important insights into how the foster care system is experienced by those most intimately involved.

CHILD PERSPECTIVES

There have been few systematic inquiries into children's own perceptions of the separation experience and how they have integrated it into their views of themselves and the world around them. One detailed investigation in this area was undertaken by Weinstein, who studied 61 children who had been placed with the Chicago Child Care Society in 1955.[1] The interviewing schedule we created was influenced by this previous research, although our emphasis was somewhat different. Both studies are concerned with understanding a child's conception of who he is, to whom he belongs, why he is not able to live with his parents, and what the future holds. These are rather basic questions and, it seemed to us, of potential importance in shaping the child's life adjustment.

The interview with the child followed a topical outline and took about 20 minutes to conduct. A tape recording was made of each interview and a typed transcript was prepared. By listening to the tape and reading the transcript, the examining psychologist was able to code each child's responses; a repeat coding operation was undertaken by a second psychologist to assess the reliability of the data. In most cases we found the reliability of the coding to be substantial.

In all, 205 children were interviewed. Of these, 56 were interviewed in their own homes, 59 in foster family homes, and 90 in institutions. The children in institutions were the oldest (mean = 11.6 years) the children in foster family homes the youngest (mean = 8.9 years), and the discharged children were in between (mean = 10.3 years). The interviews were adjusted to take into account the special circumstances that pertained to each of the three interviewing sites. For example, children in foster family homes were asked if they used their own surnames or that of foster parents; they were also asked if they were embarrassed by having a different name. Children who had returned home were asked to recall the circumstances that had prevailed while they were in care. The bulk of the questions, however, were common to all three interviewing situations.

Before reporting on the specific categories of questions, we would like to comment about the children as interviewing subjects. A number of our subjects were quite young and the questions had to be posed in simple terms. Their answers tended to be very brief and

[1] Eugene Weinstein, *The Self-Image of the Foster Child* (New York: Russell Sage Foundation, 1960).

sometimes monosyllabic. We also found that many of the children were guarded in what they had to say and seemed to defend themselves against some of the painful implications of our questions. Despite this, our psychologists were able to secure quite meaningful responses, revealing the inner emotions of the children and what they thought about the circumstances that had brought them to foster care.

From an overall perspective, it would appear that the process of separation is experienced as catastrophic or as a quite sad and unpleasant occasion by many of the children. This would be in accord with the common professional understanding of the phenomenon. The initial parting was often dramatic and frightening, and the children were frequently ill-prepared for it. Moreover, their feelings about the separation, although expressed in various ways or submerged periodically, did not seem to be resolved in a satisfactory manner.

Space does not permit displaying samples of the children's responses to all questions. We have chosen to report on those questions that provided the clearest picture of the reactions of the children. One child was asked; "How did you feel on the day you left your family?" and responded, "first that I was a bit shocked. I didn't know what would happen. They didn't say anything like you're gonna do this or like you're going into the hospital, nothing like that."

Another child who said she cried that day was asked whether she was told beforehand that she would be leaving home; she responded with the following:

No, we didn't know. It was a quarrel between my mother and my father because my mother took us to sleep in my aunt's house and from there, we never saw her again . . . from there my father picked me up and she wasn't home anymore . . . he took us home, and we asked him where was our mother, and he said that she left us.

More often, when asked about their feelings on the day they left home, the children answered that they felt "sad," "mad," or "not so good." The older children reported a greater number of occasions where separation came as a relief because of the conflicts they were having with their parents. The younger ones were most often sad. The experience seemed obviously invested with considerable emotional turmoil.

When we tabulated the coded responses of the children about how they felt on the day they left their families, we found the following:

1. For children who had returned to their own homes, 77 percent reported that they had felt sad, bad, depressed, or upset and 9 percent reported that they had felt good. The remaining responses were noncommittal.

2. For children in foster family homes, 63 percent said that they had felt sad, depressed, or upset and 10 percent, relieved or glad.

3. For children in institutions, 75 percent had been very saddened by the departure, and 10 percent said they felt relieved.

We also sought to determine how the children perceived other foster children. We were interested in understanding their concept of reasons for other children entering foster care, possibly going beyond their own particular circumstances. In their responses, the children often revealed the kind of aura that surrounded the separation phenomenon as they perceived it.

We asked the children, "What are some of the reasons children have to leave their own families and come here to live?" A number of themes emerged in the responses. One of these was the bad mother or the parent who did not like her own children or did not want to be a parent and abandoned them:

Cause the mothers don't want them.

Because the mothers are bad or the children are bad.

Cause some of the parents don't like being parents and some want to go away.

Maybe cause the mother died and the father can't take care of them, maybe cause the mother walked out on the children and left them by themselves.

Their mother don't take care of them, they just leave them—you know—there . . . or . . . they drink . . . or they don't take care of them and they have to put 'em in a house 'til they can get a better apartment or something.

Maybe the family hates the children . . . maybe they have a boy who is retarded.

Because the families are bad or the children are bad . . . living here [in foster home] is better.

They don't like them. Either the kids don't like their families or the families don't like their kinds.

For some of the children, the loss of parents is connected with their perception of severe conflict and overt fighting between the parents, which has led the parents to turn away from them. These children appear to see a linkage between their parents' ability to accept and like each other and their own children as well. The rejection by the parents is quite clear.

Well, my mother and my father had a fight and my mother left and never came back and he didn't want us and my mother didn't want us. "Who told you that they didn't want you?" Well, you could see for yourself because if they . . . if my mother wanted me the agency said that they would pay her everything and she doesn't . . . she said no. So, that shows that she doesn't really want us.

When I was young my father ran away. He ran away from my mother, cause my mother is, you know, sick. You know, in the head. And she gets mad at him sometimes. And he was washing the windows, you know, but first my grandmother told him to wash the windows but he was telling my mother to wash the windows, so they were arguing so he got, it ended up, he was washing the windows, you know. And she started saying that whoever washes the windows supposed to be a man's job and, you know, she kept on saying it. And he was quiet and washing the windows. So he got mad and threw the pails all over the place. Then he cut out, you know, he ran away, and he, he didn't come back. We ain't seen him since.

The theme of sickness and death emerges as one of the important sources of explanation held by the subjects as to why children enter foster care. Their responses reveal a conception of their preplacement situations as fraught with life-threatening hazards, and life is seen as capricious and unpredictable.

Cause well sometimes they get, um, bad and they be bad and their mothers get mad with them and they get a heart attack or something and they die like fast if they get a heart attack and sometimes they're bad cause strange things happen.

Sometimes the mother and father dies or they don't know where their mother and father went or sometimes the mother and father's sick in the hospital. And some of them live with their aunts.

Well some of the reasons are that mothers are getting killed and sometimes they might be out looking for houses like my mother [sigh].

Oh, the mothers get sick or the father dies or both parents die together.

Some of the children present a view of the parents as patently neglectful and having deviant life-styles that involve a variety of illicit activities that are implicitly or explicitly incompatible with being a proper parent.

Because sometimes their mother went out to have a good time so while their husbands are at work, they go out and whistle to the next dude and say "Hey, I got a pint. Come down and get it!"

Cause their parents don't be home so much and they go out and leave them so the other people call the police cause they don't be home with grownups. So they call the police and they take them away.

Because the mother either does something or the father. The father may start a fight or somethin', or the mother goes out with other men and the father doesn't like it, and everything else.

Because my father sometimes get my mother mad. She used to work, and he did too, and ahh . . . he used to go out in a bar and drink when he came home. He was going crazy and he used to beat her up. And, and then he used to kick her out of the house; it wasn't even his house. And then she had a whole bunch of dogs she left in the house. She used to come, she used to be, aah . . she used to tease the dogs and my father went after her with a knife . . . . I think she was my stepmother, cause everyone said my mother died.

Some of the children clearly perceive their parents, usually their mothers, as being mentally ill or incapacitated because of emotional problems, without any connotation that they are deviant or uncaring about their parental responsibilities.

Because the parents are in the hospital or they sick and they can't live with their children because they treat them the way they're not supposed to treat them. They don't mean to do things wrong . . . they can't help themselves.

Because, you know, my mother, she's having problems with herself. She gets into one of her moods and then bad things start happening. She's always sorry later.

Cause my mudder's got problems in da head. She gets crazy. She has to take pills to quiet her down. But when she goes off her rocker . . . boy!!

The reality of the parents' circumstances can strike the child as the basis for his being in care. Circumstances such as physical illness or the needs to earn income or search for an apartment are mentioned. These are seen as caused by external factors and enable the child to view the parent as not deviant or rejecting him.

Well, uh, some of the people take sick, and some of them, uh, can't, uh, find a place . . . they have to work, and, uh, they have to leave the child somewhere, and they can't find a place to leave them.

Cause my mother got hurt on the leg . . . she wanted me to come over here.

Because maybe their mother doesn't have a job—good work, or their parents separated from each other, or the mother or father might die, and, you know, the parents—they can't take care of the children anymore, so they take them to a home—they don't have enough money to buy food or clothing.

Some of the reasons is like, your mother go far, far away an' your father he can't take care of you 'cause he go to work an' everything. But see, even though my father go to work an my mother—maybe he ask her to go to work—she'd probably go to work, see. Cause I could take care of myself, cause I know how to cook an' everything.

Those children who have entered foster care because of their own behavioral difficulties clearly identify themselves as responsible for the placement. Other children sometimes view their own behavior as contributing to the breakdown in parental functioning, and there may be guilt expressed about a parent going berserk or being overwhelmed by responsibilities.

The children get messed up. They have to go to Youth House or Boys Town or a place like that.

Cause they be bad. They have to be trained to be good . . . sometimes they crazy . . . they throw rocks at the windows.

Cause they're bad to their family and they send them away.

Cause they drive their mothers up the wall. They out to all hours and go around with tough kids. The mothers go crazy. And the kids don't listen to them.

On Being a Foster Child

For the children still in care, we were interested in obtaining some perspectives on how they reconciled for themselves the duality of their relationship to substitute caretakers and their own natural parents. We were particularly interested in gaining insight into the children's view of "what makes things happen in the world." From a review of the interviews we have a general sense that although the children felt some responsibility for the factors leading to their entry into care, they felt very little control over the forces determining what would eventually happen to them, that is, whether they would continue to remain in their present environment or go on to another living arrangement. They were of the opinion that it was their parents or their social workers who would decide when and whether they might go home. A few children stated that they could go to their own homes if they wanted to but they preferred their foster homes. In general, the children projected a strong sense of helplessness. There was little in their own lives over which they felt they had any control, and there was widespread indication that they lacked faith in their own parents.

The degree to which some children felt totally disassociated from the parents is revealed by the following:

1. Of the children in foster family homes, 26 percent were unable to give the names of their mothers and 9 percent had to grope for this information; 22 percent could not give the names of their fathers and 7 percent did so with hesitation.
2. Of the children in institutions, 11 percent could not name their mothers and 8 percent did so with difficulty; 13 percent could not give the names of their fathers and 8 percent were hesitant in doing so.

The children were further questioned; "Tell me about your own family, the one you were born into. What's your mother's name? Your father's?"

Mary. ["What's her last name?"] I forget.... Her last name is—I don't know her last name. ["Do you know what your father's name is?"] I don't have him anymore.

I don't remember—don't—my real daddy's name an' I can't remember the other one's—my mother's name.

["Tell me about your family. What's your mother's name?"] She's in

Puerto Rico. ["What's her name?"] I don't know no more. ["Do you know what your father's is?"] ... ["You don't know what your father's name is, either. Do they have any other children besides you?"] In Puerto Rico. I have some family in New York. ["What family do you have in New York?"] Big family—can't even say everybody's name—don't even know them.

Larger proportions of children (nearly 33 percent) in foster homes or institutions either had no idea or were vague about the whereabouts of their parents. Similar confusion was revealed about the composition of their families.

It was most difficult to determine whether a child felt deprived because he was in foster care. Responses to questions about this tended to be guarded or somewhat superficial. However, almost 25 percent were able to distinguish between living in foster care and in one's own home in a manner that indicated they perceived some inherent disadvantage in their situations.

When asked whether "children who don't live with their own families are treated differently from children who do live with their own parents?", the responses were as follows:

I think so. Like if your mother [foster mother] tells you to stop doing that, and you say no and keep on doing it, and then your mother brings you to court and the court brings you to a convent.

Yeh—like at home you've got more freedom. If you want to go out and play you can. Here [in the institution] you have to stay in the barracks and cottage all the time.

Because when you're in the shelter the food doesn't taste right, you see, because they don't have enough time to season the food for us. At home your mother has enough to season the food.

Well they can't take them to all kinds of places like their own family can.

Yeah, they treat 'em differently. They'll mess up on them. ["What does that mean?"] They be bad on them ... They act bad.

Oh sure. Well, like there's clothes money ... and you get a certain money for a certain time for your clothes ... and well you don't get the same as if you lived with your own family. With a person who is taking care of you—they don't have the same affection and don't give like you'd give to your own child.

Yes ... can ... they get hit when they try fight, but the children who's good they, they got mothers. They don't fight, they don't get whoppin's.

Well all the time we go home and they don't go home and they have more good things than us.

Sometimes. Cause sometimes their mother doesn't treat 'em nice. Sometimes the new parents don't care for them.

Cause they are treated old.

About 10 percent regarded the foster child as receiving better treatment than other children, using as the basis for comparison the treatment they received in their own home before entering care.

Yeah. They're treated differently. Well, in a home they get treated nice. You get treated the way you want to get treated. Not the way your mother and father want to treat you.

Yup. They get more love in the shelter. And th–, and they give you new clothes.

I get clean clothes. Everytime my dress is dirty, my mother [foster mother] tells me to change it . . . put it in the hamper . . . she washes it and meanwhile it's drying . . . I put some other clothes on.

The Sentence-completion Test

We were able to administer the sentence-completion test to 215 children (59 in their own homes, 90 in institutions, 56 in foster family homes, and 10 in other living arrangements, such as homes of relatives or friends). We prepared the sentence stubs with a view to tapping some of the same domains covered by the interview:

When I was little . . . .
If I had magic power . . . .
Children who are bad . . . .
My family is . . . .
When I grow up . . . .
Children who are good . . . .
A sad time for me was when . . . .
I am living here because . . . .
The person I love best is . . . .
Brothers are . . . .
If I could choose anybody to live with, I'd choose . . . .

I felt happiest when . . . .
My mother is . . . .
Next year . . . .
A child is . . . .
My mother loves me when . . . .
The most important thing about my father is . . . .
Leaving home was . . . .

Our general impression is that the children responded even more guardedly to the sentence-completion tasks than to the interviews and that they again showed signs of being well-defended. Answers tended to be extremely concise and often concrete, avoiding emotionally charged material. However, some of the stubs were so centrally focused on a particular issue that it was difficult for the child to avoid dealing with it.

1. For the stub "I am living here because," 22 percent of the children in the institutions indicated their "bad behavior" was the reason for being in placement—almost none of the children in foster family care responded in this manner. Of institutionalized children and those in foster family care, 10 percent responded "because I belong here—it is my family." Some 23 percent of the children in foster family care responded "because I like it here"; this was true of 12 percent of the children in institutions.

2. For the stub "the person I love best," the person most often designated was the child's natural mother. This was true for 48 percent of the children tested in their homes, 40 percent of those in foster family care, and 31 percent of those in institutions. When we combined the categories of mother, father, and both parents, children in their own homes showed 70 percent responding in this way. This was true of 51 percent of the children in foster family homes and 55 percent of those in institutions. Only 9 percent of the children in foster family homes mentioned their foster parents in this regard.

3. For the stub "if I could choose anybody to live with," most children mentioned their mother, father, or both parents. This was true of 51 percent of the children in their own homes, 37 percent of those in foster family care, and 42 percent of those in institutions. Almost 13 percent of the children in all categories mentioned a sibling. For children in foster family care, 7 percent mentioned the foster parent as the person of choice.

4. For the stub "leaving home was," we find that most subjects indicated that separation was painful or sad. This was true of 46

percent of the discharged children, 60 percent of those in foster families and 71 percent of those in institutions. Ten percent of the children in their own homes spoke of their departure from home as something positive; this was true of 5 percent of those in foster family care and 7 percent of those in institutions.

This brings to a close our report on our effort to elicit subjective accounts from the children. While future research of this kind should be based on more inventive methods of involving the children in examining their own reactions to separation and placement, we believe that some useful insights have been developed from this aspect of our research.

We now consider narratives provided by the social workers based on their overall impression of the impact of the foster care experience on the children remaining in care.

PERSPECTIVES FROM THE SOCIAL WORKERS

Included in the 16-page Time III profile form we had prepared were two open-ended questions:

1. What effects do *you* think foster care is having on this child? (Please describe in detail both beneficial and/or detrimental effects.)

2. In what way(s) do you think that being in foster care has aided or hindered this child's physical and emotional health"

The answers to these questions, while often redundant, provided interesting insights into the views of the social workers about the foster care system and its consequences for the children.

When we coded the responses, according to whether the effects were seen as *beneficial* or *detrimental*, we found that for 201 children (91 percent) a beneficial effect was cited and for 95 children (43 percent), a detrimental effect.

, The fact that foster care offered an environment for normal development and provided the structure necessary for the child to mature tended to be seen overwhelmingly as the major categories of benefits. On the other hand, there was greater spread of cases among the categories identified as detrimental. First, we examine the beneficial effects and illustrate the perspectives of the social workers in their responses to the open-ended questions, basing our examples on both questions.

Beneficial Effects of Foster Care

A number of subthemes can be discerned among the benefits cited, but most frequently is a contrast established between the noxious conditions that prevailed in the child's own home and the stability, nurturance, and other positive qualities provided by the foster family home or institution.

This foster setting has provided child with a very stable environment. The natural mother has visited only twice since his placement and although she has verbalized in the past her desire to have him discharged, she has never followed through on these plans. The foster home setting has provided him with a sense of security and acceptance.

Foster care has allowed child to be taken out of extremely chaotic and destructive family constellation by court action. Foster care has provided material and educational opportunities.

Geraldine seemed to feel that she had very little self-worth. This was apparently due to her traumatic experiences before removal from the home by the court. Foster care offers all the advantages and more which are unavailable in her own home, such as nice clothes, the consistent love of a stable family, and relationships with peers.

Being abused and abandoned by own parents and given up by paternal aunt had a detrimental effect on Tommy. I feel that foster care is the best plan for him and that it has beneficial effects. These are: (a) better physical care and health, (b) improving emotional health, and (c) receiving help with medical problems associated with poor vision.

Ramona comes from a very deprived home. Her physical health is good, probably better than if she had remained with her father. Her mother had deserted four years before placement, and this rejection has scarred the child. Group parents are solicitous of the child and she is responding to their warmth and concern. She is progressing in all areas.

It has definitely aided Lillian's emotional and physical health. She was physically neglected and emotionally deprived when she lived with her natural parents. She is now much less anxious and more relaxed than previously. In foster care she has received the love and attention that she so greatly needs.

Her physical and emotional health has been aided by being with loving foster parents, in contrast to her being cared for by an immature and neglectful mother and a father who has shown no interest in her since her birth.

This was an abused neglected child placed by the court. He would probably never have survived in his natural home.

The natural mother is a drug addict. The child is being provided with a physically and emotionally secure home. He doesn't understand foster care because he doesn't see his natural parents, and only his sister occasionally. Foster care was the best solution.

Placement has helped the child grow up in a climate where he has not been exposed to constant fighting between his parents and siblings. He has also been spared severe beatings from his parents such as he received before placement.

Some of the comments of the social workers do not involve invidious comparisons between the child's natural parents and the current foster care situation. At the same time, the view of the foster care situation is suffused with highly laudatory statements indicating the worker's enthusiasm about what the child is being offered in the way of care.

This child is part of a family and knows no other family. She experiences love, warmth, understanding, and security. She receives religious and spiritual training and is maturing socially with the family, peers, and other adults. She is aware of herself, exhibits confidence, and is eager to learn and explore. She has been able to share in the love, affection, and guidance the family is able to give all of the children.

There are very good effects. She's happy that she has a family. Especially parents who can spend lots of time with her. She's become the center of this couple's life and they hers. The child was previously afraid of adults and seldom played with other children. Now she is a delightful, outgoing youngster who is articulate about her feelings. Her skin glows, she's quite active, sleeps and eats well, and enjoys good physical and emotional health.

I certainly feel that foster care has strengthened Edith's self-image. She is more assertive and outgoing than she was at admission. These changes reflect the motivation and interest of her foster parents. The agency has put much into her situation and her adjustment reflects this.

Sometimes the social workers express particularly positive feelings about the institution's or the foster home's ability to stimulate the cognitive growth of the child, especially if his natural family tended to suppress intellectual curiosity.

John is placed in a very warm, well-knit boarding family. The boarding parents are achievement-oriented and work closely with the child to help him with his current acting-out problem in the school setting. They provide consistent, firm discipline but are also quite amenable to the agency's suggestions regarding handling of the child.

He has attended a special school for children with learning problems and has received psychotherapy, chemotherapy, and visual perceptual training, all of which have helped to strengthen his ego.

In a number of situations, the social worker expresses positive views about the foster family and the child obviously benefits from their care. Yet the child's security is undermined by the failure of the natural parents to visit and the child shows feelings of deep rejection. In some cases the abandonment by the natural parents is compounded by failure of the foster parents to be responsive to the child's needs.

This child feels rejected because his father has stopped visiting. He was extremely frightened and withdrawn when he was first placed. Although he has improved in regard to social relationships, he is still a "loner" and at times is moody.

Laura has had sporadic contact with her natural parents, and the recent disappearance of these people from her life has left her somewhat confused, although she demonstrates little observable anxiety. The child has shown some insecurity and some inappropriate behavior but not necessarily completely due to separation. She witnessed the removal of a foster brother, her companion for two and one-half years, from her foster home. The circumstances were certainly detrimental to child's feelings of security and increased her sense of abandonment by her own parents.

This child has had the opportunity in foster care to develop physically. The placement offers a variety of benefits from which Roberto has profited. However, being in foster care is a burden to the child as he misses his family. His emotional growth is hindered because he cannot sense the close ties he needs from his present setting.

The child's physical needs are being well met. However, his emotional health has been hindered as he feels rejected by his natural mother and not completely accepted in his foster home.

Some foster parents actively encourage the involvement of natural parents and see this as necessary for the child's welfare.

At this point the child is adjusting beautifully in the home. Foster parents are concerned about the number of contacts between John and his natural parents. Due to marital difficulties the natural parents have not been visiting as often as they should. Foster parents feel strongly about parents being involved regularly so that a strong feeling of family will develop and minimize problems that usually occur with children in care and their relationship with their own families.

Johnny has been in the foster home since infancy. His parents have been involved from the very beginning and there is a very positive relationship between foster parents and natural parents so that Johnny's adjustment so far has remained very good.

For some social workers, the natural parents are seen as disruptive to the child's ability to make a good adjustment in the current living situation, and they are open in expressing their misgivings about the parents' continued involvement in their children's lives.

Being in foster care has definitely aided Anita's physical and emotional health in all ways. When with her natural parents, she was physically abused, neglected and emotionally deprived. Her parents' lives have become increasingly deteriorated. Since her placement at the age of two, Anita has shown increasing emotional and physical development. These impressions are supported by a recent psychological exam. She probably would have developed even more quickly if she did not have to spend weekend visits with her natural parents as ordered by the court.

In cases where children have entered foster care as infants and have remained in the same foster family homes, there often are no natural parents to deal with and the foster family is seen by the social workers as *the* family of the child. The distinction between "natural" and "foster" does not obtain. Adoption of the child by the foster family is seen as making great sense and to be encouraged.

Edward is very much a part of the foster family and they are eager to adopt him. He feels security and love in their home. He has been in this same home since infancy. He has the chance of being adopted by the foster family. The child is happy and well cared for in this home.

Since this child has been in this home most of her life, it is difficult to differentiate the terminology of foster care in the usual concept and what is considered the child's original or own home.

Detrimental Aspects of Foster Care

We now turn to the perceived detrimental effects of the foster care situation as identified for 95 (43 percent) of the 223 children for whom we received Time III profiles from the social workers. We emphasize that we are dealing with the residual cases of children who have remained in care for five years while most of their peers have returned home. We are here concerned with long-term wards of the system, where we would expect a greater concentration of problematic situations and where the sheer extension of time in which the child has been in limbo may well show the frailties of the substitute arrangements. Some of the best utilization of placement opportunities in foster care is likely to be reflected in the cases of children who have returned home and where social worker reports are no longer available. We make these comments in order to clarify that we are interested in displaying the *types* of situations that raise question about the validity of the foster care placement—*examples* of what can go wrong or be detrimental to the child. We do not intend to characterize the entire system as detrimental, since the positive comments of the social workers far outweigh those that have a negative cast.

As might be anticipated, a source of concern mentioned fairly often—20 percent of cases where a detrimental effect of foster care was reported—was the "institutionalization" of the child. This uniformly involved children in congregate institutions rather than foster family homes. The social workers expressed concern that the child would suffer loss of an individualized sense of self and the ability to enjoy more intimate types of relationships.

Group care allows for less individual attention. There have been several changes in staff and child has suffered from this.

As a result of the child being placed in foster care, he enjoys the security and the sense of physical well-being that it provides. He seems less embittered than some children who have had to survive on the "streets." William does not appear to be a person who projects a great deal of affection to others. Being in foster care and living in a group setting has made it less necessary to be very warm. However, it would be somewhat necessary in a family unit. The negative effect is that he is becoming an institutionalized child who does not desire reunion with his family.

Placement has hindered Paul's experiences in a "real world." Group living and group involvement in all aspects of placement (except the one-to-one in casework) makes little room for individuality. Poor peer relationships (manipulation by peers) has not helped build his self-esteem.

Institutionalizing child has contributed to her escape and withdrawn nature.

Placement has provided a reliable structured environment. Right now there are no outstanding effects, good or bad, for Susan seems quite accepting of placement here. However, perhaps this very acceptance may be detrimental in the long run, and years of institutionalization will result in flattened responses to the environment. Her acceptance of placement may alter in adolescence as it often does, and she may begin to question and resent the father's lack of interest.

Some social workers see the child's indeterminate status in foster care as inherently a source of disturbance, a kind of "time bomb" that may well go off later, even though the child's current adjustment seems satisfactory in some cases. The failure of the foster parents to adopt the child is sometimes mentioned as a problem.

Josefa's experiences in foster home placement have definitely been beneficial for her. She is well-accepted in her foster home and is doing fairly well academically. One detrimental effect that I can foresee is that of fully understanding and accepting her status as a foster child. Since she has had very little contact with her natural mother, she refers to her as "that other lady."

He does not appear to be much aware of himself as a foster child. He will in time, however, *probably* harbor feelings of insecurity and perhaps even hostility over not having been adopted. There is another adopted child in the home.

This child feels unloved and insecure. I feel that the longer she stays in care, the more detrimental it will be for her welfare.

Beneficial: Susan is receiving much better physical care (daily care and medical help) than she probably would in her own home. Detrimental: Her foster care situation is creating too much insecurity for her.

I strongly believe that the decision to send José to this agency was a wise one in view of his previous chaotic home situation. I do not think that the parents could have provided the type of care he has been receiving. At the same time, it is my belief that the placement was tremendously useful to the mother in straightening out her life situation. This is why, after so many years of separation, I feel that José and his mother should be reunited. José has emotional needs that can best be filled in his own family circle.

While most of the foster parents were rated quite positively by the social workers on the two occasions when the homes were rated for our project, it comes as no surprise that some of the foster families are seen as having limitations in what they have to offer the children. Some are rigid in their child-rearing tendencies, while others are overprotective.

Jane is placed in a home with three other children. She gets along well with them. The home is extremely rigid and devoid of any affection. She leads a very regimented life with too few chances for meeting children outside the home.

Physical health was definitely neglected at home and she receives much better care now. Her emotional development is seriously retarded, however, because of lack of maternal and paternal nurturing by parents or substitute parents. She is almost thirteen but very immature.

Basically all effects are beneficial. She has a good strong relationship with all in the foster family. On the negative side, foster parents have "spoiled" Sally, and this will be something of a problem as she advances in age. Also, if child were to return to her natural mother, the foster mother would be no comfort to Sally during the transitional stage.

Margaret's emotional health has been hindered somewhat due to the foster mother's "tunnel vision." Mrs. Smith is not capable of flexibility; therefore, it is difficult for her to raise children successfully.

On the detrimental side, we could consider the insecurity this child feels about what will happen to her in two or three years when the foster father retires. Also, this is a "grandparent" type of foster home, which has many regulations and limits that are a problem for many children as they approach adolescence.

I think Eve has been helped to feel that she can become part of a family. She is very well taken care of physically and there are many opportunities for enrichment. She is not being given any sense of independence, however, which is what she needs. She has many insecurities about herself and her status in foster care, which she will need help with.

I think he has been helped to gain a feeling of security within the home, although at the same time this foster family is quite over-protective of the child. He has become too dependent on the family.

I feel that foster care is good for this child, and in this home he has received a great amount of stimulation, which has resulted in a great deal of developmental progress. He does need, however, a structured surrounding where he can learn at his own pace. Sometimes the foster family's expectations are too high.

There are a number of situations reported in which the foster parents have had to take in a child with history of several previous unsuccessful placements. They have to invest in the child in a very special way to overcome the handicaps he has suffered from these earlier experiences.

It is impossible to judge what the effects are at this time. However, Danny is receiving good physical and emotional care in the home in which he is now placed. Since this placement, he has shown marked improvement in speech, socialization, and coordination (all these were lacking during prior placements). Since the beginning of agency involvement, Danny has been placed in five different homes, creating insecurity manifesting itself in physical malfunctioning. At times, the adjustment problem was severe because he was rejected by two of his foster mothers. He suffered with a mild case of hay fever, delayed speech, nervousness (lip biting), and enuresis (all symptoms have subsided in the present foster home).

COMMENTS

We have sought to provide a more enriched picture of the foster care experience by quoting directly from narrative materials secured from the children and from their social workers. It is our belief that many statistical analyses we have presented in this volume cannot fully capture what it feels like to be a child in foster care or to be a social worker concerned with the child's long-term status in care.

We trust the reader will share our view that the content of the material presented in this chapter makes clear that each child's situation reflects a complex array of forces. Sound case management in the reality of the practice situation requires a highly individualized approach to cases. Research findings such as those we report may serve as a stimulus for consideration of social policy issues or program-management procedures. The social worker who is a direct line worker, however, must take into account many individual aspects of a case in formulating an overall approach to planning for a given child's needs. The task of the researcher is to bring to bear, as background information, the wisdom that can be obtained from the examination of many cases to help support the individual judgments the worker must make.

SIXTEEN

AN OVERVIEW
AND LOOK
TO THE FUTURE

We thus conclude what is probably the only longitudinal study of children in foster care yet conducted. This was not an easy venture, although we began on this path almost a decade ago with full awareness that unusual demands would be placed on us. Many of the complexities of this kind of research were anticipated; others emerged early as we were out in the field gathering data or later as we tried to organize and make sense out of what we had collected. For a long time, we felt as though we had a tiger by the tail, determined to hold on and see the venture through to completion but not quite sure we would make it. It is thus with a sense of relief and satisfaction that we come to this final chapter.

We now feel somewhat more mature and sophisticated and are almost tempted to say, "*Now*, we could really undertake a longitudinal study and do it right!" However, fatigue and belated wisdom are sufficient to restrain our euphoria; we will gladly pass the baton to other long-distance runners, wishing them well and hoping that our work will facilitate their endeavors.

The task of conducting a longitudinal study has afforded us the opportunity of developing experience in a variety of areas, such as staying with a large sample over time (including children who have returned home as well as those remaining in care), keeping track of the movement of children within and between some 80 agencies and their movement in and out of care, administering psychological tests on a repeated basis, and securing assessment data from a variety of informants (social workers, psychologists, teachers, and parents). We have also had the benefit of data collected in parallel studies of the parents who were interviewed in a series of field surveys and the results of annual telephone research interviews with the social workers who worked with the children and their families. A major activity has been the coding and computerization of massive amounts of data. We have had to develop analytic approaches for dealing with such topics as status changes of children in care, changes in their cognitive development, school performance, and personal and social adjustment. We feel these experiences will be useful in providing orientations for future empirical studies of foster children.

Because of the sheer volume of the data collected and the fact that this book had to be limited to a reasonable number of pages, we have had to make choices about what findings to present. Even though we have provided the average reader with probably more information and tables than can be readily absorbed, we should point out that these represent only a fraction of the analyses we undertook. The computer output we produced over the last several years was so voluminous as to almost crowd us out of our offices. This volume represents the heart of our analytic effort and findings.

Having come to the end of our report, we would like to remind the reader of some of the limitations and special aspects of our sample and design so as to provide a view of our findings with an appropriate perspective. First, we emphasize the fact that the study deals exclusively with foster children who have been in care for at least 90 days and were never in care before. This means that we cannot adequately address the question of whether foster children are different from other children in the community who have not suffered separation from their parents; we have had no contrast group of community-based children to provide the basis for such comparison. Instead, we are able to compare children who have returned home with those who have remained in care; this contrast is often expressed in the form of a variable measuring length of time in care.

Since we restricted our sample to children who spent at least 90 days in care, we of course cannot describe the impact of foster care on children who experienced placement for shorter periods of time. We also do not examine the experience of children whose families have had recourse to the foster care system in the past; we deal only with a sample of new users of the system. Finally, we remind the reader that we restricted our sample to children who entered foster care under the age of 13 years. While we followed the older children until they were 18 years of age, we did not include in our study teenagers entering care. Such older children constitute an increasingly important source of new admissions to the foster care system in New York City, and they often enter care because of behavioral difficulties.

We now proceed to examine some of our major findings and comment on their implications for practice and/or social policy. We will follow this with a presentation of our research perspectives.

THE STATUS SITUATION OF FOSTER CHILDREN AND THE PROBLEM OF "DRIFT"

A most important finding of our study is the fact that 36.4 percent of our sample were still in care at the end of five years. The group discharged constituted 56.1 percent of the sample, while those placed in adoptive homes were 4.6 percent and those transferred to mental institutions or training schools, 2.9 percent. Behind these simple pieces of data lies a crucial issue about foster care, namely, *why so many children have become long-term wards of the system.* Why is this system, intended to offer *temporary* haven to children, incapable of restoring large numbers of them to their own families or in providing adoptive placements? The fact that 57 percent of the children still in care at the end of five years were unvisited by their parents, essentially abandoned, considerably colors our view of the situation.

The current period is one in which foster care has increasingly captured public attention as a source of concern. There are frequent news stories in communities across the United States about cases involving conflicts between natural, foster, or adoptive parents over custody of children caught between the claims of blood ties and those of "real" or "psychological" parents. In addition, there has been a spate of news stories, a number of them concerning foster care in New York City, which have pointed a highly critical finger at agencies providing foster care services to children. A recurrent accusation is that child welfare agencies keep children in care because of the need to utilize space and thus maintain income from their public subsidies rather than because the children need to be in care. A recent major series in the *New York Daily News*, the nation's largest newspaper, contained daily accusations with the following tone:

> There are 26,000 homeless children in New York City who have become the victims of a child care business with assets of $300 million. These children are wards of the city and state. They are the unwanted and the orphaned—children for whom permanent homes are supposedly being sought. Yet an investigation by *The News* has found that the vast majority of these children are being placed in private child care agencies that regularly deny them that opportunity to gain a permanent home. Most, in fact, remain locked in foster care for many years—many for the balance of their adolescent lives, while the private agencies to which they are assigned collect millions of tax dollars each year for their maintenance. Under their contracts with the city, the agencies are expected to care for the children while they attempt to rehabilitate their parents. If rehabilitation fails, or if the parents have died or simply disappeared, the agencies are expected to find adoptive homes for the children. But *The News* has found that a large number of these private agencies deliberately keep children off the adoption market, and a vast majority of them make little or no effort to rehabilitate natural parents to whom some children might be returned. These practices allow the agencies to keep children in long-term care and to maintain a high level of child care payments from the city. (*New York Daily News*, May 13, 1975)

The obloquy heaped on the agencies is based largely on anecdotal accounts rather than analyses of systematic data. Yet the charge that foster children are kept captive by self-serving agencies is a recurrent one and has become the central issue for planners and program managers concerned with this area of practice.

The challenge to deal more adequately with the status problems of foster children is not restricted to journalists. It is being picked up by professionals, legislators, and especially by interested laymen. The issue can no longer be avoided.

In recent years, major changes in orientation have taken place in the United States that make it necessary to define the task facing child welfare agencies in somewhat different perspective than in the recent past. It is no longer considered sufficient that a child be afforded a placement situation in which his basic needs are being cared for in terms of shelter, food, and clothing and a benign environment in which positive emotional growth can be enhanced. A newly emphasized criterion is being used to assess the adequacy of an agency's performance, namely, whether a child can be assured *permanency* in his living arrangements and *continuity* of relationship. It is not enough that he might be placed in a foster family home that offers him family-like care. If he cannot regard the people he is living with as *his* family on a permanent basis, his situation is increasingly regarded as reflecting something less than an adequate resolution of his life situation.

The notion that all children should be living with their natural or adoptive families and that foster care should not be a permanent status has taken on such force in recent years that we face the prospect of a radical shift in the expectations placed on service providers in child welfare. The first revolution in child welfare was the closing down of the mass congregate institutions and the expansion of foster family care as a major alternative living arrangement. The second may soon be upon us—a massive effort to make the foster care status a time-limited one.

The radical alteration in thinking about foster children has been stimulated by a number of developments in recent years. These have included:

1. Increased success in placing older, handicapped, and minority children for adoption. In the not-too-distant past these children tended to be seen as permanent wards of the foster care system.
2. The development of assertiveness by foster parents and adoptive parents who have organized themselves and have shown strong interest in freeing children for adoption.
3. A changed perspective regarding the rights of natural parents vis-à-vis the rights of the child. There is increasing acceptance of the ideas set forth by Goldstein, Freud, and Solnit, maintaining that continuity of relationship is a critical criterion in decision making about living arrangements for children.[1]
4. There is evidence that court surveillance of the foster care system, through routine periodic review of cases, can succeed in moving significant numbers of children into adoption.[2]

[1] Joseph Goldstein, Anna Freud, and Albert J. Solnit, *Beyond the Best Interests of the Child* (New York: Free Press, 1973).

[2] Trudy Bradley Festinger, "The New York Court Review of Children in Foster Care," *Child Welfare* 54 (1975): 211–45.

We emerge from our research with the view that all children should be afforded permanency in their living arrangements if at all possible. This general orientation makes sense to us for a variety of reasons, which we shall outline below. However, we should clarify that we do not come to our position on the basis of our study of the condition of the children over a five-year period. As we indicate later in this chapter, our findings do not show that children who remained in foster care fared less well with respect to intellectual abilities, school performance, and personal and social adjustment compared to those who returned to their own homes. It is important to emphasize that we support the move to free children from an impermanent status in foster care on grounds other than the fact that the children are being ruined by staying where they are. The empirical data we have gathered do not support such a jaundiced view of the system of foster care for children.

On what basis do we then add our voices to those who clamor for an end to impermanency for foster children? If it does not particularly harm them to stay in care, compared to those who have gone home, why be so concerned about their continuing in placement until reaching the age of 18 years? We respond to these questions as follows.

We are not completely sure that continued tenure in foster care over extended periods is not in itself harmful to children. On the level at which we were able to measure the adjustment of the children we could find no such negative effect. However, we feel that our measures of adjustment are not without problems, and we are not sure that our procedures have captured the potential feelings of pain and impaired self-image that can be created by impermanent status in foster care. We fear that in the inner recesses of his heart, a child who is not living with his own family or who is not adopted may come to think of himself as being less than first-rate, as an unwanted human being. We do not apologize for our lack of success in assessing this quality because we view the measurement of the phenomenon (i.e., of feeling "wanted" or "belonging") as an extraordinarily difficult task. We attempted to assess the children's self-image through direct interviews (Time II) and such devices as the sentence-completion test. However, our subjects were apparently quite well defended in this area, and we were only able to catch a glimpse of the underlying feelings.

It would appear to us on first glance that the impermanent status suffered by many children in our sample, compounded by the massive failure of the parents to visit (57 percent of the children by the end of the five-year period), must be viewed as being potentially a profound insult to the child's sense of self-identity. We would therefore support efforts to free children for adoption if strong efforts to restore natural parents to effective functioning are not successful.

Furthermore, providing long-term foster care to children is a very costly affair, particularly for a service that may not be desirable on an extended basis. We have elsewhere published the results of our analysis of the cost involved in the care of the children in our sample as well as what it would cost to continue care until 18 years of age for those not yet discharged.[3] Among the findings we reported were the following:

1. For our sample of 624 children and including all their siblings in care not in our sample, the cost for their care for the first four years of our study was $11,771,915.

2. For children in our sample and their siblings, who had not left foster care at the end of four years we projected that it would cost $23,625,027 to care for the children until they reached 18 years of age.

3. We estimated that the cost of maintaining in foster care an infant child entering the system in 1971 and staying in care for the full 18 years of childhood as $122,500. This contrasted with an estimate made in 1970, calculated for families in the general population, that the 18-year cost of rearing a child for an urban family with two children in the North Carolina region was $25,560 based on a low-cost estimate.[4]

4. Among the 161 families with children remaining in foster care at the end of four years of our study, at least four families appeared likely to cost the community over $500,000 in foster care fees each. The four families taken together would require 335 cumulative years of service at an estimated cost of $2,508,028—providing no additional children were born and entered foster care. These families ranged in size from five to eight children.

[3] David Fanshel and Eugene B. Shinn, Dollars and Sense in the Foster Care of Children: A Look at Cost Factors (New York: Child Welfare League of America, 1972).
[4] Jean Pennock, "Child Rearing Costs at Two Levels of Living by Family Size," Family Economics Review (December, 1970): 16–18.

As part of the effort to rationalize the delivery of service, it is important to be sure that foster care—a most expensive service—is utilized on a long-term basis only where absolutely essential. Keeping children in care who do not belong in the system is to be doubly condemned; it is against the interest of the child's well-being and is an unnecessary drain on society's resources.

Another strong argument for providing the children with a sense of permanency is the fact, of which we became aware after five years of field-data collection, that many children are in long-term care through lack of systematic case management and accountability mechanisms rather than through design. With the frequent turnover of social workers that characterized the system during the period of our study[5] and the absence of a management information system to provide aggregated data about the status of the children, we felt that planning for our subjects was often interrupted and not followed through in systematic fashion. We were aware, for example, that information on the frequency of parental visiting was not available to managers of the system. Without such information, it is difficult to see how effective program management could be carried out.

A final reason for strongly espousing the end to impermanency for foster children arises from data previously cited. In Table 13.1 we report that at Time II (two and one-half years after the child's entry into care), 26 percent of the children in care were judged by their social workers to be unaware that they were not living with their own parents and at Time III, 20 percent of the children were so described. It was also reported that at Time II, 60 percent of the children appeared to treat the child caring person as if he or she were the natural parent; this was true of 69 percent of the children at Time III. Responses by the social workers to other items indicated that many of the children had become well ensconced in their settings and had adapted to the child caring person as the psychological parent. After years in the same setting, and given the failure of many natural parents to visit, it seems hardly likely that these children could be removed without severe consequences. The words of Goldstein, Freud, and Solnit take on a special cogency for

[5] Deborah Shapiro, "Occupational Mobility and Child Welfare Workers: An Exploratory Study," *Child Welfare* 53 (1974): 5–13.

such children, "Once the prior tie has been broken, the foster or other temporary placements can no longer be considered temporary. They may develop into or substantially begin to become psychological parent–child relationships, which in accord with the continuity guideline deserve recognition as a common-law adoption."[6]

The increased promotion of subsidized adoptions for children who have experienced long-term placements in stable foster family care situations would seem to be highly desirable. It may strike some readers that the transformation of a home from "foster" to "adoptive" is an insignificant paper transaction since the child continues to dwell in the very same setting in which he has resided for a number of years with the same routines and the same family members to relate to. However, many observers of the foster care phenomenon feel that the knowledge that the family cares enough about their ward to make the relationship legally binding has great psychological significance. While there has been no testing of this assumption, many practitioners consider it preferable for a child to know that his placement has been finalized than to have him remain in the more transient foster care status. This issue requires systematic investigation.[7]

One decided advantage of subsidized adoption is that it is a less expensive living arrangement for the community to support. While the adoptive family continues to receive a board payment, it has been estimated that the cost of care is reduced to about half the normal foster care fee because agency services are no longer required.[8]

Having indicated our support for the notion of permanency for foster children, we must make clear that it is based on our concern that efforts be made to work with the natural parents as the preferred solution to the child's status problem, as indicated below.

[6] Joseph Goldstein, Anna Freud, and Albert J. Solnit, *Beyond the Best Interests of the Child*, p. 39.

[7] See Roberta G. Andrews, "When is Subsidized Adoption Preferable to Long-Term Foster Care?" *Child Welfare* 50 (1971): 194–200; Kenneth Watson, "Subsidized Adoption: A Crucial Investment," *Child Welfare* 51 (1972): 220–30; Vivian Hargrave, Joan Shireman, and Peter Connor, *Where Love and Need Are One: A Report on the Use of Subsidies to Increase Adoption of Black Children* (Chicago: Illinois Department of Children and Family Services, 1975).

[8] Personal communication from Carol J. Parry, Assistant Commissioner, Special Services for Children, New York City Department of Social Services, November 1975.

PARENTS AND THEIR CHILDREN IN FOSTER CARE

While our study has focused on the children who have experienced foster care, their parents have also loomed large in our consideration. In chapter 4 we emphasize an important finding, namely, the failure of many parents to visit their children, particularly those still in care at the end of five years. We were taken aback by the discovery that 57 percent of the children in care at the end of our study were unvisited by their parents. This struck us as a depressing and intolerable state of affairs. We further observed that there is indication from three other studies that the massive abandonment of children in foster care is a nationwide phenomenon.[9]

The phenomenon of unvisited foster children suggests that parental visiting behavior must be understood more fully and measures taken to cope with the problem. Policymakers and program managers ought to be especially concerned about the matter because: (a) there is evidence in our data that the well-being of the children is influenced by patterns of parental visiting and (b) parental visiting is the best variable we found among various available predictors regarding the discharge of children from foster care. With respect to the latter consideration, we emphasize the fact that 86 percent of the children whose parents were uniformly *high* visitors—that is, who never flagged in their visiting—were eventually discharged from care. This was true of only 41 percent of the children of parents who were uniformly infrequent in their visiting and 36 percent of those whose visiting patterns deteriorated over time. Thus, the failure to ensure that parental visiting takes place loads the dice against a child's return to his own home.

We were impressed with the fact that parental visiting was linked to the amount of casework activity invested in a case and that such activity explained a significant amount of unique variance in parental visiting. More careful monitoring of parental visiting and judicious casework intervention where visiting falters, particularly early in the child's placement, seems to us to be a prime respon-

[9] See Henry S. Maas and Richard E. Engler, Jr., *Children in Need of Parents* (New York: Columbia University Press, 1959), p. 380; Alan R. Gruber, *Foster Home Care in Massachusetts* (Boston: Governor's Commission on Adoption and Foster Care, Commonwealth of Massachusetts, 1973), p. 18; Edmund V. Mech, *Public Welfare Services for Children and Youth in Arizona* (Tucson: Joint Interim Committee on Health and Welfare, 29th Legislature, State of Arizona, 1970), p. 72.

sibility faced by an agency offering foster care services to children. We have elsewhere expressed the following view about parental visiting:

> It ought to be mandatory for all agencies to keep a log on the visitation of parents to their children in foster care. This information should be readily available as part of the computerized management information systems currently being developed in this area of service. The requirement that this information be available should be formalized into state law, and agency practices in this regard should be carefully monitored by the state departments of social service as part of their licensing function. Like the frequent monitoring of body temperature information for assessing the health of patients in hospitals, the visitation of children should be carefully scrutinized as the best indicator we have concerning the long-term fate of children in care. Consider the fact that 66 percent of the children who received no visits during the first year of care were still in care five years later.[10]

From a research perspective, we feel we have only begun to scratch the surface in accounting for the frequency of parental visiting. In our multiple regression analyses of the visiting phenomenon assessed at four occasions, the maximum amount of variance accounted for was 28 percent (at Time II). This indicates to us that there are many forces at play, beyond the variables we used, that might contribute to our understanding of why parents fail to visit. There is particular need to determine the manner in which agency practices serve to encourage or discourage parental visiting. The report of Jenkins and Norman from their analysis of parental interviews suggests that parents often see their own problems and agency practices as a deterrent to visiting:

> Only one-fourth of all mothers said that they had no problems visiting their children; the rest reported one or more complaints or difficulties. Of those with problems about half of the mothers said their own illness prevented them from visiting as much as they would have liked. Of the other major problems mentioned, over one-third of all mothers mentioned the distance from the child and the lack of travel money as creating problems. The foster care establishment was blamed for setting inconvenient visiting times by about 20 percent of

---

[10] David Fanshel, "Parental Visiting of Children in Foster Care: Key to Discharge?" *Social Service Review* 49 (1975): 513.

mothers, and the same percentage accused agencies of trying to keep the mothers away. Eleven percent of the mothers blamed the foster parents themselves for making visiting difficult. Finally, one-third of the mothers felt that visiting was upsetting emotionally for themselves, and one-fourth said that it was disturbing for the child.[11]

We believe that the phenomenon of parental visiting deserves more intense research than it has received thus far. A research project that specifically focuses on this phenomenon might make a substantial contribution to our knowledge. It is important to know in greater detail how parents approach the matter of visiting their children; for instance, understanding their obligations, their attitudes toward visiting, and the interplay of psychological and reality factors (including agency practices). We are impressed by the fact that, despite their obvious handicaps, parents who had suffered mental illness—and where this was the major reason for placement—were able to moblize themselves to visit their children on a higher level than many other groups of parents (categorized by reason for placement). Obviously, emotional impairments are not the only sources of difficulty in accounting for parental failure to visit.

Our finding that the caseworker's evaluation of the mother is a significant predictor of visiting behavior suggests that we need to know more profoundly how individuals relate to their parental responsibilities. While suffering severe mental illness, some adults may nevertheless retain a strong sense of parenthood involving firm identification with and commitments to their children. On the other hand, there are adults who are apparently intact emotionally and in their ability to function in many areas of their lives but who seem entirely undeveloped as parental figures. Foster care appears saturated with such parental types; the massive abandonment of children in care is a reflection of this. In the context of studying visitation patterns, we need to learn more about the dynamics of states of parenthood in which a true sense of parental feeling and commitment has not been achieved. There is very pressing need to determine whether undeveloped or damaged parental functioning—as evidenced by the request for placement and in the early failure to visit—is amenable to casework and other methods of influence and

---

[11] Shirley Jenkins and Elaine Norman, *Beyond Placement: Mothers View Foster Care* (New York: Columbia University Press, 1975), p. 67.

treatment. For all of the vast experience of child welfare agencies in dealing with failing parents, the professional literature with respect to diagnosis and treatment that has emerged from this area of practice is relatively meager. This is another indication that service to parents of children in placement is the most manifest and blatant area of failure in service delivery that one can find as one reviews the foster care phenomenon.

PARENTAL VISITING AND THE WELL-BEING OF THE CHILDREN

It is one thing to demonstrate that there is a correlation of parental visiting and other parental characteristics with the discharge of children from care. It is a more difficult task to determine the consequences of parental performance for the overall well-being of the children. Our extensive data analyses have firmly convinced us of the need to study children for continued evidence of parental interest in the form of visiting. Although it did not emerge uniformly as a significant predictor of changes in the children, we nevertheless were impressed with the frequency with which significant variance in change measures was accounted for by parental visiting. Consider the following comparisons between frequently and infrequently visited children:

1. Highly visited children showed significantly greater gains in nonverbal IQ scores from Time I to Time II (see Table 8.2).
2. Highly visited children showed significantly greater gains in verbal IQ scores over the full five years of the study (see Table 8.4).
3. Children who were highly visited showed more significant gains from Time I to Time II in a summary measure of their emotional adjustment as measured by the figure-drawing tests (see Table 11.8).
4. Children who were highly visited showed significant changes in CBC scores (Child Behavioral Characteristics) from Time I to Time II for the composite scores of: (a) responsibility and (b) agreeableness. From Time II to Time III high parental visiting was a positive predictor of change for: (a) defiance–hostility (negative correlation) and (b) emotionality–tension (negative correlation). For Time I to Time III, parental visiting helped predict change in: (a) agreeableness,

(b) defiance–hostility (negative correlation), and (c) emotionality–tension (negative correlation) (see Table 12.9).

5. A higher level of parental visiting was a significant predictor of an overall positive assessment by the child's classroom teacher (see Table 14.12).

While there were some outcome measures where parental visiting was not a significant predictor of change (e.g., school performance and the psychologists' clinical assessment of the emotional condition of the children), we nevertheless are impressed with the occasions cited above where visiting proved to be a significant regressor variable. Considering the many influences acting on the child, the finding of such positive "traces" seemed to us to warrant consideration of parental visiting as a phenomenon to be encouraged by agencies in the interest of the child's emotional well-being. Our positive view of the influence of parental visiting is supported by the results of research by others.[12]

One caveat to our benign perspective about parental visiting must be introduced on the basis of the findings reported in chapter 13. Children who remain in foster care for as long as five years and who continue to be visited by parents are subject to certain strains that are less noticeable in unvisited children. The visited children are perceived by their social workers as having greater difficulty in coping with the foster care environment. Having two sets of parents in their lives requires considerable adaptation and can obviously be a source of emotional confusion.

Lest we appear to be providing the reader with a confusing message, some elaboration of our views is in order. In the main, we strongly support the notion that continued contact with parents, even when the functioning of the latter is marginal, is good for most foster children. Our data suggest that total abandonment by parents is associated with evidence of emotional turmoil in the children. We can think of no more profound insult to a child's personality than evidence that the parent thinks so little of the relationship with him

---

[12] See Eugene A. Weinstein, *The Self-Image of the Foster Child* (New York: Russell Sage Foundation, 1960), pp. 68–69; M. L. Kellmer Pringle and L. Clifford, "Conditions Associated with Emotional Maladjustment among Children in Care," *Education Review* 14 (1962): 112–23; Jacquelyne A. Gallop, "*Three Factors Affecting the Reactions of Children to Foster Family Care*, doctoral dissertation, Catholic University of America (1972).

that there is no motivation to visit and see how he is faring. Good care in the hands of loving foster parents or institutional child care staff can mitigate the insult but cannot fully compensate for it. It is our view that the parents continue to have significance for the child even when they are no longer visible to him.[13]

At the same time, we are saying that continued visiting by parents of children who are long-term wards of the foster care system, while beneficial, is not without stress. It is not easy for the child to juggle two sets of relationships, and the caseworkers report that some children show signs of strain in the process. We maintain, however, that this is a healthier state of affairs than that faced by the child who must reconcile questions about his own worth as a human being with the fact of parental abandonment. In the main, children are more able to accept additional concerned and loving parental figures in their lives, with all the confusions inherent in such a situation, than to accept the loss of meaningful figures.[14]

[13] For an account of one foster child's effort to reunite and identify with his family, see Fernando Colon, "In Search of One's Past: An Identity Trip," *Family Process* 12 (1973): 429–38.

[14] One of the authors (D.F.) heard a similar viewpoint expressed by Dr. Albert J. Solnit before hearings on foster care of children conducted jointly by the U.S. Senate Subcommittee on Children and Youth and the House of Representatives Select Subcommittee on Education, on December 1, 1975 in Washington, D.C. Dr. Solnit is a co-author of *Beyond the Best Interests of the Child* (1973) and is director of the Child Study Center at Yale University. In correspondence with Dr. Solnit about his statement, he indicates a somewhat different position on the role of natural parents with respect to children in foster care from the one taken here. The dissimilar orientations need to be considered by those who are involved in the formulation of social policy for children in foster care. Dr. Solnit expressed support for the multiple involvement of foster parents and natural parents in the lives of foster children on the assumption that "the children were in foster care as a temporary measure and would be returning to their natural parents." He goes on to state:

> If the foster care is permanent there probably should be a case-by-case determination as to whether the biological or natural parents can and should continue their contact. In other words, if the permanent foster parents are indeed the psychological parents their decision and comfort should be determining since they should now have all the options and authority as well as the responsibility to be the permanent psychological parents of the child. Once children are changed from one set of parents to another, those parents who are the current and permanently committed parents should have their permanency supported by the way in which they are allowed to take on the full custodial responsibility and authority.
>
> Under many circumstances I would hope that they would feel comfortable and see the advantage of prior parental persons being able to retain a useful contact. Therefore, I can't completely agree with the point of view you have put forth. (Communication from Albert J. Solnit to David Fanshel, August 30, 1976.)

We are aware that many of the parents of the children in our study have given evidence that they are sorely troubled human beings. Their visiting can be unpredictable and sporadic and can generate distressing feelings in the child. For some foster parents, child care workers, and social workers faced with the aftermath of a parent's visit, the question may arise as to whether it is worth the turmoil evidenced in the child to encourage the parents to visit. Our response is an emphatic *yes*. It is better for the child to have to cope with *real* parents who are obviously flawed in their parental behavior, who bring a mixture of love and rejection, than to reckon with *fantasy* parents who play an undermining role on the deeper level of the child's subconscious.

The matter of levels of child adaptation being observed is an important consideration in our thinking and helps explain the mixed findings we report. A child being cared for by loving foster parents may, on a surface level, seem at peace with the world. On a deeper level, however, the abandonment by natural parents can impose a profound sense of loss and the child's ease with himself can be markedly impaired.

While we are concerned with the problem of "drift" in foster care, as revealed by our data, we do not support the increasing tendency of many critics of the foster care system to make short shrift of natural parents who have failed their children.[15] Lifting the banner for foster parents and adoptive parents, there is a much too cavalier readiness to early terminate the rights of natural parents, even when there has been no real effort to assist these hapless victims of poor service delivery. We agree with the statement of the Joint Commission on Mental Health of Children that "total displacement of the natural family is a drastic and painful procedure to be followed only when it is clearly in the best interest of the child."[16]

In addition to our concern for the well-being of the foster children who have need for their own parents, we are also con-

---

[15] These comments were included in the testimony of one of the authors (David Fanshel) before Congressional hearings on foster care of children conducted jointly by the U.S. Senate Subcommittee on Children and Youth and the House of Representatives Select Subcommittee on Education, on December 1, 1975 in Washington, D.C.

[16] *Crisis in Child Mental Health: Challenge for the 1970's*, Report of the Joint Commission on Mental Health of Children (New York: Harper and Row, 1969), p. 64.

cerned with the rights of the adults involved. *The termination of parental rights reflects one of the most extreme forms of state power. It should be used most gingerly and judiciously. People should not be penalized because they are poor, because they are mentally ill, or because they are afflicted with drug addiction or alcoholism. They should not be penalized because it is less expensive for society to terminate their rights and allow others, endowed with better economic means, to replace them as the parents of their children.*

Because natural parents are potentially a precious resource for foster children, we would urge augmented federal funding to increase the capacity of local communities to render service to parents of children in foster care in new, more meaningful, and imaginative ways. We would particularly emphasize case advocacy efforts by child welfare workers seeking to enlist more responsible and more effective service delivery to parents from medical care facilities, mental hospitals, addiction services agencies, housing departments, and public assistance departments. New legislation should provide for field experiments in which the interface between child welfare agencies and other social service and health systems serving the parents of children in foster care is organized in more rational fashion.

HOW OUR STUDY CHILDREN FARED

One of our major interests in studying the children over time was to assess whether continued status in foster care increased the risk of impairment with respect to mental abilities or in the emotional sphere. We do not find that the longer a child spends in foster care, the more likely he is to show signs of deterioration. We observe the following:

1. The logarithm of time spent in care was a significant predictor of IQ change for the first two-and-one-half-years of the study (Times I–II). Contrary to expectations, the longer children spent in care, the more likely they were to show enhanced IQs. They fared significantly better than the children who returned home. No such differentiation was found for the second two-and-one-half-year period (Times II–III). When we considered the full five-year span (Times I–III), length

of time in care was again a significant predictor; tenure in care was positively related to enhancement in IQ.

2. Length of stay in foster care was not a significant predictor of change in school performance for any of the three time spans considered.

3. Length of stay in foster care failed to emerge as a significant predictor of change with respect to both figure-drawing scores and the global assessment of the emotional condition of the children by our examining psychologists.

In general, we have developed the perspective that continued tenure in foster care is not demonstrably deleterious with respect to IQ change, school performance, or the measures of emotional adjustment we employed. We do not say that the children are in a condition that is always reassuring—but staying in care as opposed to returning home does not seem to compound the difficulties of the children.

We need to distinguish between our observation that continued tenure in foster care per se is evidently not deleterious for the children involved and predictive of the degree of emotional impairment we find among them. We wish to develop this point further.

Mental Health Status of Foster Children

Unlike some studies in the mental health field, our work has not relied exclusively on a single classification of our subjects in order to locate them on a continuum reflecting their mental health status. For example, in the well-known study of Srole and colleagues, a procedure was used by which psychiatrists rated research protocols (in the form of survey data) that permitted subjects to be classified as: (a) well, (b) having mild symptom formation, (c) having moderate symptom formation, and (d) impaired.[17]

Our approach to child assessment was not based on a single classification system but on a variety of measures because we lacked confidence in any single approach to the assessment task. Furthermore, we lacked the resources to have each child's situation assessed by pairs of psychiatrists, even if such an approach ap-

---

[17] Leo Srole, Thomas S. Langner, Stanley T. Michael, Marvin K. Opler, and Thomas A. C. Rennie, *Mental Health in the Metropolis: the Midtown Manhattan Study* (New York: McGraw Hill, 1962), pp. 395–407.

pealed to us. Because of the absence of a simple classification, our emphasis has been on comparative scores and the analysis of variance accounted for (in the scores of the various measures we used) by variables we were interested in, such as length of time in care and age and sex of the child. This may leave some readers feeling frustrated because we do not end with simple statements to the effect that "X percent of the children were at such and such level of impairment," and so forth. We do, however, have some clues about proportions of the children who are seen as impaired from single items we have used in our several approaches to appraisal.

For the reader who is interested in this kind of information, we summarize here some of our findings that provide data about the mental health status of our subjects in more categorical form:

1. In Table 11.12 we report that 52 percent of the subjects were always rated "normal" by our examining psychologists, while another 25 percent moved from an "abnormal" or "suspect" classification to normal by the third round of testing. On the other hand, 12 percent of the subjects were always rated as suspect or abnormal, while another 12 percent moved from an earlier rating of normal to a suspect or abnormal classification in the final round of testing. Thus, about 25 percent of the subjects were seen as emotionally impaired at the end of our study.

2. When caseworkers were asked to rate the subjects still in care at the end of five years on the degree of difficulty experienced in their care, for 30 percent there was reported "no difficulty" and 40 percent, "slight" difficulty; 17 percent were rated as showing "moderate" difficulty, while another 12 percent were rated as showing "substantial" difficulty. Thus, we again see that about 30 percent were rated as showing what would appear to be significant difficulty.[18]

3. When school teachers were asked to give RSPA ratings for the subjects in their classes, their ratings on the scale called "overall emotional adjustment" were as follows: (a) 9 percent "very well adjusted," (b) 27 percent "well adjusted," and (c) 33 percent having "moderately adequate adjustment." On the more pathological end of the scale, 24 percent of the children were rated as "poorly" and 7 percent, "very poorly" adjusted. Thus, about 31 percent of the children remaining in care were seen as showing adjustment problems.

[18] Source was Time III Child Profile Form, a mailed questionnaire sent to the social workers responsible for the children's cases.

4. When parents of children discharged from foster care were interviewed by our psychologists in the final round of testing (Time III), they were asked whether their children had appeared to be under a strain during the past year. Their responses were distributed as follows: 68 percent of the children showed no strain, 19 percent showed strain sometimes, and 13 percent often. When asked if they considered their children to be nervous, the responses were distributed as follows: 51 percent were "no, not at all," 30 percent "somewhat, a bit," and 20 percent "yes, quite so."

We, of course, have no contrast group of children who did not experience foster care with whom to compare our subjects. In the main, whether we report the judgments of social workers, examining psychologists, parents, or teachers it would seem that 25–33 percent of our subjects show signs of emotional impairment.

We do not know what the distribution of emotional disorders is among low-income children in the general population on the basis of our own work. However, other investigators provide some sense of the parameters that exist. For adults, Srole and others found that 23.4 percent were impaired.[19] In a study by Langner and others, a random sample of 1034 children between six and 12 years of age were described by their mothers in two-hour home interviews conducted in New York City.[20] The mother's report on each child was rated by at least two psychiatrists on five-point scales of impairment. Of these children, 12 percent were rated 4 or 5 on the 5 point scale of total impairment, indicating marked or severe impairment, which could be considered grounds for immediate intervention. Of the children in welfare families, 36 percent had moderate or worse (3+) ratings in developmental impairment and 20 percent had symptom impairment (4+).

In 1969, the Joint Commission on Mental Health of Children estimated that for the general population, 0.6 percent of the children were psychotic and another 2–3 percent were severely disturbed. It was also estimated that "an additional 8 to 10 percent of our young people are afflicted with emotional problems (neuroses and the like)

---

[19] Leo Srole et al., *Mental Health in the Metropolis*, p. 138.
[20] Thomas S. Langner, Edward L. Greene, Joseph H. Herson, Jean D. Jameson, Jeanne A. Goff, John Rostkowski, and David Zykorie, "Psychiatric Impairment in Welfare and Non-welfare Children," *Welfare in Review* (March–April 1969): 10–21.

and are in need of specialized services." It was further reported that there are in the United States some 2,500,000 children with "well-marked behavior difficulties including the more serious mental and nervous disorders."[21]

Since Langner and his associates found that there was greater prevalence of impairment among black children and among welfare families, our report of emotional impairment of 25–33 percent of our sample, depending on the source of information, seems to be quite in line with his data. Our foster care sample was preponderately black and Puerto Rican (almost three-fourths of our sample) and drawn heavily from single-parent households where public assistance was the main source of support. Given the social circumstances of these families, our estimates of impairment are not surprising.

While we suggest that foster children tend to reflect the populations from which they derive—and also point out that children who remain in care appear to fare no worse than those who return home—we do not wish this to become a source of complacency. We share the alarm of the Joint Commission on Mental Health of Children that the personalities of large numbers of children in the United States, particularly minority and impoverished children, are being damaged. Because of the special circumstances experienced by foster children—loss of parents through abandonment, illness, and other factors, including placement and replacement—they must be seen as having a special kind of vulnerability. Having become the wards of the public, they are entitled to the most careful and skilled attention to their emotional problems. We are particularly mindful of the fact that our study was limited to five years. It is possible that the problems faced by these children will unfold and their impairments show greater severity as they move into young adulthood.

While we would tend to place greater stress on the status problems of foster children and actions taken to facilitate their return home or placement in adoptive homes, we nevertheless would hold the system accountable for monitoring the emotional

---

[21] *Crisis in Child Mental Health*, pp. 253–54.

health of the children and, where indicated, for providing therapeutic help in the quantity and quality required. In this regard, we would emphasize the following:

1. Children in foster care should be carefully scrutinized and their problems systematically appraised for signs of emotional difficulty. The use of staff conferences involving those in a position to observe the child are usually helpful. Psychiatric and psychological examinations should be utilized when more deeply seated signs of disturbance are evidenced.

2. Individualized treatment should be offered children in need of help; whether treatment takes the form of intensive casework help, group therapy, or individual psychiatric attention should depend on the child's needs. *All* children should have the opportunity to deal with their concerns about being in foster care and what their future living arrangements are apt to be like. They also should have the opportunity to sort out the complicated sets of relationships involving substitute and natural parental figures and siblings.

3. Foster parents and institutional child-caring persons should be selected from among those who have qualities such as described in the Child Welfare League of America's *Standards for Foster Family Care Service.*[22] They should be persons who:

a. are able to give affection and care to a child in order to meet his needs;

b. have the capacity to be giving without expectation of immediate returns;

c. are able to maintain meaningful relationships, free from chronic severe conflict, with members of their own families and with persons outside the family;

d. give evidence of flexibility and modifiability in their expectations, attitudes, and behavior in relation to the needs and problems of children and ability to use help when it is needed to meet problems of family living;

e. have the ability to accept the child's relationship with his parents and with the agency, without any marked tendency to be over-possessive.

[22] Taken from a list appearing in Child Welfare League of America, *Standards for Foster Family Care Service* (New York: 1959), pp. 34–35.

FOSTER PARENTS
AND INSTITUTIONAL CHILD CARE PERSONNEL

We can think of no greater influence on the well-being of foster children while they are in care than those who directly minister to their needs. Foster parents are obviously crucial to the system of foster care since they take on responsibility for a total living arrangement when a child is placed in their homes. Despite important differences, their responsibilities closely approximate those of natural parents who rear their own children. Approximately 260,430 children were cared for in foster family homes in the United States during 1971.[23] Foster parents perform an extraordinary service to deprived children. The emergence of the foster family as a major national resource for children has been very much a contribution of child welfare programs in the United States. The emphasis on foster family care for young children has been increasingly emulated by countries around the world as a preferred form of care. In our view, in no other area of American life has voluntarism reached such a stunning level of participatory effort. The taking in of children who are strangers on such a vast scale has no parallel in the social life of this country.

That foster parents have an influence on their wards has been demonstrated by our data. As reported in chapter 8, we found that the "democratic permissiveness" index derived from the FPAF was significantly correlated with nonverbal IQ gains for the Times I–II and Times II–III comparisons and for change over the full five years of the study. We were surprised to find that an index measuring the intellectual climate of the foster home was not significantly associated with change in IQ. On the other hand, a permissive foster family environment seemed to "loosen up" the child, and the atmosphere the family provided appeared conducive to growth as reflected in the performance part of the IQ tests.[24]

[23] Telephone conversation reported by Paul E. Mott with Alice Alderman, National Center for Social Statistics, Social and Rehabilitation Service, U.S. Department of Health, Education, and Welfare. Reported in Paul E. Mott, *Foster Care and Adoptions: Some Key Policy Issues*, report prepared for the Subcommittee on Children and Youth of the Committee on Labor and Public Welfare of the United States Senate (Washington, D.C.: U.S. Government Printing Office, 1975), p. 7.

[24] We interpret the correlations to indicate that foster parents rated low on either democratic permissiveness or intellectual climate would exhibit a negative influence with respect to IQ gain or behavioral change.

When we studied changes in behavior scores achieved by the children as assessed by the CBC form, the foster parent index we entitled "intellectual climate" proved to be a significant predictor of changes in several areas of observed behavior for all time comparisons. The index predicted changes in such scores as agreeableness, emotionality–tension, defiance–hostility, likability, and unmotivated–laziness. We were impressed that here the intellectual climate developed by foster parents seemed to play such a strong role, rather than the style of discipline (democratic permissiveness).

That foster parent qualities played a role in IQ gain and behavioral change suggests that foster parent selection is a critical task for agencies, since the qualities of these caretakers could help induce positive change or be the source of regressive behavior. We know that the selection process is a difficult one and the judgments involved are prone to a fair amount of human error.[25] The matter takes on importance because there is an increasing tendency to view foster parents of children who have experienced long-term care as a likely resource for the adoption of such children. In a recent analysis of newly computerized information describing children in foster care in New York City, it was found that almost 8 percent of the children discharged from care were adopted on a subsidized basis by their foster parents; this was true of 23 percent of the children six to nine years of age. Subsidized adoption by foster parents was a particularly important resource for black Protestant children.[26]

We developed a perspective about the quality of the foster homes on the basis of ratings made on the two occasions when social workers filled out the FPAF.

The foster parents providing care to the children in our study were, in the main, viewed positively by the social workers. It was extremely rare for the latter to rate the home as providing less than "excellent" or "good" physical care, and about 85 percent of the homes were rated as being "warm and affectionate" to the child on both rating occasions.

---

[25] Martin Wolins, *Selecting Foster Parents* (New York: Columbia University Press, 1963).

[26] David Fanshel and John Grundy, *Computerized Data for Children in Foster Care: First Analyses from a Management Information Service in New York City* (New York: Child Welfare Information Services, 1975), pp. 40–46.

The workers were asked, "With regard to the specific challenges presented by this child's situation and considering the goals set for the placement, what is your overall appraisal of the way the foster parents fulfilled their tasks?" At Time I the ratings were 35.1 percent "excellent" performance, 42.6 percent "good" performance, 16.9 percent "adequate" performance, 3.4 percent "somewhat less than adequate" performance, and 1.4 percent "poor" performance. At Time II, the ratings were 40.8 percent "excellent" performance, 43.4 percent "good" performance, 10.5 percent "adequate" performance, 4.6 percent "somewhat less than adequate" performance, and 0.7 percent "poor" performance. Thus, at Time I, about 77 percent of the foster parents were rated as "excellent" or "good" in their performance and this climbed to 84 percent at Time II.[27]

These appraisals would indicate that the social workers had a generally positive view of the placement situations in which the children were located and would probably view a majority of the homes as quite acceptable if subsidized adoption were to be considered for the children.

When we examined the situation of our institutionalized subjects, we viewed the child care workers as one of the most important sources of influence since they were the adults who were in most frequent contact with these children. We did not have available the more elaborate kinds of assessments we had secured about the foster parents but nevertheless came up with an interesting significant predictor of both IQ and behavioral change, namely, the years of experience of the child-care worker. We found that children who were exposed to the younger, inexperienced child care staff, as opposed to those who had been in their jobs for over three years, showed significantly greater gains in IQ for Times II–III comparisons and for the full five years (Times I–III). We have conjectured that the younger child care counselors served as a source of intellectual stimulation. They are often college-trained persons who use institutional work as transitional careers. We suspect they bring an intellectual freshness to their jobs, which redounds to the benefit of the children. From a more negative

[27] See David Fanshel and John Grundy, "Foster Parenthood: A Replication and Extension of Prior Studies," Columbia University School of Social Work, April 15, 1971 (Mimeographed.)

perspective, we have concern that some children are exposed to "institutionalized" adults among the more experienced staff, whose care may be adequate but insufficiently stimulating to the children.

When we analyzed forces contributing to behavioral change, as measured by the CBC indexes, we found that for the second half of the study (reflecting changes from Time II to Time III), exposure to inexperienced child care staff was predictive of positive change in four CBC index scores, and for a similar number of indexes for the Times I–III comparisons. The findings again suggest the salutary influence of child care workers who are less embedded in institutional life.

Overall, we emerge from our longitudinal investigation with a sense of the saliency of "people" variables in understanding how children fare in foster care. The child as a predictor of himself (as secured from developmental histories provided by the parents), the natural parent, the foster parent or child care worker, and the social worker are all potential sources of significant predictions of changes to be observed in the child as he gets older. Although they are never consistent as a source of influence, we have observed sufficient "traces" from these "people" variables in our many analyses to persuade us that they must loom large in any future major effort to account for what happens to foster children.

We simply echo the concerns of many observers of foster care when we stress the need for *stability* of living arrangements for these children who have already suffered discontinuities that can undermine their emotional stability. We are mindful of the fact that during the five years we were in the field gathering our longitudinal data we witnessed a great deal of turnover among the social workers who had key roles to play in the lives of our subjects. On the face of it, such turnover is deplorable and efforts should be made to overcome this problem.

SCHOOL PERFORMANCE

Chapters 9 and 10 are devoted to assessment of the school performance of the foster children. As far as we are aware, ours is the first detailed account of what these children are like as students, in terms of what their problems are and how their performance was influenced over time by a variety of factors. We have reported that a majority of children in our study were performing below their age-appropriate level. Using a summary measure based on an average of 11 subjects, we found that 59 percent of our subjects were performing below their age-appropriate level following their entry into foster care, and this was true of 55 percent at the midpoint of our study. At the end of five years, we found that 53 percent of our subjects were performing below their age-appropriate level.

We found no major difference in school performance when we compared children remaining in foster care for five years compared to those discharged for a period of three to five years. A sizable number of children showed improvement in performance toward the latter part of our study.

We would emphasize the need for a concentrated effort to enhance the school performance of foster children, since this obviously has serious implications for their future ability to be well-employed, self-sustaining adults. Investment in this area should have high priority.

FUTURE RESEARCH

As we contemplate possible future emphases of research on foster children, we advance the following suggestions to those who would fund new enterprises:

1. That a premium be placed on rooting research activity more squarely within service programs using data routinely gathered, preferably through computerized management information systems.

2. That theoretical causal models of the discharge phenomenon be developed and tested using important new tools of causal analysis, such as "path analysis."

3. That measurements of the condition of children be strengthened and greater clarity be developed regarding choice of instruments and modes of data collection for various purposes in studies of foster children.

Toward Computerization

In the course of conducting this lengthy investigation, in which we have become as deeply immersed in a field of practice as any researchers could hope to be, we have developed a fairly strong view about strategies for maximizing the payoff of future research developments dealing with the foster care of children. We believe that the locus of research should be moved from a university base into the heart of practice and that data should be generated on a *routine basis* by service providers as service is delivered, rather than through the vehicle of special research "projects." Our viewpoint derives from the following considerations:

1. Because longitudinal investigations are extremely expensive ventures to mount, it is highly doubtful that investigations similar to the one we report here will be funded in the foreseeable future. This is true even though a longitudinal design is most appropriate for the study of foster children.

2. In the course of carrying out our study we realized that much of the fact-gathering undertaken by us was potentially within the routine data-gathering capability of agencies, assuming the desire to obtain such information. We estimate that many of the variables included in our study could be systematically collected in situ. The data would not necessarily take the same form as those prepared in a research context, but satisfactory equivalents could be developed. It is also our belief that such data are potentially more useful to agencies than the voluminous narratives now being stored in case records.

3. The necessity of having computerized management information systems as a basis for sounder management of human services has been increasingly recognized, and steps are under way in a number of cities to develop such system. They provide a basis for case monitoring and establishing accountability for the provision of foster care to children.[28] The superiority of routinized data-gathering over the approach of special "projects" is that the latter take too much time to bring to fruition and cannot produce reports that are sufficiently timely to meet ongoing management requirements. By contrast, computerized management information systems can be organized with a programmed capacity for producing analytic reports on a demand basis.

[28] See David W. Young, "Management Information Systems in Child Welfare: An Agency Experience," *Child Welfare* 53 (1974): 102–11; Ann M. Rothschild, "An Agency Evaluates its Foster Care Service," *Child Welfare* 53 (1974); 42–50.

During the past two years, one of the authors (David Fanshel) has had the experience of providing research consultation to a newly developed computerized information system organized in New York City. Child Welfare Information Services (CWIS) is designed to provide information about children in foster care. At any given time, CWIS has about 30,000 children accounted for in its active data file. In the course of working with this system, it has become clear that the phenomenon of service delivery can be seen as having features that make it analogous to a longitudinal study. Clients enter the system as it proceeds in time and exit at later periods. On any day, one can obtain a cross-sectional view of the client population currently being served, but to probe more deeply about the careers of children in foster care it is necessary to follow the same children (a cohort) over time. When this is done, the analyst becomes involved in something akin to a longitudinal investigation. For example, in using such computerized data, one has to be able to deal with the analytic problem of accounting for change in subjects over time or accounting for variance in later outcomes (e.g., discharges) by use of data collected earlier. These are the problems that have occupied us in this study.

The experience of having conducted a longitudinal study has sensitized the authors to the important variables that need to be included in the assessment of outcomes such as discharge. Current experience in the analysis of such computerized data has already produced results that appear promising as aids to program management and social policy formulation.[29]

The Need for Causal Models of Discharge

One of the research tasks that requires immediate attention is the development of a multicausal statistical model appropriate for analysis of the discharge of children from foster care. In chapter 5 we report the results of four simple multiple regression analyses of the discharge phenomenon, each from the perspective of a different time occasion. These analyses show a number of significant predictors: (a) the age of the child, (b) his ethnicity, (c) the frequency of

---

[29] David Fanshel and John Grundy, *Computerized Data for Children in Foster Care.*

parental visiting, (d) the amount of casework invested in the situation, and (e) evaluation of the mother. The maximum amount of variance accounted for in our analyses was 31 percent; this was the result of the prediction effort at Time III. Considering the importance of bringing discharge under statistical control, this is far from a satisfactory state of affairs. It may not be an exaggeration to say that if the factors accounting for release of children from care cannot be better defined and accounted for, the capacity to rationalize service-delivery efforts is markedly impaired. How can we determine where to direct our programmatic efforts to secure the early discharge of children from care if we have such limited understanding of the causal forces at play? Efforts to increase the variance in discharge accounted for by the addition to our analysis of new and more powerful variables should, therefore, be assigned high priority.

Efforts to enhance predictability might well range in new directions such as the employment of variables on a more macroscopic level than previously employed, that is, descriptions of agency structures and of the interplay between child welfare and other agencies delivering service to parents.[30] There is also need for a richer description of the characteristics of the natural parents, including the kinds of impairments from which they suffer, their material resources, the quality of their family relationships, their child-rearing practices, and their attitude toward restoring a home for the foster child.

There is danger in adding more variables to the prediction effort than can be handled efficiently. From a phenomenological standpoint, however, the discharge of children from foster care is determined by a complex interplay of forces. Likely candidate items for inclusion are as follows:

1. Characteristics of the child:
   a. age at entry into care;
   b. birth status (in wedlock/out of wedlock);

---

[30] In their well-known study, *Children in Need of Parents*, Maas and Engler posit the existence of "collaborative" and "noncollaborative" networks of agencies in the communities that they studied. They report, "Collaborative networks showed greater incidence of adoption while noncollaborative networks showed lower incidence of adoption, but higher return home rates." Henry S. Maas and Richard E. Engler, Jr., *Children in Need of Parents* (New York: Columbia University Press, 1959), p. 330.

    c. physical health status;
    d. mental health status (and behavioral characteristics);
    e. school performance history;
    f. deviant behaviors (if any).
2. Characteristics of the child's family:
    a. number of children;
    b. number of children in care;
    c. paternity of children (single father/multiple fathers);
    d. source of family income;
    e. material circumstances;
    f. relationship with extended family.
3. Characteristics of the child's mother:
    a. age
    b. race–ethnicity–religion;
    c. number of births experienced;
    d. age at first birth;
    e. relationship to child's father;
    f. physical health status;
    g. mental health status;
    h. occupation and source of income;
    i. disabling conditions;
    j. attitudes toward restoration of home for child;
    k. frequency and quality of contacts with foster child;
    l. patterns of agency service utilization;
    m. child-rearing practices.
4. Characteristics of the child's father:
    a. age;
    b. race–ethnicity–religion;
    c. acknowledgment of paternity of foster child;
    d. number of children fathered;
    e. occupation and source of income;
    f. contribution to support of foster child;
    g. physical health status;
    h. mental health status;
    i. disabling conditions;
    j. attitudes toward restoration of home for child;
    k. frequency and quality of contacts with foster child;
    l. patterns of agency service utilization;
    m. child-rearing practices.
5. Characteristics of agency service provision:
    a. goals of agency for child (specified/unspecified);
    b. plans for child's discharge (staying in care/return home/adoption/other);
    c. frequency of case contacts with child and parents;
    d. stability of staffing (i.e., turnover of social workers);

e. internal agency resources available;
f. training and experience of the social workers;
g. goals for care set by licensing and administrative agencies;
h. patterns of case monitoring (i.e., whether goal-oriented activity);
i. external agency resources utilized.

Each of the items cited above could constitute a crucial element in determining whether a child is discharged from foster care. In the aggregation of cases, however, the interplay of forces can be quite complex, with only some of the variables contributing significant amounts of explained variance. We would expect to find some redundancy among variables, while others can play a mediating role in their interaction with still other variables.

There is a strong need for a theoretical multicausal model to underpin analytic efforts to understand the discharge phenomenon. We have established that ethnicity is linked to parental visiting and discharge, that qualities of the mother, parental visiting, and the amount of casework attention are significant predictors of discharge. However, more complex models of causal inference should be developed in consort with practitioners and these models tested through procedures such as path analysis. We do not suggest this move toward more complex analytic work because it has become almost routine in some circles to use multicausal models. Rather, the complex interplay of forces affecting the discharge of foster children demands a more parsimonious theoretical formulation and a major attempt at causal analysis.

Future studies of discharge status will require that attention be given to the temporal element in the career of foster children. It is one thing to develop linear causal models that enable the investigator to predict discharge at the time that the child enters foster care. It is a more difficult task to develop models that take into account the fact that predictive variables may change after one or two years. Therefore, the theoretical models to be tested will probably need to vary according to the temporal vantage point assumed by the investigator. This obviously adds to the complexity of the task of "understanding" discharge.

It also seems advantageous to us, in contemplating future investigations, to partition foster care populations into more meaningful groupings for analytic purposes. In our study, we have included under the single rubric of "foster child" an infant who has entered care shortly after being born out of wedlock to a teenage mother who is unable to care for it, a toddler in care because of suspected abuse by a parent, and a teenager who appears likely to engage in violent behavior. The taxonomy of foster child description warrants research attention, perhaps using newly available computerized clustering programs.[31]

Measurement Tasks

Our experience in assessing the foster children from different perspectives using various data-gathering approaches has given us a strong sense of the need for refinement of measurement techniques. We are convinced that our decision to use multiple informants rather than a single rating procedure was correct. The child, his parents, his social worker, and his teacher have their unique as well as shared perspectives on his situation. Each should be tapped to provide cross-validation of the portrait that is developed. Nevertheless, the correlations among the perceptions of various reporters in our study were not higher than .3 or .4 for most phenomena under study.

CONCLUDING NOTE

Foster children tend to come largely out of the ghettos and poverty areas of our country in what seems to be almost a random process. There is no research in the literature to indicate that entrance into foster care can be predicted. In our discussions with professional workers in this field, we have come to share the view that foster children and their families have their counterparts in large numbers in the communities from which they come and that they are probably not highly differentiated from them. There are many vulnerable families in communities across the country who teeter on the edge of dismemberment. Why disaster strikes one family and

---

[31] See Jerrold Rubin and Herman P. Freedman, *A Cluster Analysis and Taxonomy System for Grouping and Classifying Data* (New York: IBM Corporation, New York Scientific Center, 1967).

causes its disintegration and not another, seemingly equally deprived, is not fully known.

We have no faith in the ability to predict or prevent the entrance of children into foster care. True prevention would require strong support for *all* families in their child-rearing efforts, particularly the most impoverished. If such support is not forthcoming for the increasing number of vulnerable families in our country, more children will inevitably wind up in foster care. Cutting public assistance budgets, ending support for public housing, terminating mental health after-care clinics, and closing down community-based health facilities—all grim phenomena of this recent period—are sure ways to increase the number of families where parental breakdown will occur and children will require foster care.

While under current conditions we see little that child welfare agencies can do to cut off the flow of children entering care, we do have some hope that once a child enters care, a goal-oriented approach can be developed to maximize the likelihood of his departure. More rational deployment of the resources of agencies should be focused on early goal setting and monitoring of cases to ensure that children do not "drift" in foster care. With computer-assisted case planning, we anticipate marked improvement in the way services are delivered to children.

Foster children are among the most deprived of all children in our society. The way care is organized for them and the concern and love that are provided them are profound reflections on all of us.

APPENDIX

ANALYSIS
OF ATTRITION

A major task confronting the investigator in a longitudinal investigation is that of accounting for cases that are lost over the course
of data-collection efforts. It came as no surprise in an enterprise such
as ours that attrition in the sample took place as the study proceeded.
The phenomenon manifested itself mainly with the cases involving
children discharged from foster care; keeping informed about the
children remaining in care was not a problem since the agencies were
very cooperative in providing information.

Five years is a relatively long period in which to maintain the
integrity of a sample, particularly when the subjects come from very
poor and often disorganized families. The parents of the children were
known to be beset with serious personal and social problems that
frequently were the cause of family breakup and the original entrance
of the children into foster care. In most cases the father was not
present and the mother was carrying on under difficult circumstances.
It was not unusual to have a mother enter a mental or general hospital
or to be unavailable because of other disabilities, e.g., drug addiction or
alcoholism. Often the parent moved suddenly without leaving a
forwarding address.

Some parents simply saw no point in cooperating with a study that
focused on events that had taken place several years earlier. Either
recalling the separation period was too painful, and something to be
avoided, or it was viewed as one of many life crises that had been
successfully navigated and was simply no longer of interest.

In the psychological testing program considerable effort was
invested in finding the homes of the discharged children in order to set
up appointments for testing them. The psychologists made repeated
visits to a home if there was any chance of success in reaching the

parent and making an appointment. It was not unusual to make five or six visits to a home before abandoning the effort.

The matter of attrition needs to be considered from several perspectives. First, whenever there is presented a cross-sectional view of the prevalence of problems for the group that has remained under research scrutiny, one must keep in mind the potential effect of sample loss. Secondly, wherever data are presented showing the saliency of predictor variables in accounting for change in a measure of the children, the revealed dependencies might have been altered if the full sample had been available.

To determine the nature of the attrition problem, mainly as related to the representativeness of the discharged children for whom data had been secured, a number of analyses were undertaken to compare children for whom reports existed or were lacking. The analyses were concerned with the following phenomena: (1) Time III school reports, (2) Times II and III intelligence testing, and (3) interviews with parents of discharged children at Time III to secure information about the symptomatic behavior of subjects.

SCHOOL REPORTS

The third and final school survey (reported in chapter 9) took place in 1971. At that time, 223 out of 477 study children of school age (47 percent) were covered by returned forms. We attempted to assess the representativeness of the group for whom we had received school reports by undertaking comparisons with those eligible but not covered (254 children). We ascertained the following:

1. There was no significant difference in the proportion of male children for the reported (46.5 percent) and the unreported group (47.0 percent).
2. There was no significant difference in the mean ages of the two groups.
3. Ethnic differences between the two groups were not statistically significant although black Catholic and white Catholic and white Protestant children tended to be underrepresented and Jewish children overrepresented.
4. There was no significant difference between the reported and unreported groups when they were compared by reason for place-

ment. Children who came into care because of their behavior problems tended to be underreported and abandoned children tended to be overreported.

5. There were only trivial differences between the reported and unreported groups in mean Total Deviation IQ scores for all three testing occasions.

6. There were only trivial differences between the reported and unreported groups with respect to assessment of emotional condition of the subjects on the three testing occasions.

7. For most child behavior characteristics (CBC) Time I scores there were no significant differences between the reported and unreported groups. This was true of alertness–intelligence, learning difficulty, unmotivated–laziness, defiance–hostility, likability, infantilism, withdrawal, appetite, overcleanliness, sex inhibition, and assertiveness. The group for whom Time III school reports were received were perceived significantly more positively on the CBC Time I score called agreeableness and significantly lower on emotionality–tension.

PSYCHOLOGICAL TESTING

As reported in chapter 7, 63 percent of the sample of 624 children were tested on all three testing occasions. An additional 15 percent of the subjects were tested at Times I and II only, and 13 percent at Time I only. Sixteen children were tested at various times (Times I and III, II and III, II only, and III only). Forty children (6.5 percent) were never tested. To determine whether sample loss reflected a bias in who was seen, an analysis was made of the mean IQ scores achieved by the two groups (tested/not tested) in earlier rounds of testing.

The results of this analysis, given in the accompanying table, show no bias reflected in the attrition situation that appears to favor retention in the sample of children with higher scores. The tested and nontested groups at Times II and III are essentially in a state of parity with respect to their prior IQ scores.

Time II Testing

	Mean	SD	N
Time I Deviation Verbal IQ	99.98	14.99	407
Group I (not tested at Time II)	102.58	13.49	66
Group 2 (tested at Time II)	99.48	15.21	341
	$t = 1.539$; $p = .125$		
Time I Deviation Nonverbal IQ	99.96	14.96	407
Group I (not tested at Time II)	100.05	15.17	66
Group 2 (tested at Time II)	99.94	14.92	341
	$t = 0.052$; $p > .500$		
Time I Deviation Total IQ	100.02	14.97	577
Group 1 (not tested at Time II)	100.39	16.24	92
Group 2 (tested at Time II)	99.95	14.72	485
	$t = 0.257$; $p > .500$		

Time III testing

	Mean	SD	N
Time II Deviation Verbal IQ	99.99	14.95	375
Group 1 (not tested at Time III)	101.47	17.90	77
Group 2 (tested at Time III)	99.61	14.06	298
	$t = 0.970$; $p = .333$		
Time II Deviation Nonverbal IQ	100.02	14.90	375
Group 1 (not tested at Time III)	100.83	15.86	77
Group 2 (tested at Time III)	99.82	14.64	298
	$t = 0.532$; $p > .500$		
Time II Deviation Total IQ	100.10	15.13	490
Group 1 (not tested at Time III)	100.10	15.13	97
Group 2 (tested at Time III)	99.88	14.16	393
	$t = 0.658$; $p > .500$		

PARENT INTERVIEWS

At Time III, the examining psychologists interviewed parents of 137 children; these constituted 39 percent of the discharged children. With respect to the representativeness of the children covered by the interviews, our analysis shows the following:

1. There was no significant difference in the proportion of male children for the interview group (49.6 percent) and the attrition group (50.6 percent).

2. There was almost the same proportion in both groups for

children who had entered care for child behavior (15.3 percent versus 15.5 percent), neglect and abuse (13.9 percent versus 13.7 percent), and abandonment (6.6 percent versus 8.2 percent). Mental hospitalization of the mother as a reason for placement was more characteristic of the interviewed group than the attrition group (29.9 percent versus 18.5 percent).

3. The difference in age between the two groups was trivial.

4. There was a higher proportion of Puerto Rican children for the interviewed group, somewhat fewer black children, and somewhat fewer white children. The differences were not statistically significant at the .05 level.

5. When the psychologists' assessments of the emotional condition of the children at Time I were examined, the differences between the interviewed and the attrition cases were found to be trivial.

6. When the two types of cases, interviewed and attrition, were compared for their Time I CBC scores, most comparisons failed to show significant differences. This was true of the following CBC indexes: alertness–intelligence, learning difficulty, agreeableness, defiance–hostility, likability, emotionality–tension, withdrawal, appetite, sex precociousness, sex inhibition, and overcleanliness. Significant differences were found for the following index scores, showing more positive types of behavior for the interviewed group: responsibility, unmotivated–laziness, and infantilism.

7. There was no significant difference between the two groups with respect to their mean Time I Total Deviation IQ scores (99.7 versus 101.4).

INDEX

PUBLICATIONS
OF THE CHILD WELFARE
AND FAMILY WELFARE
RESEARCH PROGRAM

Borgatta, Edgar F., and David Fanshel. "The Child Behavior Characteristics (CBC) Form: Revised Age-Specific Forms." *Multivariate Behavioral Research*, 5 (January 1970), 49–81.

Fanshel, David. "The Exit of Children from Foster Care: An Interim Research Report." *Child Welfare*, 50 (February 1971), 65–81.

—"Parental Failure and Consequences for Children: The Drug Abusing Mother Whose Children Are in Foster Care." *American Journal of Public Health* (June 1974), 604–12.

—"Parental Visiting of Children in Foster Care: Key to Discharge?" *Social Service Review*, 49 (December 1975), 493–514.

—"Status Changes of Children in Foster Care: Final Results of the Columbia University Longitudinal Study." *Child Welfare*, 55 (March 1976), 143–171.

Fanshel, David, and Eugene B. Shinn. *Children in Foster Care: A Longitudinal Investigation.* New York: Columbia University Press, 1977.

—*Dollars and Sense in the Foster Care of Children.* New York: Child Welfare League of America, 1972 (47 pages).

Jenkins, Shirley. "Filial Deprivation in Parents of Children in Foster Care." *Children*, 14 (January–February 1967), 8–12.

—"Separation Experience of Parents Whose Children Are in Foster Care." *Child Welfare*, 48 (June 1969), 334–40.

Jenkins, Shirley, and Elaine Norman. *Beyond Placement: Mothers View Foster Care.* New York: Columbia University Press, 1975 (152 pages).

—"Families of Children in Foster Care." *Children*, 16 (July–August 1969), 155–59.

—*Filial Deprivation and Foster Care.* New York: Columbia University Press, 1972 (296 pages).

Norman, Elaine. "Some Correlates of Behavioral Expectations: A Role Study of Mothers with Children in Foster Care Placement." Unpublished Ph.D. dissertation, City University of New York, 1972 (204 pages).

Shapiro, Deborah. "Agency Investment in Foster Care: A Follow-Up." *Social Work*, 18 (November 1973), 3–9.

—"Agency Investment in Foster Care: A Study." *Social Work*, 17 (July 1972), 20–28.

—"Occupational Mobility and Child Welfare Workers: An Exploratory Study." *Child Welfare*, 53 (January 1974), 5–13.

PUBLICATIONS

—"Professional Education and the Child Welfare Worker: An Exploratory Study," in *Approaches to Innovation in Social Work Education*. New York: Council on Social Work Education, 1974; pp. 82–91.

—*Agencies and Foster Children*. New York: Columbia University Press, 1976 (218 pages).